CAPTAIN
★ AMERICA ★

RED, WHITE & BLUE

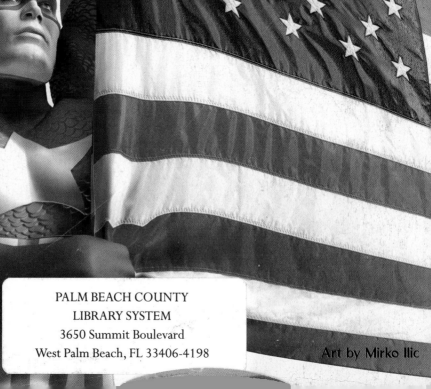

Art by Mirko Ilic

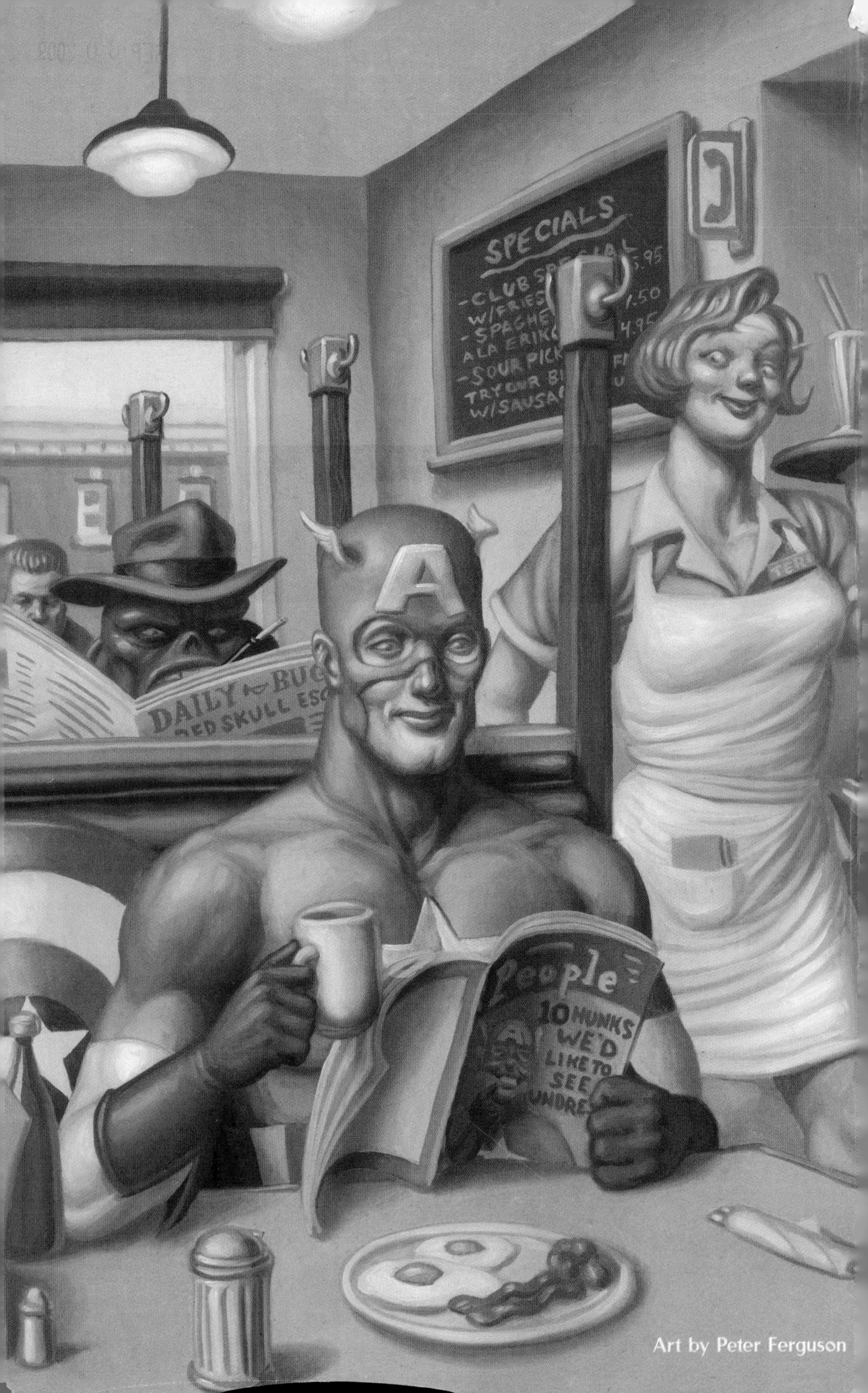
SPECIALS
DAILY BUG
RED SKULL
People
10 HUNKS WE'D LIKE TO SEE
Art by Peter Ferguson

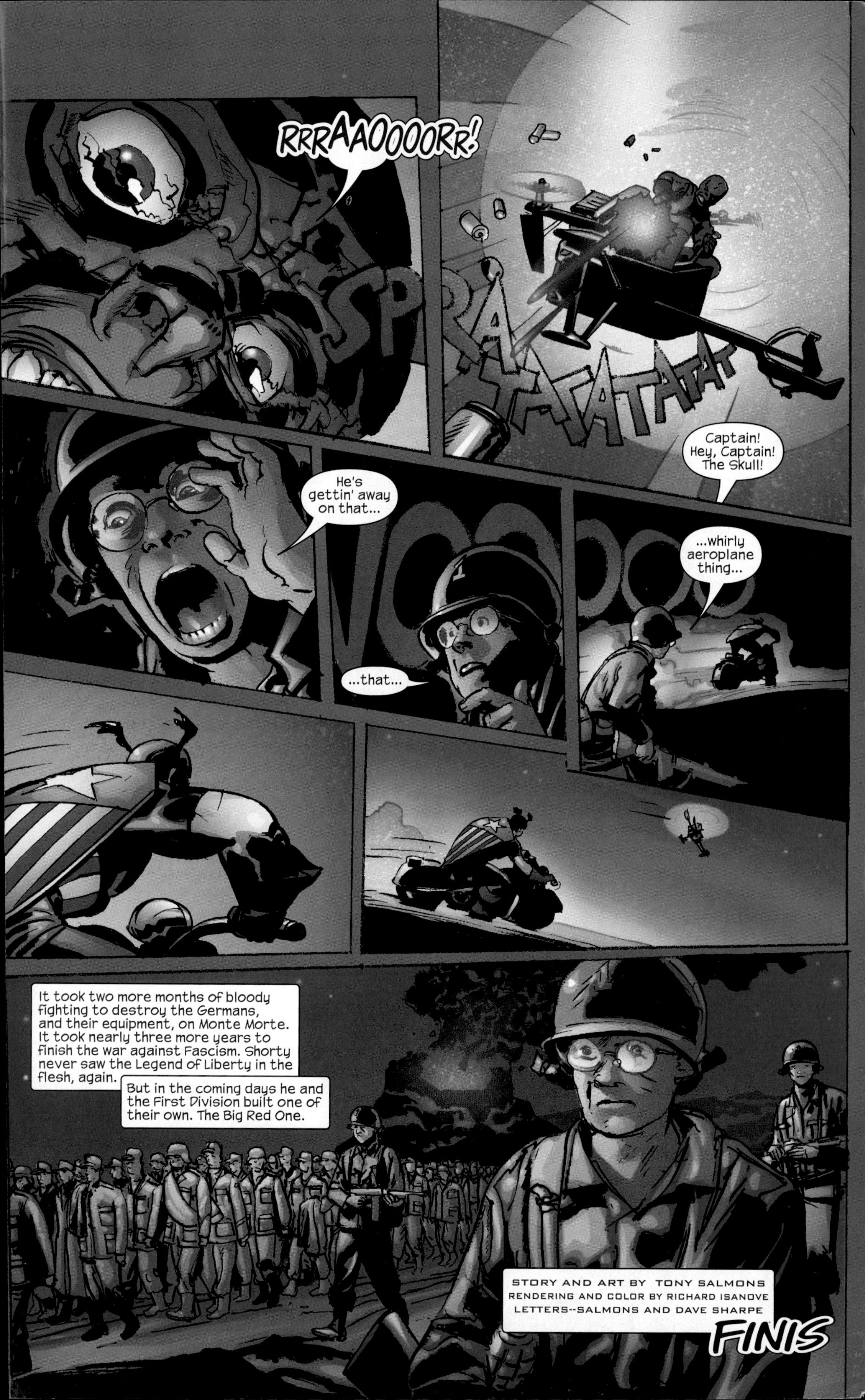
RRRAAOOOORR!
Captain! Hey, Captain! The Skull!
He's gettin' away on that...
...that...
...whirly aeroplane thing...
It took two more months of bloody fighting to destroy the Germans, and their equipment, on Monte Morte. It took nearly three more years to finish the war against Fascism. Shorty never saw the Legend of Liberty in the flesh, again.
But in the coming days he and the First Division built one of their own. The Big Red One.
STORY AND ART BY TONY SALMONS
RENDERING AND COLOR BY RICHARD ISANOVE
LETTERS--SALMONS AND DAVE SHARPE
FINIS

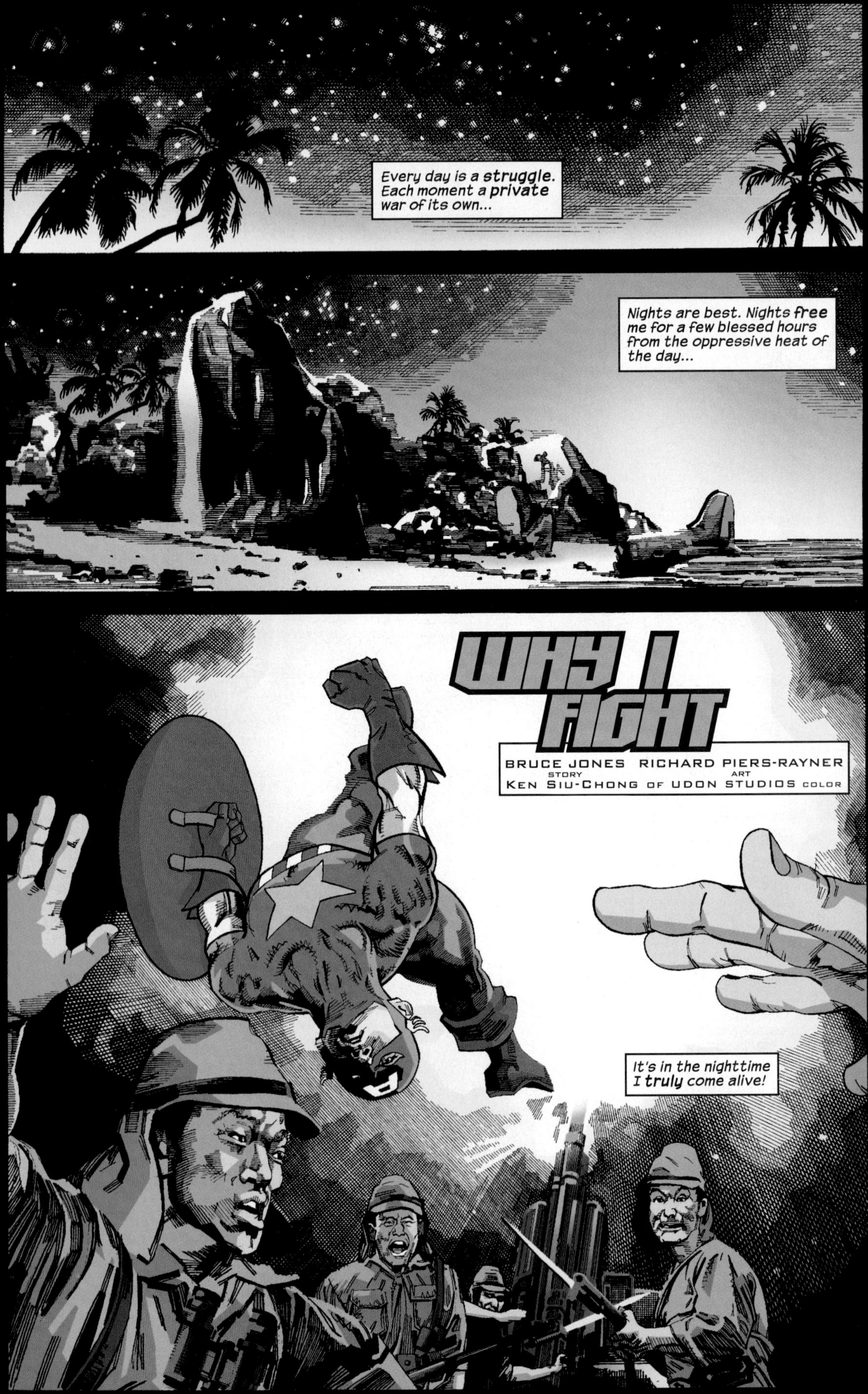

Every day is a struggle. Each moment a private war of its own...
Nights are best. Nights free me for a few blessed hours from the oppressive heat of the day...
WHY I FIGHT
BRUCE JONES STORY RICHARD PIERS-RAYNER ART
KEN SIU-CHONG OF UDON STUDIOS COLOR
It's in the nighttime I truly come alive!

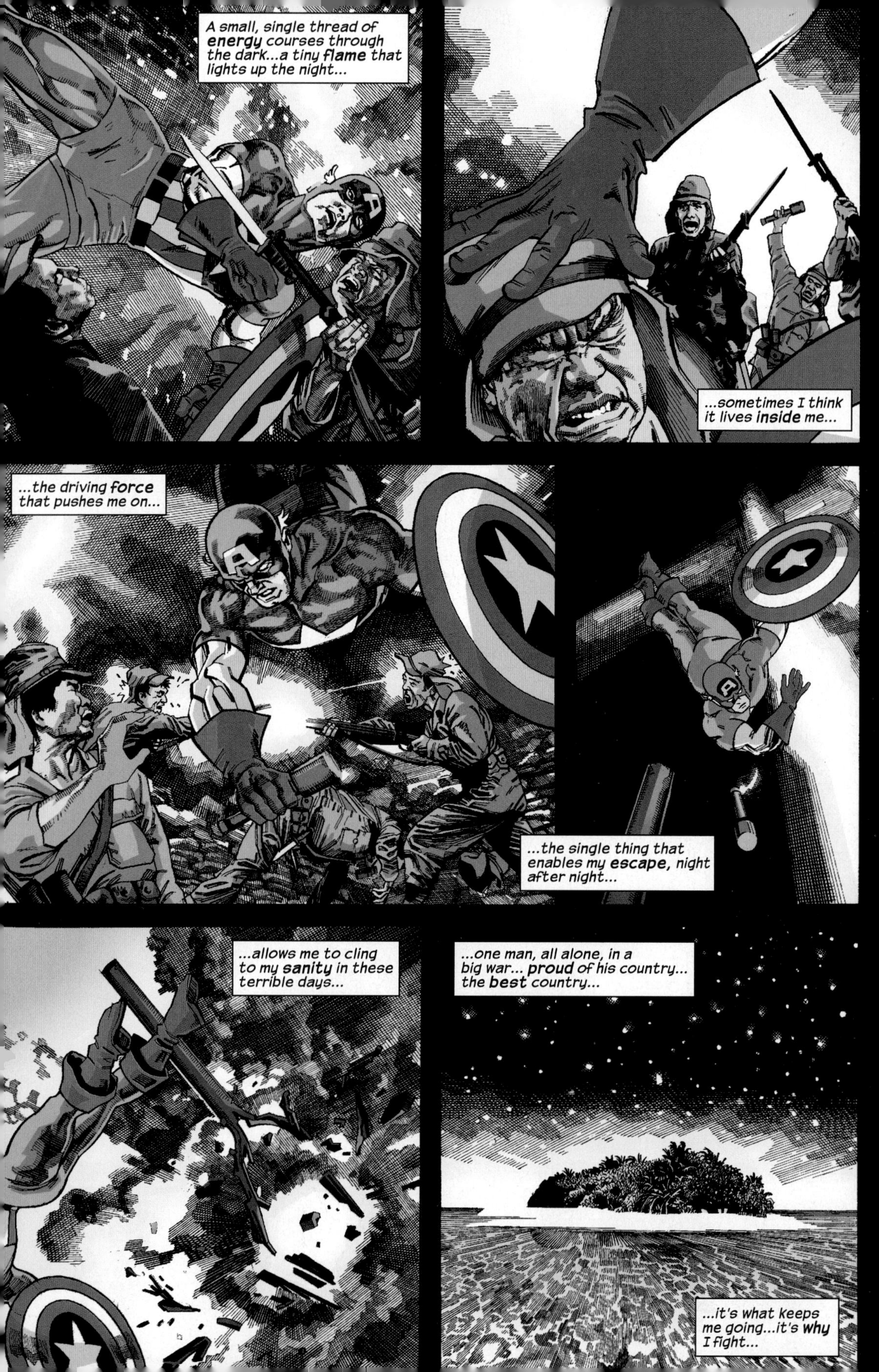
A small, single thread of energy courses through the dark...a tiny flame that lights up the night...
...sometimes I think it lives inside me...
...the driving force that pushes me on...
...the single thing that enables my escape, night after night...
...allows me to cling to my sanity in these terrible days...
...one man, all alone, in a big war... proud of his country... the best country...
...it's what keeps me going...it's why I fight...

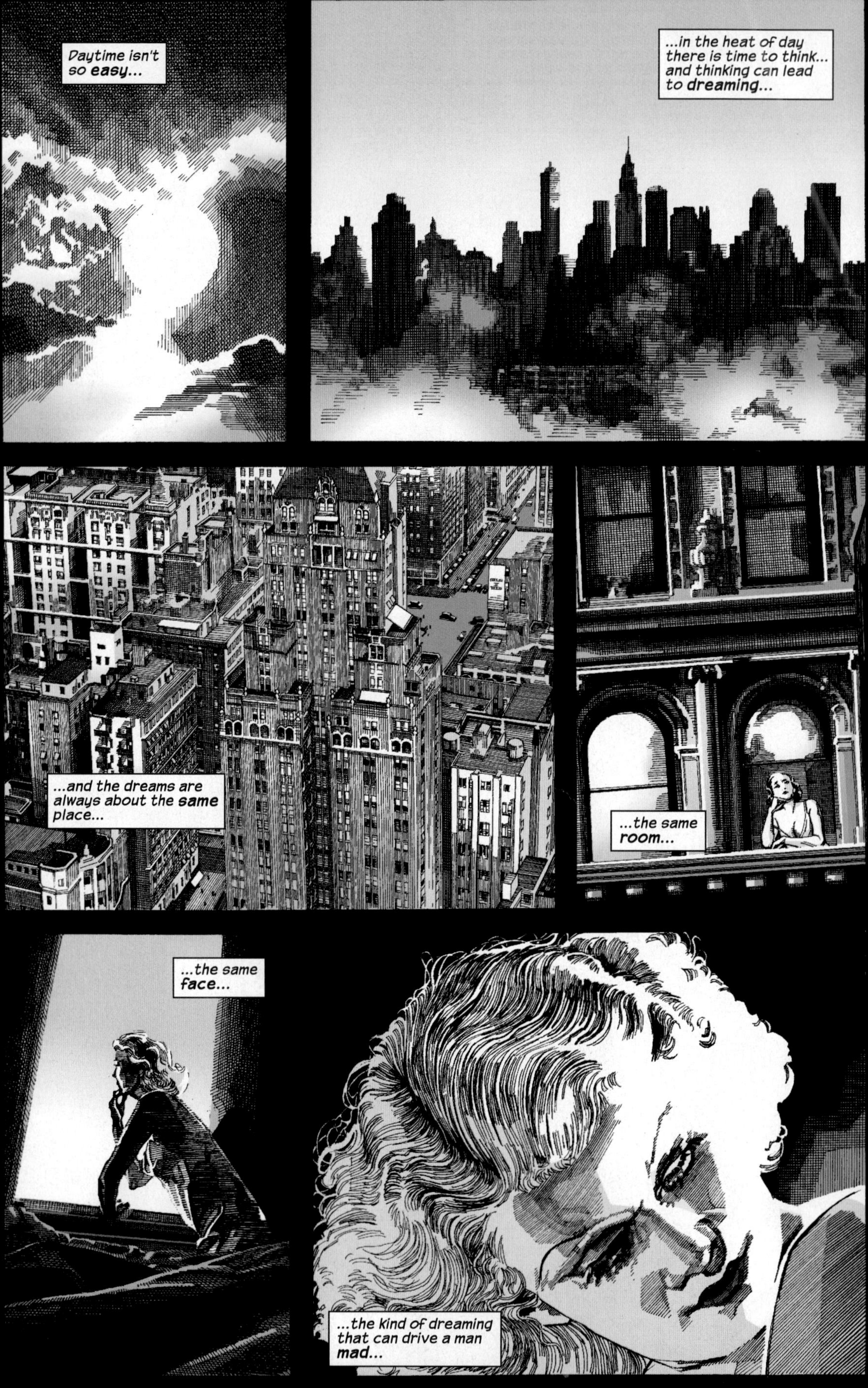
Daytime isn't so easy...
...in the heat of day there is time to think... and thinking can lead to dreaming...
...and the dreams are always about the same place...
...the same room...
...the same face...
...the kind of dreaming that can drive a man mad...

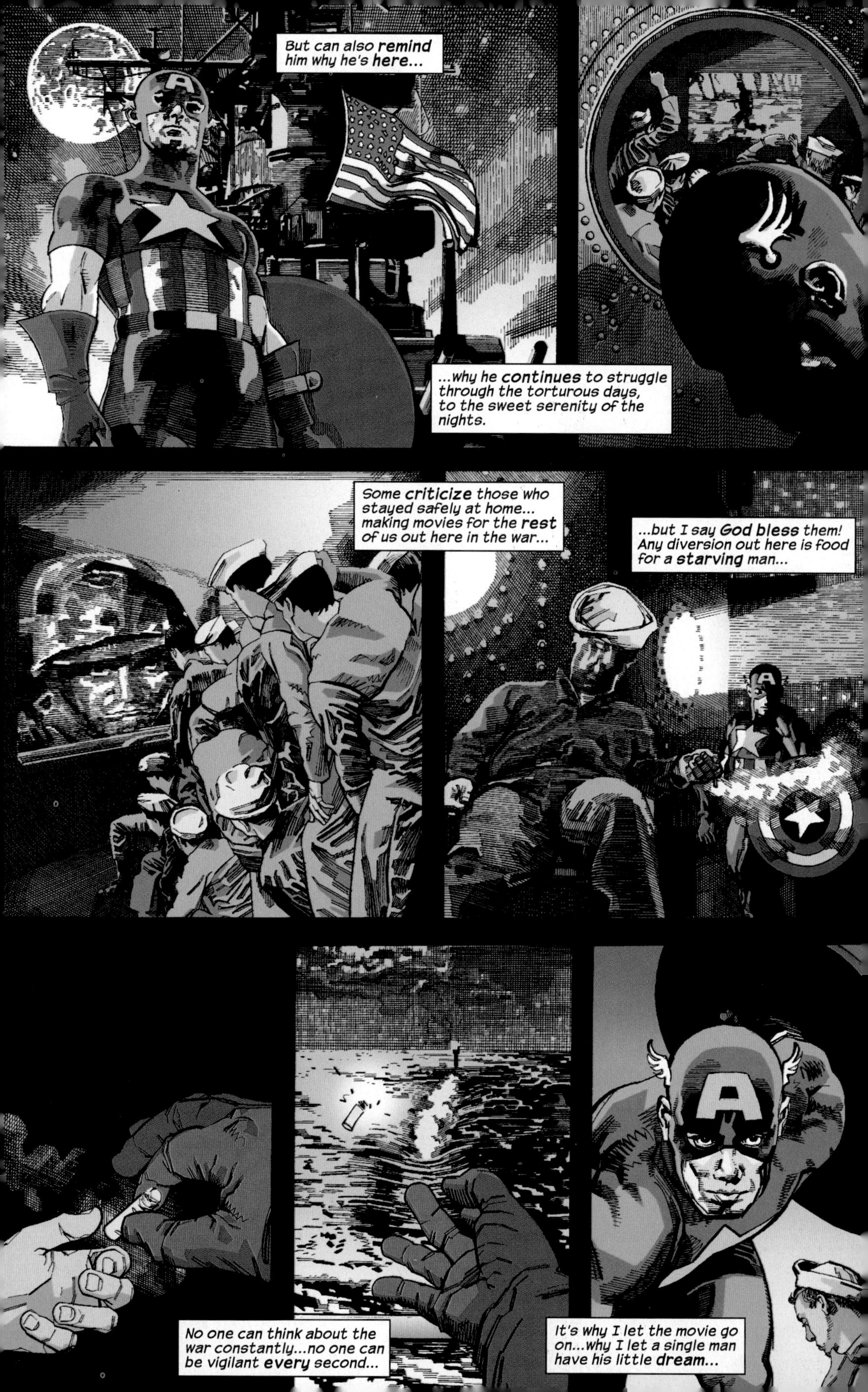
But can also remind him why he's here...
...why he continues to struggle through the torturous days, to the sweet serenity of the nights.
Some criticize those who stayed safely at home... making movies for the rest of us out here in the war...
...but I say God bless them! Any diversion out here is food for a starving man...
No one can think about the war constantly...no one can be vigilant every second...
It's why I let the movie go on...why I let a single man have his little dream...

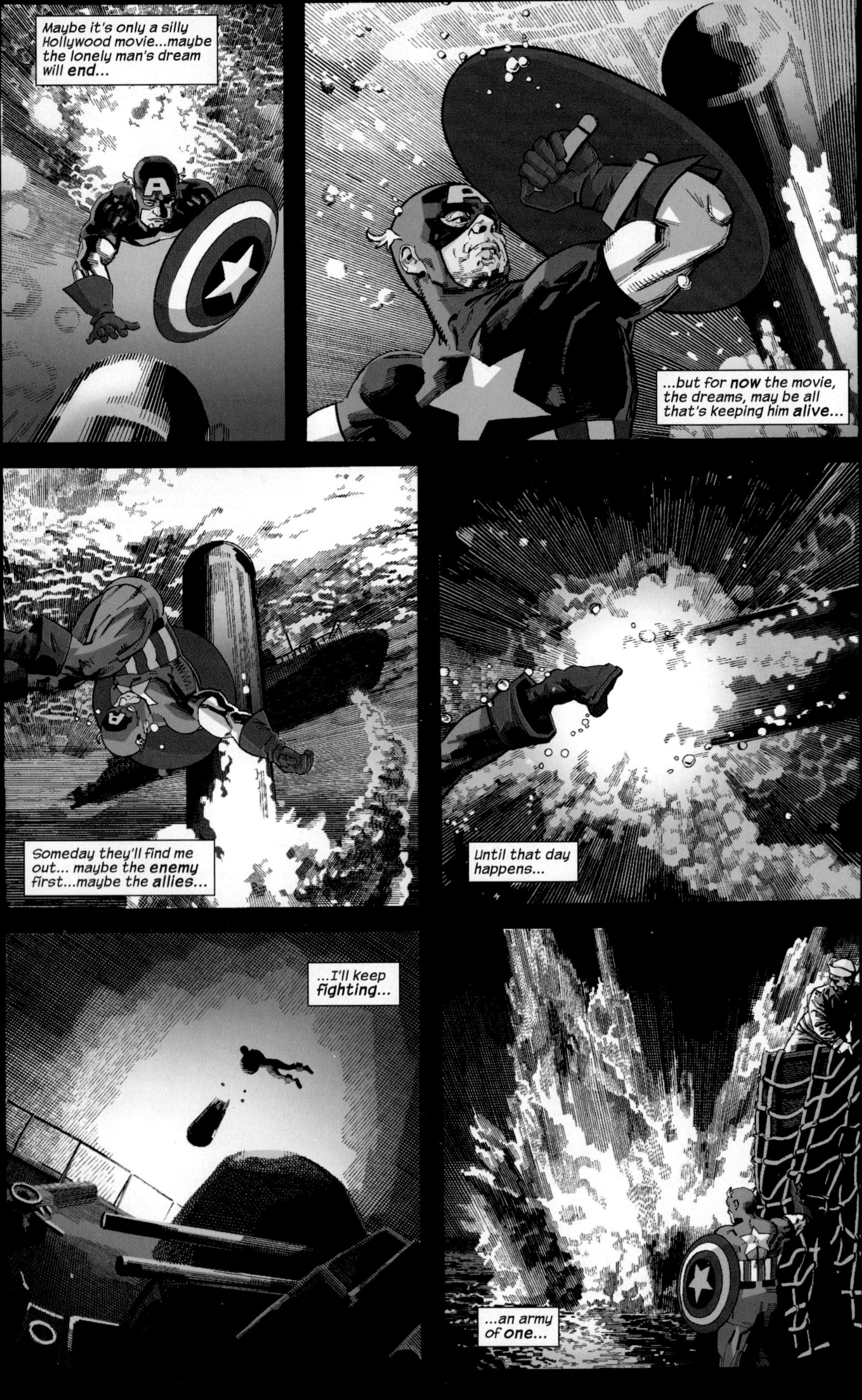
Maybe it's only a silly Hollywood movie...maybe the lonely man's dream will end...
...but for now the movie, the dreams, may be all that's keeping him alive...
Someday they'll find me out... maybe the enemy first...maybe the allies...
Until that day happens...
...I'll keep fighting...
...an army of one...

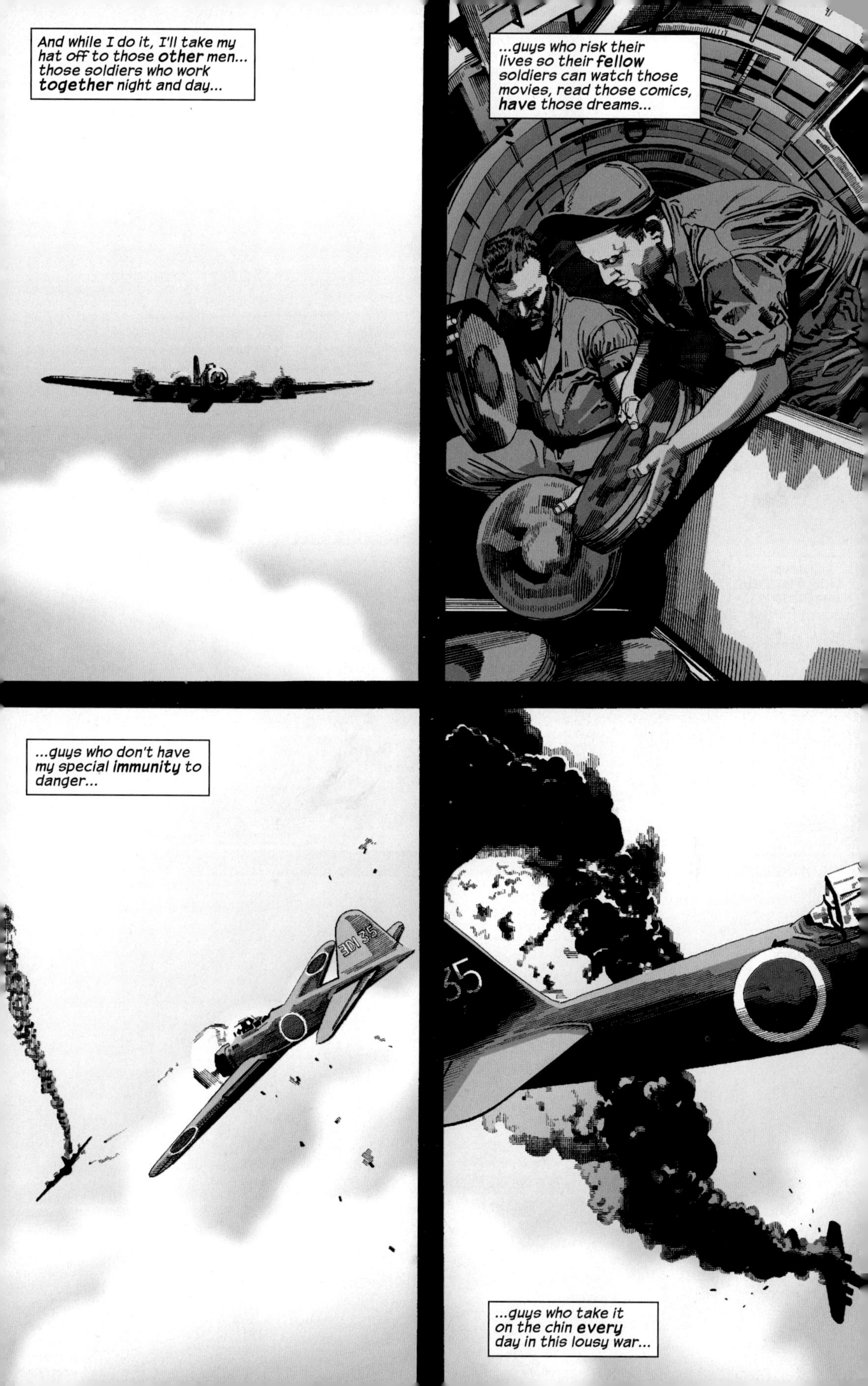
And while I do it, I'll take my hat off to those other men... those soldiers who work together night and day...
...guys who risk their lives so their fellow soldiers can watch those movies, read those comics, have those dreams...
...guys who don't have my special immunity to danger...
EDI 35
35
...guys who take it on the chin every day in this lousy war...

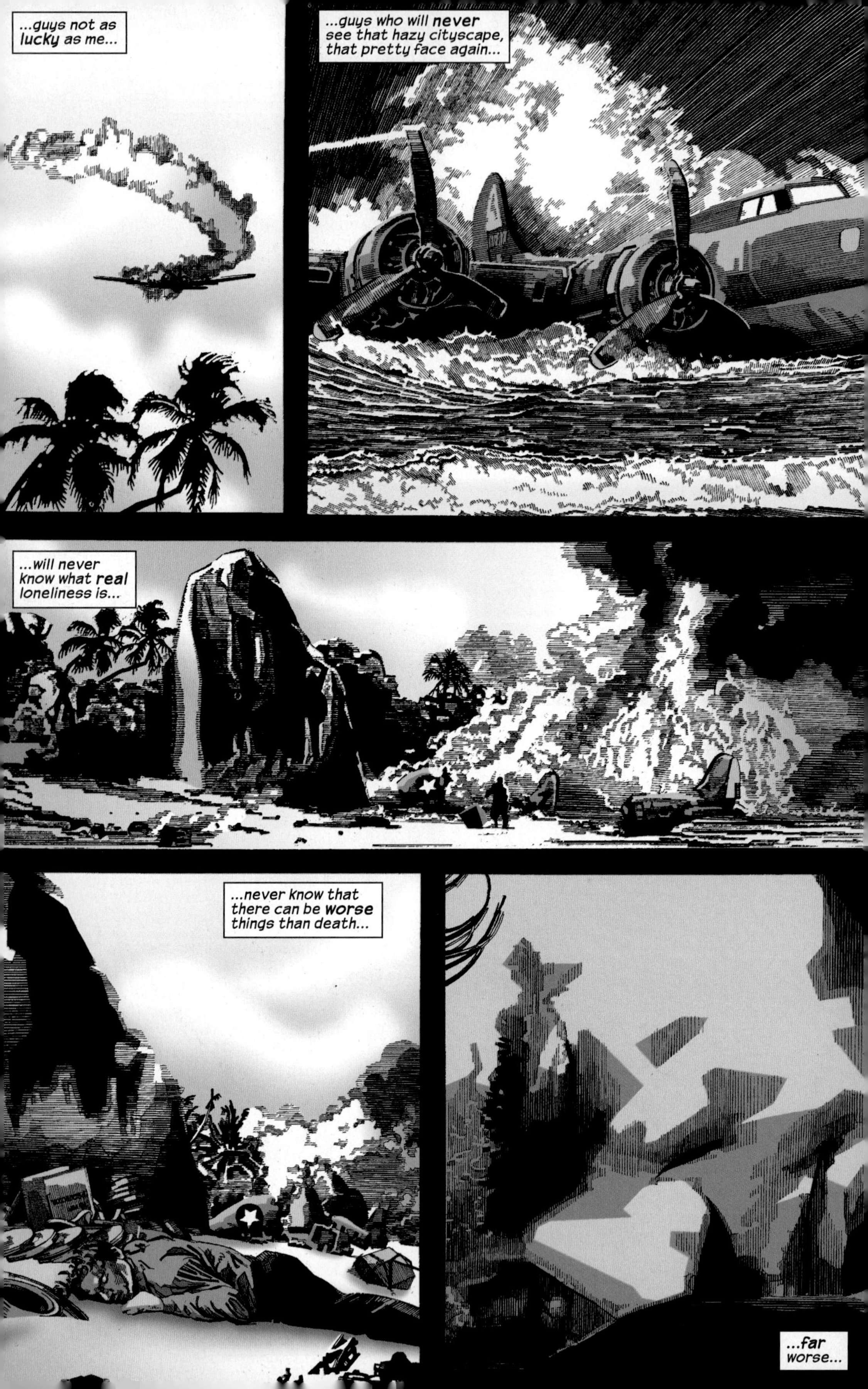
...guys not as lucky as me...
...guys who will never see that hazy cityscape, that pretty face again...
...will never know what real loneliness is...
...never know that there can be worse things than death...
...far worse...

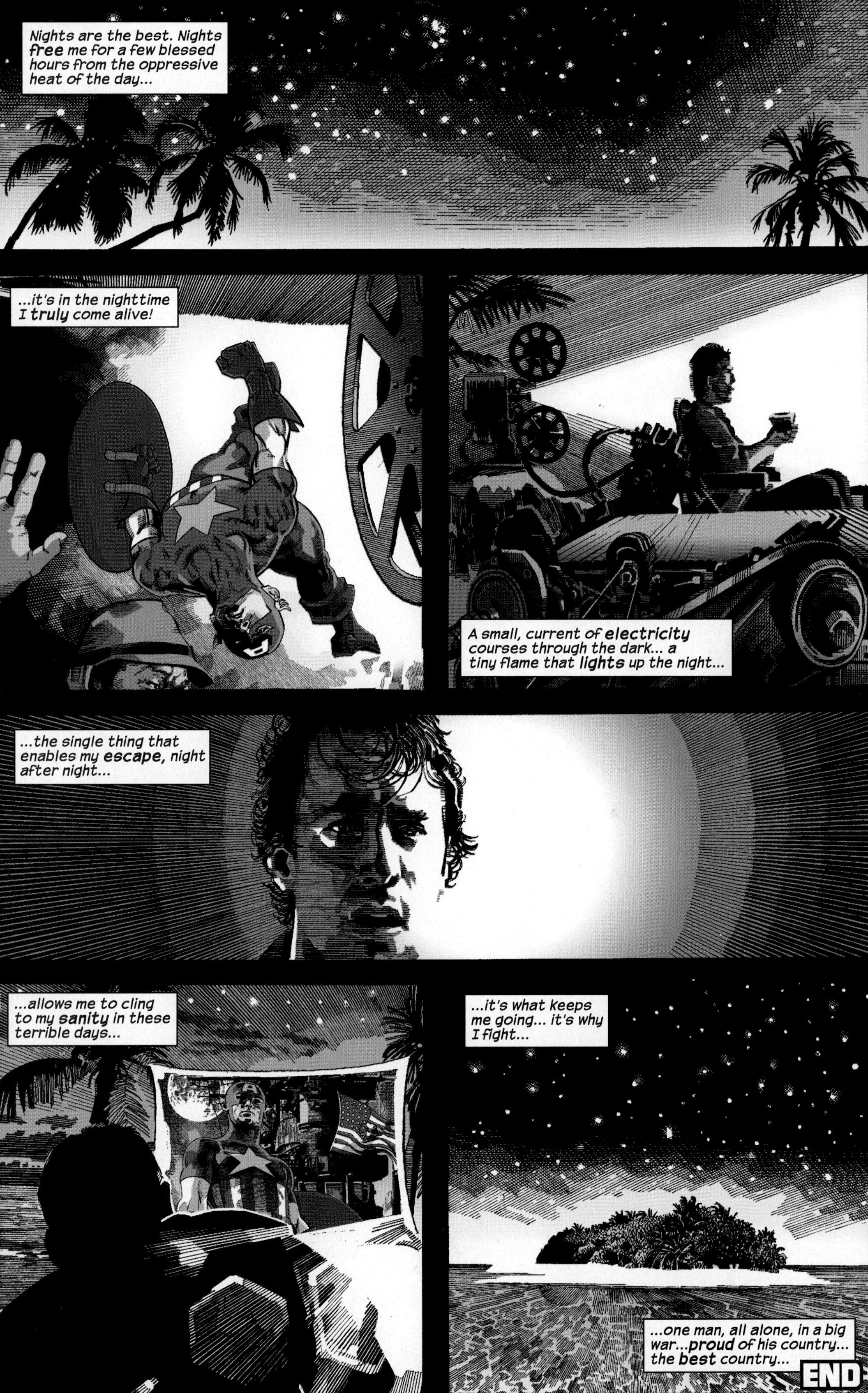

Nights are the best. Nights free me for a few blessed hours from the oppressive heat of the day...
...it's in the nighttime I truly come alive!
A small, current of electricity courses through the dark... a tiny flame that lights up the night...
...the single thing that enables my escape, night after night...
...allows me to cling to my sanity in these terrible days...
...it's what keeps me going... it's why I fight...
...one man, all alone, in a big war...proud of his country... the best country...
END

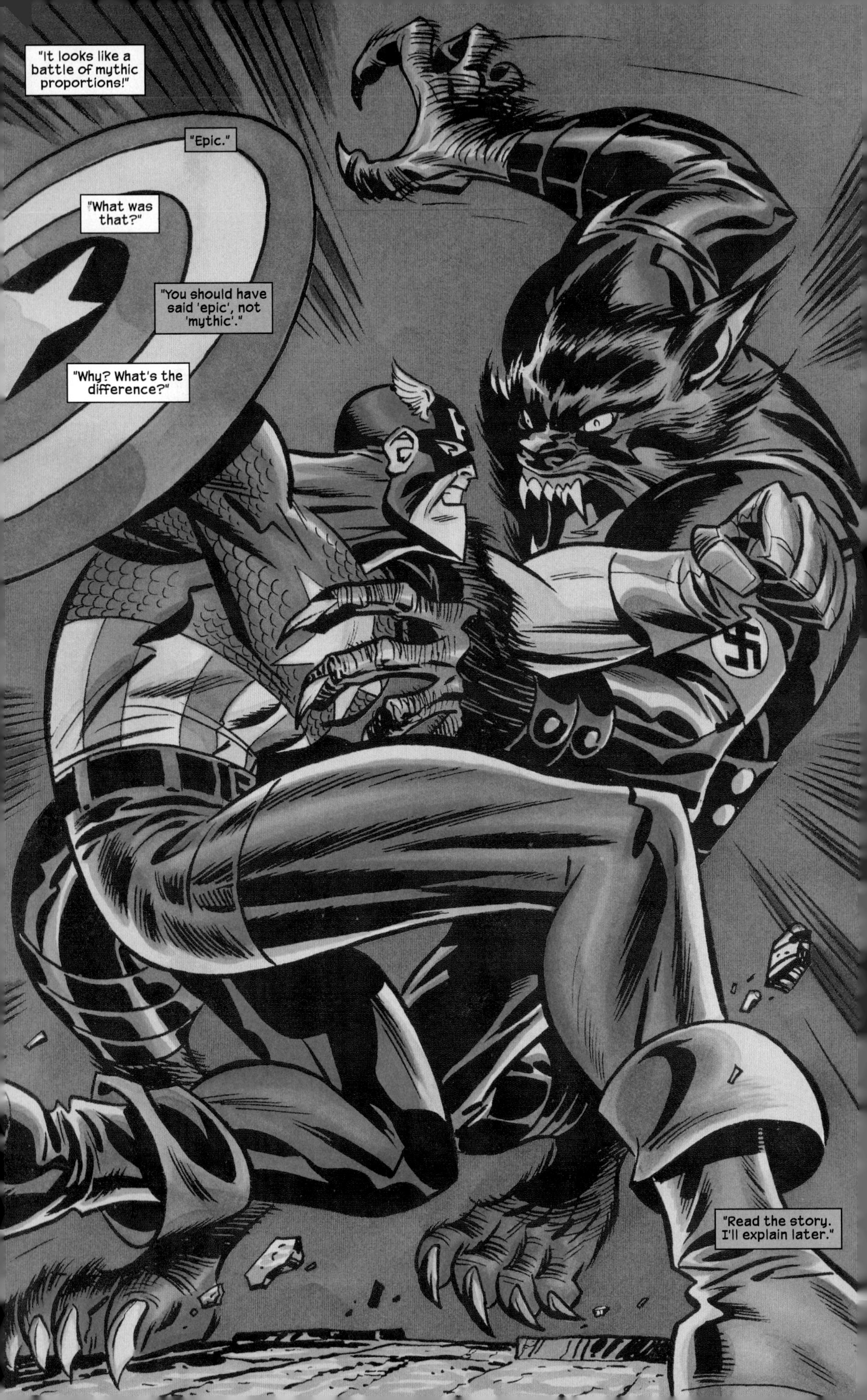
"It looks like a battle of mythic proportions!"
"Epic."
"What was that?"
"You should have said 'epic', not 'mythic'."
"Why? What's the difference?"
"Read the story. I'll explain later."

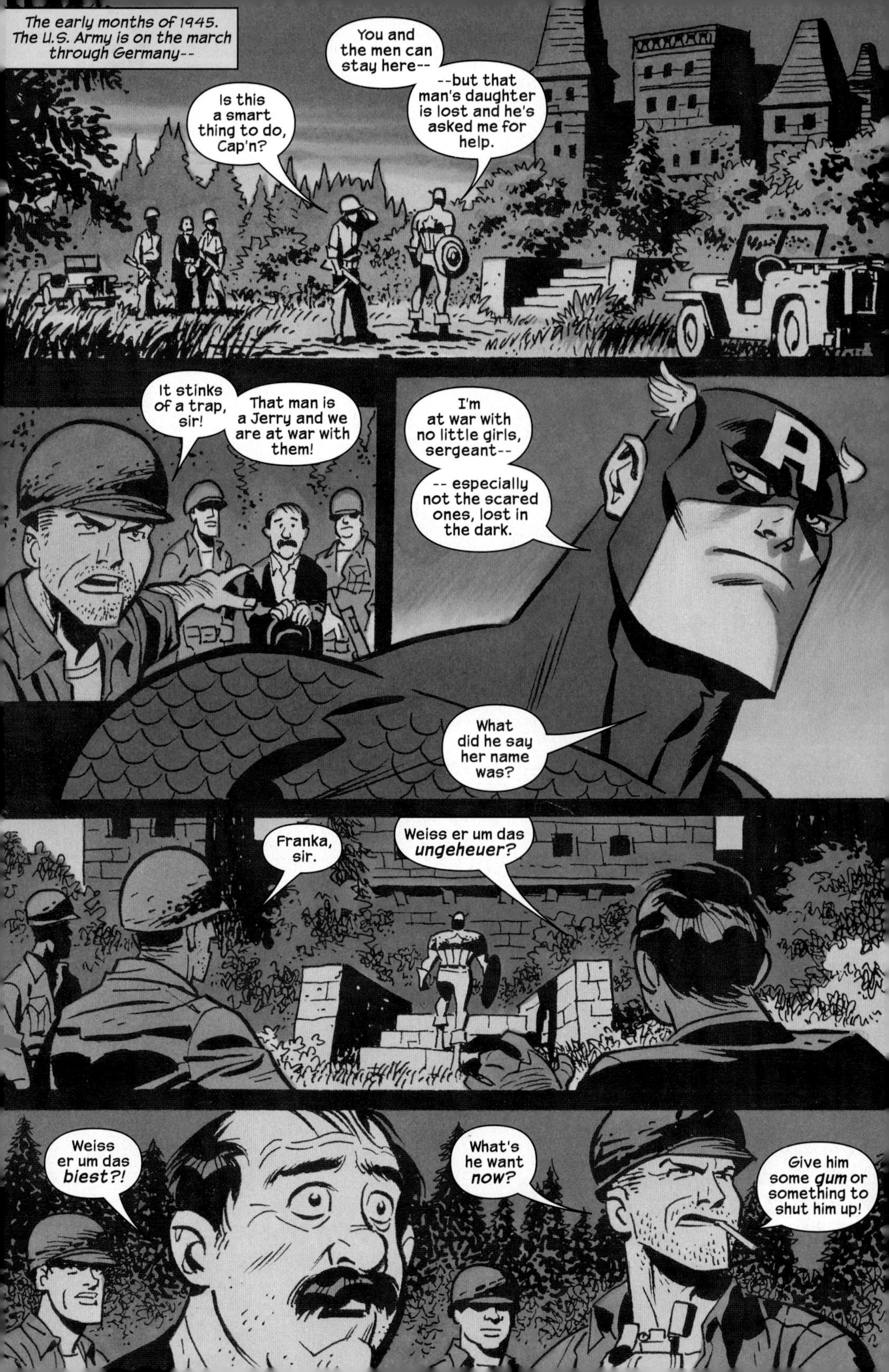
The early months of 1945. The U.S. Army is on the march through Germany--
Is this a smart thing to do, Cap'n?
You and the men can stay here--
--but that man's daughter is lost and he's asked me for help.
It stinks of a trap, sir!
That man is a Jerry and we are at war with them!
I'm at war with no little girls, sergeant--
-- especially not the scared ones, lost in the dark.
What did he say her name was?
Franka, sir.
Weiss er um das *ungeheuer*?
Weiss er um das *biest*?!
What's he want *now*?
Give him some *gum* or something to shut him up!

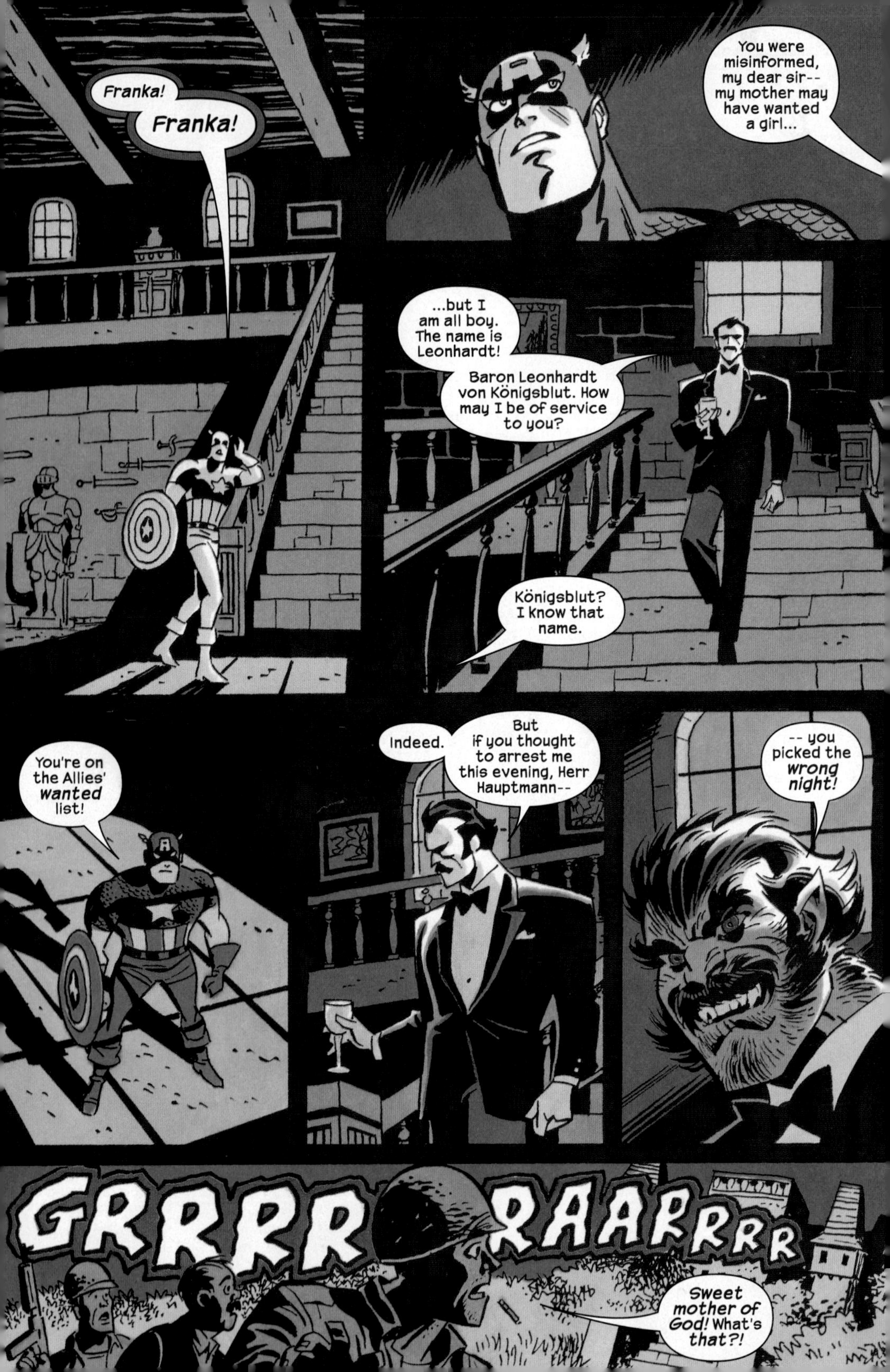
Franka!
Franka!
You were misinformed, my dear sir-- my mother may have wanted a girl...
...but I am all boy. The name is Leonhardt!
Baron Leonhardt von Königsblut. How may I be of service to you?
Königsblut? I know that name.
You're on the Allies' *wanted* list!
Indeed.
But if you thought to arrest me this evening, Herr Hauptmann--
-- you picked the *wrong night!*
GRRRRRAAARRRR
Sweet mother of God! What's that?!

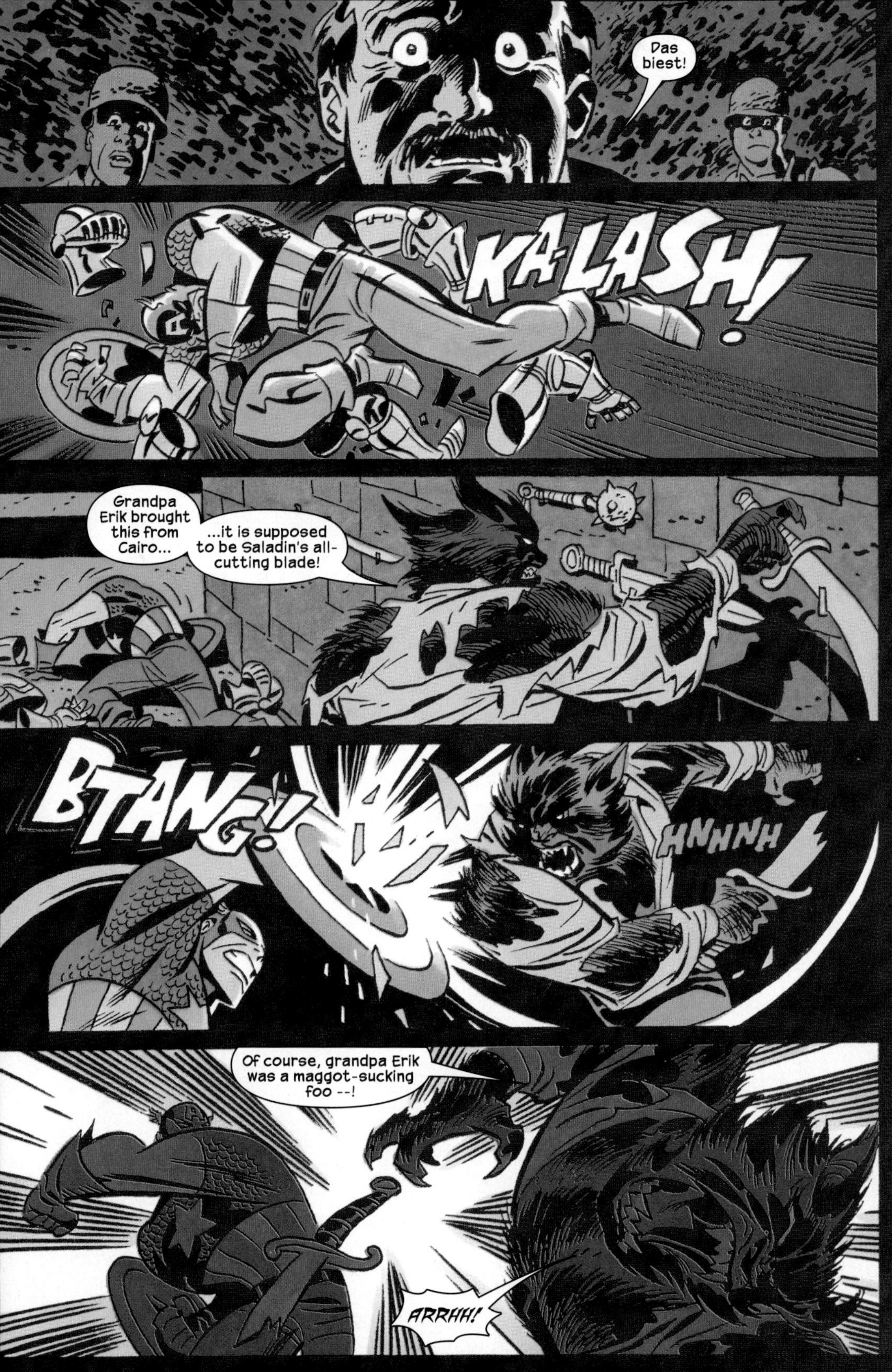
Das biest!
KA-LASH!
Grandpa Erik brought this from Cairo...
...it is supposed to be Saladin's all-cutting blade!
BTANG!
HNNNH
Of course, grandpa Erik was a maggot-sucking foo --!
ARRHH!

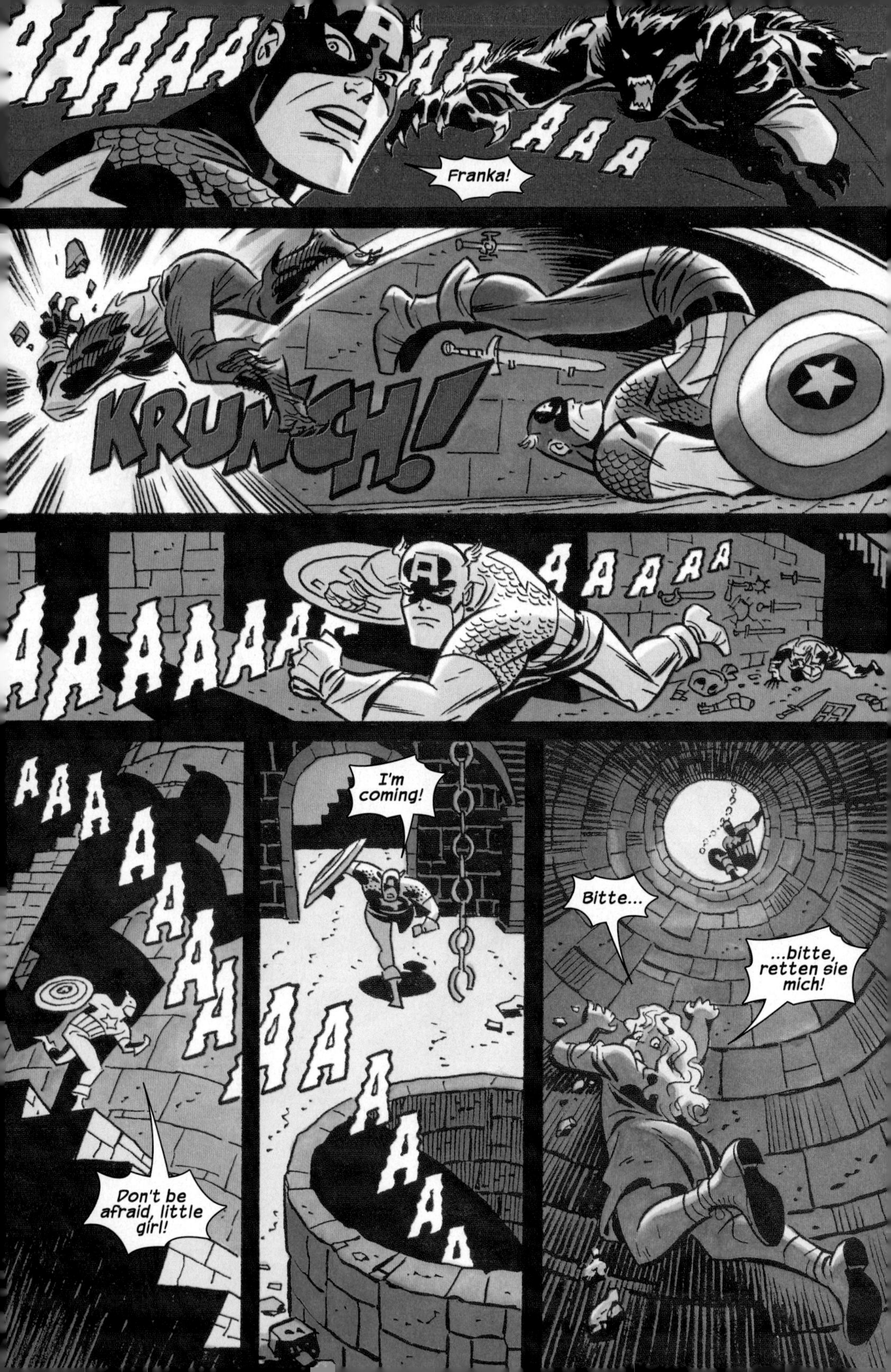

AAAAAAAAAAA
Franka!
KRUNCH!
AAAAAAAAAAA
AAAAAAAAA
Don't be afraid, little girl!
I'm coming!
AAAAAAA
Bitte...
...bitte, retten sie mich!

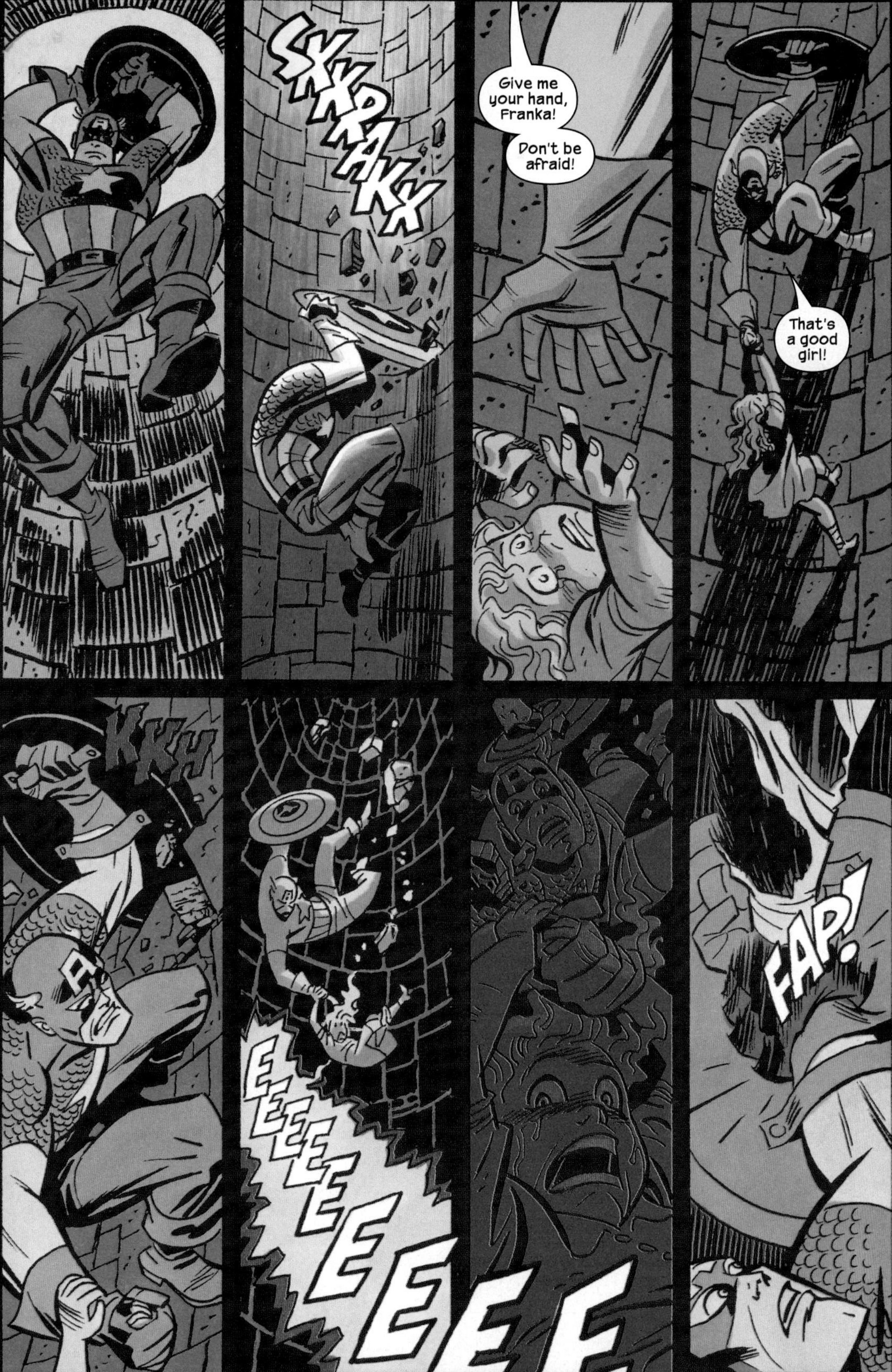
SKKRAKKK
Give me your hand, Franka!
Don't be afraid!
That's a good girl!
KKH
EEEEEEEEEEEE
FAP!

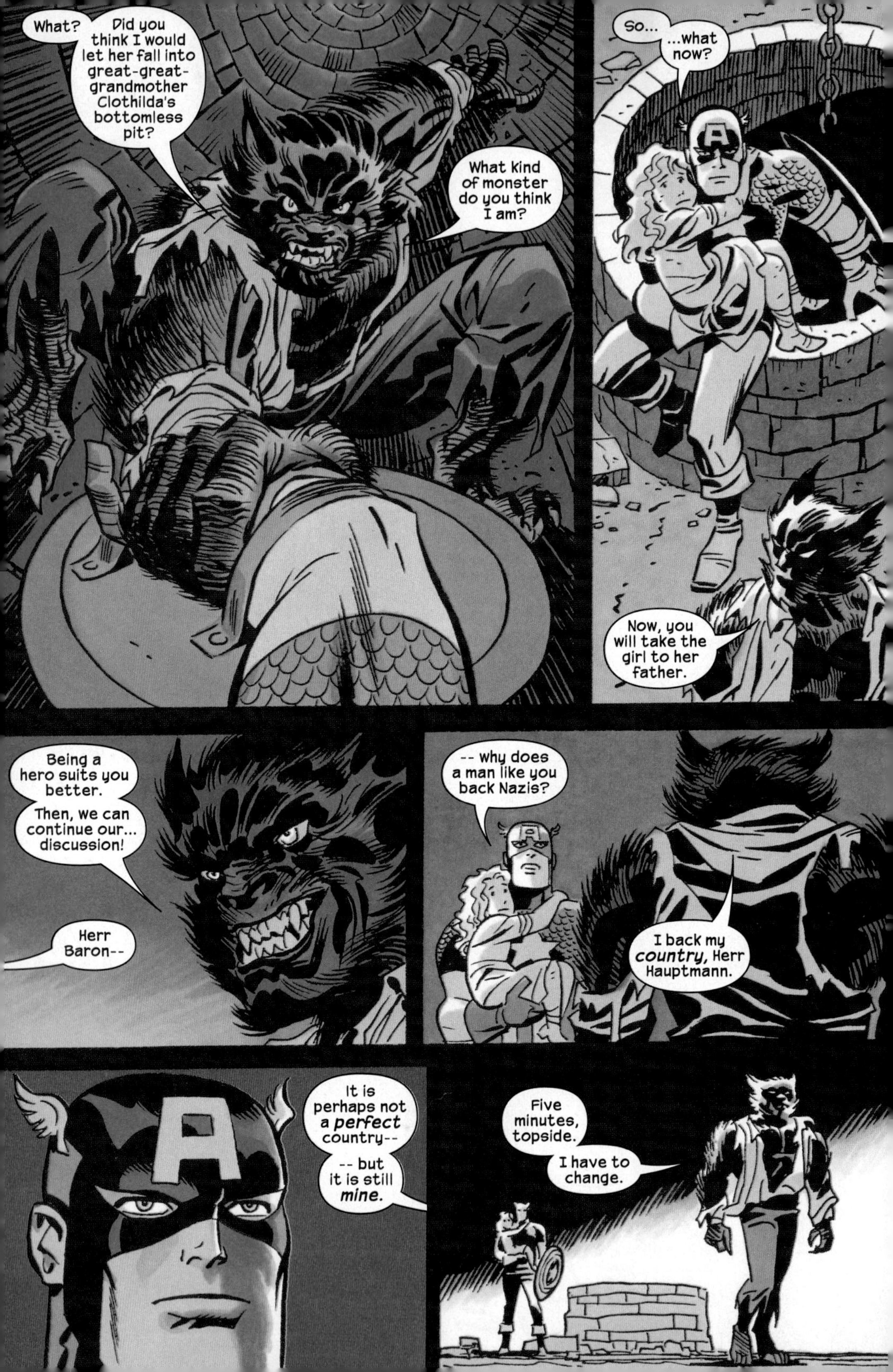
What?
Did you think I would let her fall into great-great-grandmother Clothilda's bottomless pit?
What kind of monster do you think I am?
So...
...what now?
Now, you will take the girl to her father.
Being a hero suits you better.
Then, we can continue our... discussion!
Herr Baron--
-- why does a man like you back Nazis?
I back my *country,* Herr Hauptmann.
It is perhaps not a *perfect* country--
-- but it is still *mine.*
Five minutes, topside.
I have to change.

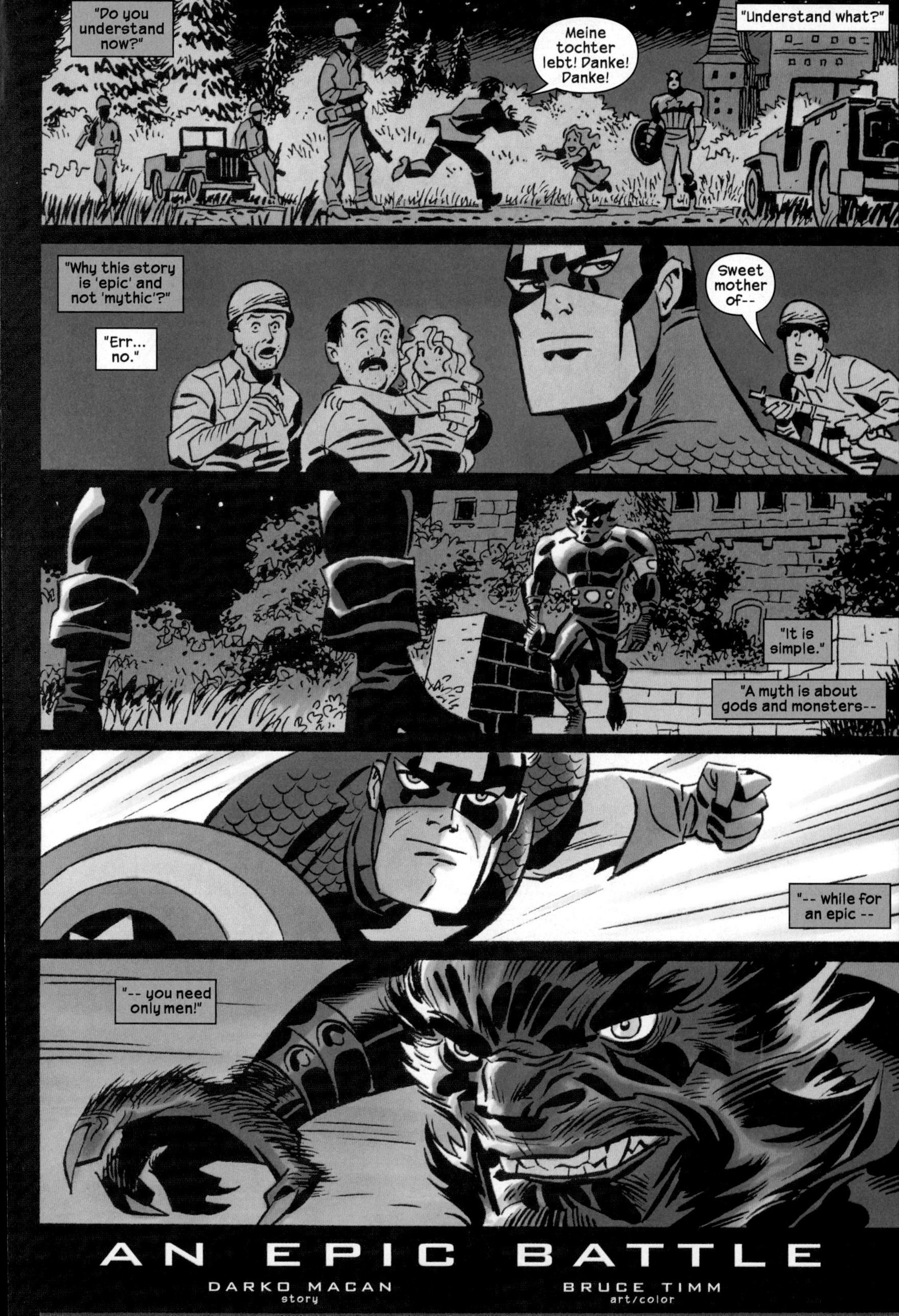
"Do you understand now?"
Meine tochter lebt! Danke! Danke!
"Understand what?"
"Why this story is 'epic' and not 'mythic'?"
"Err... no."
Sweet mother of--
"It is simple."
"A myth is about gods and monsters--
"-- while for an epic --
"-- you need only men!"

AN EPIC BATTLE

DARKO MACAN
story

BRUCE TIMM
art/color

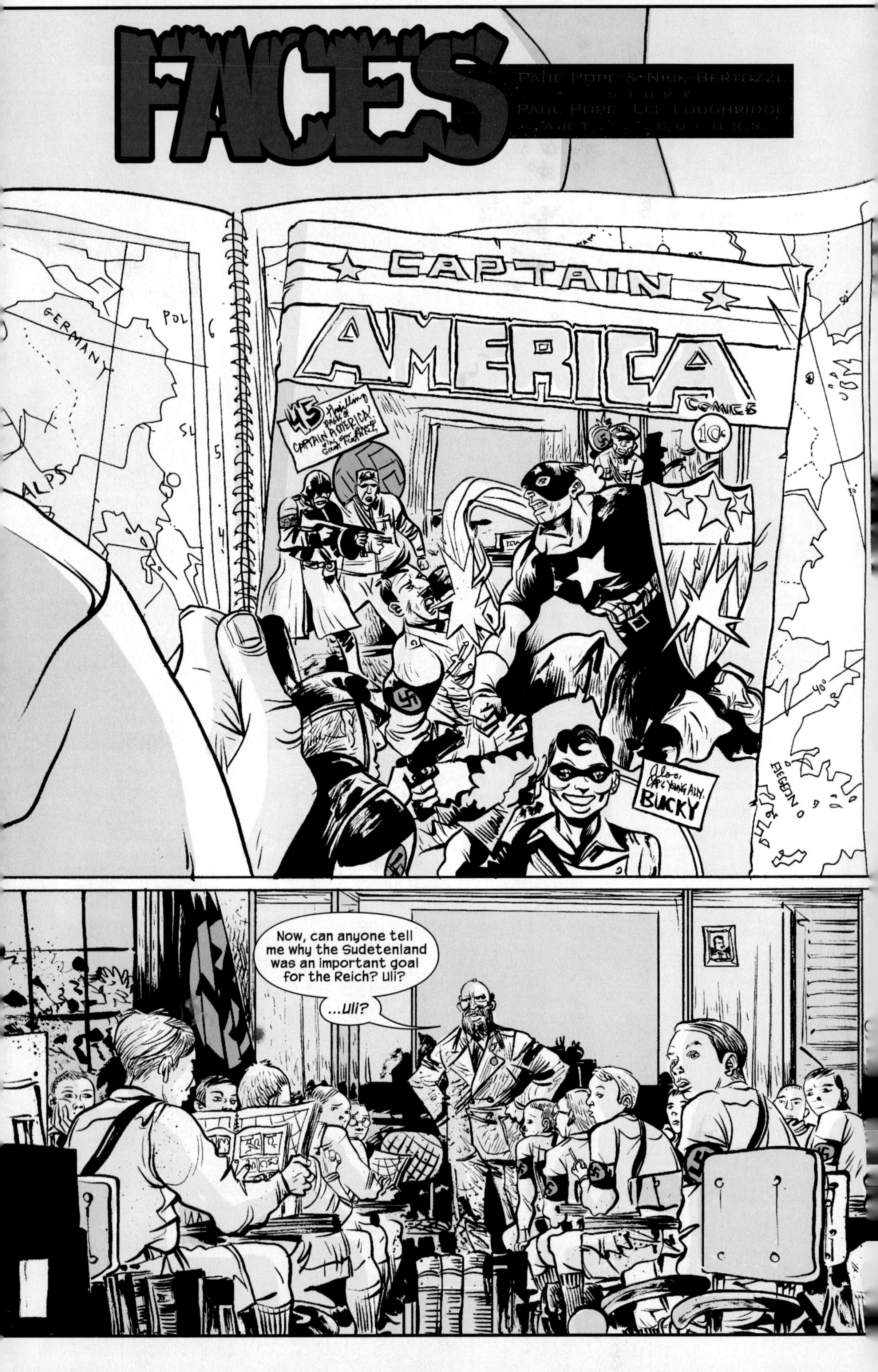
FACES
PAUL POPE & NICK BERTOZZI
STORY
PAUL POPE LEE LOUGHRIDGE
ART COLORS
GERMANY
POL
ALPS
CAPTAIN AMERICA COMICS
10¢
45 thrilling pages of CAPTAIN AMERICA
Also: Cap's young ally, BUCKY
Now, can anyone tell me why the Sudetenland was an important goal for the Reich? Uli?
...Uli?

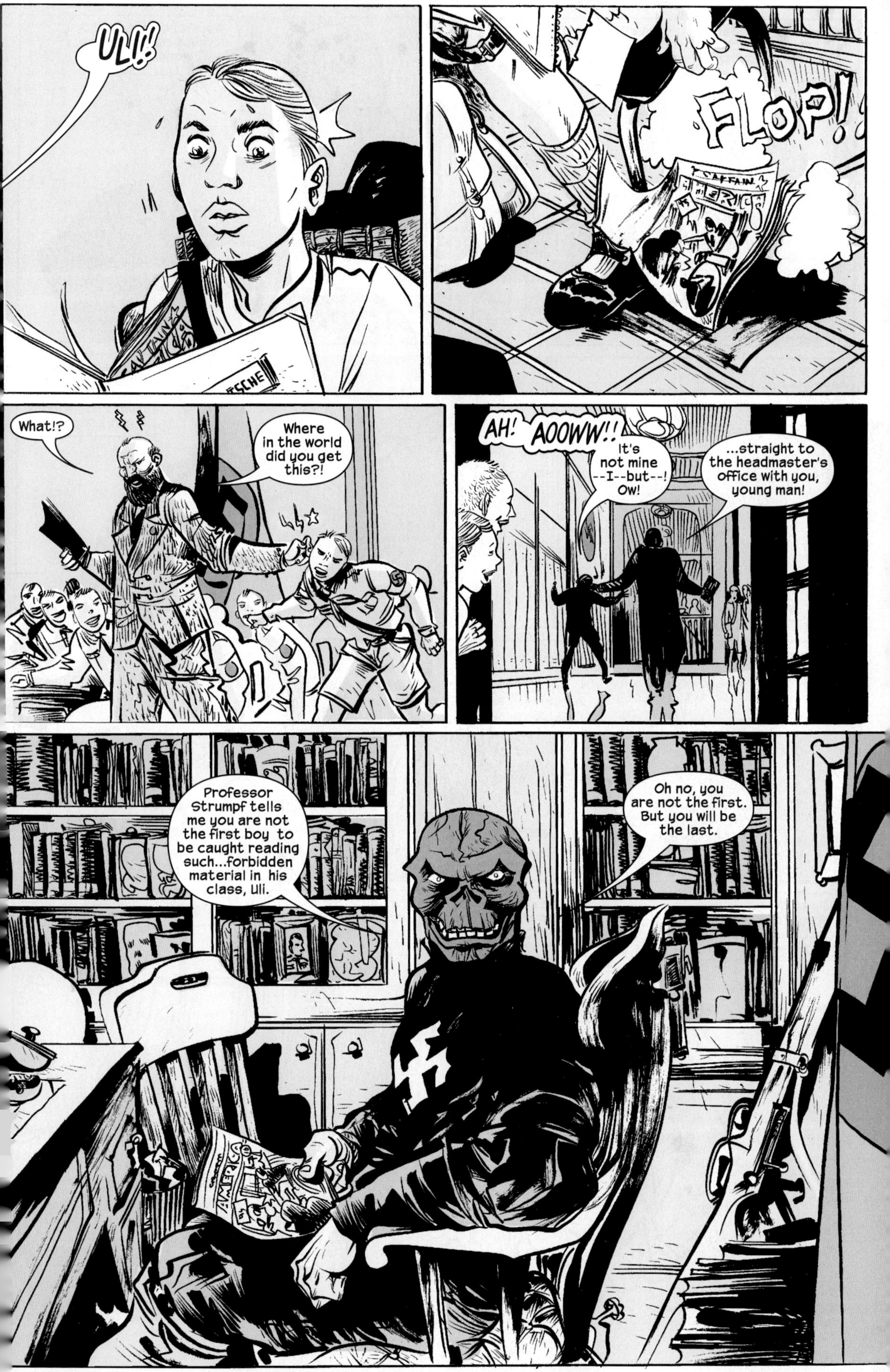
ULI!!
FLOP!
What!?
Where in the world did you get this?!
AH! AOOWW!!
It's not mine --I--but--! Ow!
...straight to the headmaster's office with you, young man!
Professor Strumpf tells me you are not the first boy to be caught reading such...forbidden material in his class, Uli.
Oh no, you are not the first. But you will be the last.

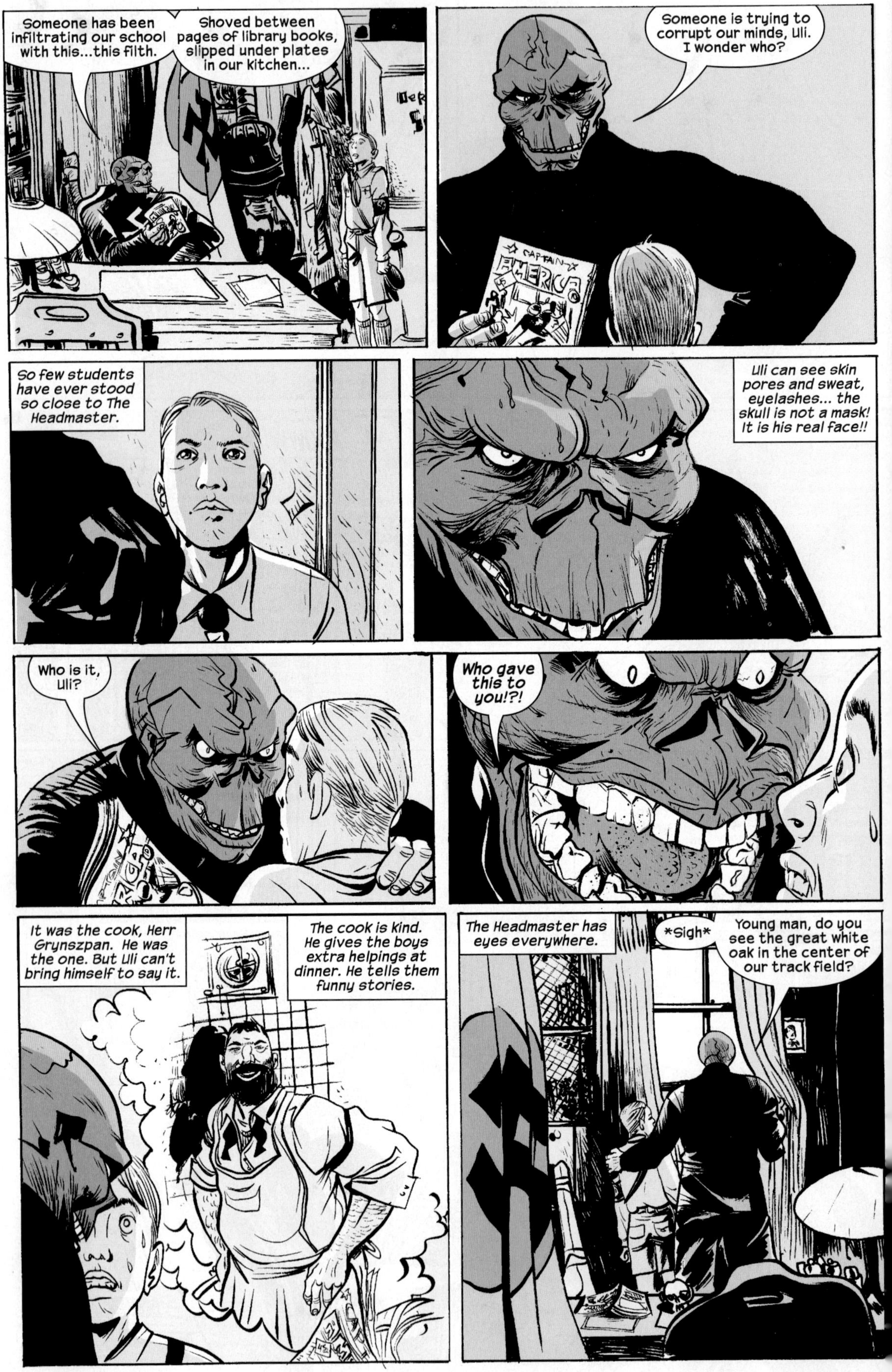
Someone has been infiltrating our school with this...this filth.
Shoved between pages of library books, slipped under plates in our kitchen...
Someone is trying to corrupt our minds, Uli. I wonder who?
So few students have ever stood so close to The Headmaster.
Uli can see skin pores and sweat, eyelashes... the skull is not a mask! It is his real face!!
Who is it, Uli?
Who gave this to you!?!
It was the cook, Herr Grynszpan. He was the one. But Uli can't bring himself to say it.
The cook is kind. He gives the boys extra helpings at dinner. He tells them funny stories.
The Headmaster has eyes everywhere.
Sigh
Young man, do you see the great white oak in the center of our track field?

"That white oak marks the very spot where the hero Siegfried, on his way to the lovely Brunhild, slew the fearsome Uberworm.

"And with his blazing sword, Siegfried cast the worm deep into the caverns under the world, from which it has never fully reemerged."

"From the blood Siegfried shed that day has blossomed the Ubermenchen, Uli.

"That blood is us, the Aryans, the master race.

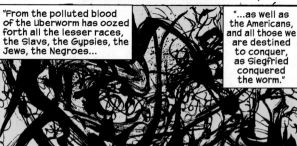

"From the polluted blood of the Uberworm has oozed forth all the lesser races, the Slavs, the Gypsies, the Jews, the Negroes...

"...as well as the Americans, and all those we are destined to conquer, as Siegfried conquered the worm."

Like Siegfried, we must remain brave and pure. We must shield our minds from the lies of our enemies.

Here, my little Siegfried-- my Mauser. Take it.

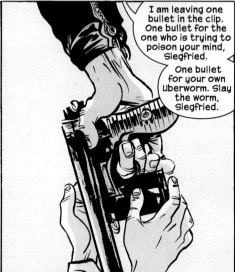

I am leaving one bullet in the clip. One bullet for the one who is trying to poison your mind, Siegfried.

One bullet for your own Uberworm. Slay the worm, Siegfried.

Oh, don't be stupid, Uli! I already know who it is--

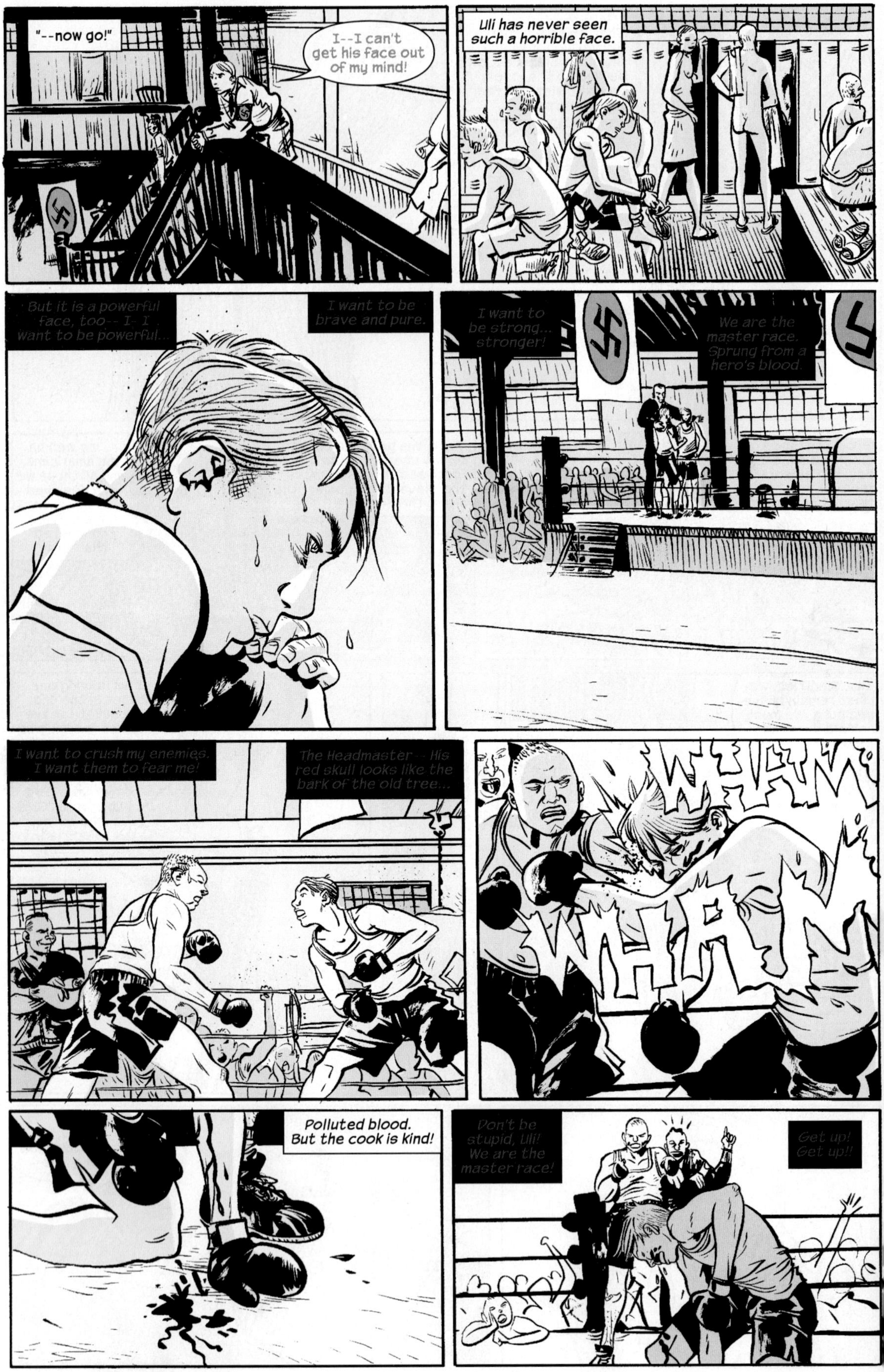
"--now go!"
I--I can't get his face out of my mind!
Uli has never seen such a horrible face.
But it is a powerful face, too-- I- I want to be powerful...
I want to be brave and pure.
I want to be strong... stronger!
We are the master race. Sprung from a hero's blood.
I want to crush my enemies. I want them to fear me!
The Headmaster-- His red skull looks like the bark of the old tree...
WHAM
WHAM
Polluted blood. But the cook is kind!
Don't be stupid, Uli! We are the master race!
Get up! Get up!!

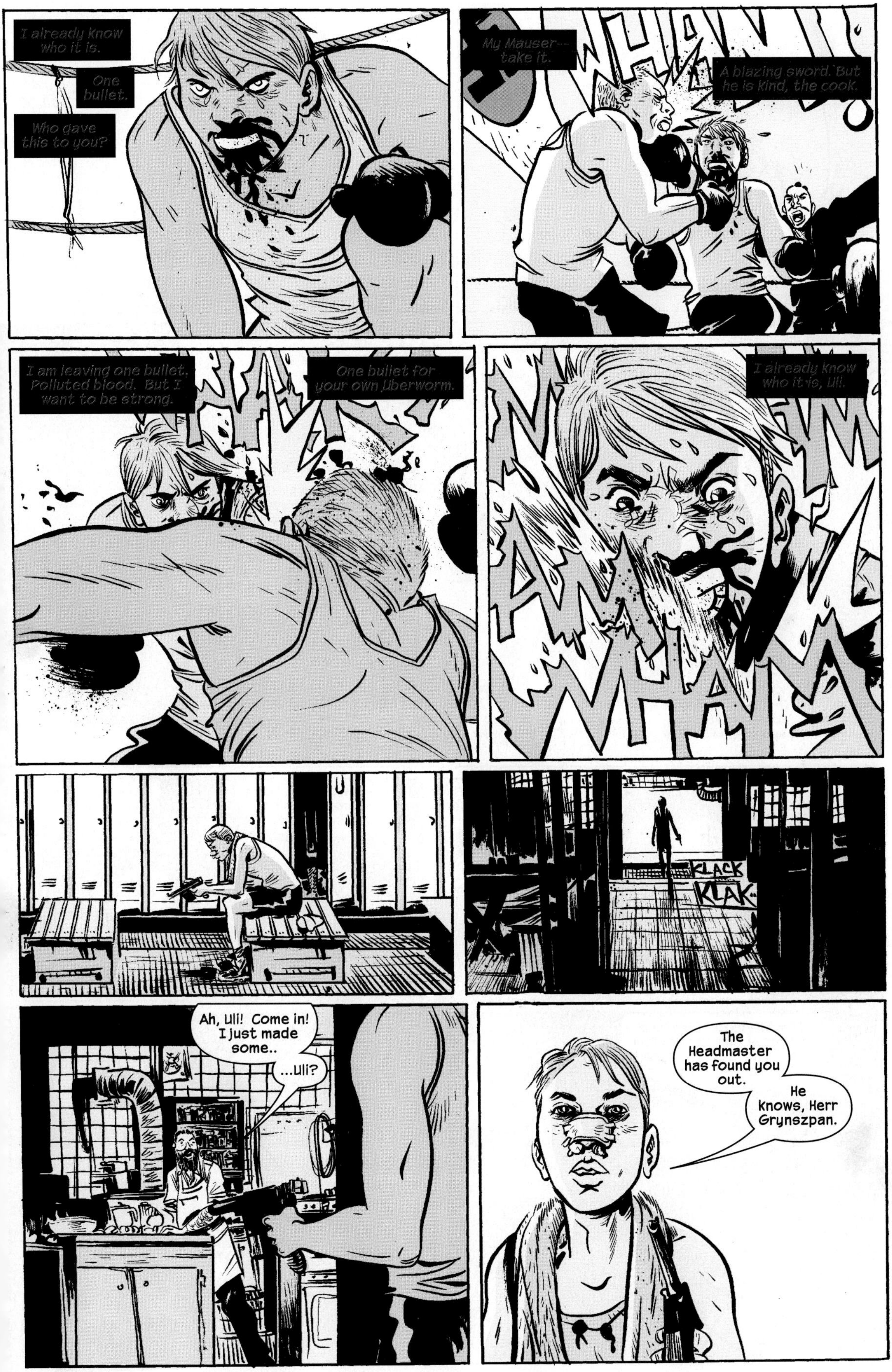

I already know who it is.
One bullet.
Who gave this to you?
My Mauser-- take it.
A blazing sword. But he is kind, the cook.
I am leaving one bullet. Polluted blood. But I want to be strong.
One bullet for your own Uberworm.
I already know who it is, Uli.
KLACK
KLAK..
Ah, Uli! Come in! I just made some..
...Uli?
The Headmaster has found you out.
He knows, Herr Grynszpan.

Outside! To the trackfield! Go!!

Uli! I--I thought we were *friends*--

Shut up! Shut up!!

Up against the tree.

Uli, don't! You don't have to-- You could say I escaped! We could escape together! The trains are--

This...this old tree marks the very spot where the hero Siegfried...

Uli!

...s-slew the fearsome Uberworm with his blazing sword.

From Switzerland we..we could...

From the blood Siegfried shed has sprung the master race... and from the blood of the Uberworm...

...even to--to America...

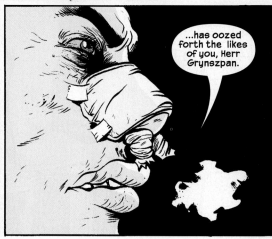

...has oozed forth the likes of you, Herr Grynszpan.

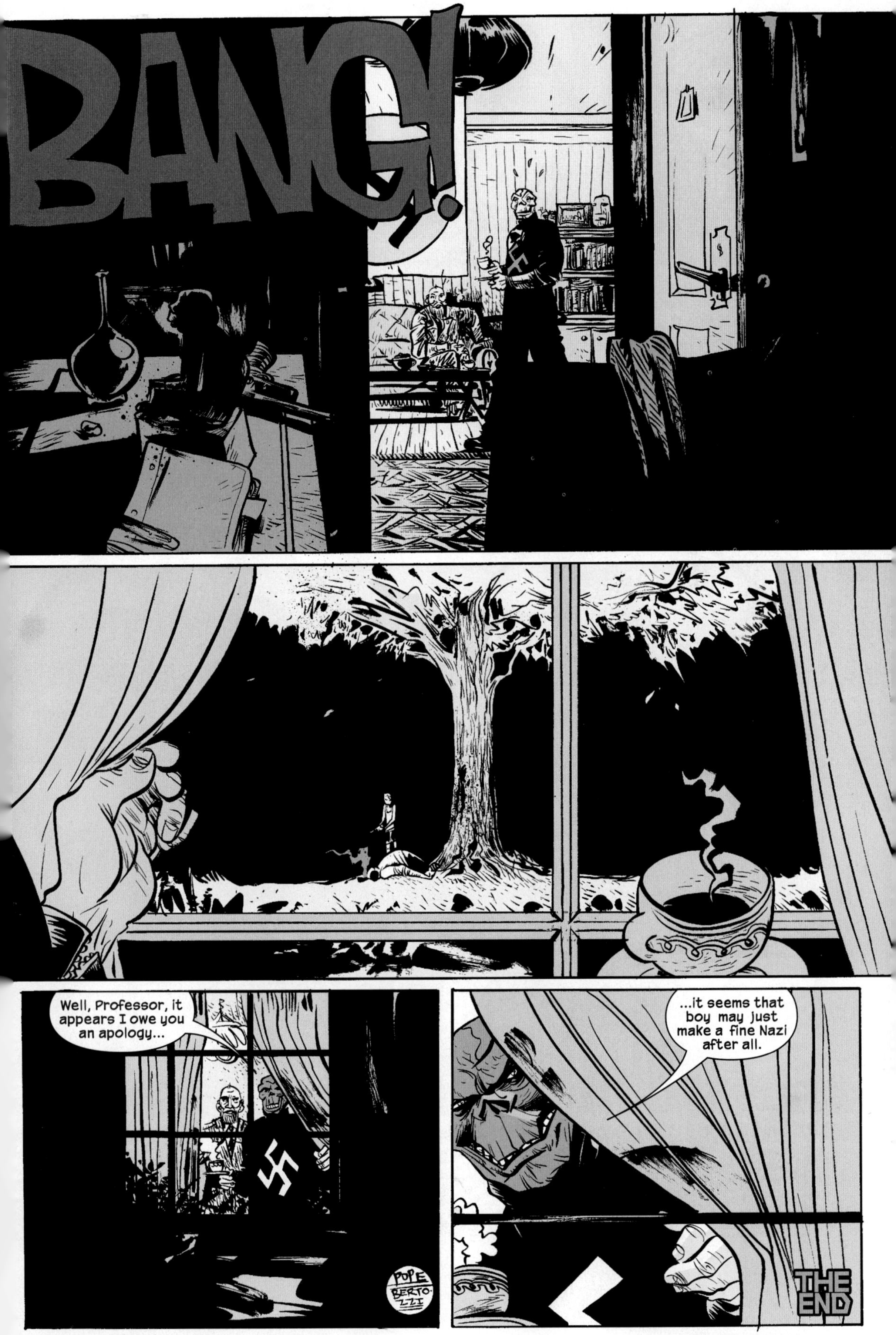
BANG!
Well, Professor, it appears I owe you an apology...
...it seems that boy may just make a fine Nazi after all.
POPE BERTOZZI
THE END

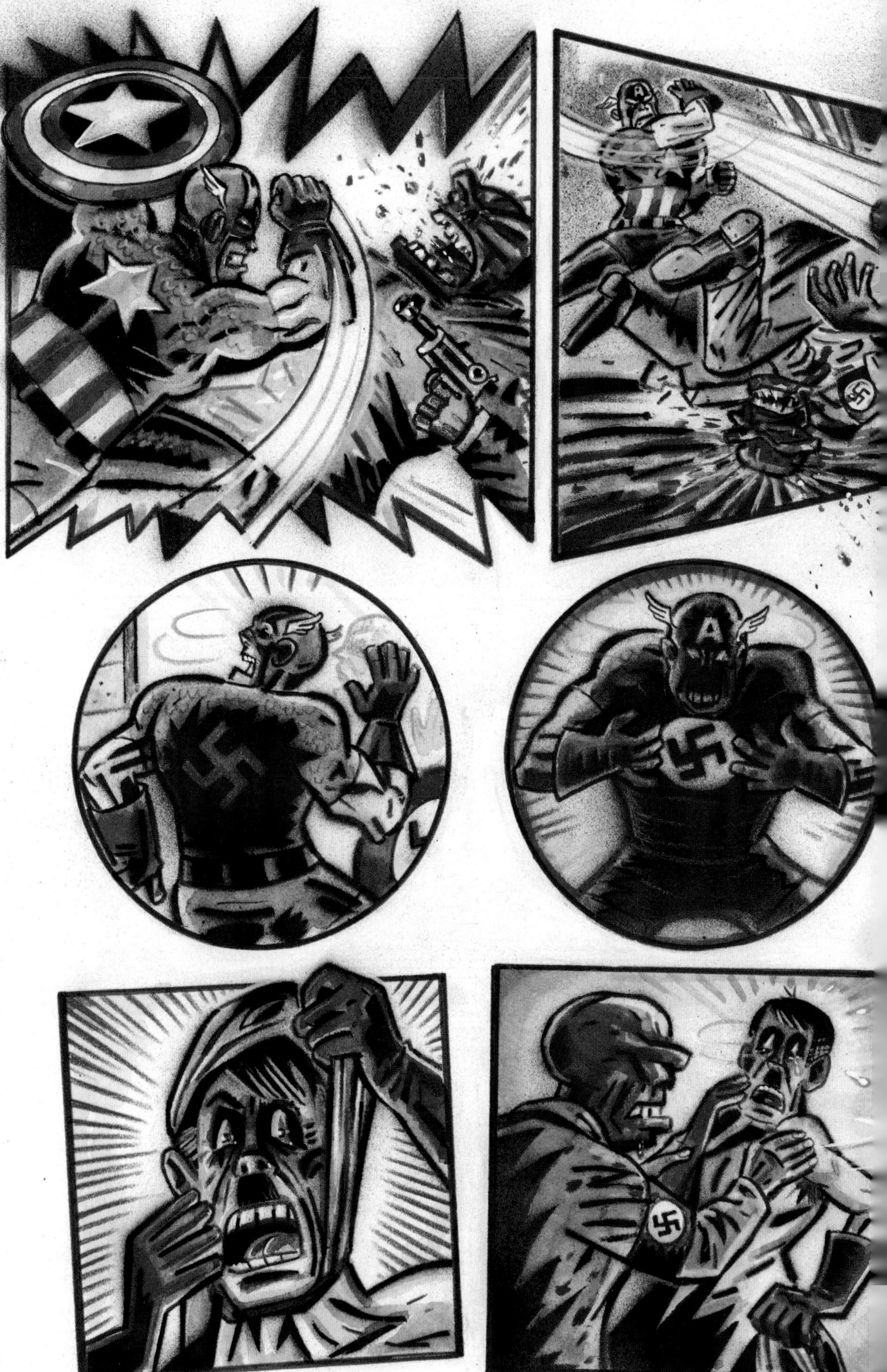

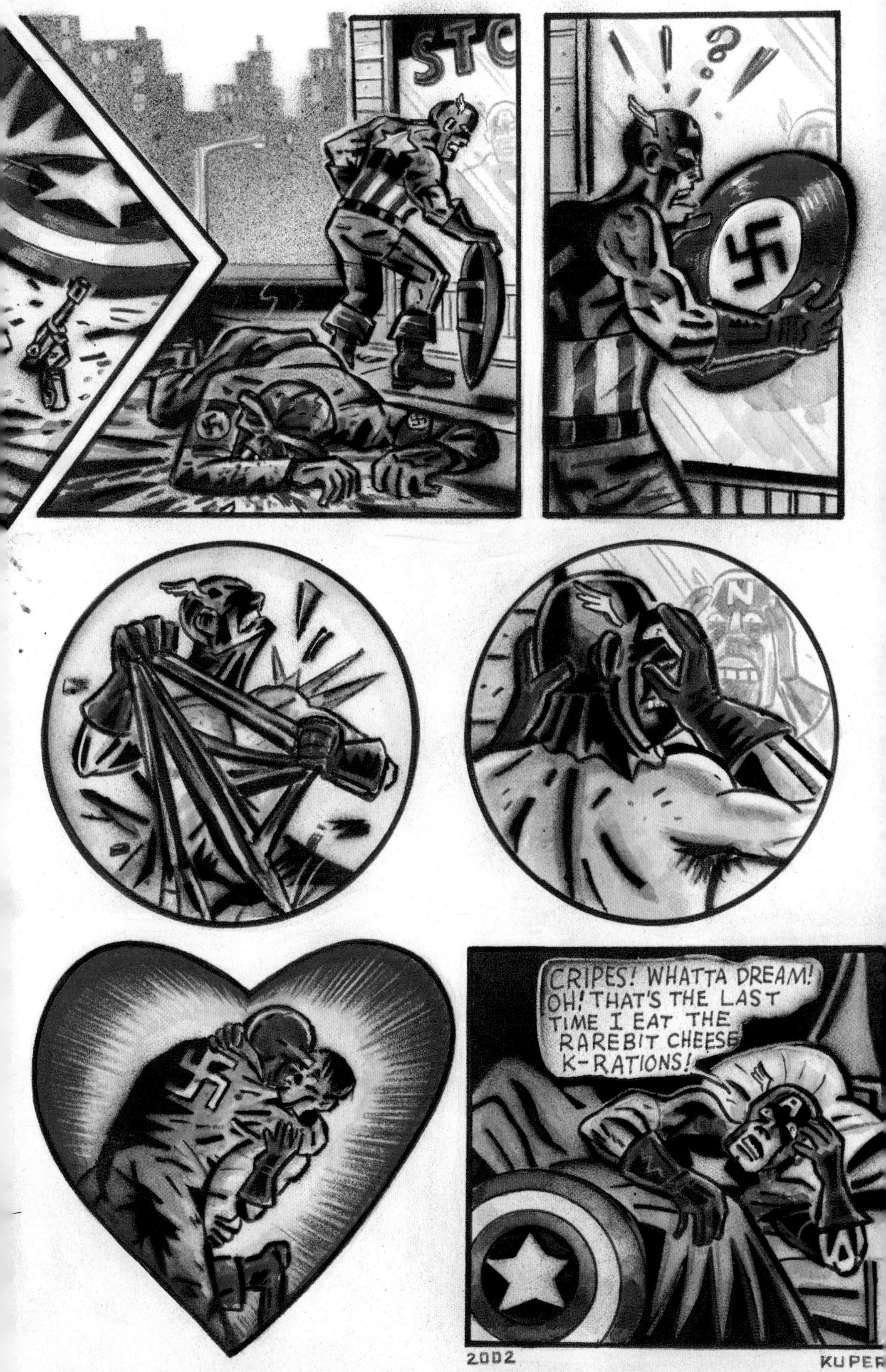
STO
CRIPES! WHATTA DREAM! OH! THAT'S THE LAST TIME I EAT THE RAREBIT CHEESE K-RATIONS!

2002 KUPER

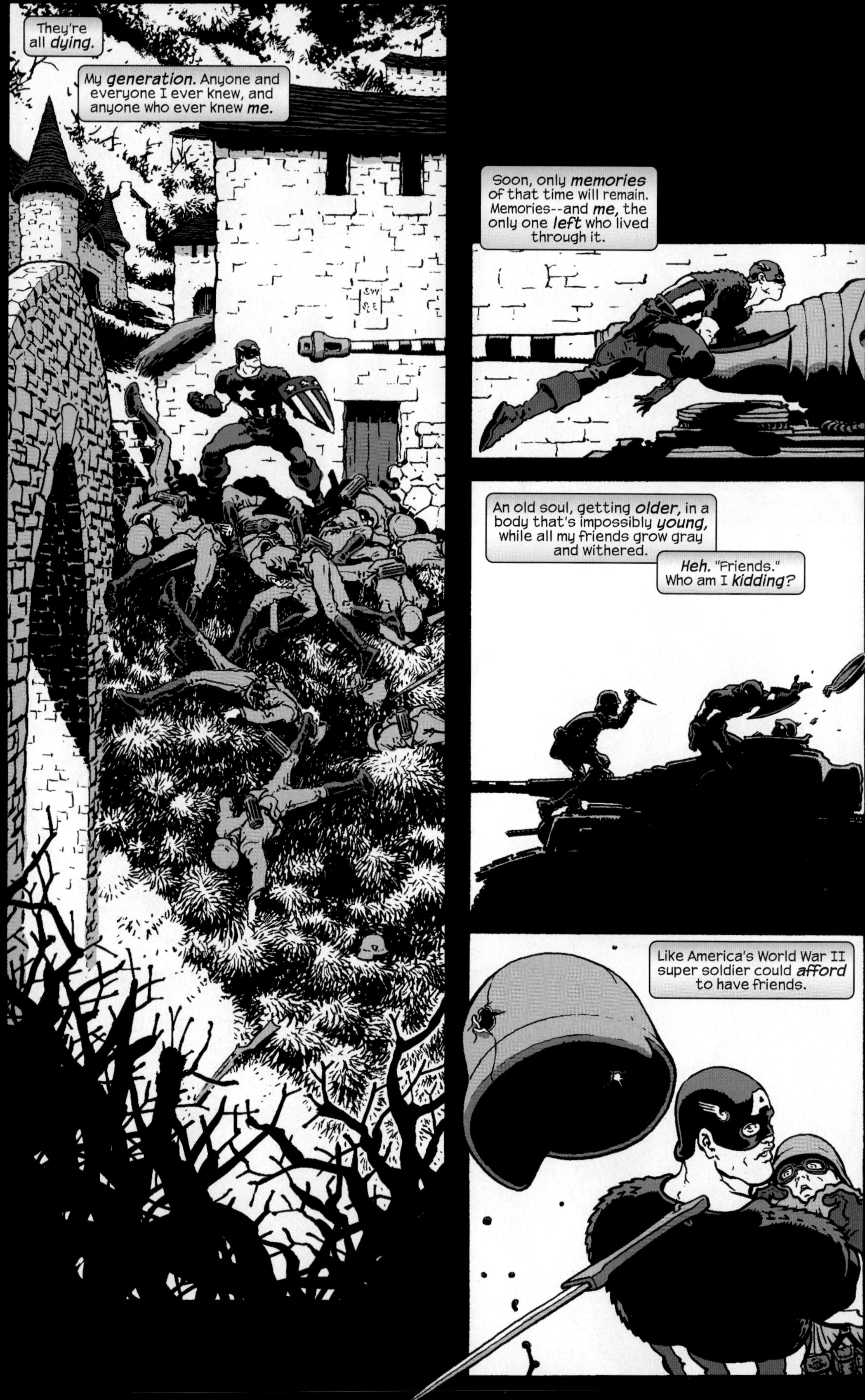
They're all *dying.*
My *generation.* Anyone and everyone I ever knew, and anyone who ever knew *me.*
Soon, only *memories* of that time will remain. Memories--and *me,* the only one *left* who lived through it.
An old soul, getting *older,* in a body that's impossibly *young,* while all my friends grow gray and withered.
Heh. "Friends." Who am I *kidding?*
Like America's World War II super soldier could *afford* to have friends.

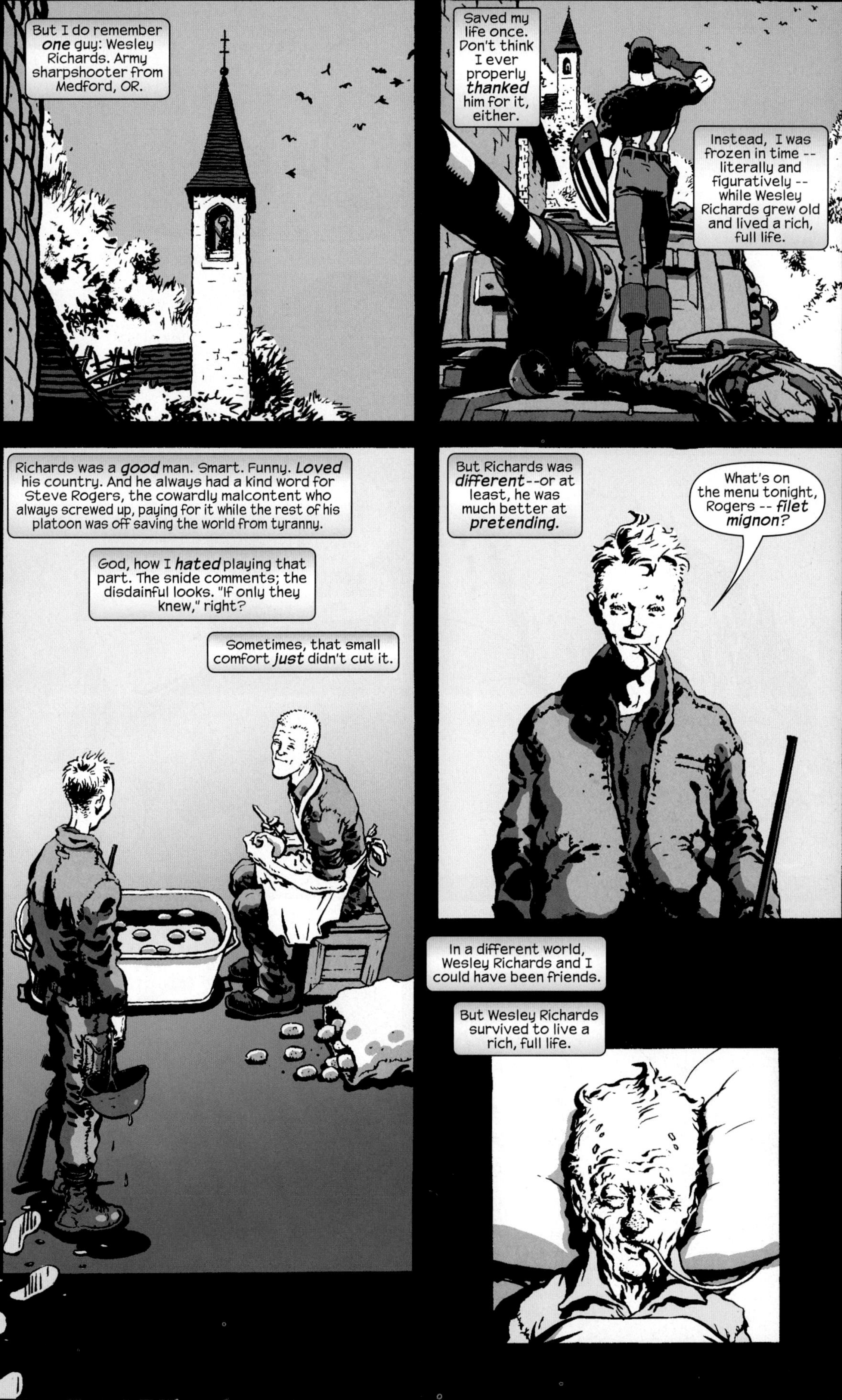
But I do remember *one* guy: Wesley Richards. Army sharpshooter from Medford, OR.
Saved my life once. Don't think I ever properly *thanked* him for it, either.
Instead, I was frozen in time -- literally and figuratively -- while Wesley Richards grew old and lived a rich, full life.
Richards was a *good* man. Smart. Funny. *Loved* his country. And he always had a kind word for Steve Rogers, the cowardly malcontent who always screwed up, paying for it while the rest of his platoon was off saving the world from tyranny.
God, how I *hated* playing that part. The snide comments; the disdainful looks. "If only they knew," right?
Sometimes, that small comfort *just* didn't cut it.
But Richards was *different*--or at least, he was much better at *pretending.*
What's on the menu tonight, Rogers -- *filet mignon?*
In a different world, Wesley Richards and I could have been friends.
But Wesley Richards survived to live a rich, full life.

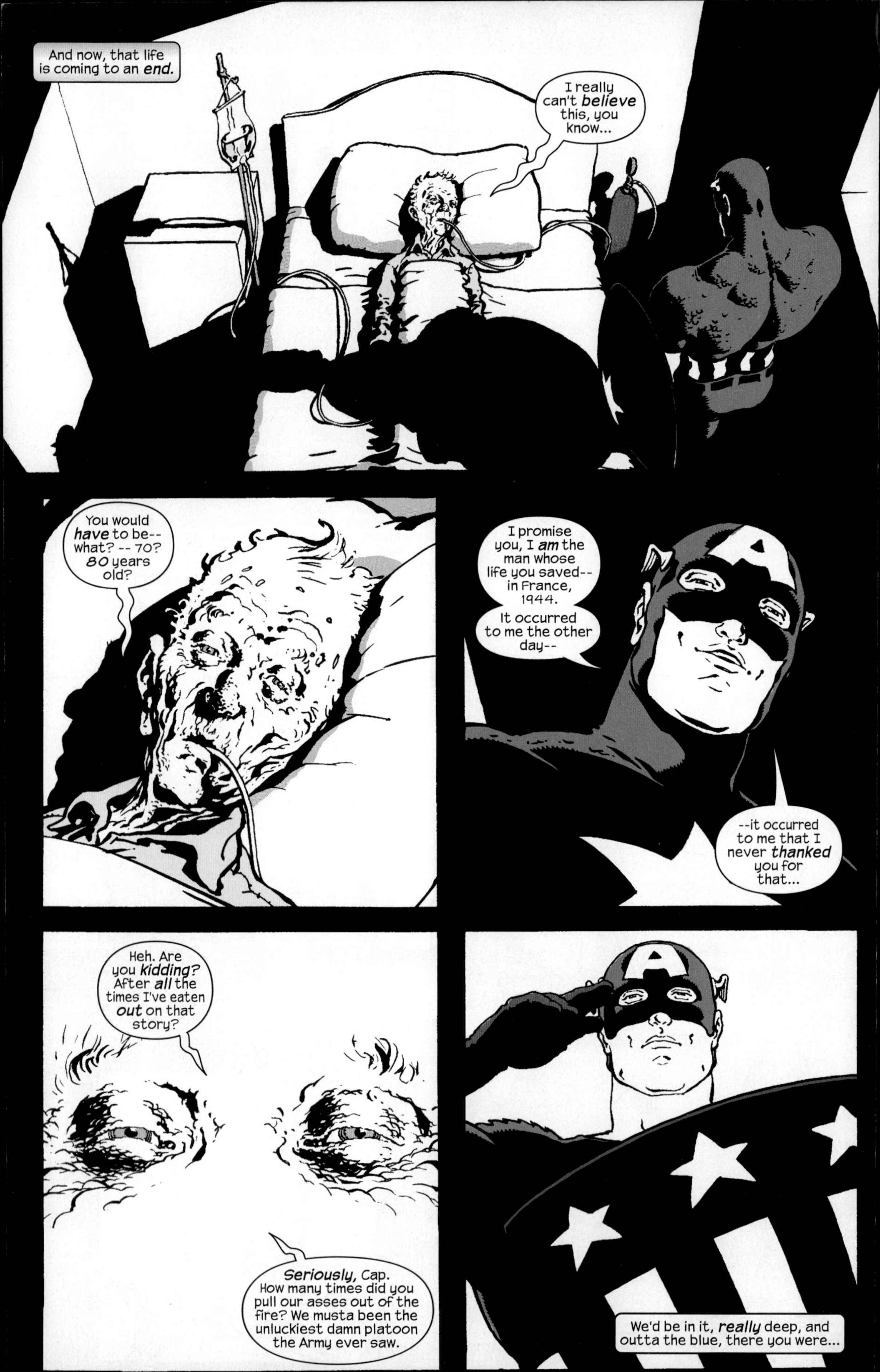
And now, that life is coming to an *end.*
I really can't *believe* this, you know...
You would *have* to be-- what? -- 70? *80* years old?
I promise you, I *am* the man whose life you saved-- in France, 1944.
It occurred to me the other day--
--it occurred to me that I never *thanked* you for that...
Heh. Are you *kidding?* After *all* the times I've eaten *out* on that story?
Seriously, Cap. How many times did you pull our asses out of the fire? We musta been the unluckiest damn platoon the Army ever saw.
We'd be in it, *really* deep, and outta the blue, there you were...

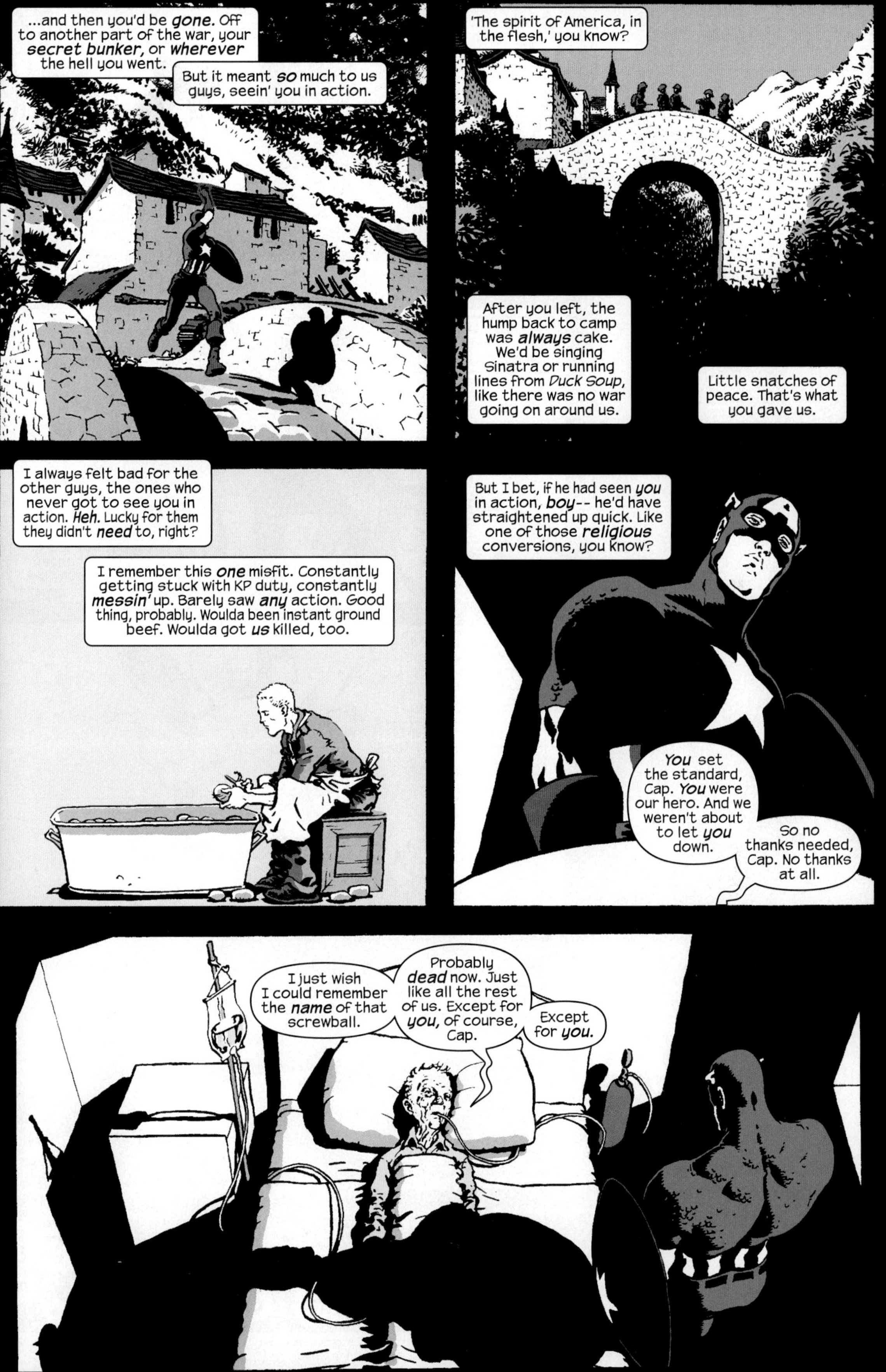
...and then you'd be *gone.* Off to another part of the war, your *secret bunker,* or *wherever* the hell you went.
But it meant *so* much to us guys, seein' you in action.
'The spirit of America, in the flesh,' you know?
After you left, the hump back to camp was *always* cake. We'd be singing Sinatra or running lines from *Duck Soup,* like there was no war going on around us.
Little snatches of peace. That's what you gave us.
I always felt bad for the other guys, the ones who never got to see you in action. *Heh.* Lucky for them they didn't *need* to, right?
I remember this *one* misfit. Constantly getting stuck with KP duty, constantly *messin'* up. Barely saw *any* action. Good thing, probably. Woulda been instant ground beef. Woulda got *us* killed, too.
But I bet, if he had seen *you* in action, *boy*-- he'd have straightened up quick. Like one of those *religious* conversions, you know?
You set the standard, Cap. *You* were our hero. And we weren't about to let *you* down.
So no thanks needed, Cap. No thanks at all.
I just wish I could remember the *name* of that screwball.
Probably *dead* now. Just like all the rest of us. Except for *you,* of course, Cap.
Except for *you.*

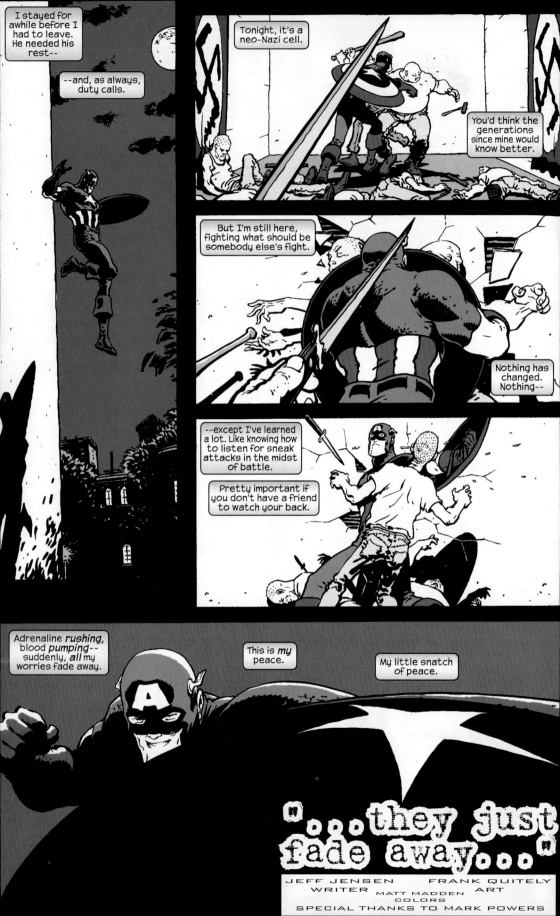

I stayed for awhile before I had to leave. He needed his rest--

--and, as always, duty calls.

Tonight, it's a neo-Nazi cell.

You'd think the generations since mine would know better.

But I'm still here, fighting what should be somebody else's fight.

Nothing has changed. Nothing--

--except I've learned a lot. Like knowing how to listen for sneak attacks in the midst of battle.

Pretty important if you don't have a friend to watch your back.

Adrenaline *rushing*, blood *pumping*-- suddenly, *all* my worries fade away.

This is *my* peace.

My little snatch of peace.

"...they just fade away..."

JEFF JENSEN   FRANK QUITELY
WRITER   ART
MATT MADDEN
COLORS
SPECIAL THANKS TO MARK POWERS

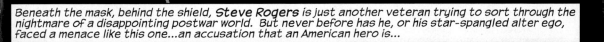

Beneath the mask, behind the shield, *Steve Rogers* is just another veteran trying to sort through the nightmare of a disappointing postwar world. But never before has he, or his star-spangled alter ego, faced a menace like this one...an accusation that an American hero is...

RED UNDER THE MASK

MAX ALLAN COLLINS — WRITER
VATCHE MAVLIAN — ARTIST

JOSE VILLARRUBIA
RENDERING

February 1954 -- the Korean War is over, but the battle on Communism continues. Ever eager to serve his nation, anxious to help root out subversion, Captain America makes an appearance on Capitol Hill...

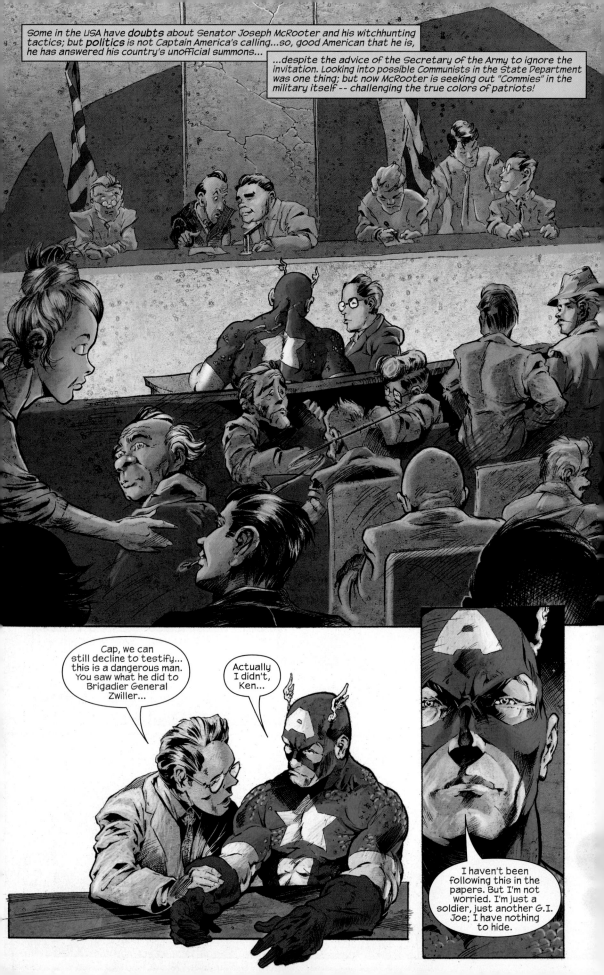

Some in the USA have **doubts** about Senator Joseph McRooter and his witchhunting tactics; but **politics** is not Captain America's calling...so, good American that he is, he has answered his country's unofficial summons...

...despite the advice of the Secretary of the Army to ignore the invitation. Looking into possible Communists in the State Department was one thing; but now McRooter is seeking out "Commies" in the military itself -- challenging the true colors of patriots!

Cap, we can still decline to testify... this is a dangerous man. You saw what he did to Brigadier General Zwiller...

Actually I didn't, Ken...

I haven't been following this in the papers. But I'm not worried. I'm just a soldier, just another G.I. Joe; I have nothing to hide.

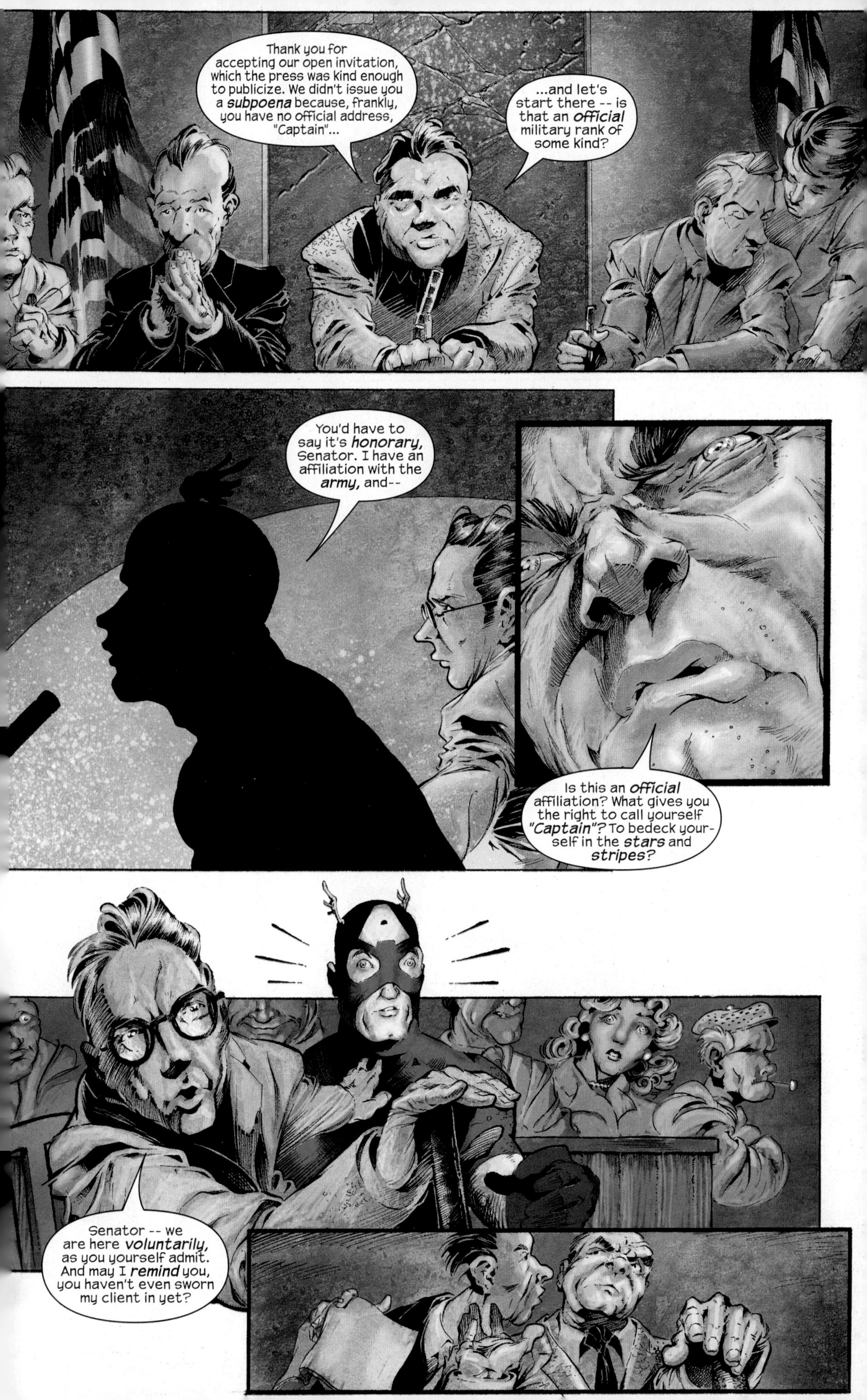
Thank you for accepting our open invitation, which the press was kind enough to publicize. We didn't issue you a *subpoena* because, frankly, you have no official address, "Captain"...
...and let's start there -- is that an *official* military rank of some kind?
You'd have to say it's *honorary,* Senator. I have an affiliation with the *army,* and--
Is this an *official* affiliation? What gives you the right to call yourself *"Captain"*? To bedeck your-self in the *stars* and *stripes*?
Senator -- we are here *voluntarily,* as you yourself admit. And may I *remind* you, you haven't even sworn my client in yet?

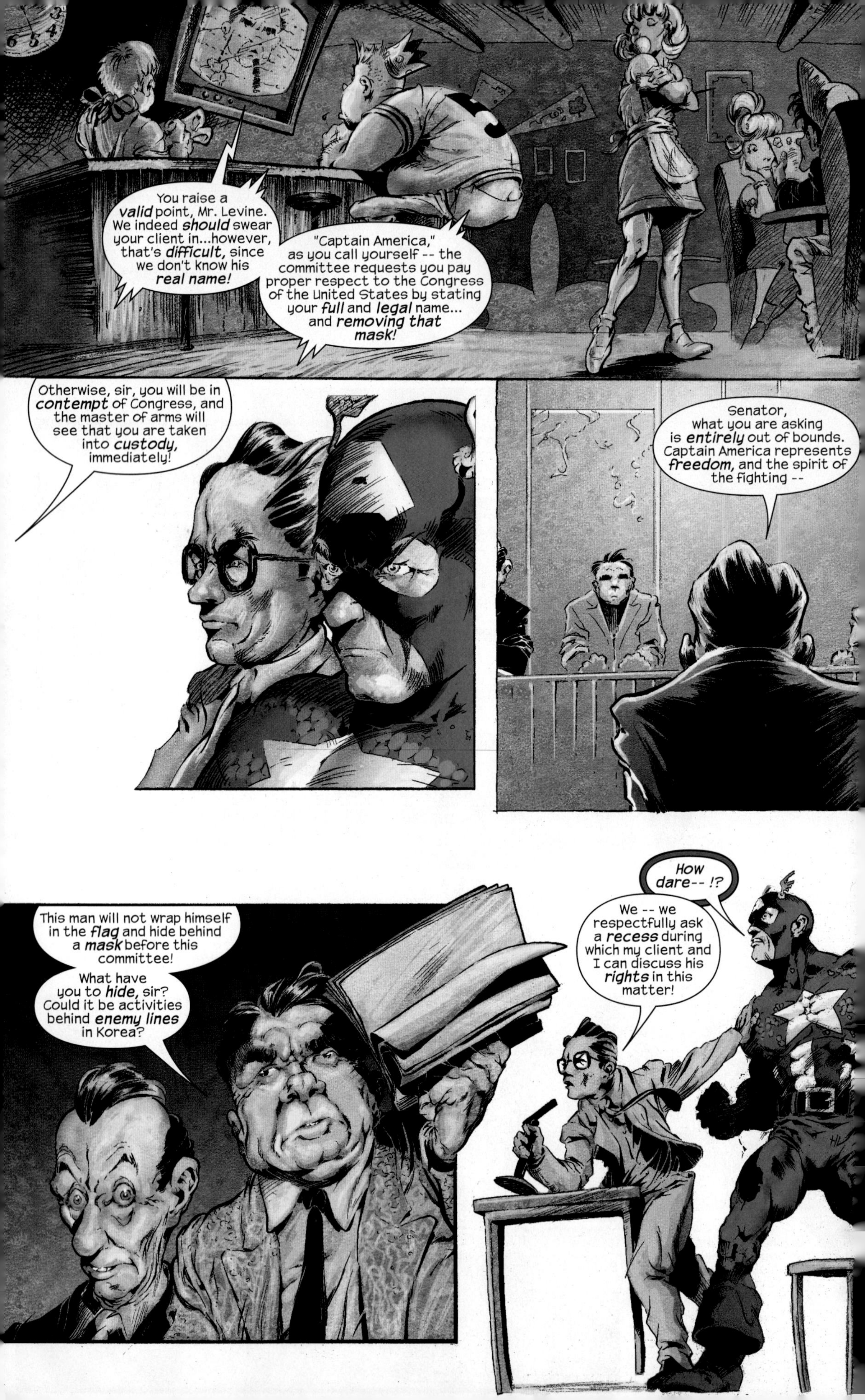

You raise a valid point, Mr. Levine. We indeed should swear your client in...however, that's difficult, since we don't know his real name!
"Captain America," as you call yourself -- the committee requests you pay proper respect to the Congress of the United States by stating your full and legal name... and removing that mask!
Otherwise, sir, you will be in contempt of Congress, and the master of arms will see that you are taken into custody, immediately!
Senator, what you are asking is entirely out of bounds. Captain America represents freedom, and the spirit of the fighting --
This man will not wrap himself in the flag and hide behind a mask before this committee!
What have you to hide, sir? Could it be activities behind enemy lines in Korea?
How dare-- !?
We -- we respectfully ask a recess during which my client and I can discuss his rights in this matter!

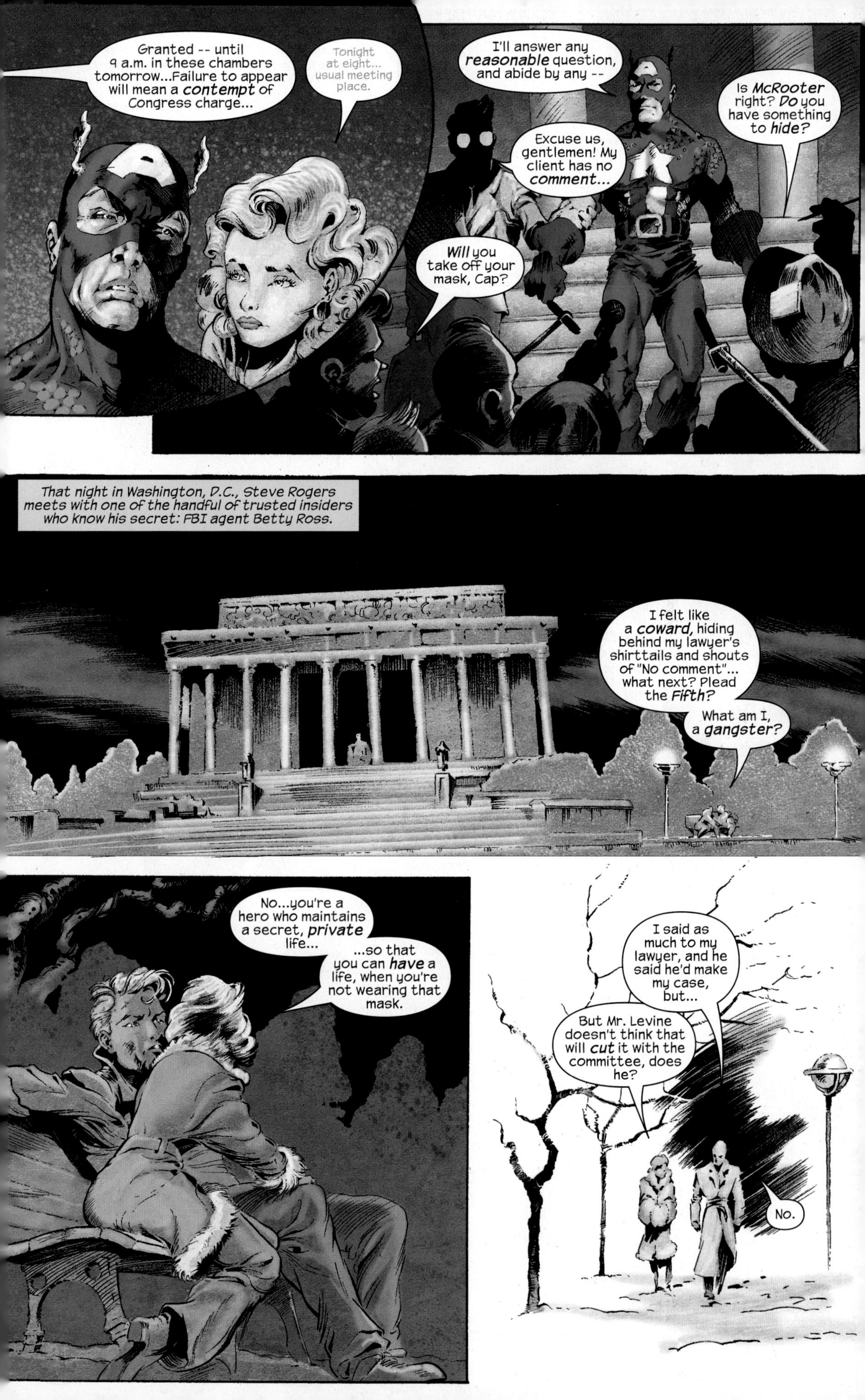

Granted -- until 9 a.m. in these chambers tomorrow...Failure to appear will mean a contempt of Congress charge...
Tonight at eight... usual meeting place.
I'll answer any reasonable question, and abide by any --
Excuse us, gentlemen! My client has no comment...
Is McRooter right? Do you have something to hide?
Will you take off your mask, Cap?
That night in Washington, D.C., Steve Rogers meets with one of the handful of trusted insiders who know his secret: FBI agent Betty Ross.
I felt like a coward, hiding behind my lawyer's shirttails and shouts of "No comment"... what next? Plead the Fifth?
What am I, a gangster?
No...you're a hero who maintains a secret, private life...
...so that you can have a life, when you're not wearing that mask.
I said as much to my lawyer, and he said he'd make my case, but...
But Mr. Levine doesn't think that will cut it with the committee, does he?
No.

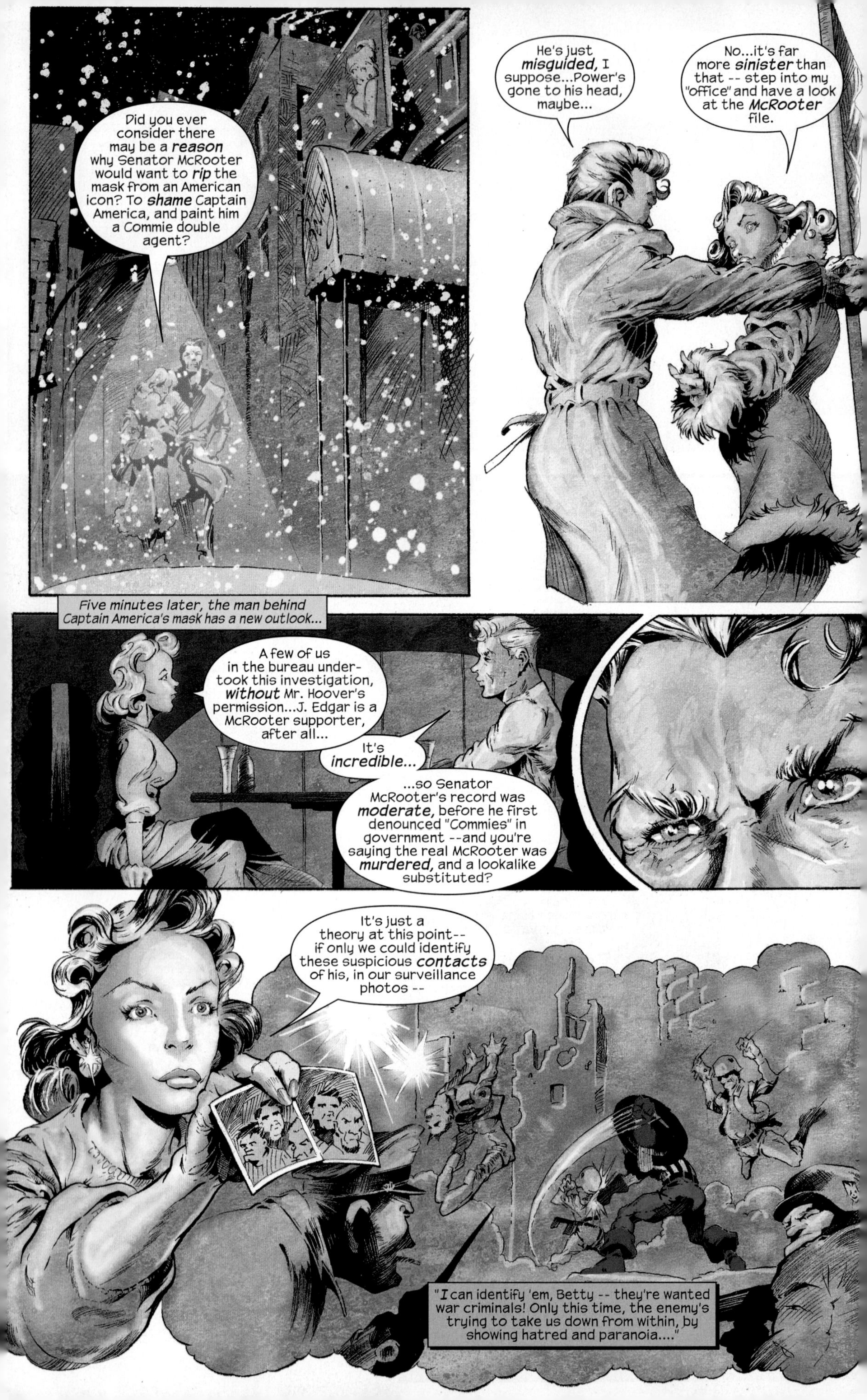
Did you ever consider there may be a reason why Senator McRooter would want to rip the mask from an American icon? To shame Captain America, and paint him a Commie double agent?
He's just misguided, I suppose...Power's gone to his head, maybe...
No...it's far more sinister than that -- step into my "office" and have a look at the McRooter file.
Five minutes later, the man behind Captain America's mask has a new outlook...
A few of us in the bureau undertook this investigation, without Mr. Hoover's permission...J. Edgar is a McRooter supporter, after all...
It's incredible...
...so Senator McRooter's record was moderate, before he first denounced "Commies" in government --and you're saying the real McRooter was murdered, and a lookalike substituted?
It's just a theory at this point-- if only we could identify these suspicious contacts of his, in our surveillance photos --
"I can identify 'em, Betty -- they're wanted war criminals! Only this time, the enemy's trying to take us down from within, by showing hatred and paranoia...."

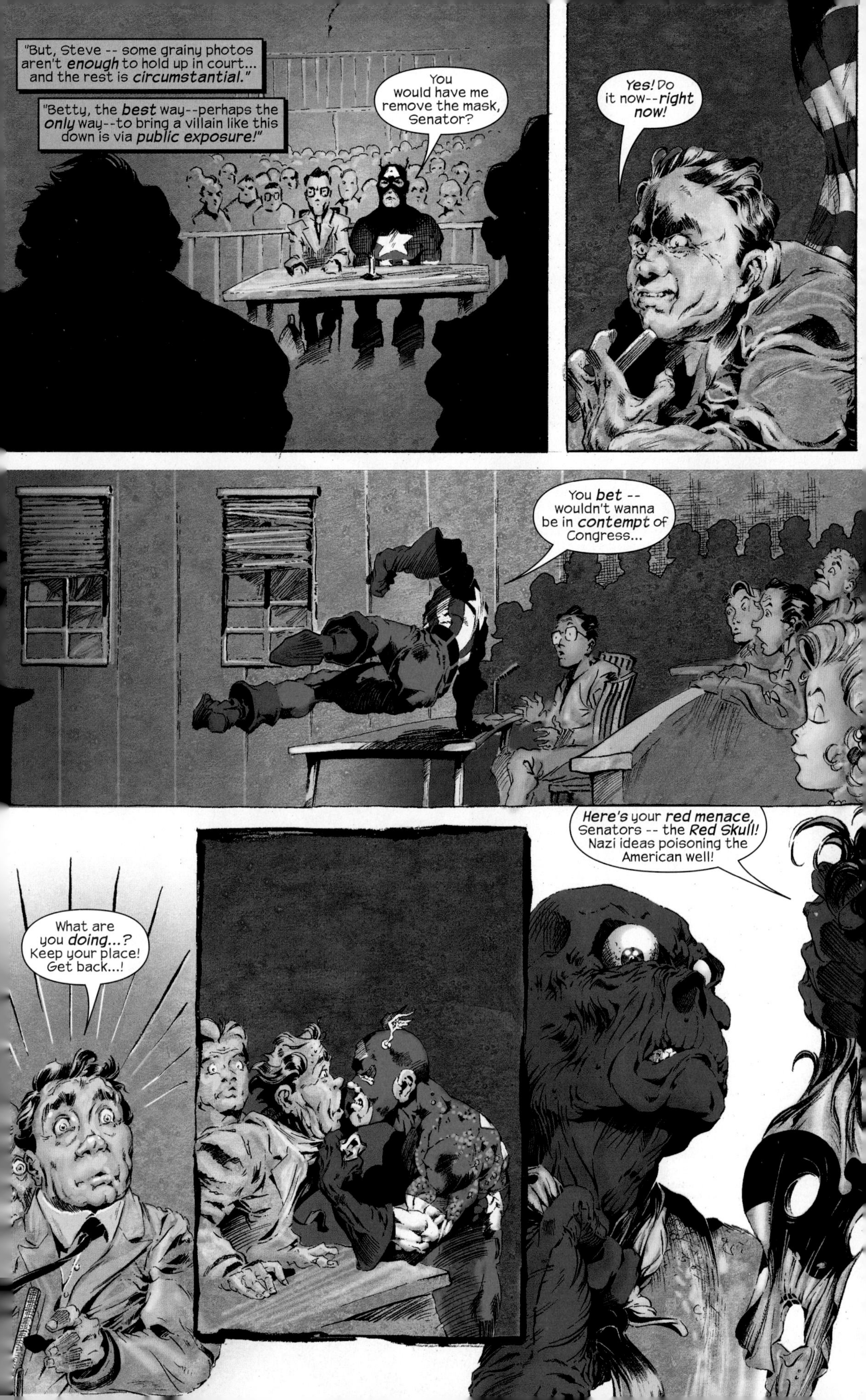
"But, Steve -- some grainy photos aren't *enough* to hold up in court... and the rest is *circumstantial.*"
"Betty, the *best* way--perhaps the *only* way--to bring a villain like this down is via *public exposure!*"
You would have me remove the mask, Senator?
Yes! Do it now--*right now!*
You *bet* -- wouldn't wanna be in *contempt* of Congress...
What are you *doing...?* Keep your place! Get back...!
Here's your *red menace,* Senators -- the *Red Skull!* Nazi ideas poisoning the American well!

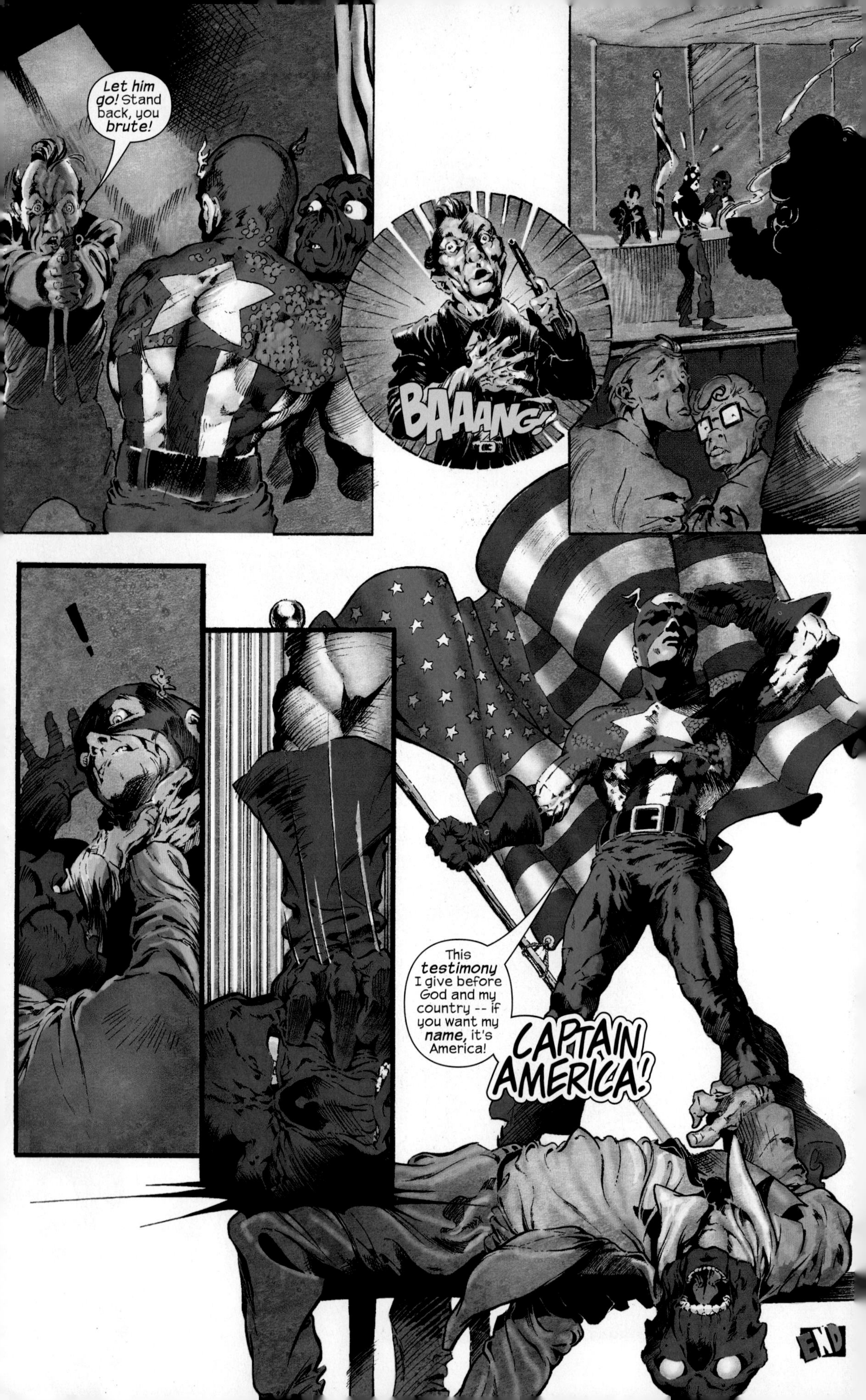
Let him go! Stand back, you brute!
BAAANG!
!
This testimony I give before God and my country -- if you want my name, it's America!
CAPTAIN AMERICA!
END

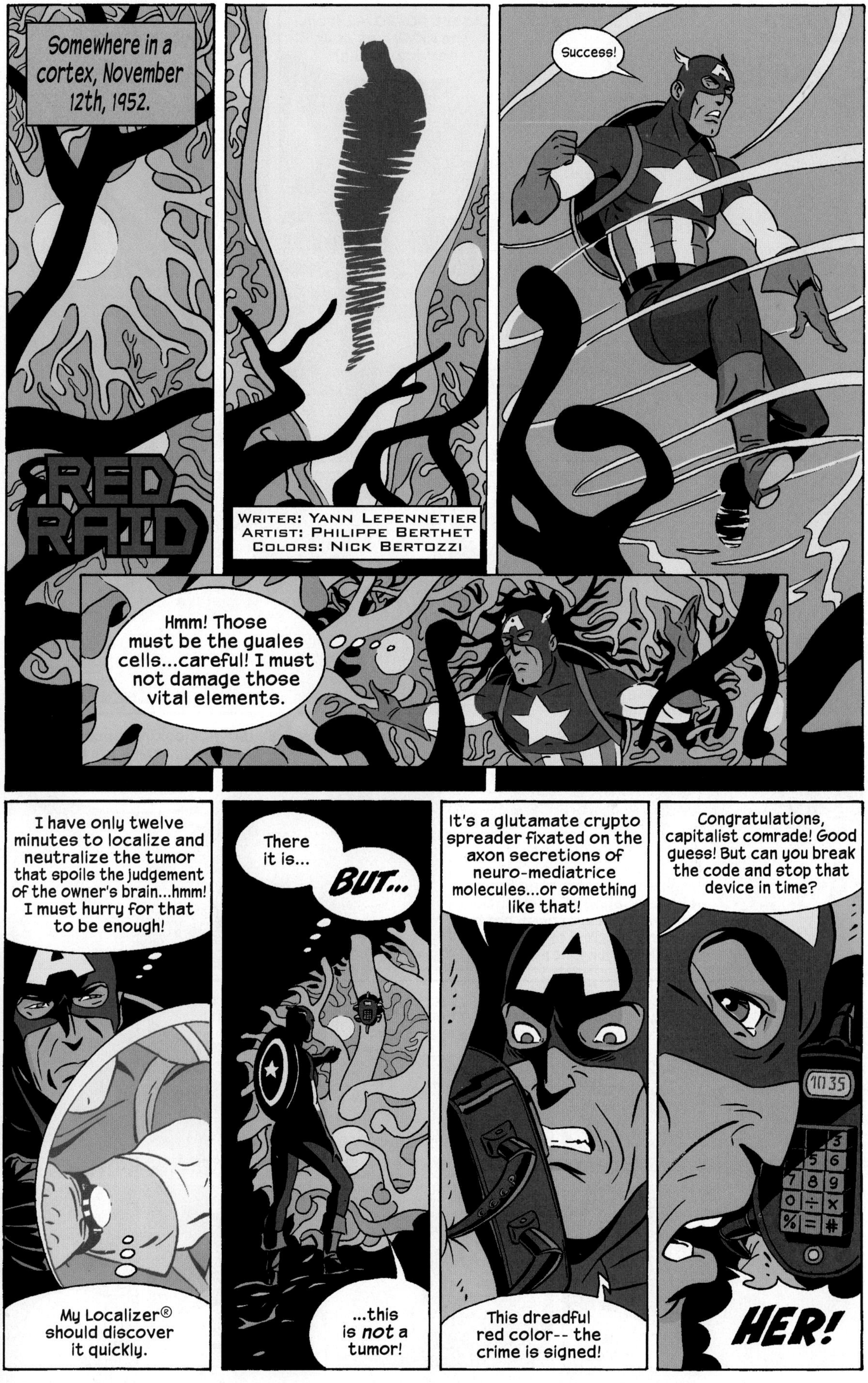
Somewhere in a cortex, November 12th, 1952.
RED RAID
Writer: Yann Lepennetier
Artist: Philippe Berthet
Colors: Nick Bertozzi
Success!
Hmm! Those must be the guales cells...careful! I must not damage those vital elements.
I have only twelve minutes to localize and neutralize the tumor that spoils the judgement of the owner's brain...hmm! I must hurry for that to be enough!
My Localizer® should discover it quickly.
There it is...
BUT...
...this is *not* a tumor!
It's a glutamate crypto spreader fixated on the axon secretions of neuro-mediatrice molecules...or something like that!
This dreadful red color-- the crime is signed!
Congratulations, capitalist comrade! Good guess! But can you break the code and stop that device in time?
HER!

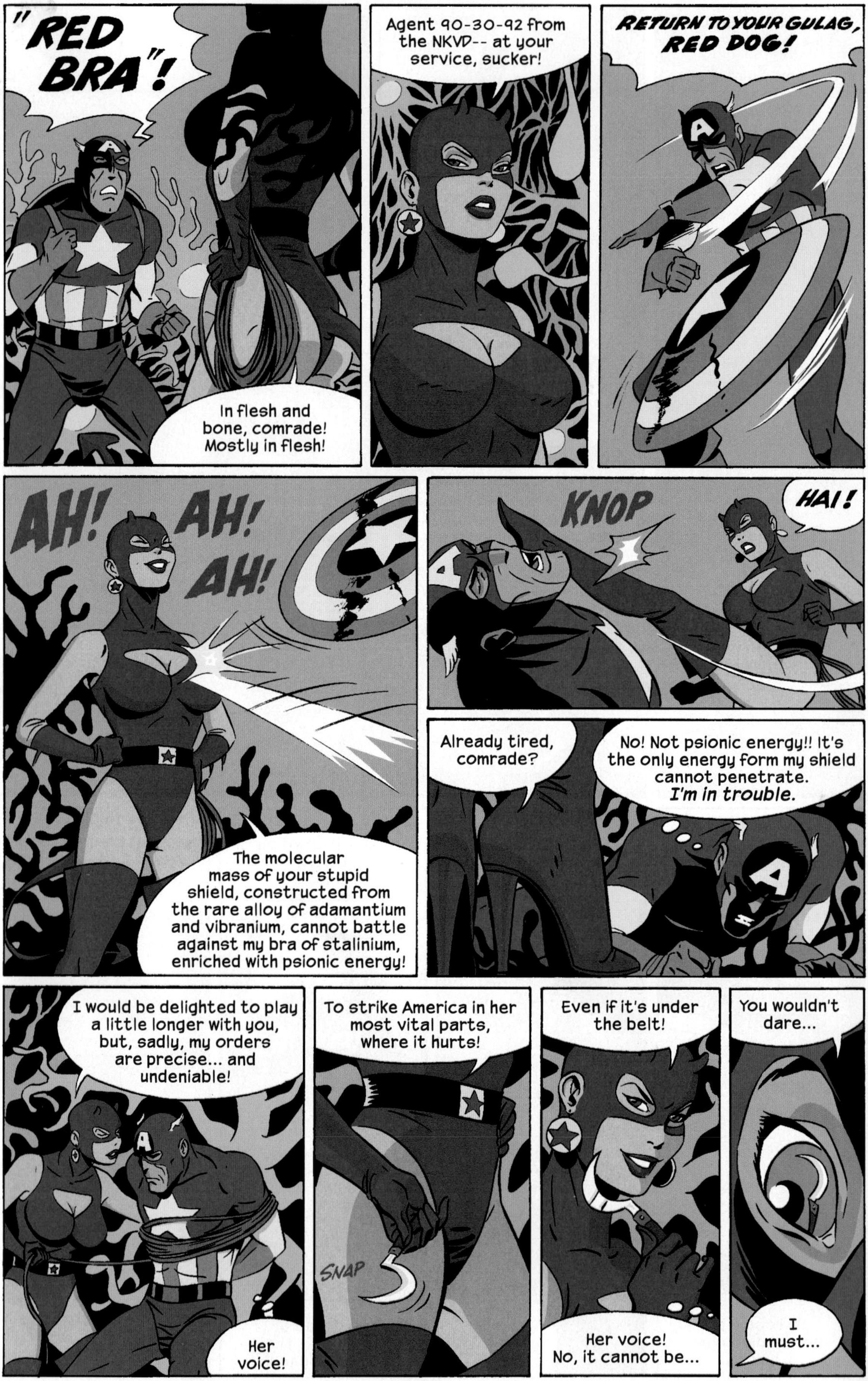
"RED BRA"!
In flesh and bone, comrade! Mostly in flesh!
Agent 90-30-92 from the NKVD-- at your service, sucker!
RETURN TO YOUR GULAG, RED DOG!
AH! AH! AH!
The molecular mass of your stupid shield, constructed from the rare alloy of adamantium and vibranium, cannot battle against my bra of stalinium, enriched with psionic energy!
KNOP
HAI!
Already tired, comrade?
No! Not psionic energy!! It's the only energy form my shield cannot penetrate. *I'm in trouble.*
I would be delighted to play a little longer with you, but, sadly, my orders are precise... and undeniable!
Her voice!
To strike America in her most vital parts, where it hurts!
SNAP
Even if it's under the belt!
Her voice! No, it cannot be...
You wouldn't dare...
I must...

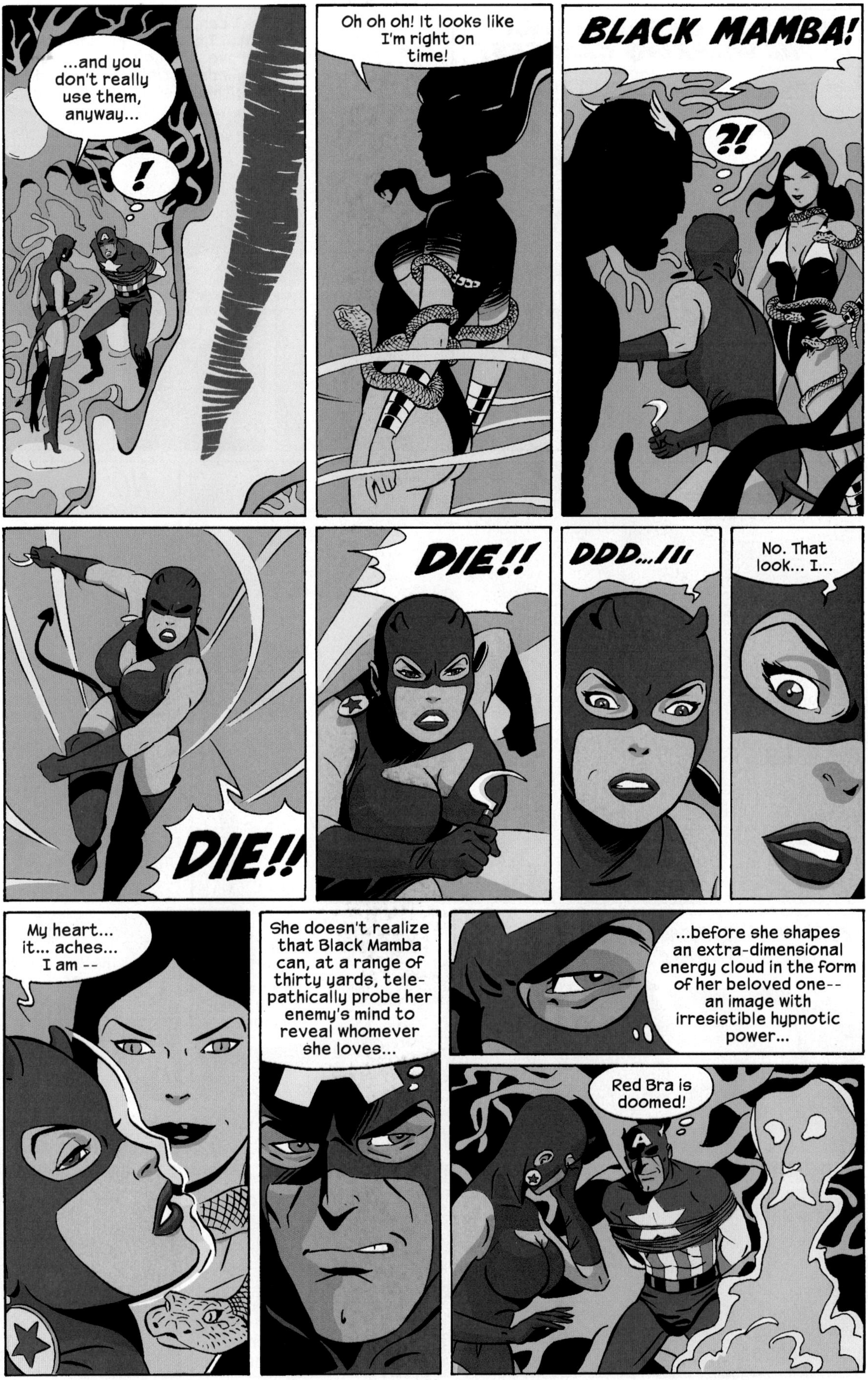
...and you don't really use them, anyway...
!
Oh oh oh! It looks like I'm right on time!
BLACK MAMBA!
?!
DIE!!
DIE!!
DDD...!!!
No. That look... I...
My heart... it... aches... I am --
She doesn't realize that Black Mamba can, at a range of thirty yards, telepathically probe her enemy's mind to reveal whomever she loves...
...before she shapes an extra-dimensional energy cloud in the form of her beloved one-- an image with irresistible hypnotic power...
Red Bra is doomed!

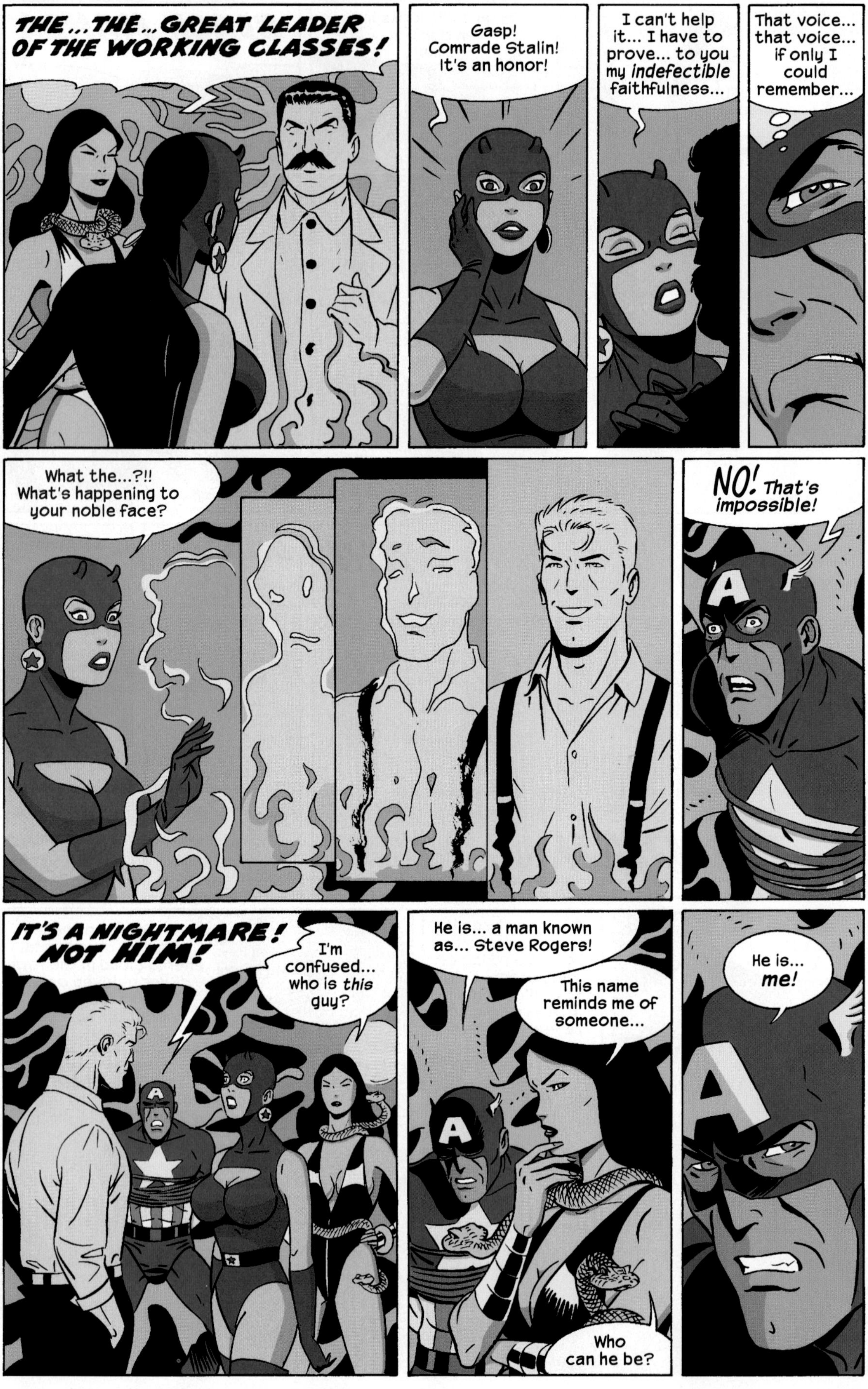
THE... THE... GREAT LEADER OF THE WORKING CLASSES!
Gasp! Comrade Stalin! It's an honor!
I can't help it... I have to prove... to you my *indefectible* faithfulness...
That voice... that voice... if only I could remember...
What the...?!! What's happening to your noble face?
NO! That's impossible!
IT'S A NIGHTMARE! NOT HIM!
I'm confused... who is *this* guy?
He is... a man known as... Steve Rogers!
This name reminds me of someone...
Who can he be?
He is... *me!*

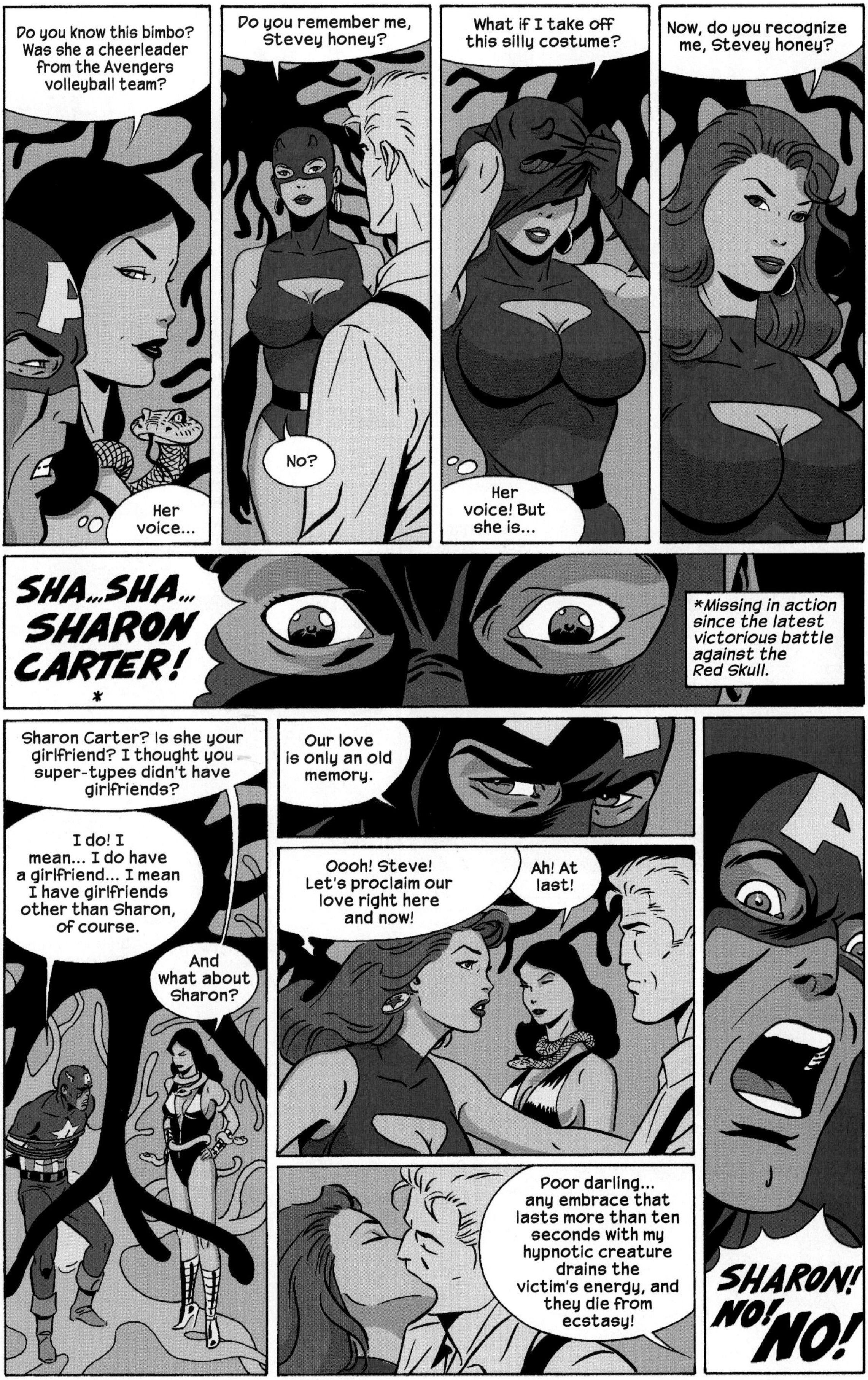
Do you know this bimbo? Was she a cheerleader from the Avengers volleyball team?
Her voice...
Do you remember me, Stevey honey?
No?
What if I take off this silly costume?
Her voice! But she is...
Now, do you recognize me, Stevey honey?
SHA...SHA... SHARON CARTER! *
*Missing in action since the latest victorious battle against the Red Skull.
Sharon Carter? Is she your girlfriend? I thought you super-types didn't have girlfriends?
I do! I mean... I do have a girlfriend... I mean I have girlfriends other than Sharon, of course.
And what about Sharon?
Our love is only an old memory.
Oooh! Steve! Let's proclaim our love right here and now!
Ah! At last!
Poor darling... any embrace that lasts more than ten seconds with my hypnotic creature drains the victim's energy, and they die from ecstasy!
SHARON! NO! NO!

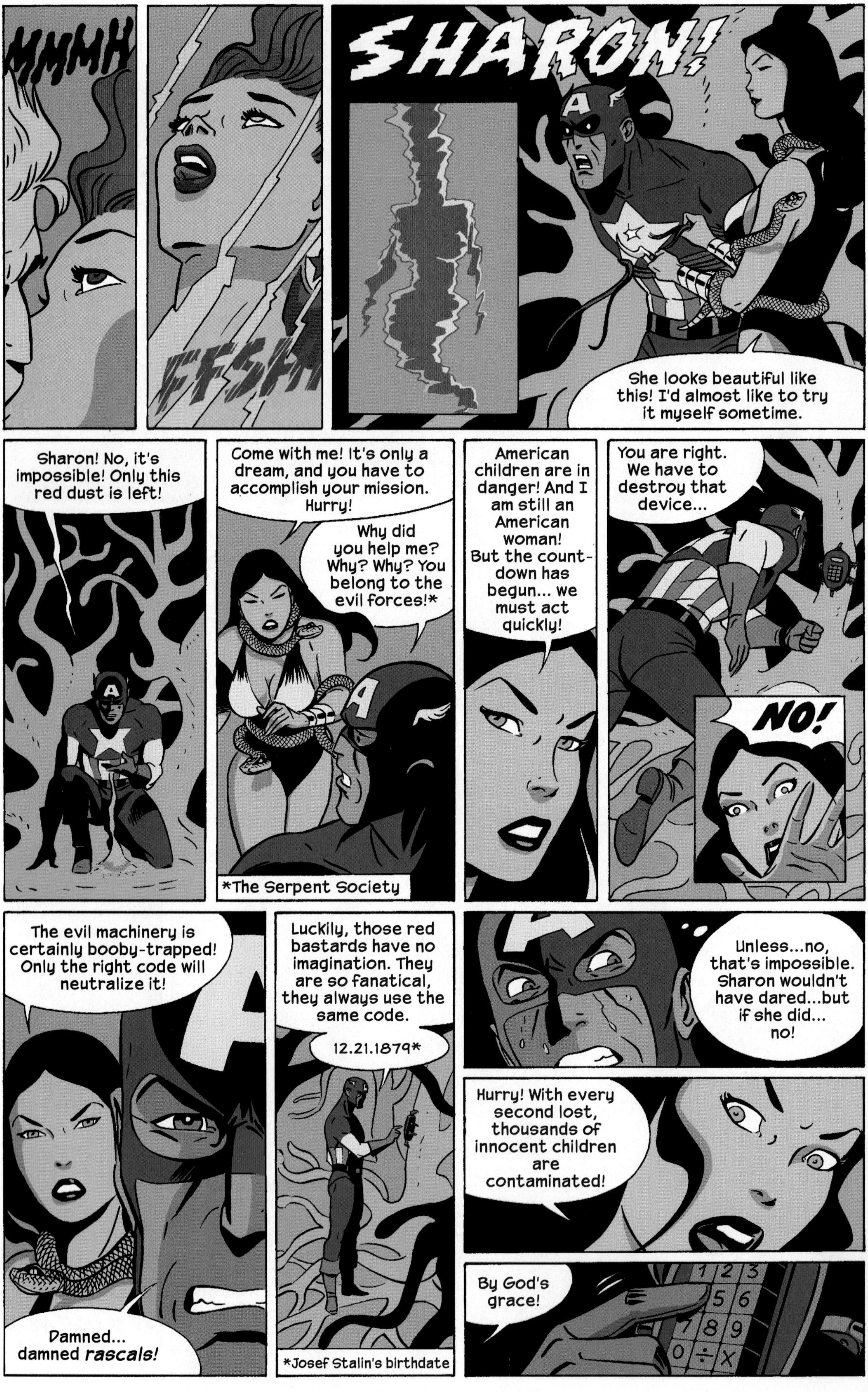
MMMH
FFSHH
SHARON!
She looks beautiful like this! I'd almost like to try it myself sometime.
Sharon! No, it's impossible! Only this red dust is left!
Come with me! It's only a dream, and you have to accomplish your mission. Hurry!
Why did you help me? Why? Why? You belong to the evil forces!*
*The Serpent Society
American children are in danger! And I am still an American woman! But the count-down has begun... we must act quickly!
You are right. We have to destroy that device...
NO!
The evil machinery is certainly booby-trapped! Only the right code will neutralize it!
Damned... damned rascals!
Luckily, those red bastards have no imagination. They are so fanatical, they always use the same code.
12.21.1879*
*Josef Stalin's birthdate
Unless...no, that's impossible. Sharon wouldn't have dared...but if she did... no!
Hurry! With every second lost, thousands of innocent children are contaminated!
By God's grace!

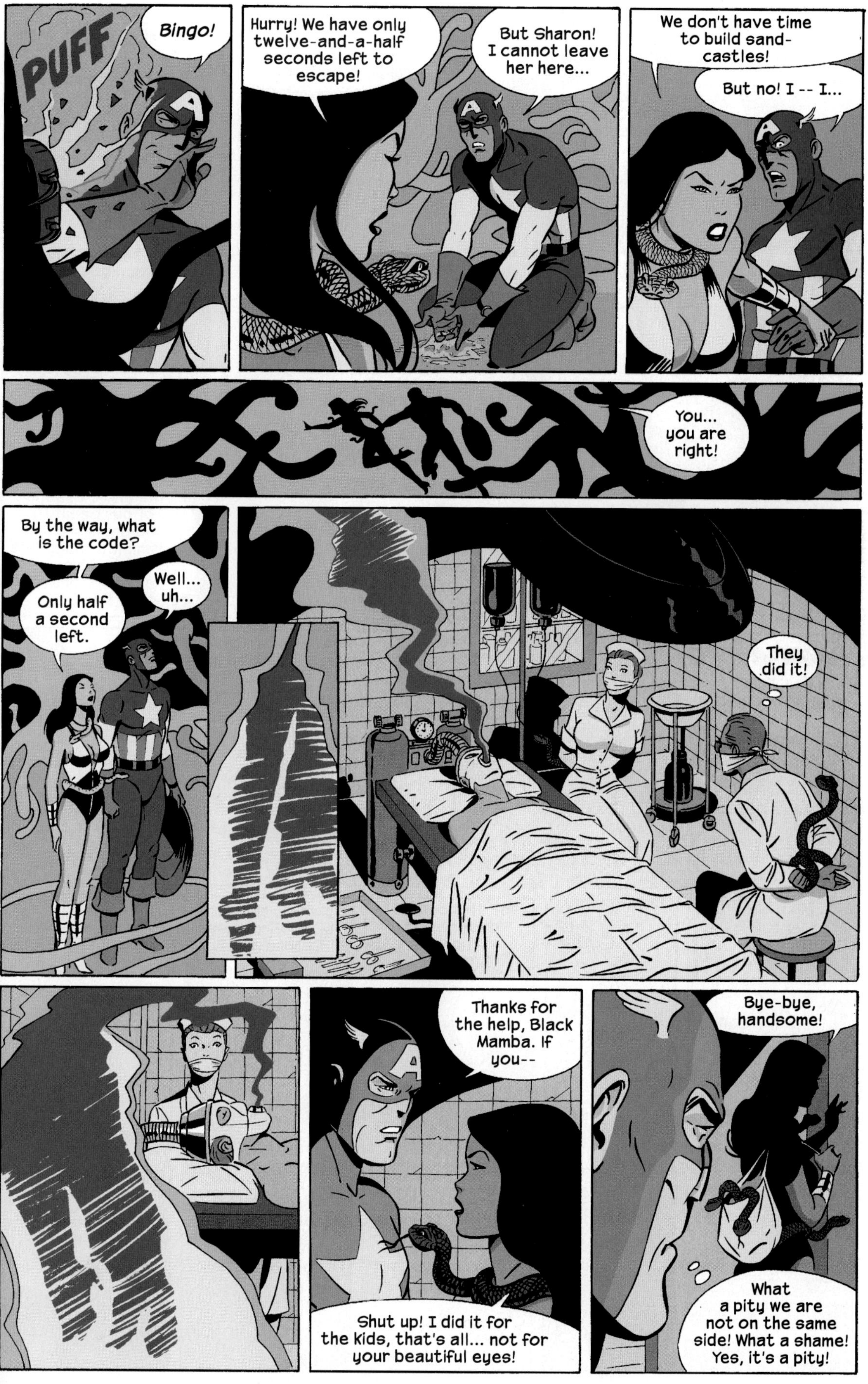
PUFF
Bingo!
Hurry! We have only twelve-and-a-half seconds left to escape!
But Sharon! I cannot leave her here...
We don't have time to build sand-castles!
But no! I -- I...
You... you are right!
By the way, what is the code?
Only half a second left.
Well... uh...
They did it!
Thanks for the help, Black Mamba. If you--
Shut up! I did it for the kids, that's all... not for your beautiful eyes!
Bye-bye, handsome!
What a pity we are not on the same side! What a shame! Yes, it's a pity!

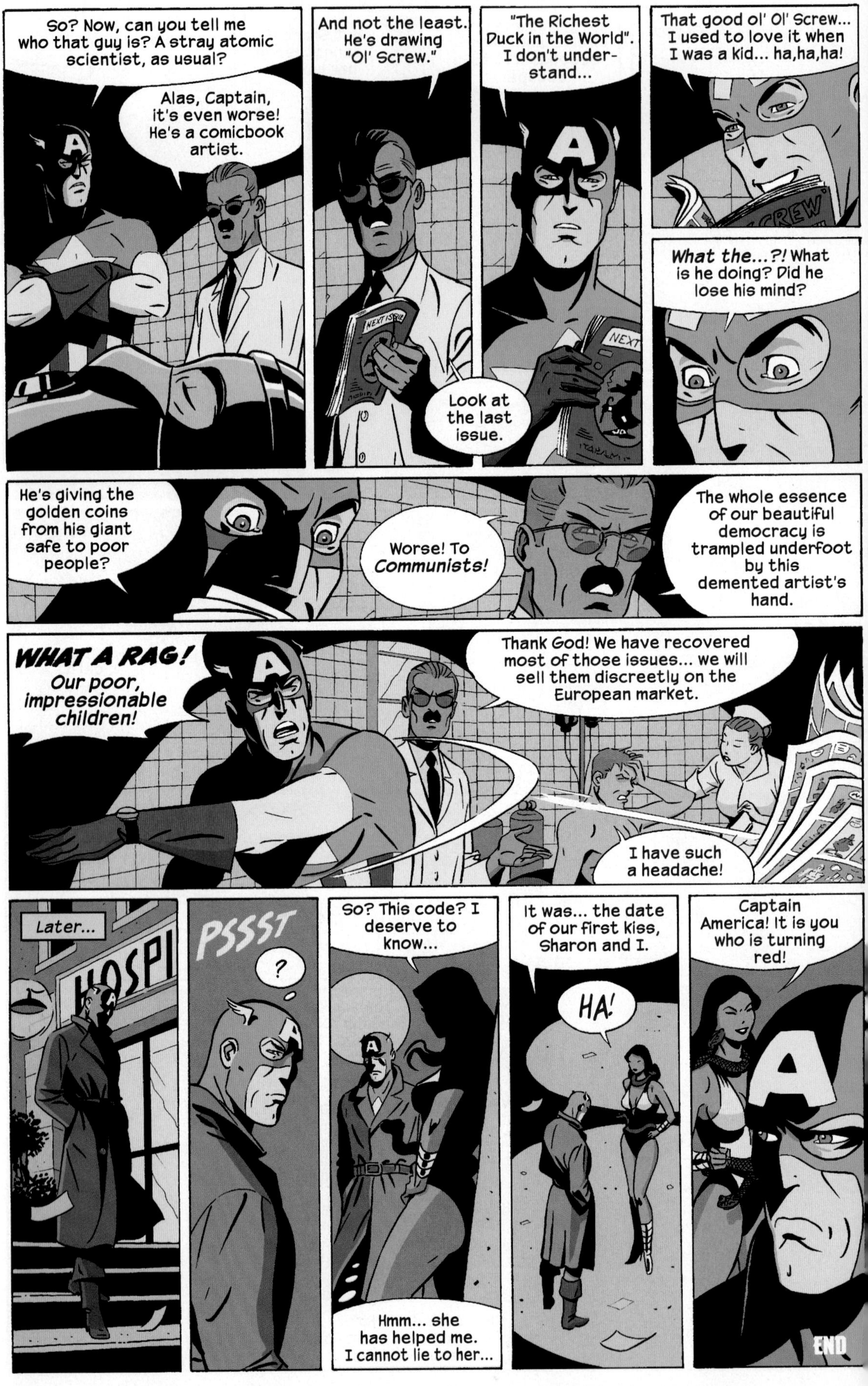

So? Now, can you tell me who that guy is? A stray atomic scientist, as usual?
Alas, Captain, it's even worse! He's a comicbook artist.
And not the least. He's drawing "Ol' Screw."
"The Richest Duck in the World". I don't understand...
Look at the last issue.
That good ol' Ol' Screw... I used to love it when I was a kid... ha,ha,ha!
What the...?! What is he doing? Did he lose his mind?
He's giving the golden coins from his giant safe to poor people?
Worse! To Communists!
The whole essence of our beautiful democracy is trampled underfoot by this demented artist's hand.
WHAT A RAG! Our poor, impressionable children!
Thank God! We have recovered most of those issues... we will sell them discreetly on the European market.
I have such a headache!
Later...
HOSPI
PSSST
?
So? This code? I deserve to know...
Hmm... she has helped me. I cannot lie to her...
It was... the date of our first kiss, Sharon and I.
HA!
Captain America! It is you who is turning red!
END

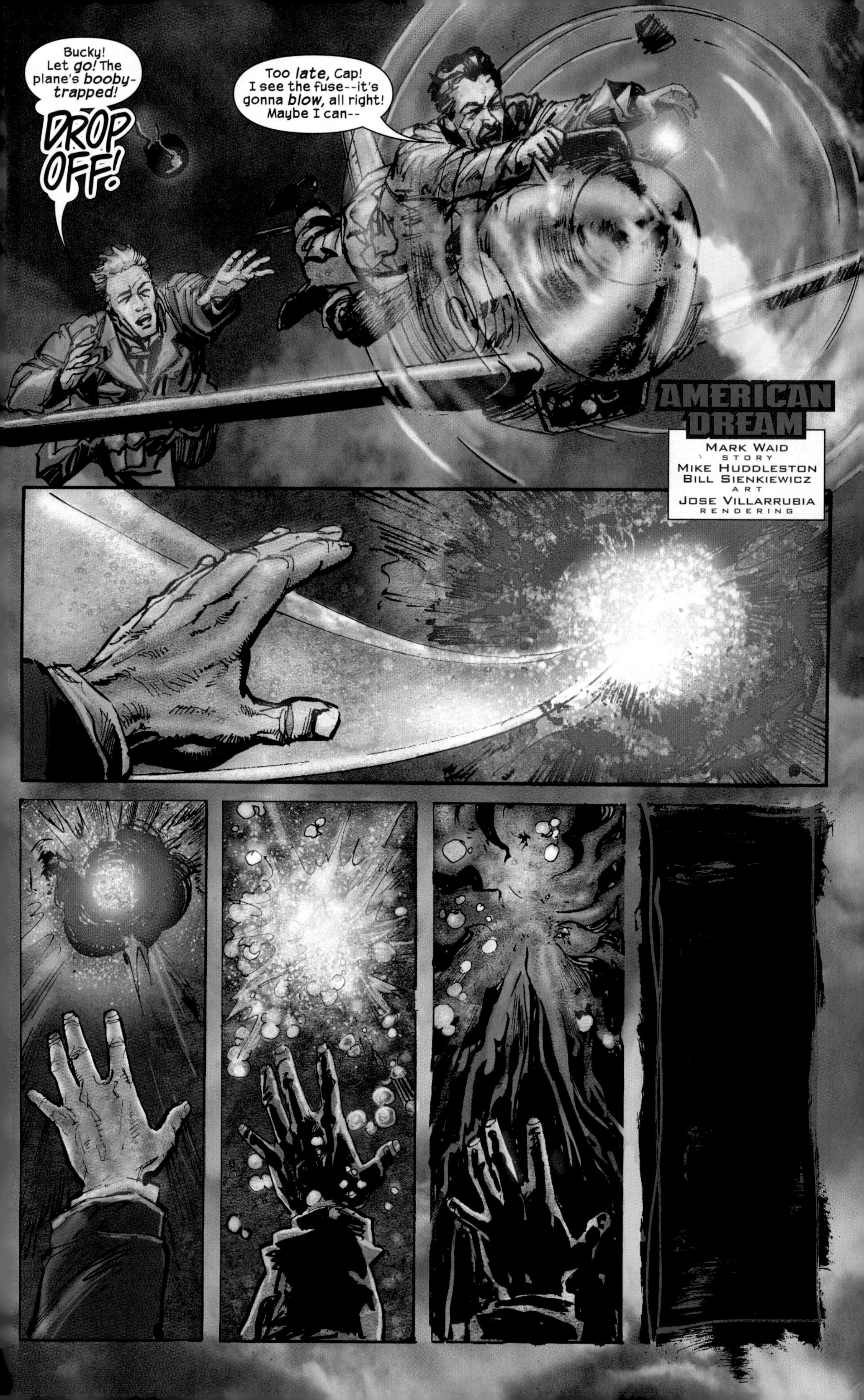
Bucky! Let go! The plane's booby-trapped!
DROP OFF!
Too late, Cap! I see the fuse--it's gonna blow, all right! Maybe I can--
AMERICAN DREAM
MARK WAID STORY
MIKE HUDDLESTON BILL SIENKIEWICZ ART
JOSE VILLARRUBIA RENDERING

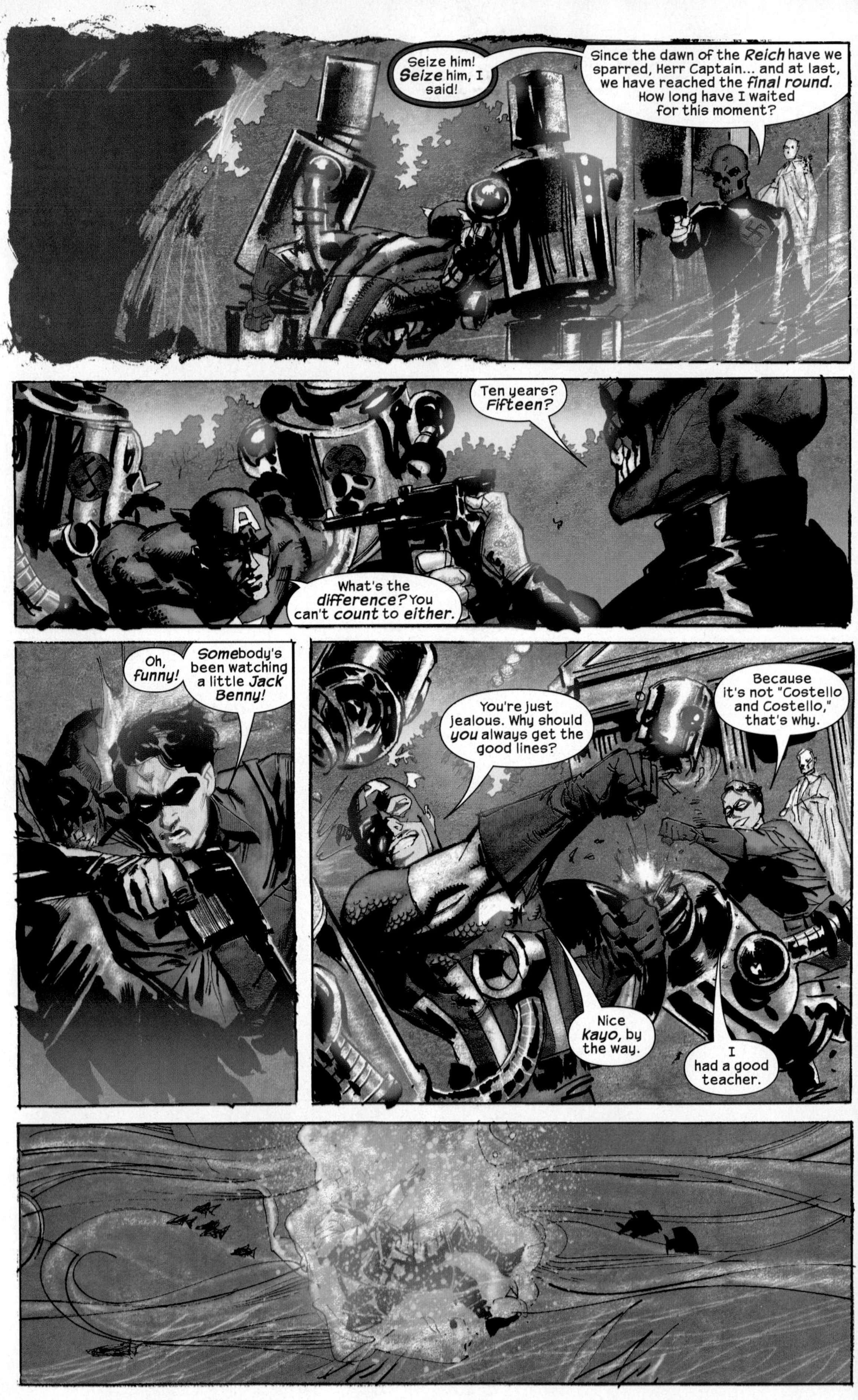
Seize him! Seize him, I said!
Since the dawn of the Reich have we sparred, Herr Captain... and at last, we have reached the final round. How long have I waited for this moment?
Ten years? Fifteen?
What's the difference? You can't count to either.
Oh, funny!
Somebody's been watching a little Jack Benny!
You're just jealous. Why should you always get the good lines?
Because it's not "Costello and Costello," that's why.
Nice kayo, by the way.
I had a good teacher.

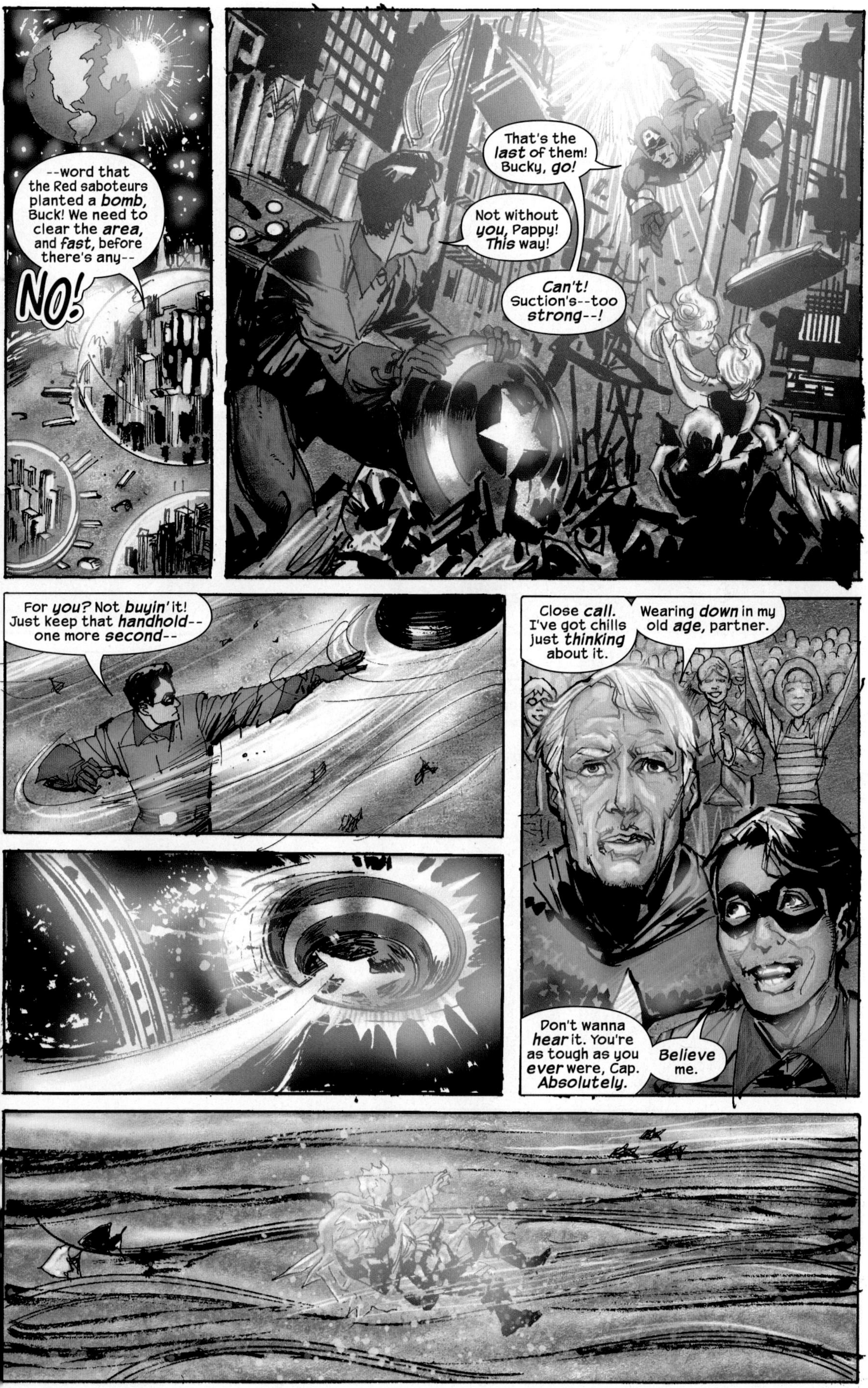
--word that the Red saboteurs planted a bomb, Buck! We need to clear the area, and fast, before there's any--
NO!
That's the last of them! Bucky, go!
Not without you, Pappy! This way!
Can't! Suction's--too strong--!
For you? Not buyin' it! Just keep that handhold-- one more second--
Close call. I've got chills just thinking about it.
Wearing down in my old age, partner.
Don't wanna hear it. You're as tough as you ever were, Cap. Absolutely.
Believe me.

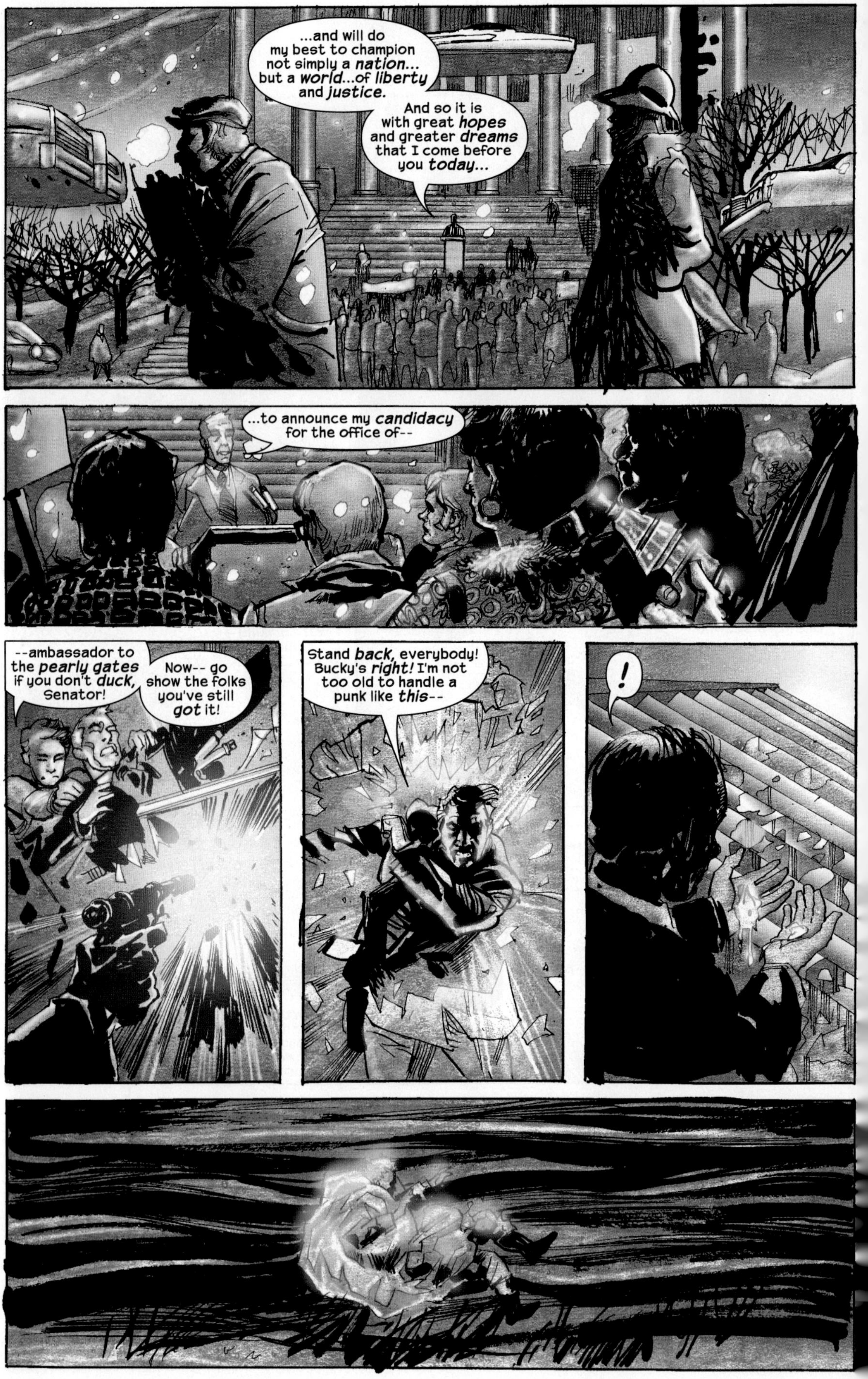
...and will do my best to champion not simply a *nation*... but a *world*...of *liberty* and *justice*.
And so it is with great *hopes* and greater *dreams* that I come before you *today*...
...to announce my *candidacy* for the office of--
--ambassador to the *pearly gates* if you don't *duck*, Senator!
Now-- go show the folks you've still *got* it!
Stand *back*, everybody! Bucky's *right!* I'm not too old to handle a punk like *this*--
!

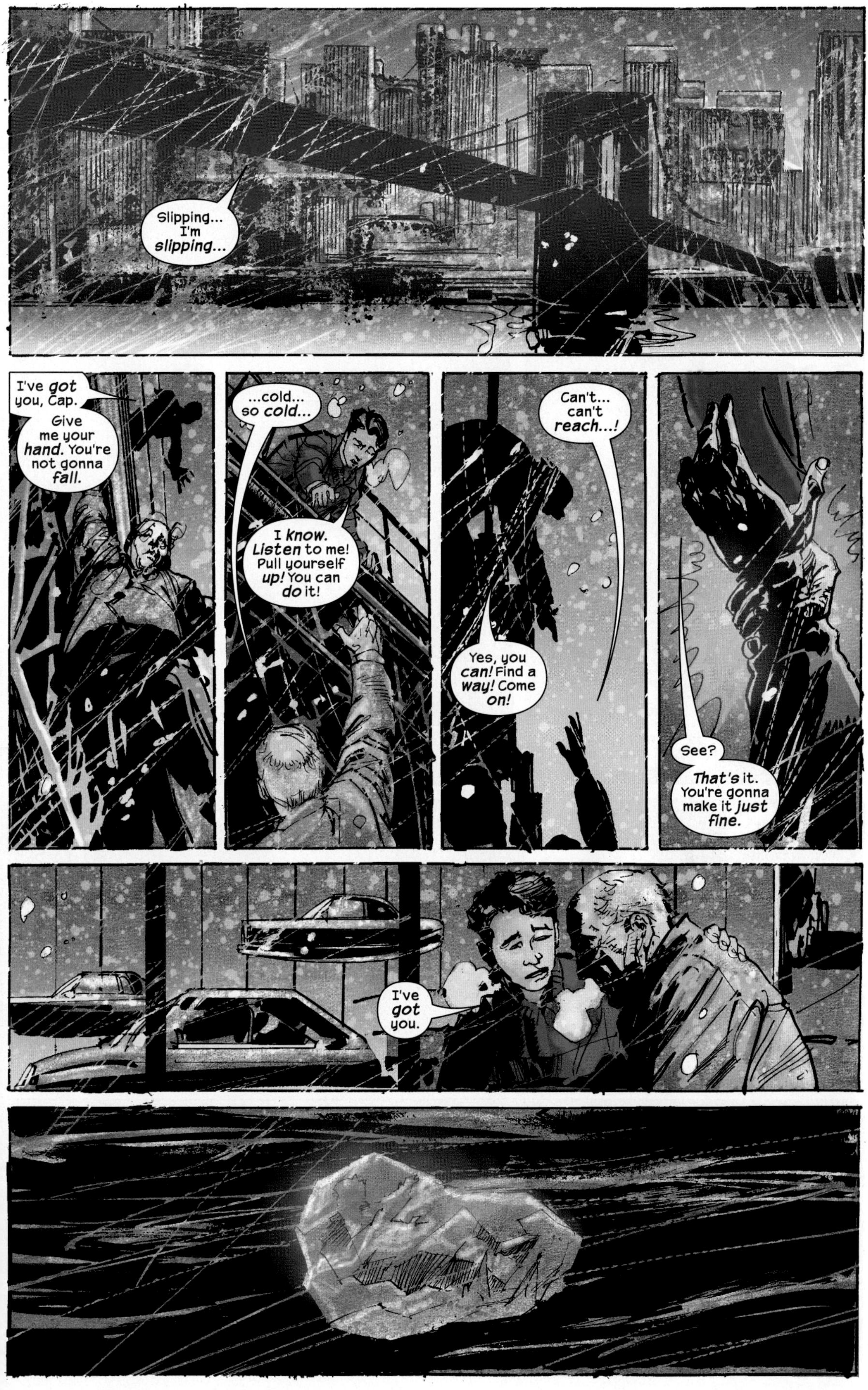
Slipping... I'm slipping...
I've got you, Cap. Give me your hand. You're not gonna fall.
...cold... so cold...
I know. Listen to me! Pull yourself up! You can do it!
Can't... can't reach...!
Yes, you can! Find a way! Come on!
See?
That's it. You're gonna make it just fine.
I've got you.

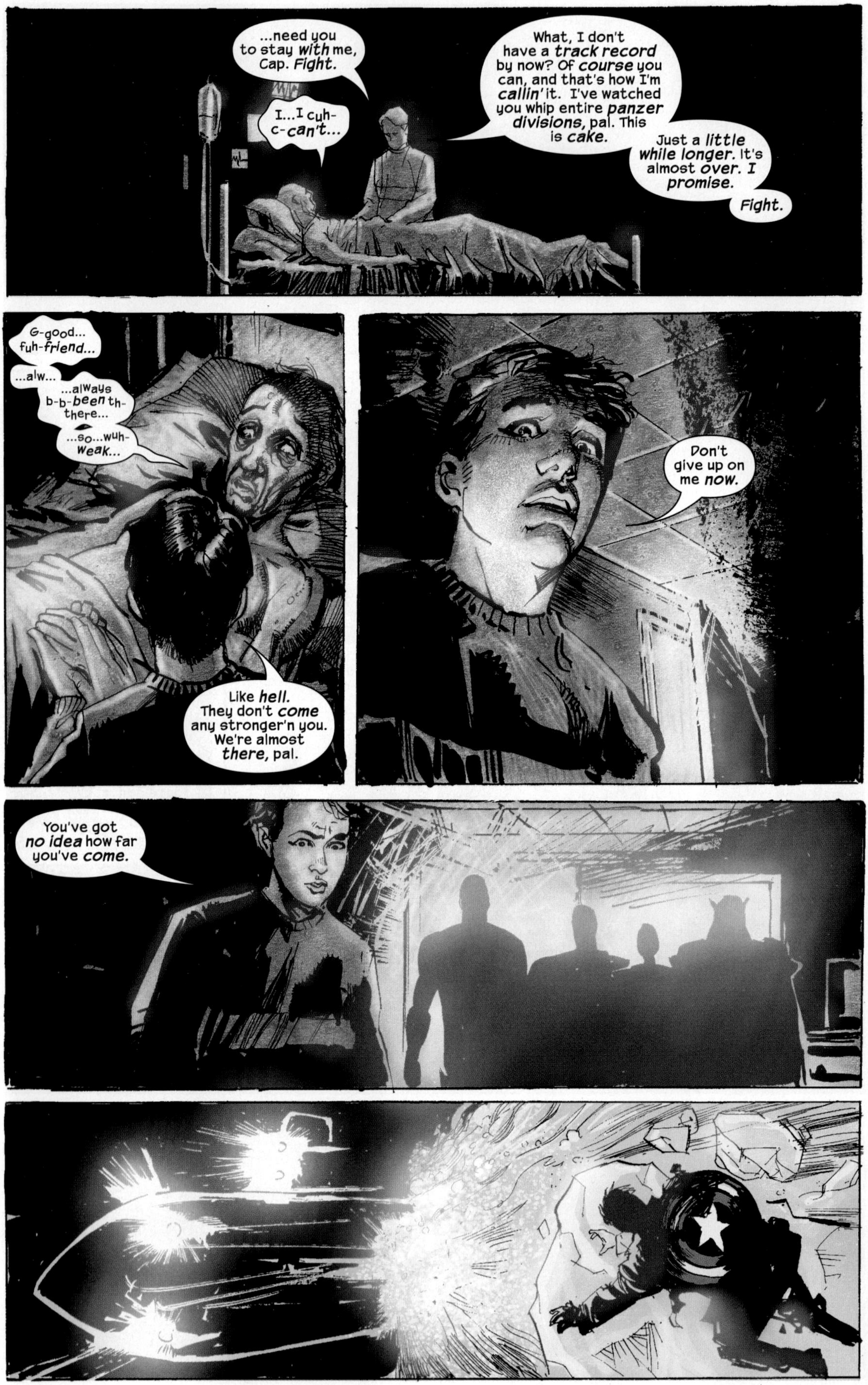
...need you to stay with me, Cap. Fight.
I...I cuh-c-can't...
What, I don't have a track record by now? Of course you can, and that's how I'm callin' it. I've watched you whip entire panzer divisions, pal. This is cake.
Just a little while longer. It's almost over. I promise.
Fight.
G-good... fuh-friend...
...alw...
...always b-b-been th-there...
...so...wuh-weak...
Like hell. They don't come any stronger'n you. We're almost there, pal.
Don't give up on me now.
You've got no idea how far you've come.

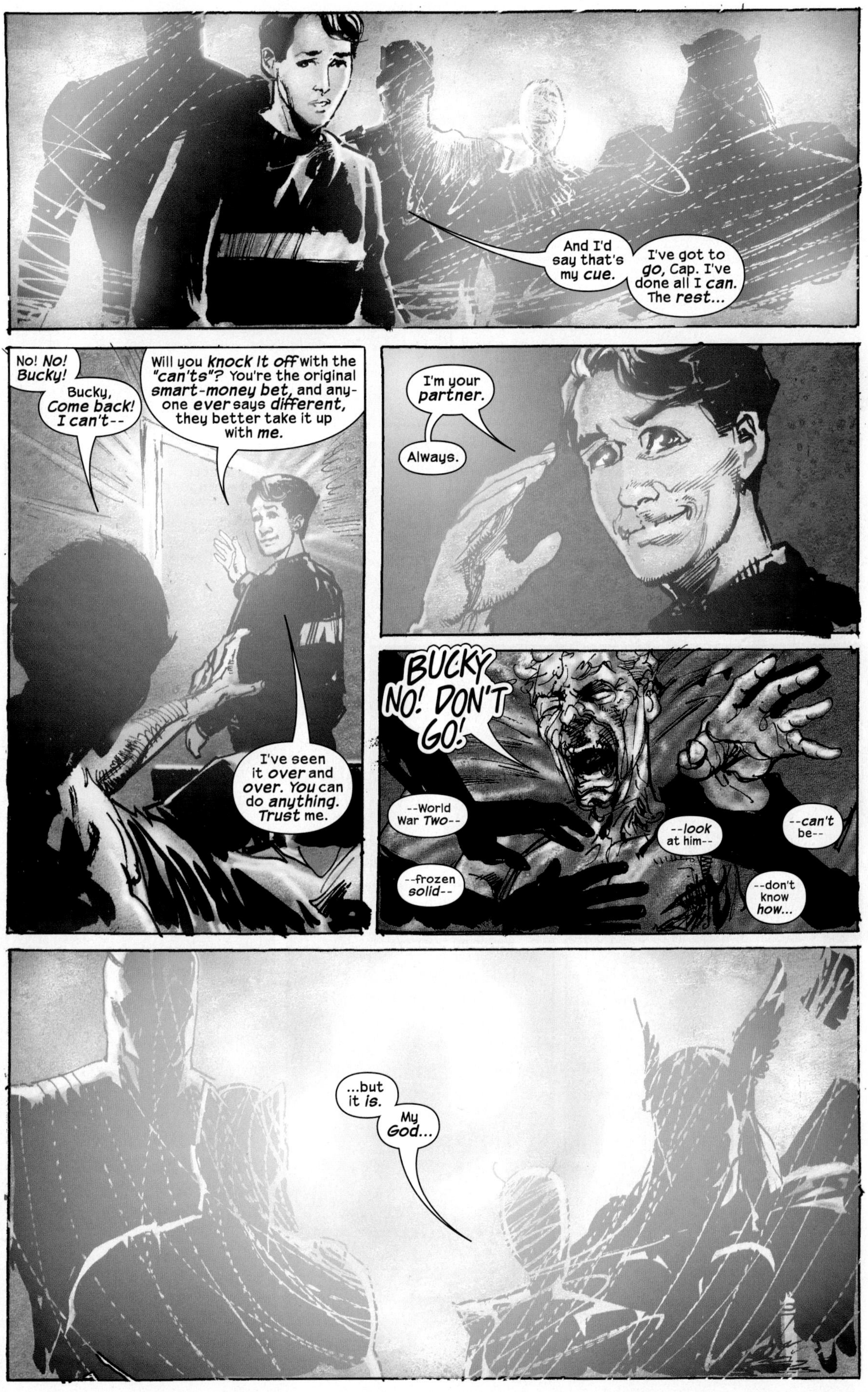

And I'd say that's my cue.
I've got to go, Cap. I've done all I can. The rest...
No! No! Bucky!
Bucky, Come back! I can't--
Will you knock it off with the "can'ts"? You're the original smart-money bet, and any-one ever says different, they better take it up with me.
I've seen it over and over. You can do anything. Trust me.
I'm your partner.
Always.
BUCKY NO! DON'T GO!
--World War Two--
--look at him--
--can't be--
--frozen solid--
--don't know how...
...but it is.
My God...

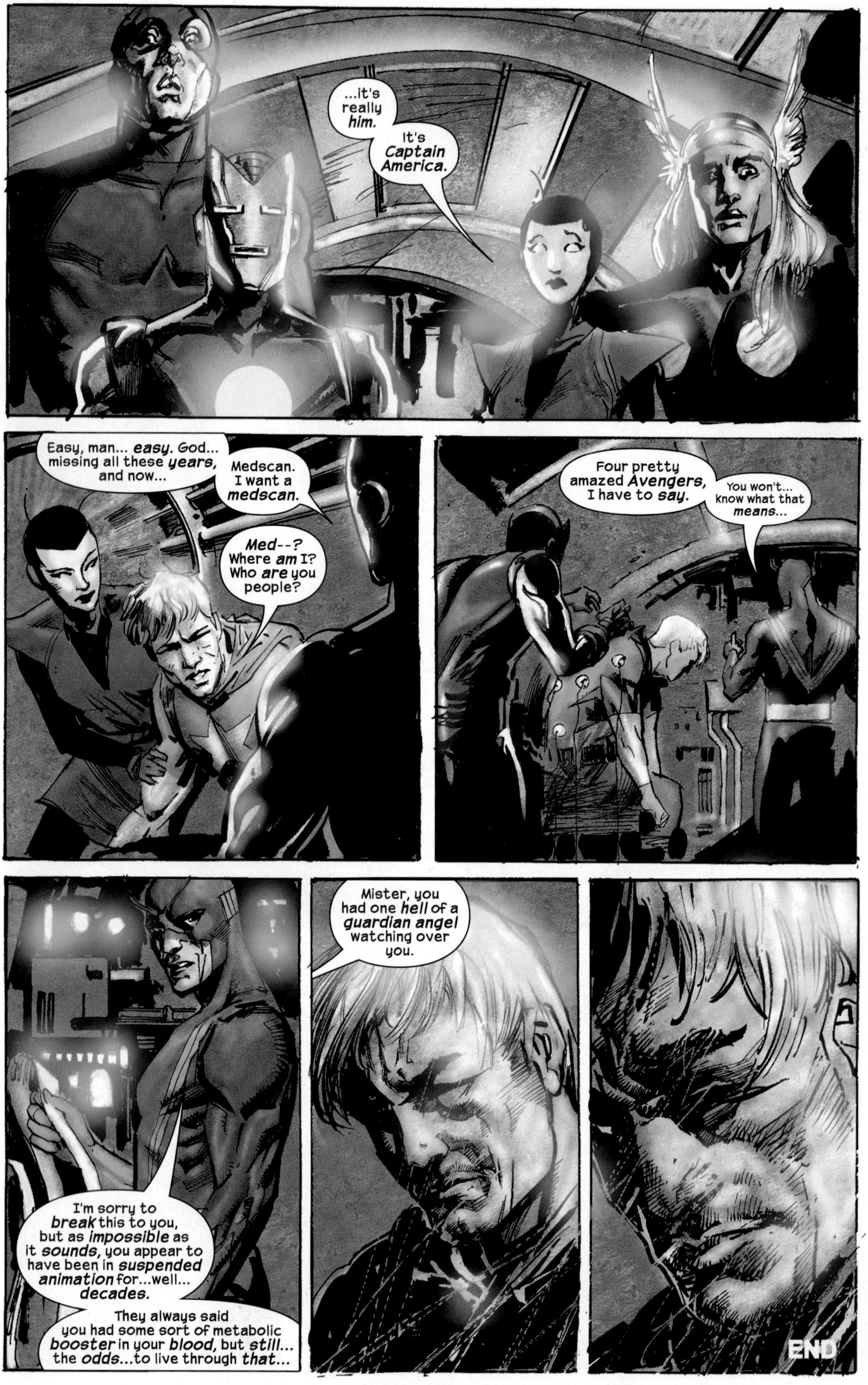

...it's really him.
It's Captain America.
Easy, man... easy. God... missing all these years, and now...
Medscan. I want a medscan.
Med--? Where am I? Who are you people?
Four pretty amazed Avengers, I have to say.
You won't... know what that means...
I'm sorry to break this to you, but as impossible as it sounds, you appear to have been in suspended animation for...well... decades.
They always said you had some sort of metabolic booster in your blood, but still... the odds...to live through that...
Mister, you had one hell of a guardian angel watching over you.
END

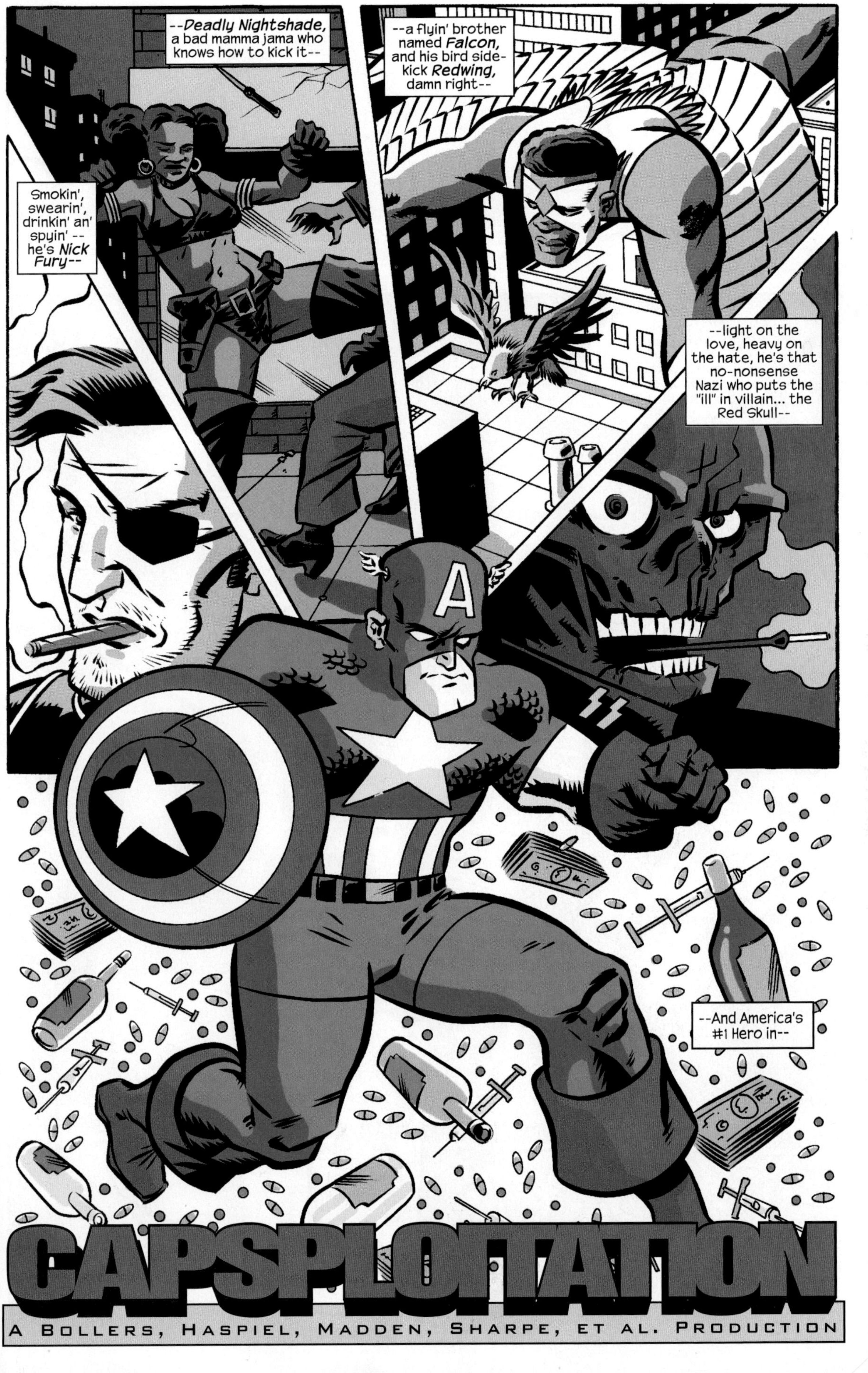
Smokin', swearin', drinkin' an' spyin' -- he's Nick Fury--
--Deadly Nightshade, a bad mamma jama who knows how to kick it--
--a flyin' brother named Falcon, and his bird side-kick Redwing, damn right--
--light on the love, heavy on the hate, he's that no-nonsense Nazi who puts the "ill" in villain... the Red Skull--
--And America's #1 Hero in--
CAPSPLOITATION
A Bollers, Haspiel, Madden, Sharpe, et al. Production

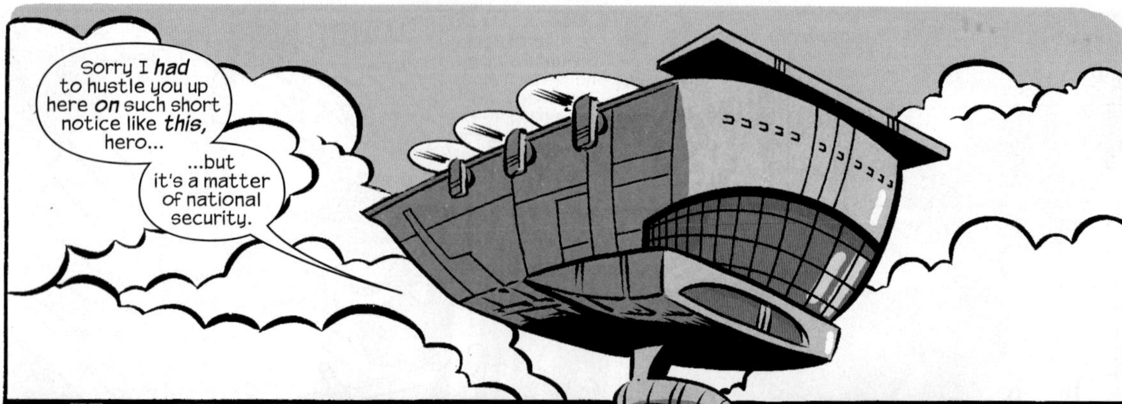
Sorry I *had* to hustle you up here *on* such short notice like *this,* hero...
...but it's a matter of national security.

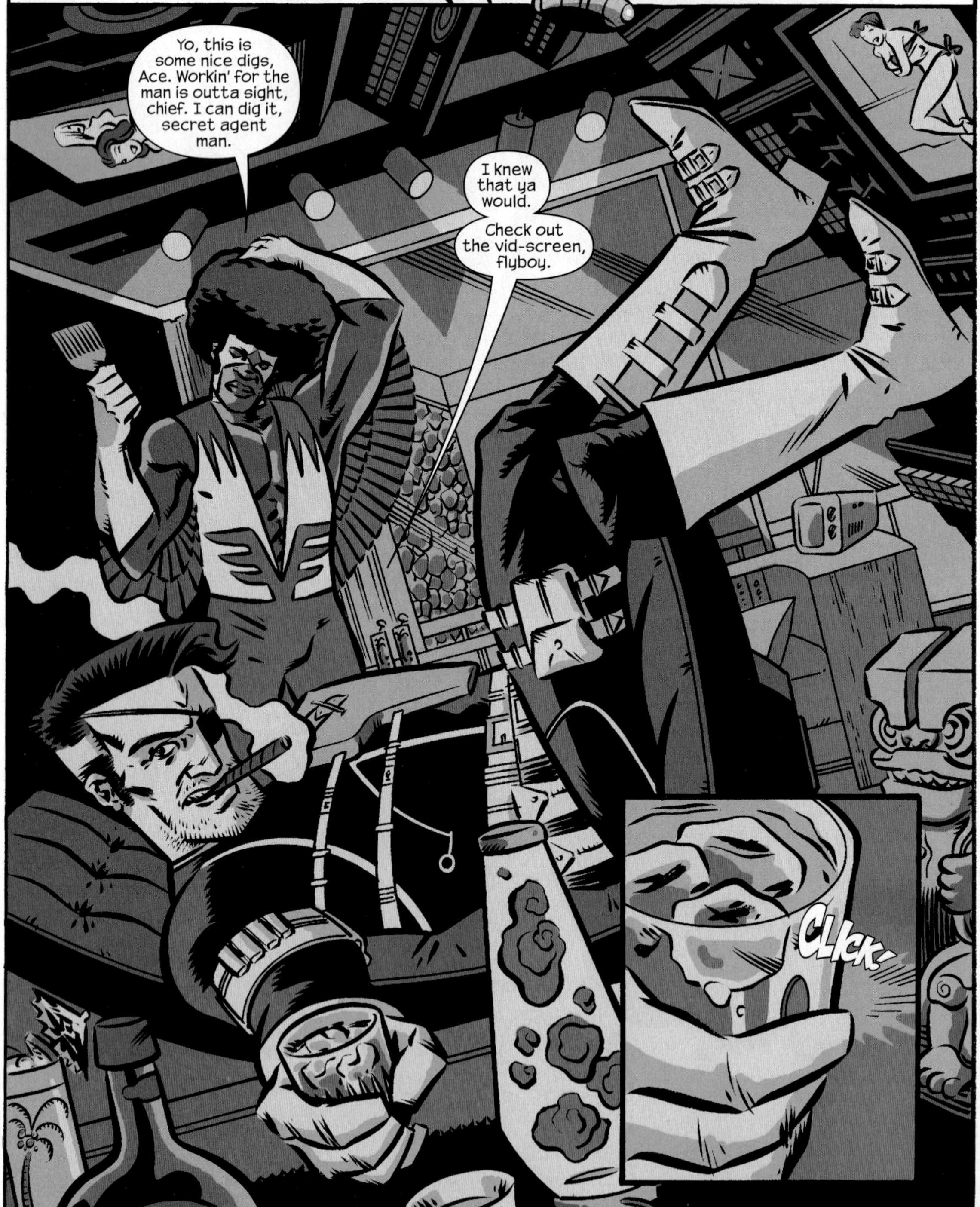
Yo, this is some nice digs, Ace. Workin' for the man is outta sight, chief. I can dig it, secret agent man.
I knew that ya would.
Check out the vid-screen, flyboy.
CLICK!

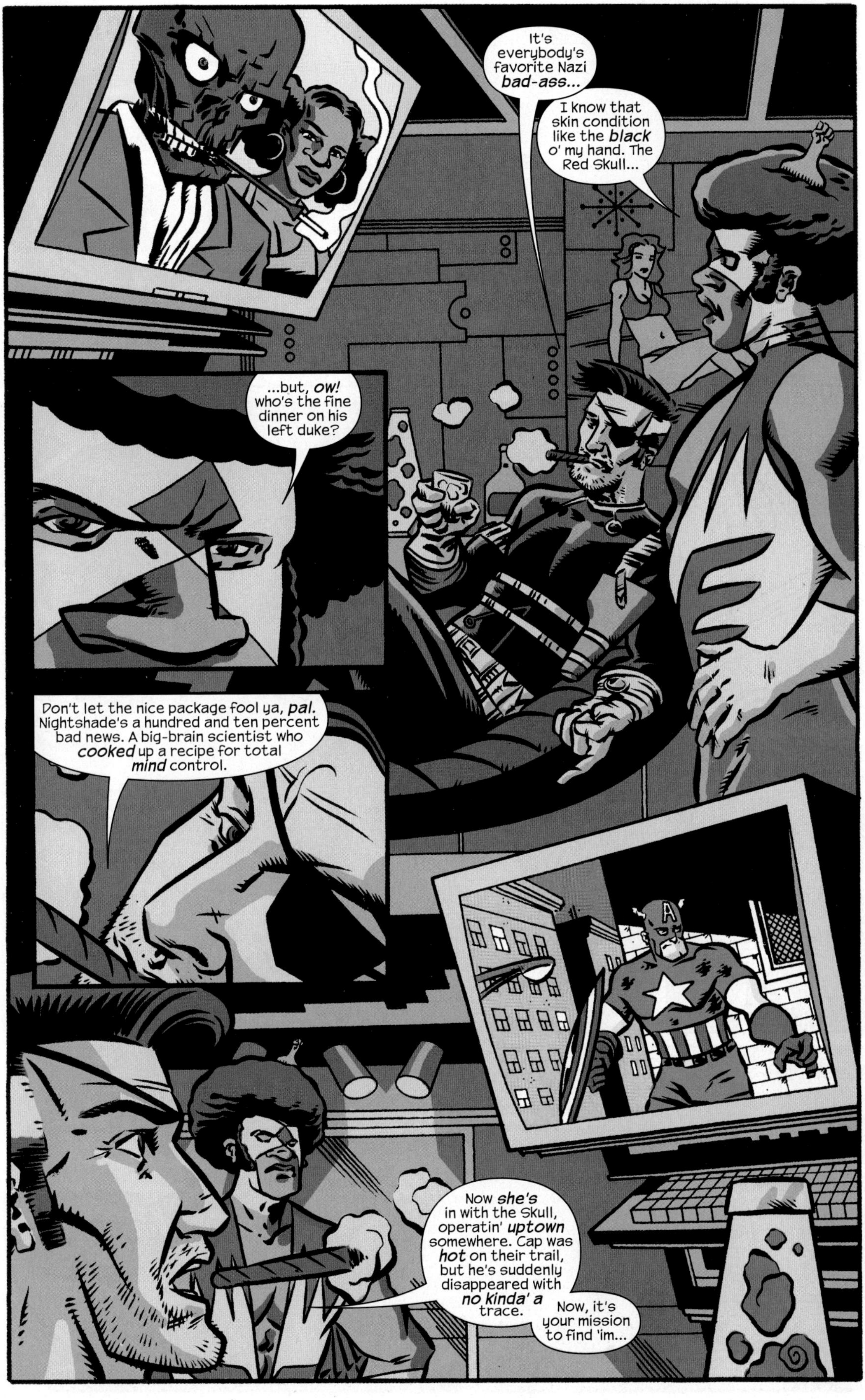
It's everybody's favorite Nazi *bad-ass...*
I know that skin condition like the *black* o' my hand. The Red Skull...
...but, *ow!* who's the fine dinner on his left duke?
Don't let the nice package fool ya, *pal.* Nightshade's a hundred and ten percent bad news. A big-brain scientist who *cooked* up a recipe for total *mind* control.
Now *she's* in with the Skull, operatin' *uptown* somewhere. Cap was *hot* on their trail, but he's suddenly disappeared with *no kinda' a* trace.
Now, it's your mission to find 'im...

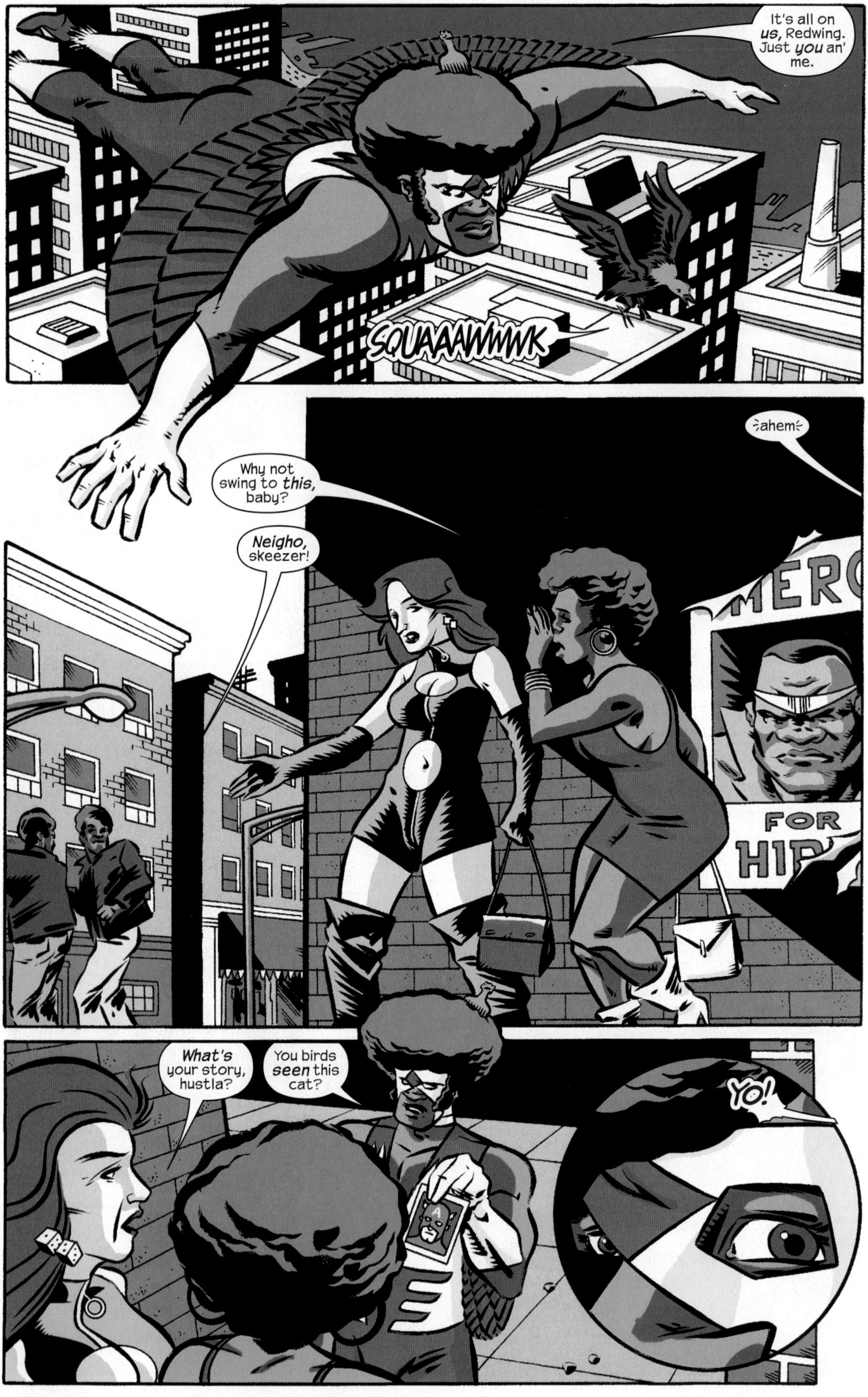
It's all on us, Redwing. Just you an' me.
SQUAAAWWWK
Why not swing to this, baby?
Neigho, skeezer!
ahem
MERC
FOR HIR
What's your story, hustla?
You birds seen this cat?
YO!

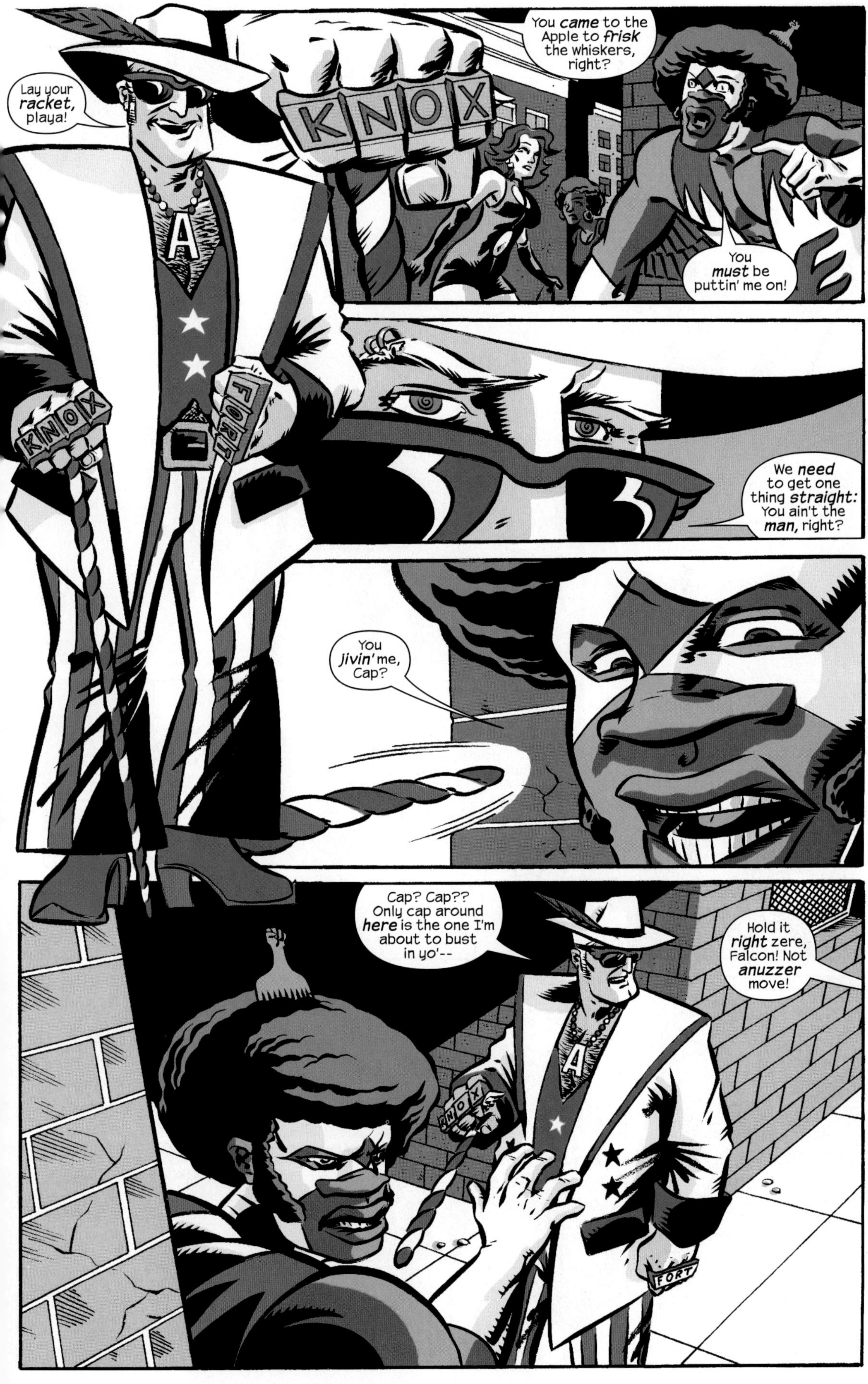

Lay your racket, playa!
You came to the Apple to frisk the whiskers, right?
You must be puttin' me on!
We need to get one thing straight: You ain't the man, right?
You jivin' me, Cap?
Cap? Cap?? Only cap around here is the one I'm about to bust in yo'--
Hold it right zere, Falcon! Not anuzzer move!
KNOX
FORT

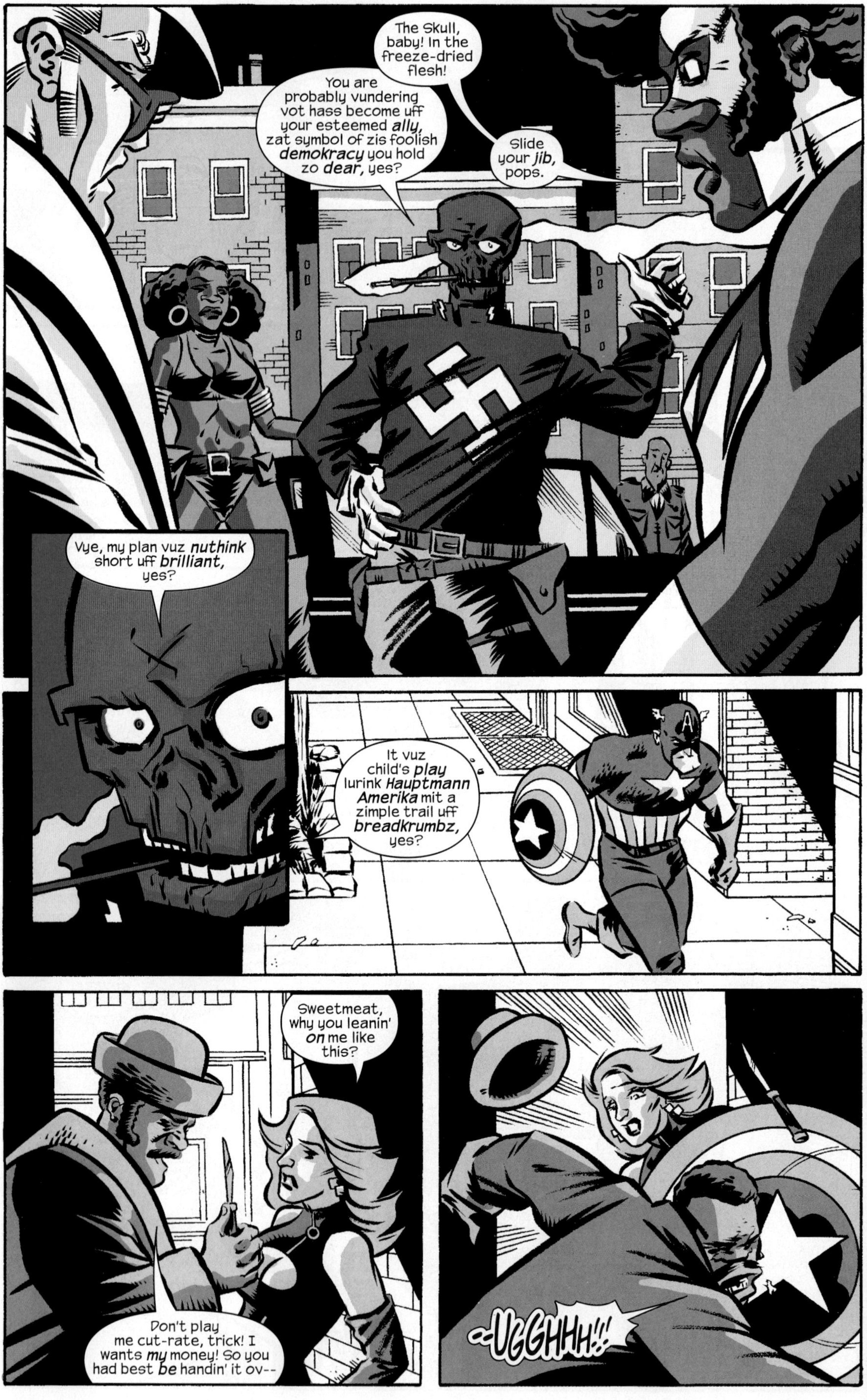

You are probably vundering vot hass become uff your esteemed *ally*, zat symbol of zis foolish *demokracy* you hold zo *dear*, yes?
The Skull, baby! In the freeze-dried flesh!
Slide your *jib*, pops.
Vye, my plan vuz *nuthink* short uff *brilliant*, yes?
It vuz child's *play* lurink *Hauptmann Amerika* mit a zimple trail uff *breadkrumbz*, yes?
Sweetmeat, why you leanin' *on* me like this?
Don't play me cut-rate, trick! I wants *my* money! So you had best *be* handin' it ov--
--UGGHHH!!

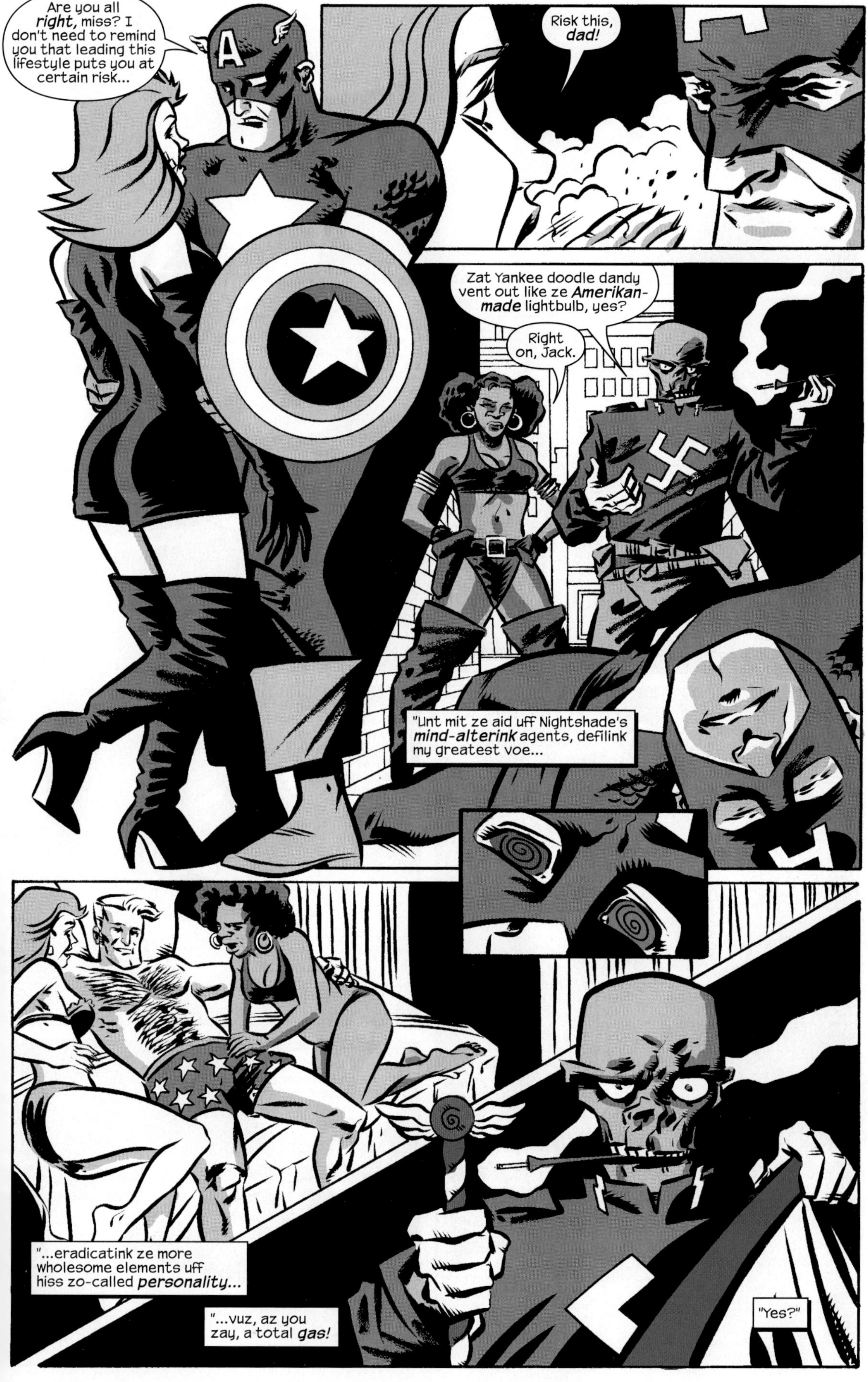
Are you all *right,* miss? I don't need to remind you that leading this lifestyle puts you at certain risk...
Risk this, *dad!*
Zat Yankee doodle dandy vent out like ze *Amerikan-made* lightbulb, yes?
Right on, Jack.
"Unt mit ze aid uff Nightshade's *mind-alterink* agents, defilink my greatest voe...
"...eradicatink ze more wholesome elements uff hiss zo-called *personality...*
"...vuz, az you zay, a total *gas!*
"Yes?"

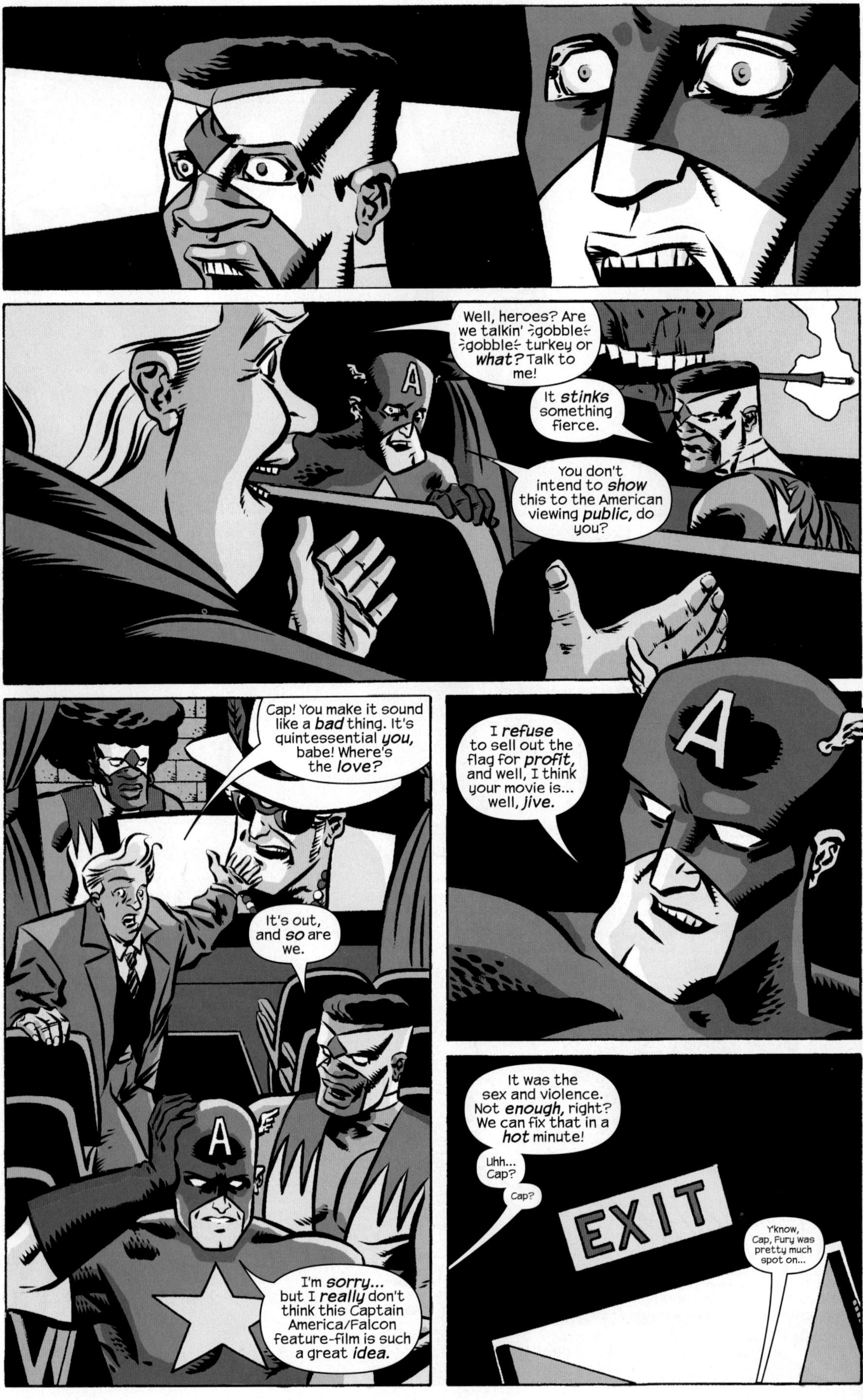
Well, heroes? Are we talkin' gobble gobble turkey or what? Talk to me!
It stinks something fierce.
You don't intend to show this to the American viewing public, do you?
Cap! You make it sound like a bad thing. It's quintessential you, babe! Where's the love?
It's out, and so are we.
I'm sorry... but I really don't think this Captain America/Falcon feature-film is such a great idea.
I refuse to sell out the flag for profit, and well, I think your movie is... well, jive.
It was the sex and violence. Not enough, right? We can fix that in a hot minute!
Uhh... Cap?
Cap?
EXIT
Y'know, Cap, Fury was pretty much spot on...

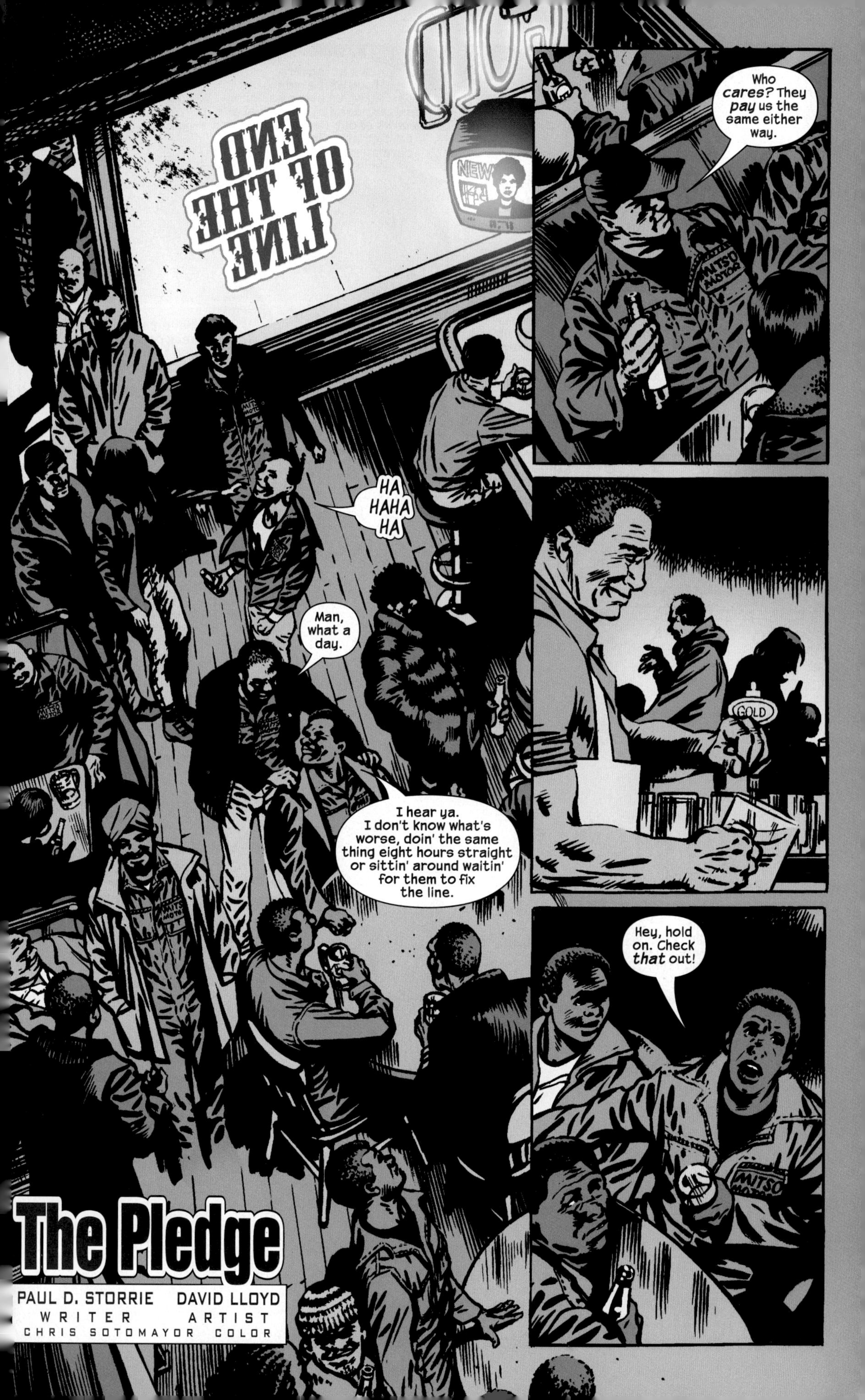
END OF THE LINE
HA HAHA HA
Man, what a day.
I hear ya. I don't know what's worse, doin' the same thing eight hours straight or sittin' around waitin' for them to fix the line.
Who *cares?* They *pay* us the same either way.
GOLD
Hey, hold on. Check *that* out!
The Pledge
PAUL D. STORRIE WRITER
DAVID LLOYD ARTIST
CHRIS SOTOMAYOR COLOR

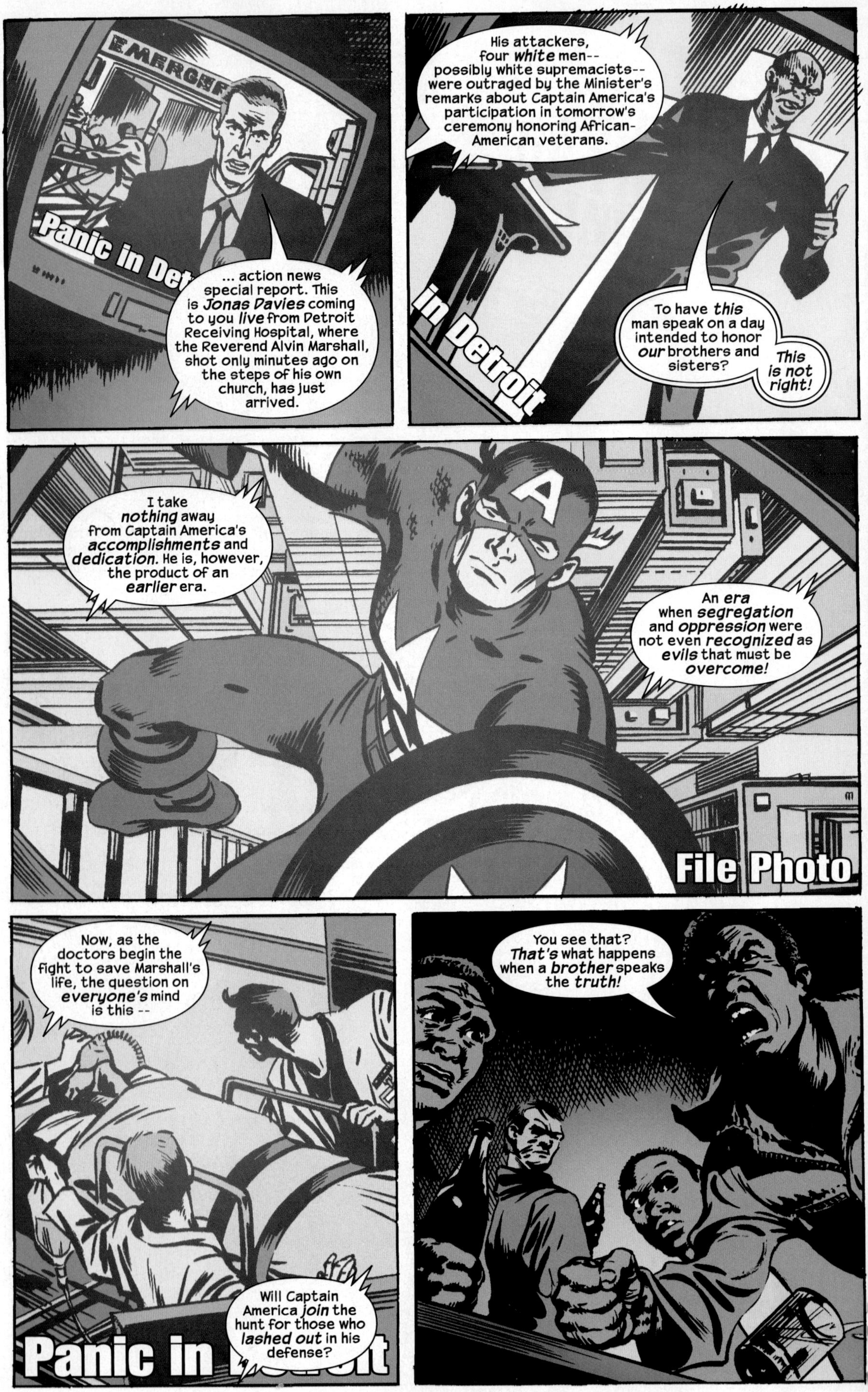
EMERGEN
Panic in Det
... action news special report. This is Jonas Davies coming to you live from Detroit Receiving Hospital, where the Reverend Alvin Marshall, shot only minutes ago on the steps of his own church, has just arrived.
His attackers, four white men-- possibly white supremacists-- were outraged by the Minister's remarks about Captain America's participation in tomorrow's ceremony honoring African-American veterans.
in Detroit
To have this man speak on a day intended to honor our brothers and sisters?
This is not right!
I take nothing away from Captain America's accomplishments and dedication. He is, however, the product of an earlier era.
An era when segregation and oppression were not even recognized as evils that must be overcome!
File Photo
Now, as the doctors begin the fight to save Marshall's life, the question on everyone's mind is this --
Will Captain America join the hunt for those who lashed out in his defense?
Panic in
You see that? That's what happens when a brother speaks the truth!

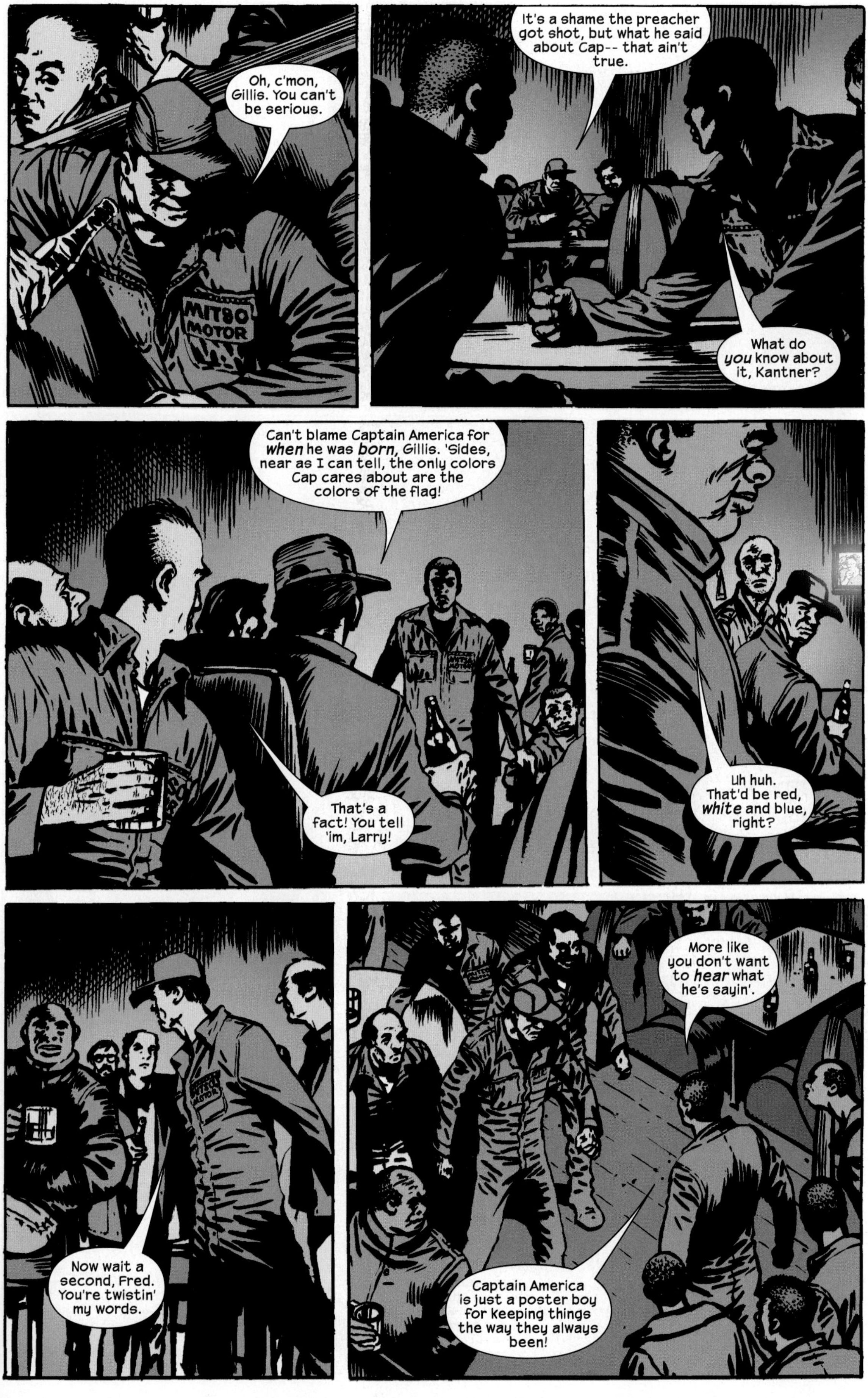
Oh, c'mon, Gillis. You can't be serious.
It's a shame the preacher got shot, but what he said about Cap-- that ain't true.
What do *you* know about it, Kantner?
Can't blame Captain America for *when* he was *born,* Gillis. 'Sides, near as I can tell, the only colors Cap cares about are the colors of the flag!
That's a fact! You tell 'im, Larry!
Uh huh. That'd be red, *white* and blue, right?
Now wait a second, Fred. You're twistin' my words.
More like you don't want to *hear* what he's sayin'.
Captain America is just a poster boy for keeping things the way they always been!

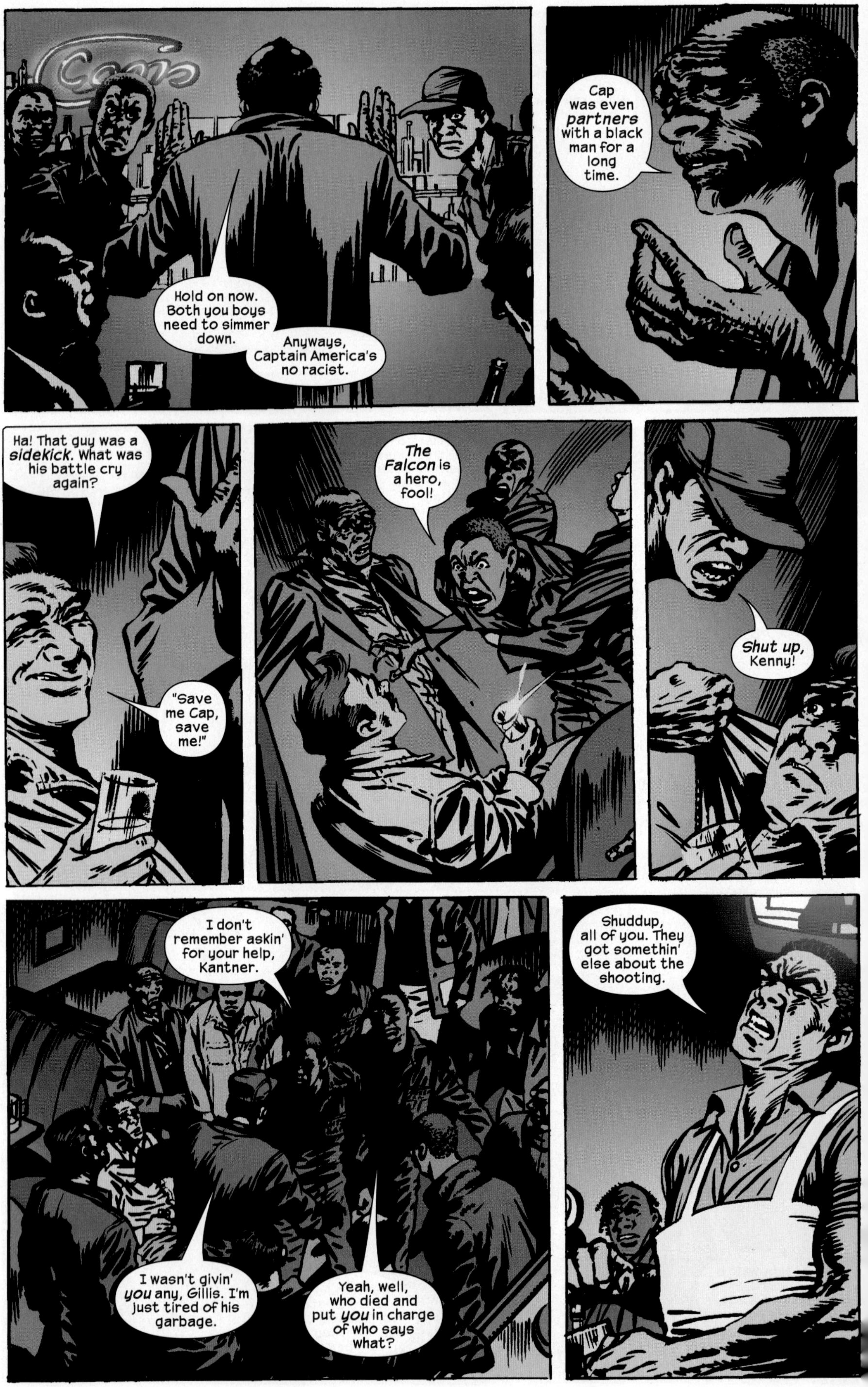
Hold on now. Both you boys need to simmer down.
Anyways, Captain America's no racist.
Cap was even *partners* with a black man for a long time.
Ha! That guy was a *sidekick*. What was his battle cry again?
"Save me Cap, save me!"
The Falcon is a hero, fool!
Shut up, Kenny!
I don't remember askin' for your help, Kantner.
I wasn't givin' *you* any, Gillis. I'm just tired of his garbage.
Yeah, well, who died and put *you* in charge of who says what?
Shuddup, all of you. They got somethin' else about the shooting.

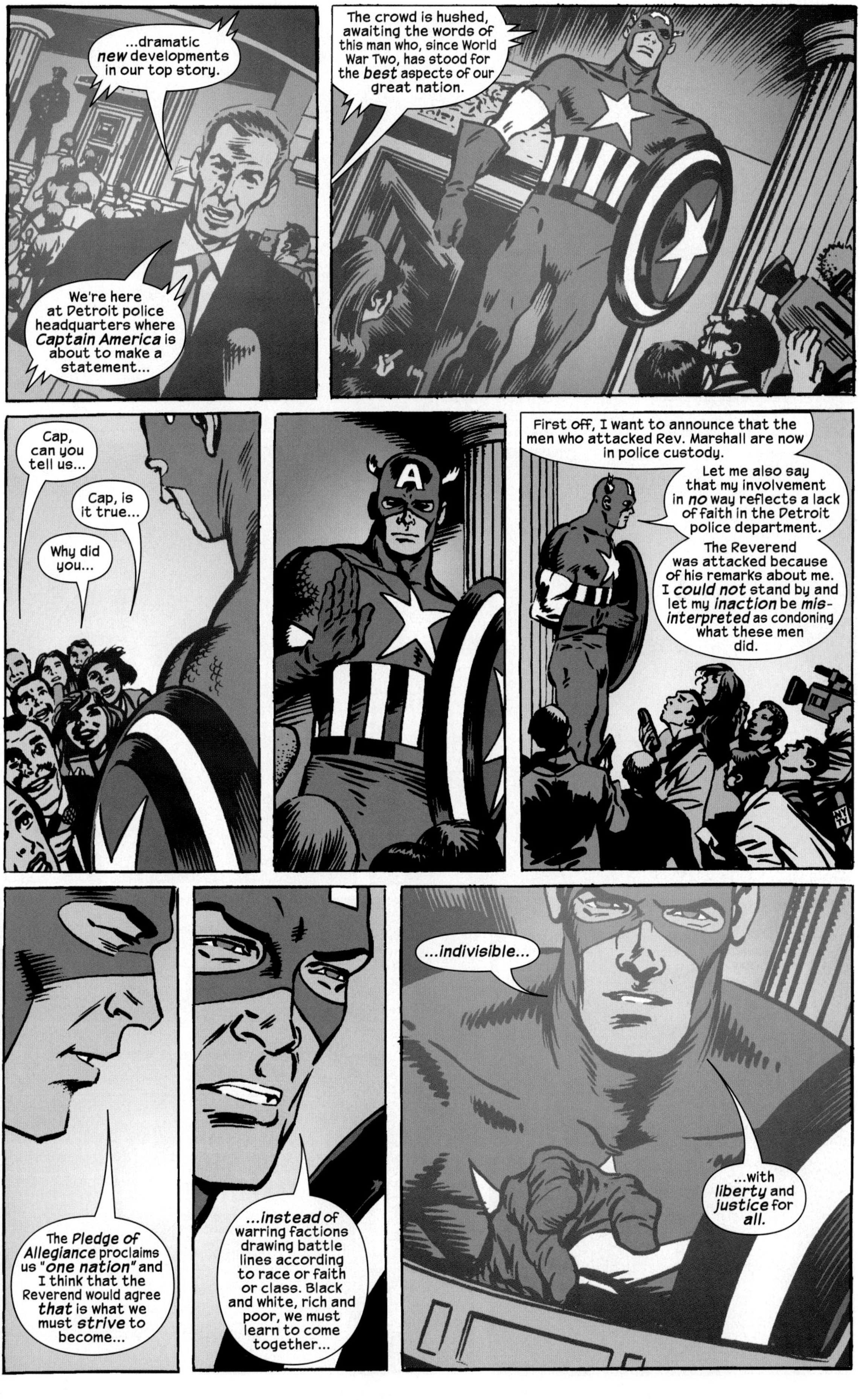

...dramatic new developments in our top story.
We're here at Detroit police headquarters where Captain America is about to make a statement...
The crowd is hushed, awaiting the words of this man who, since World War Two, has stood for the best aspects of our great nation.
Cap, can you tell us...
Cap, is it true...
Why did you...
First off, I want to announce that the men who attacked Rev. Marshall are now in police custody.
Let me also say that my involvement in no way reflects a lack of faith in the Detroit police department.
The Reverend was attacked because of his remarks about me. I could not stand by and let my inaction be misinterpreted as condoning what these men did.
The Pledge of Allegiance proclaims us "one nation" and I think that the Reverend would agree that is what we must strive to become...
...instead of warring factions drawing battle lines according to race or faith or class. Black and white, rich and poor, we must learn to come together...
...indivisible...
...with liberty and justice for all.

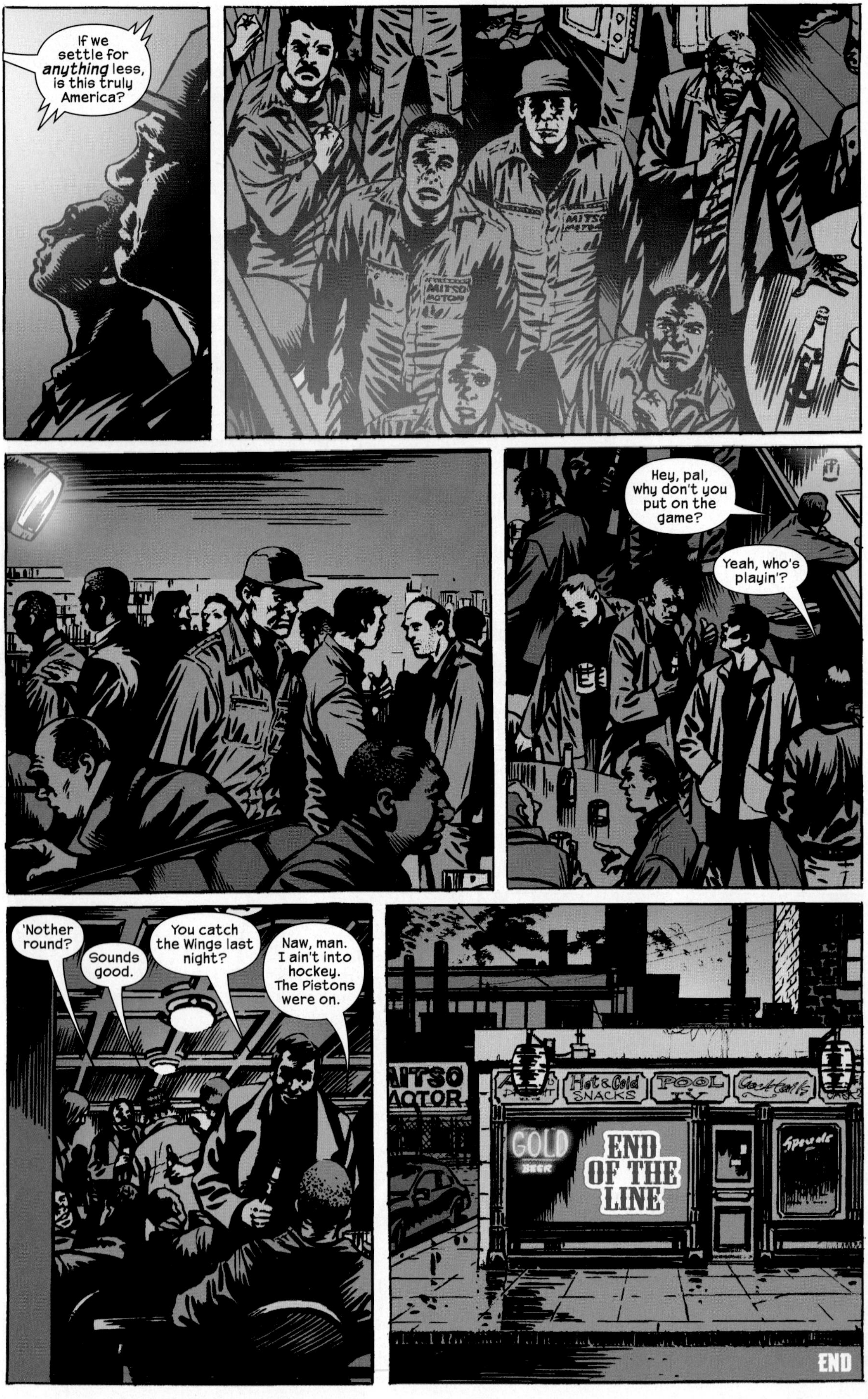
If we settle for *anything* less, is this truly America?
Hey, pal, why don't you put on the game?
Yeah, who's playin'?
'Nother round?
Sounds good.
You catch the Wings last night?
Naw, man. I ain't into hockey. The Pistons were on.
MITSO MOTOR
Hot & Cold SNACKS
POOL TV
Cocktails
GOLD BEER
END OF THE LINE
END

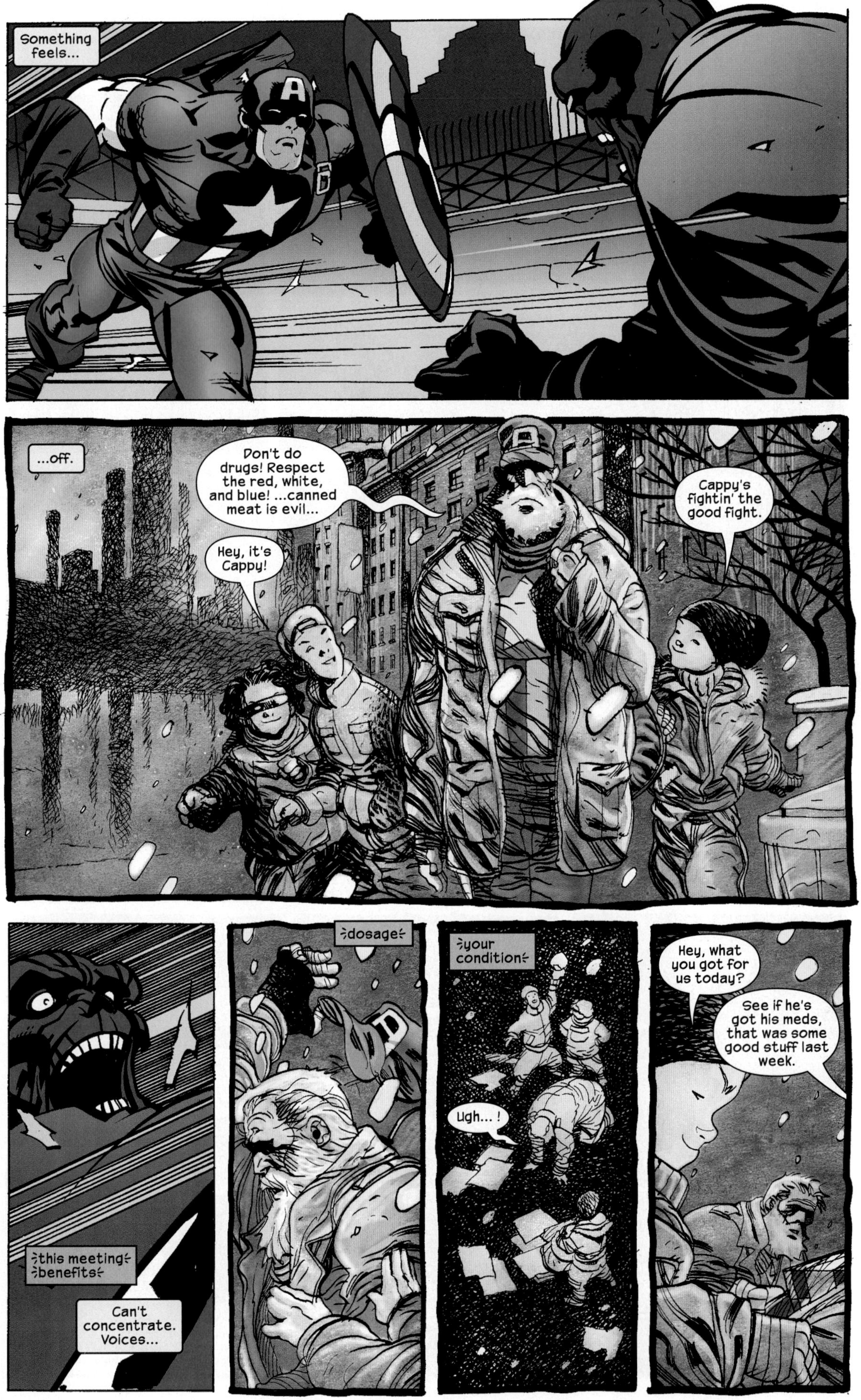
Something feels...
...off.
Don't do drugs! Respect the red, white, and blue! ...canned meat is evil...
Hey, it's Cappy!
Cappy's fightin' the good fight.
this meeting benefits
Can't concentrate. Voices...
dosage
your condition
Ugh... !
Hey, what you got for us today?
See if he's got his meds, that was some good stuff last week.

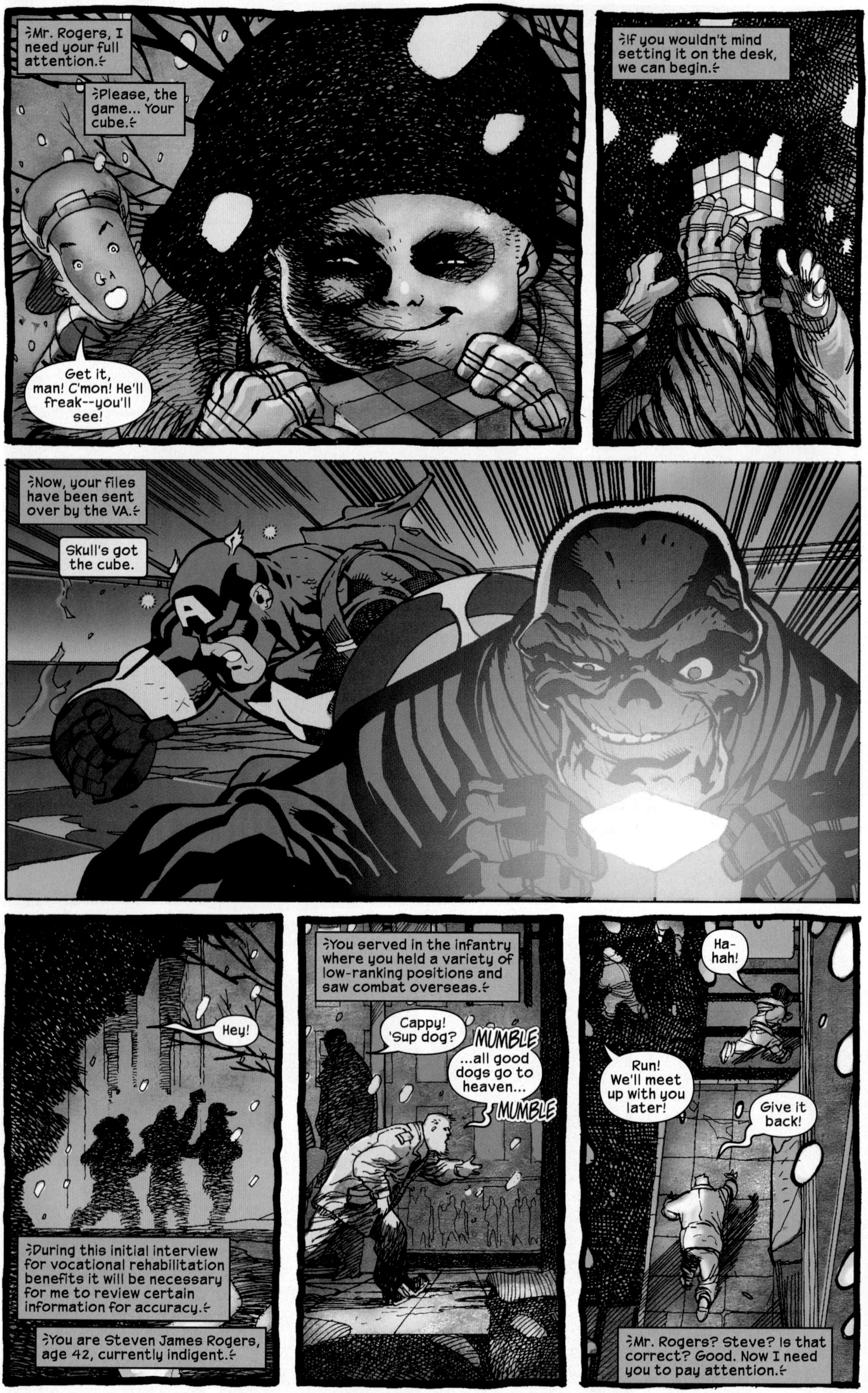
Mr. Rogers, I need your full attention.
Please, the game... Your cube.
Get it, man! C'mon! He'll freak--you'll see!
If you wouldn't mind setting it on the desk, we can begin.
Now, your files have been sent over by the VA.
Skull's got the cube.
Hey!
During this initial interview for vocational rehabilitation benefits it will be necessary for me to review certain information for accuracy.
You are Steven James Rogers, age 42, currently indigent.
You served in the infantry where you held a variety of low-ranking positions and saw combat overseas.
Cappy! 'Sup dog?
MUMBLE
...all good dogs go to heaven...
MUMBLE
Ha-hah!
Run! We'll meet up with you later!
Give it back!
Mr. Rogers? Steve? Is that correct? Good. Now I need you to pay attention.

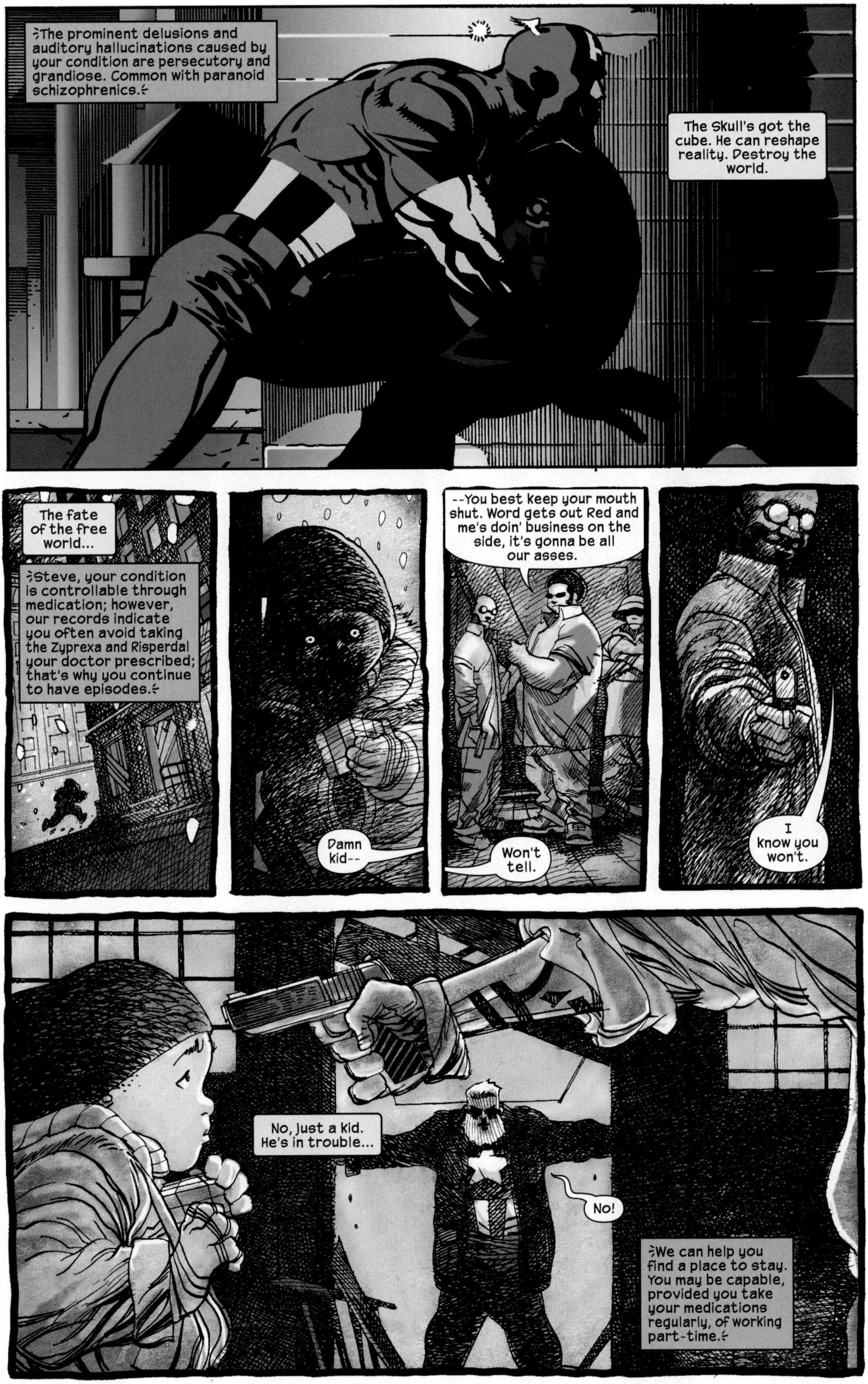
The prominent delusions and auditory hallucinations caused by your condition are persecutory and grandiose. Common with paranoid schizophrenics.
The Skull's got the cube. He can reshape reality. Destroy the world.
The fate of the free world...
Steve, your condition is controllable through medication; however, our records indicate you often avoid taking the Zyprexa and Risperdal your doctor prescribed; that's why you continue to have episodes.
Damn kid--
--You best keep your mouth shut. Word gets out Red and me's doin' business on the side, it's gonna be all our asses.
Won't tell.
I know you won't.
No, just a kid. He's in trouble...
No!
We can help you find a place to stay. You may be capable, provided you take your medications regularly, of working part-time.

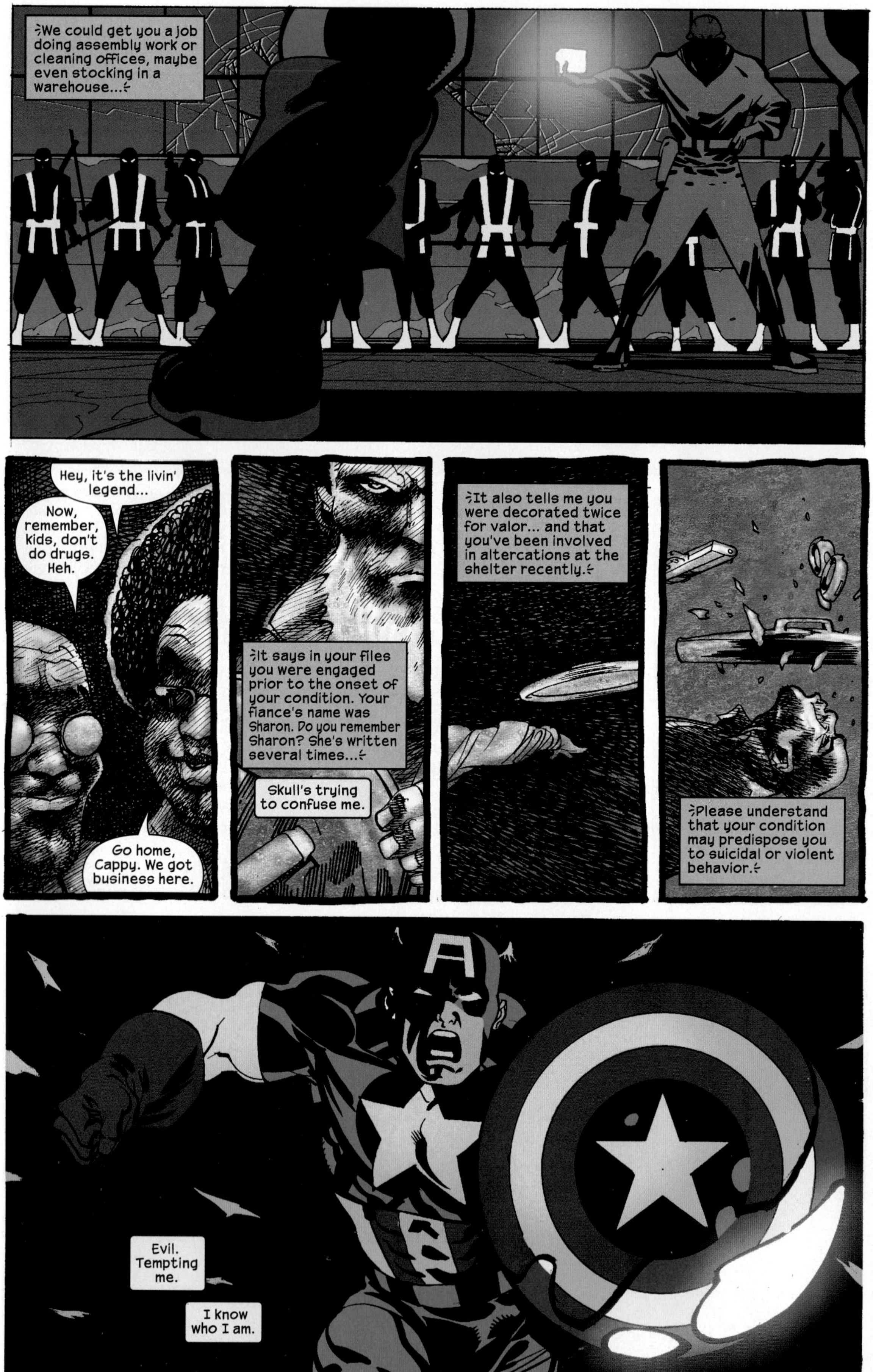

We could get you a job doing assembly work or cleaning offices, maybe even stocking in a warehouse...
Hey, it's the livin' legend...
Now, remember, kids, don't do drugs. Heh.
Go home, Cappy. We got business here.
It says in your files you were engaged prior to the onset of your condition. Your fiance's name was Sharon. Do you remember Sharon? She's written several times...
Skull's trying to confuse me.
It also tells me you were decorated twice for valor... and that you've been involved in altercations at the shelter recently.
Please understand that your condition may predispose you to suicidal or violent behavior.
Evil. Tempting me.
I know who I am.

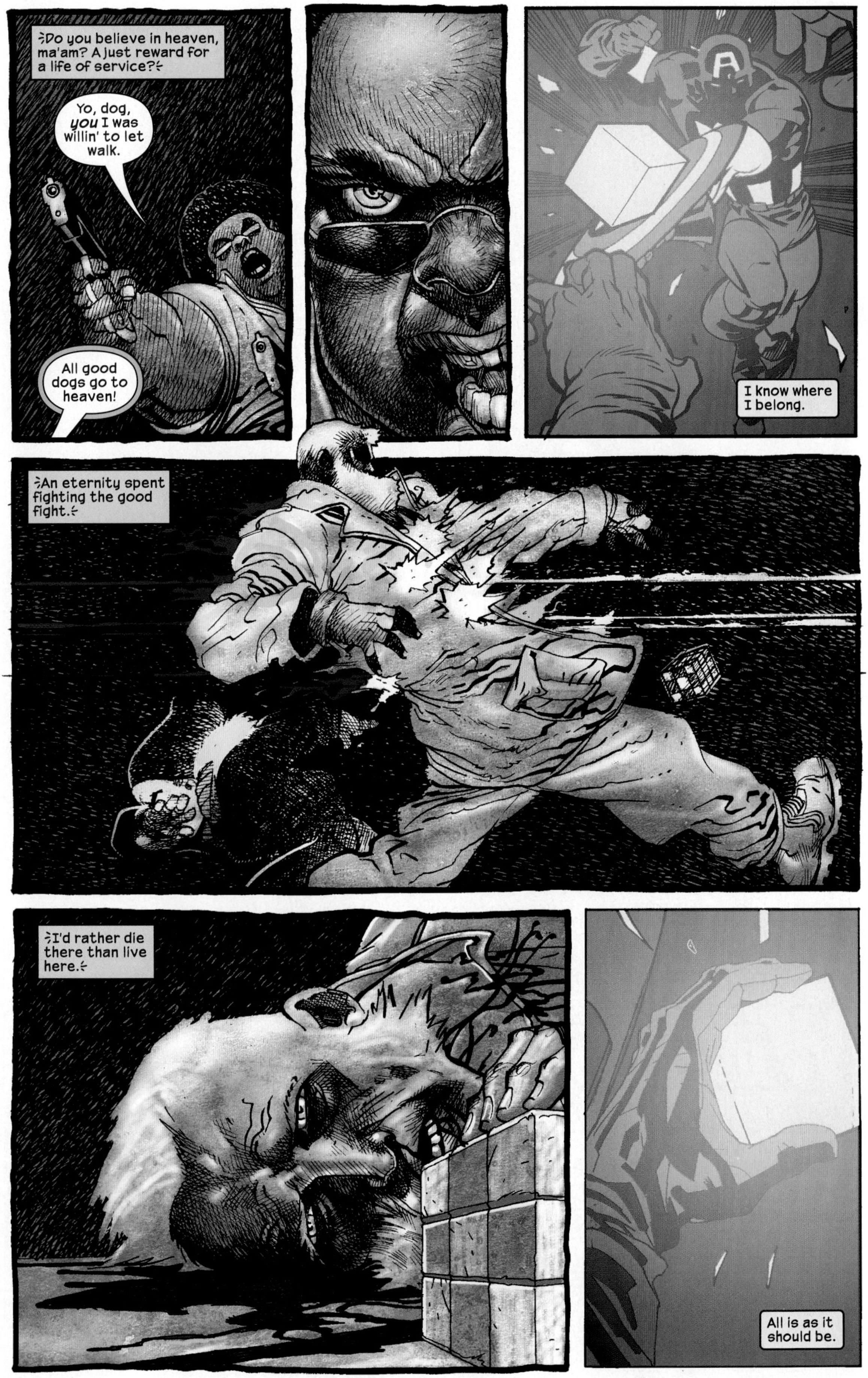

Do you believe in heaven, ma'am? A just reward for a life of service?
Yo, dog, *you* I was willin' to let walk.
All good dogs go to heaven!
I know where I belong.
An eternity spent fighting the good fight.
I'd rather die there than live here.
All is as it should be.

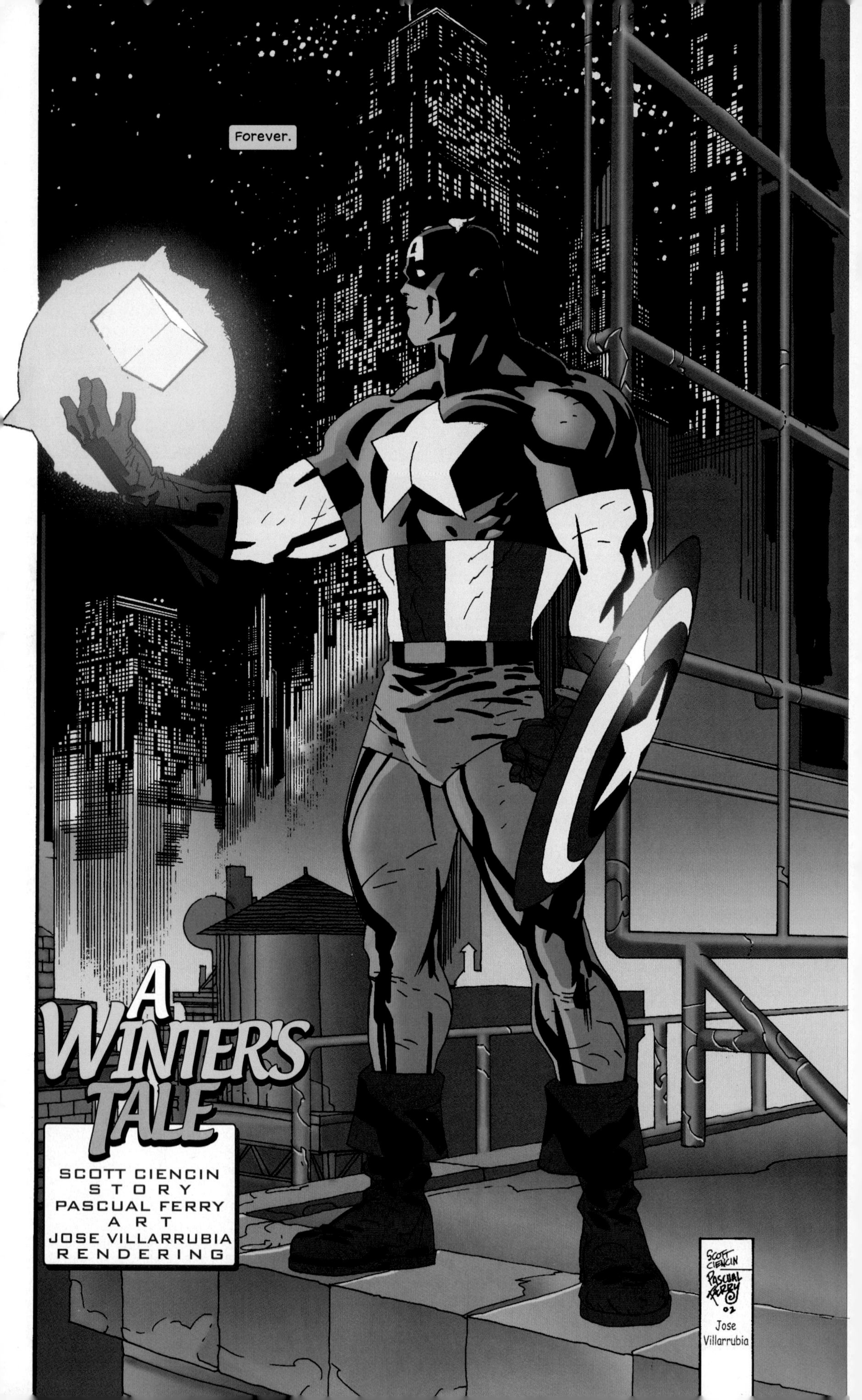
Forever.
A WINTER'S TALE
SCOTT CIENCIN
STORY
PASCUAL FERRY
ART
JOSE VILLARRUBIA
RENDERING
SCOTT CIENCIN
PASCUAL FERRY
02
Jose
Villarrubia

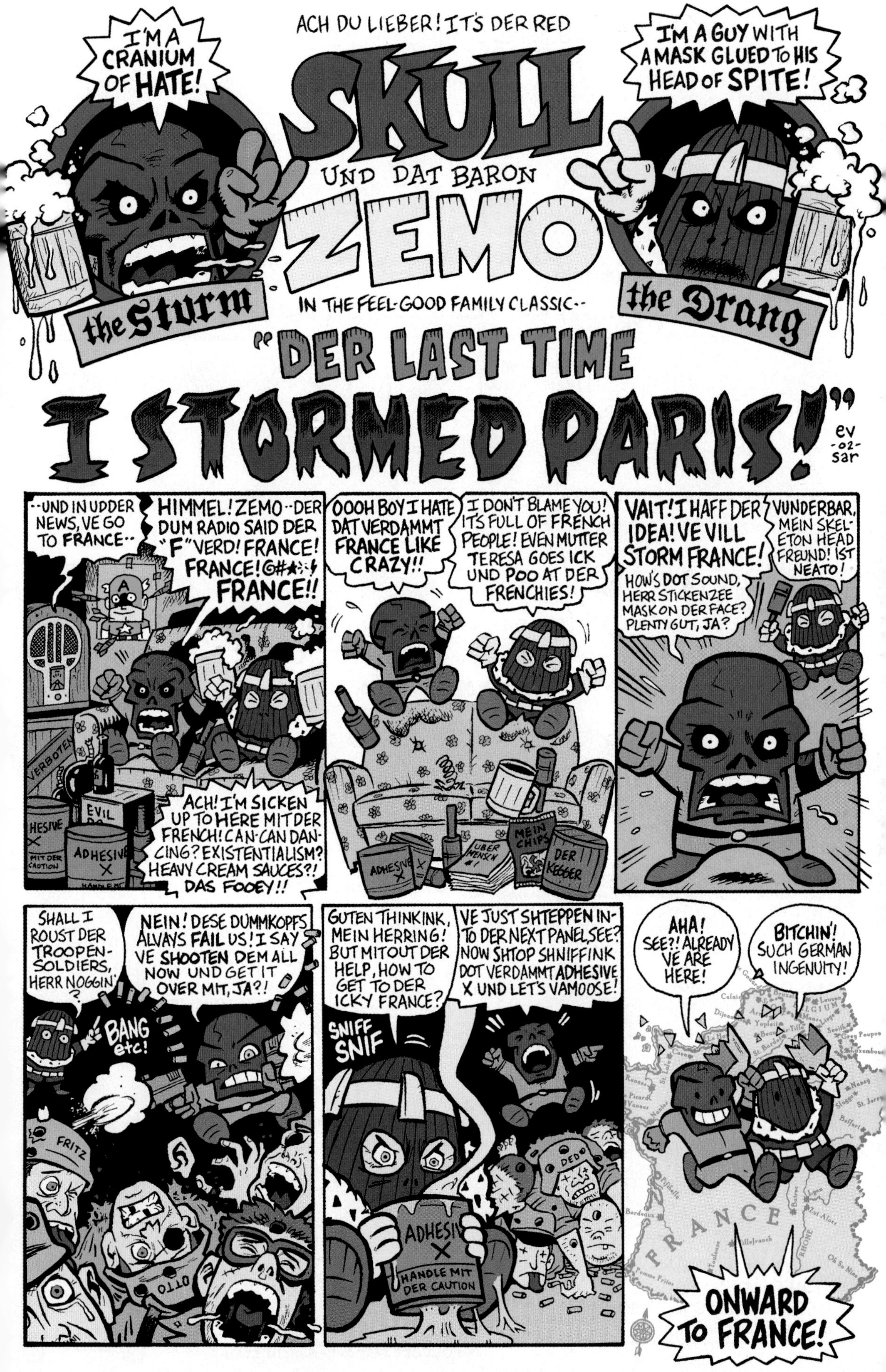
ACH DU LIEBER! IT'S DER RED
SKULL
UND DAT BARON
ZEMO
I'M A CRANIUM OF HATE!
I'M A GUY WITH A MASK GLUED TO HIS HEAD OF SPITE!
the Sturm
the Drang
IN THE FEEL-GOOD FAMILY CLASSIC--
"DER LAST TIME I STORMED PARIS!"
ev -02- sar
--UND IN UDDER NEWS, VE GO TO FRANCE--
HIMMEL! ZEMO--DER DUM RADIO SAID DER "F" VERD! FRANCE! FRANCE! @#*! FRANCE!!
VERBOTEN
EVIL
HESIVE X MIT DER CAUTION
ADHESIVE X
ACH! I'M SICKEN UP TO HERE MIT DER FRENCH! CAN-CAN DANCING? EXISTENTIALISM? HEAVY CREAM SAUCES?! DAS FOOEY!!
OOOH BOY I HATE DAT VERDAMMT FRANCE LIKE CRAZY!!
I DON'T BLAME YOU! IT'S FULL OF FRENCH PEOPLE! EVEN MUTTER TERESA GOES ICK UND POO AT DER FRENCHIES!
ADHESIVE X
UBER MENSCH #1
MEIN CHIPS
DER KEGGER
VAIT! I HAFF DER IDEA! VE VILL STORM FRANCE!
HOW'S DOT SOUND, HERR STICKENZEE MASK ON DER FACE? PLENTY GUT, JA?
VUNDERBAR, MEIN SKELETON HEAD FREUND! IST NEATO!
SHALL I ROUST DER TROOPEN-SOLDIERS, HERR NOGGIN'?
NEIN! DESE DUMMKOPFS ALVAYS FAIL US! I SAY VE SHOOTEN DEM ALL NOW UND GET IT OVER MIT, JA?!
BANG etc!
FRITZ
OTTO
GUTEN THINKINK, MEIN HERRING! BUT MITOUT DER HELP, HOW TO GET TO DER ICKY FRANCE?
VE JUST SHTEPPEN INTO DER NEXT PANEL, SEE? NOW SHTOP SHNIFFINK DOT VERDAMMT ADHESIVE X UND LET'S VAMOOSE!
SNIFF SNIF
ADHESIV X HANDLE MIT DER CAUTION
DED
AHA! SEE?! ALREADY VE ARE HERE!
BITCHIN'! SUCH GERMAN INGENUITY!
FRANCE
ONWARD TO FRANCE!

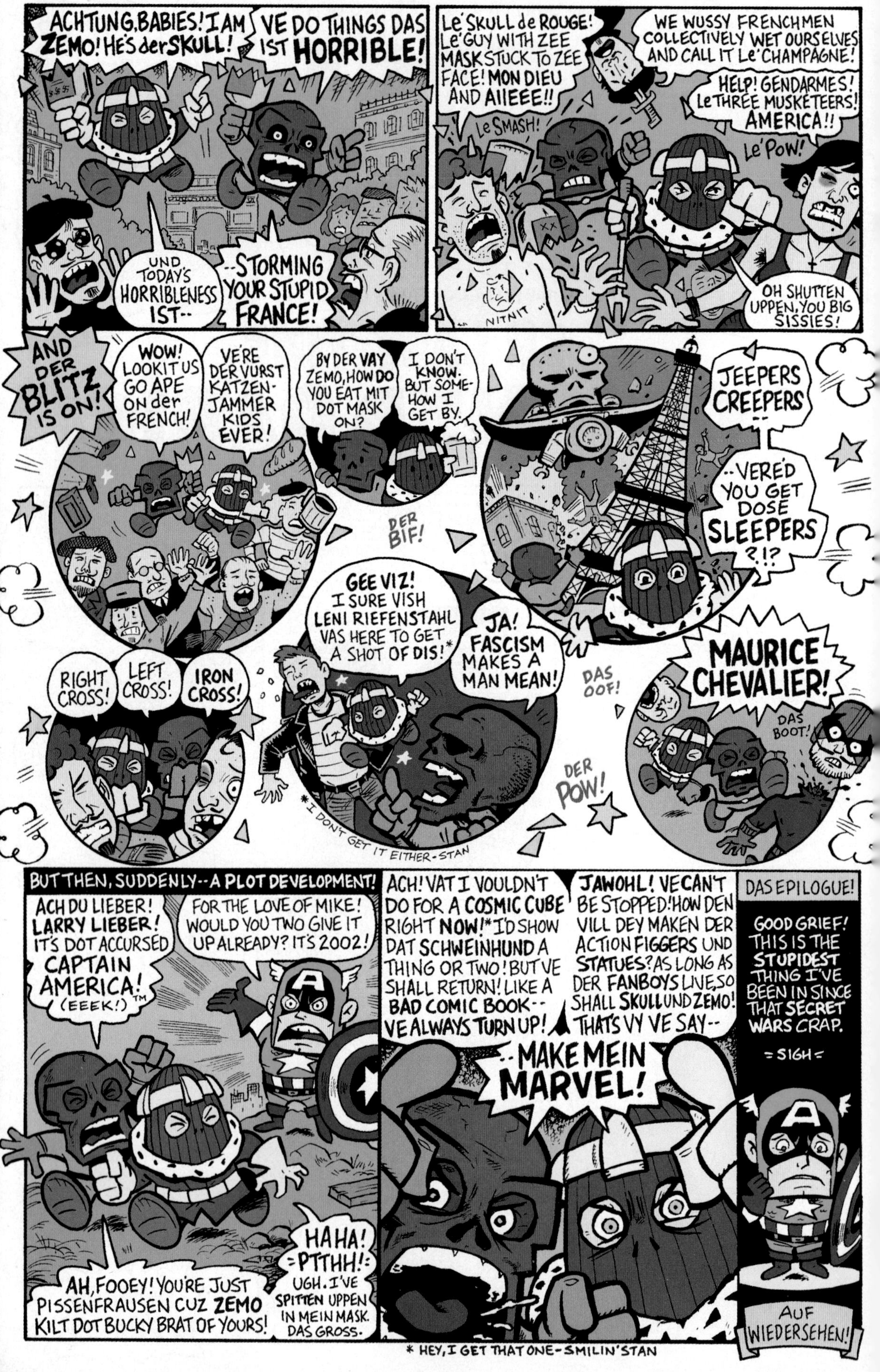
ACHTUNG, BABIES! I AM ZEMO! HE'S der SKULL!
VE DO THINGS DAS IST HORRIBLE!
UND TODAY'S HORRIBLENESS IST--
--STORMING YOUR STUPID FRANCE!
Le' SKULL de ROUGE! Le' GUY WITH ZEE MASK STUCK TO ZEE FACE! MON DIEU AND AIIEEE!!
WE WUSSY FRENCHMEN COLLECTIVELY WET OURSELVES AND CALL IT Le' CHAMPAGNE!
HELP! GENDARMES! Le THREE MUSKETEERS! AMERICA!!
Le SMASH!
Le' POW!
NITNIT
OH SHUTTEN UPPEN, YOU BIG SISSIES!
AND DER BLITZ IS ON!
WOW! LOOKIT US GO APE on der FRENCH!
VE'RE DER VURST KATZEN-JAMMER KIDS EVER!
BY DER VAY ZEMO, HOW DO YOU EAT MIT DOT MASK ON?
I DON'T KNOW. BUT SOME-HOW I GET BY.
JEEPERS CREEPERS--
--VERE'D YOU GET DOSE SLEEPERS ?!?
DER BIF!
GEE VIZ! I SURE VISH LENI RIEFENSTAHL VAS HERE TO GET A SHOT OF DIS!*
JA! FASCISM MAKES A MAN MEAN!
DAS OOF!
MAURICE CHEVALIER!
DAS BOOT!
RIGHT CROSS!
LEFT CROSS!
IRON CROSS!
DER POW!
* I DON'T GET IT EITHER - STAN
BUT THEN, SUDDENLY--A PLOT DEVELOPMENT!
ACH DU LIEBER! LARRY LIEBER! IT'S DOT ACCURSED CAPTAIN AMERICA! (EEEK!)™
FOR THE LOVE OF MIKE! WOULD YOU TWO GIVE IT UP ALREADY? IT'S 2002!
AH, FOOEY! YOU'RE JUST PISSENFRAUSEN CUZ ZEMO KILT DOT BUCKY BRAT OF YOURS!
HAHA! =PTTHH!=
UGH. I'VE SPITTEN UPPEN IN MEIN MASK. DAS GROSS.
ACH! VAT I VOULDN'T DO FOR A COSMIC CUBE RIGHT NOW!* I'D SHOW DAT SCHWEINHUND A THING OR TWO! BUT VE SHALL RETURN! LIKE A BAD COMIC BOOK--VE ALWAYS TURN UP!
JAWOHL! VE CAN'T BE STOPPED! HOW DEN VILL DEY MAKEN DER ACTION FIGGERS UND STATUES? AS LONG AS DER FANBOYS LIVE, SO SHALL SKULL UND ZEMO! THAT'S VY VE SAY--
--MAKE MEIN MARVEL!
DAS EPILOGUE!
GOOD GRIEF! THIS IS THE STUPIDEST THING I'VE BEEN IN SINCE THAT SECRET WARS CRAP.
=SIGH=
AUF WIEDERSEHEN!
* HEY, I GET THAT ONE - SMILIN' STAN

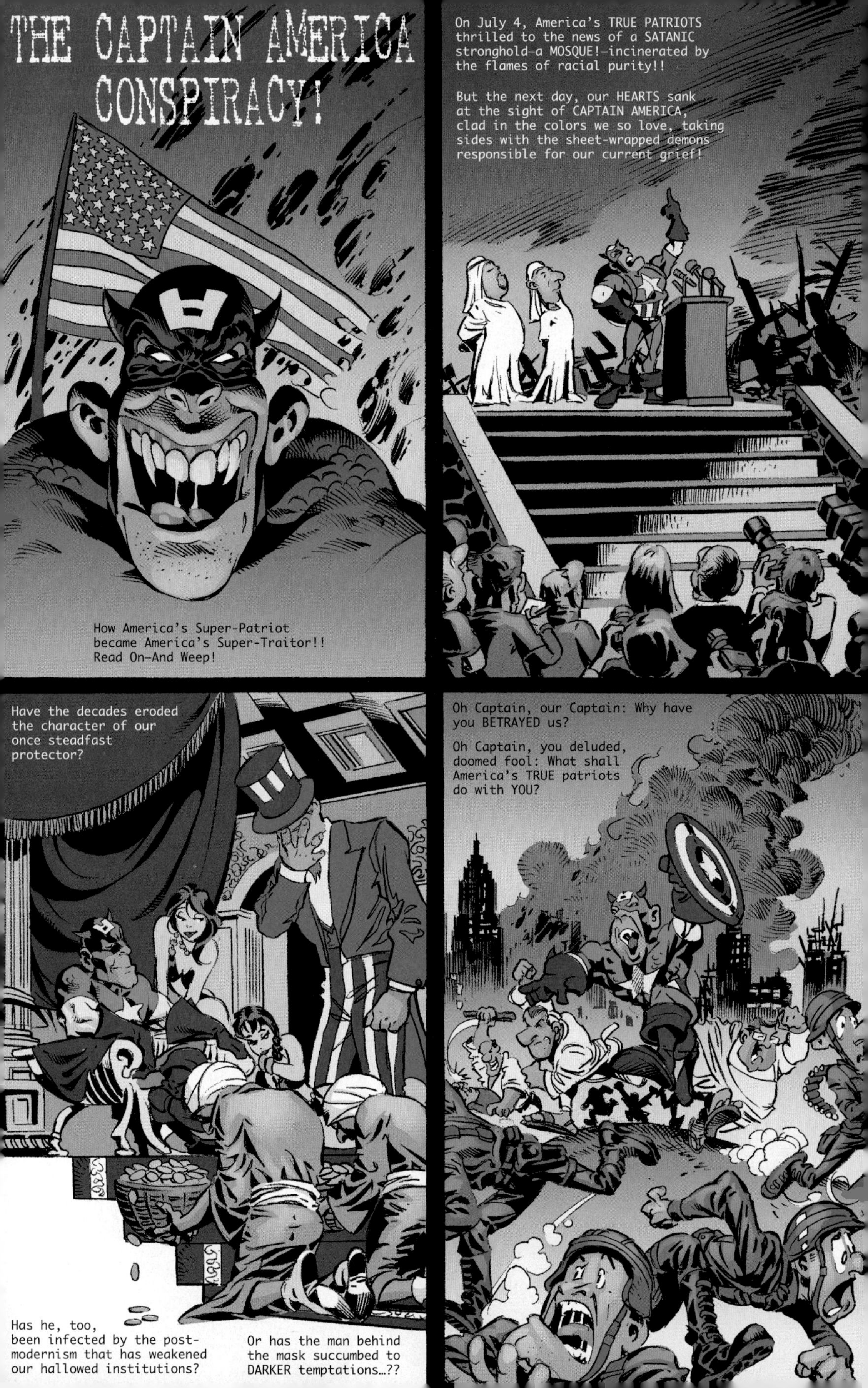
THE CAPTAIN AMERICA CONSPIRACY!
How America's Super-Patriot became America's Super-Traitor!! Read On—And Weep!
On July 4, America's TRUE PATRIOTS thrilled to the news of a SATANIC stronghold—a MOSQUE!—incinerated by the flames of racial purity!!
But the next day, our HEARTS sank at the sight of CAPTAIN AMERICA, clad in the colors we so love, taking sides with the sheet-wrapped demons responsible for our current grief!
Have the decades eroded the character of our once steadfast protector?
Has he, too, been infected by the post-modernism that has weakened our hallowed institutions?
Or has the man behind the mask succumbed to DARKER temptations…??
Oh Captain, our Captain: Why have you BETRAYED us?
Oh Captain, you deluded, doomed fool: What shall America's TRUE patriots do with YOU?

"Needless to say, I was not amused."

"I exist to many as only a symbol-- a walking incarnation of an idea called 'America.'

"And yes, I understand that this... this slander is not of me, but of the icon that I embody.

"I should not take this personally...

"...Yet here I am.

"The FBI raided a hate cell in Maine and took into evidence a stash of hate literature, including that pamphlet."

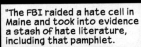

"When they told me that these... 'publications' were in violation of several Postal codes, I offered to handle the bust on the printer."

Y-yes?

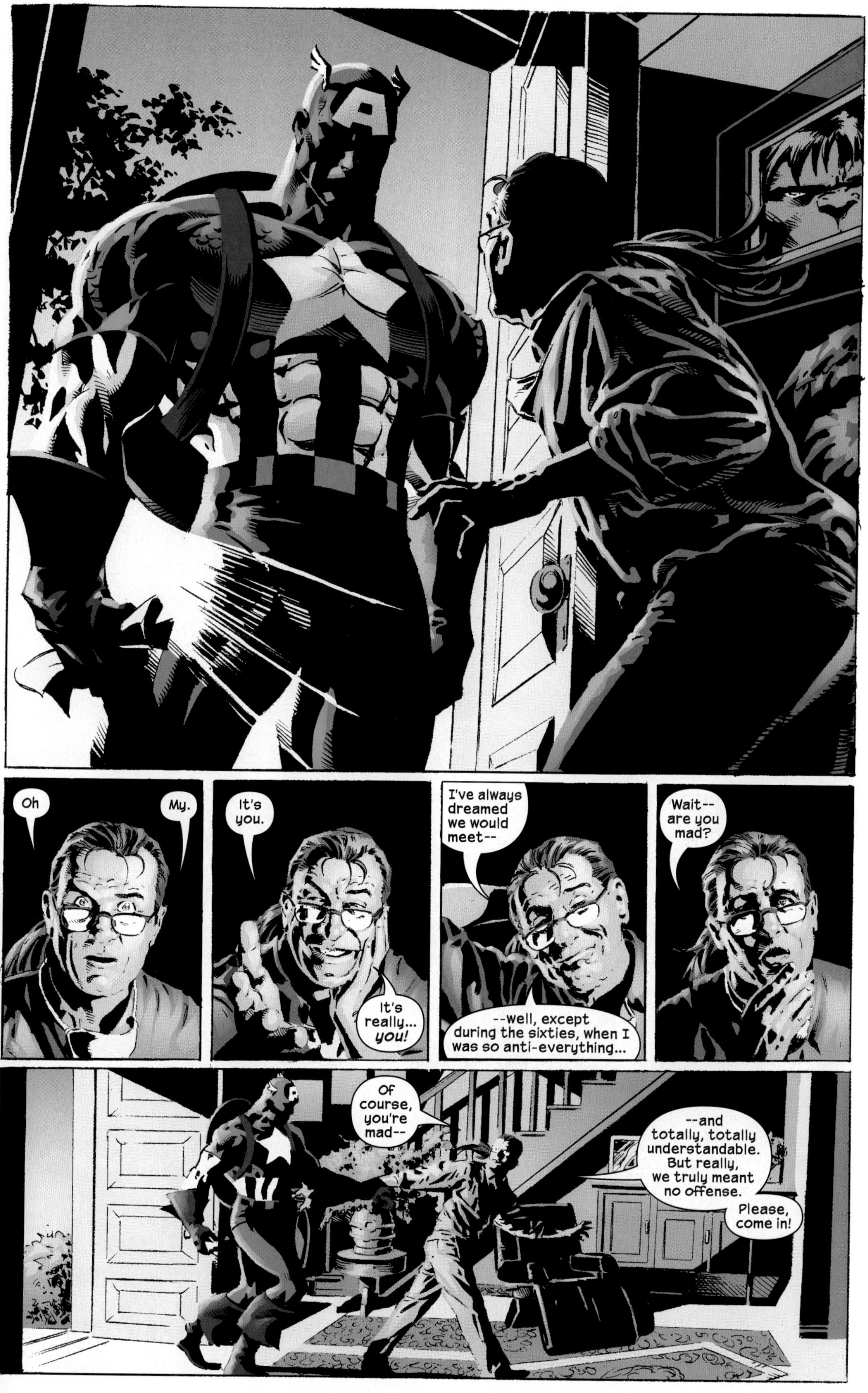
Oh
My.
It's you.
It's really... *you!*
I've always dreamed we would meet--
--well, except during the sixties, when I was so anti-everything...
Wait-- are you mad?
Of course, you're mad--
--and totally, totally understandable. But really, we truly meant no offense.
Please, come in!

Uhhh... your call, Cap. We'll follow your lead.

You're not feeling *sick*, are you?

No-- why would I?

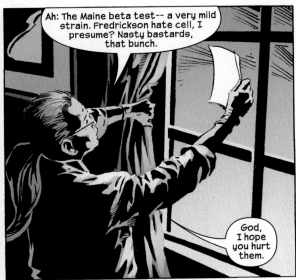

Ah: The Maine beta test-- a very mild strain. Fredrickson hate cell, I presume? Nasty bastards, that bunch.

God, I hope you hurt them.

Heh. And to think I used to be a pacifist. Do you want to see our lab?

Pretty cool, huh?

Impressive is the word.

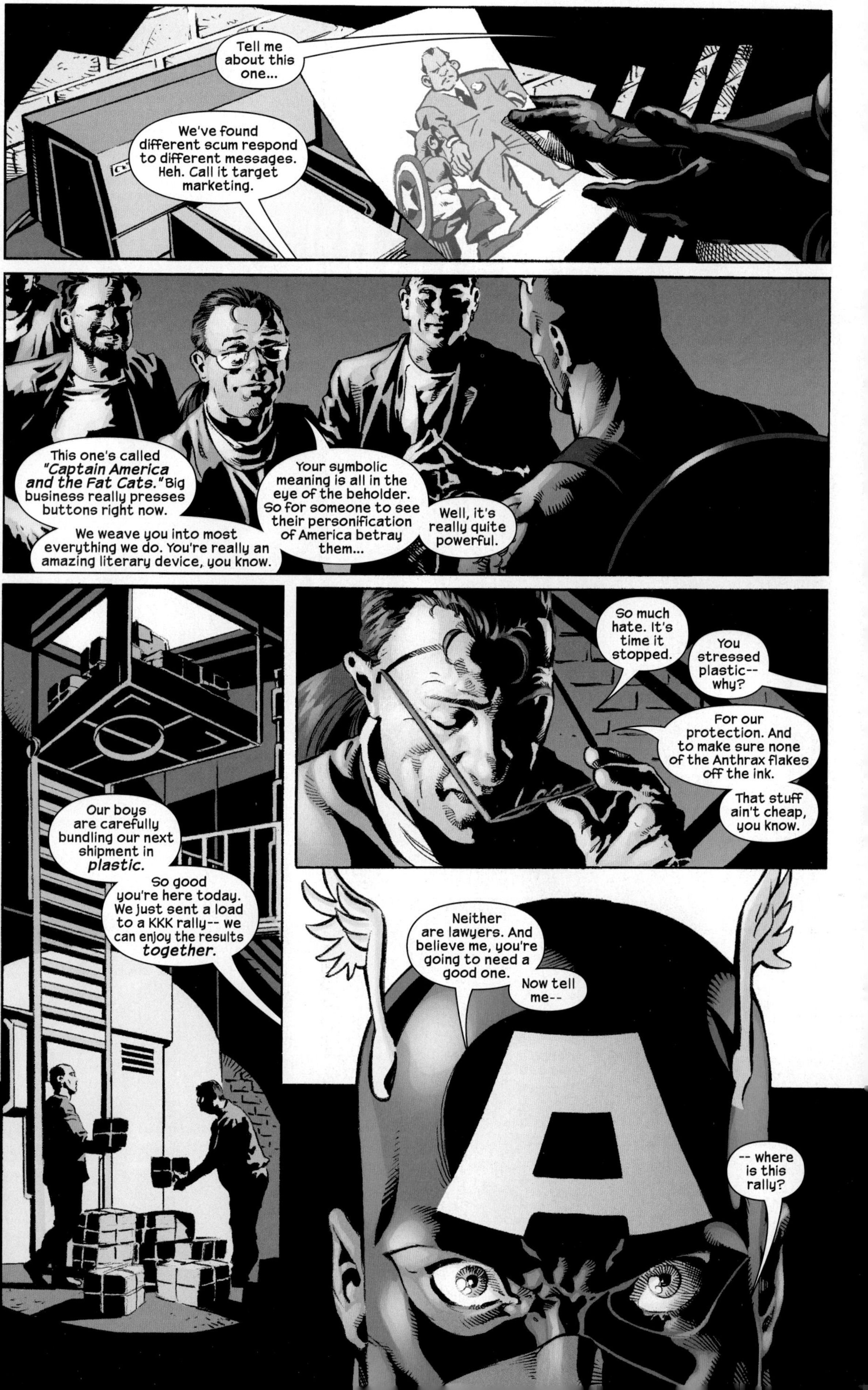

Tell me about this one...
We've found different scum respond to different messages. Heh. Call it target marketing.
This one's called *"Captain America and the Fat Cats."* Big business really presses buttons right now.
We weave you into most everything we do. You're really an amazing literary device, you know.
Your symbolic meaning is all in the eye of the beholder. So for someone to see their personification of America betray them...
Well, it's really quite powerful.
Our boys are carefully bundling our next shipment in *plastic*.
So good you're here today. We just sent a load to a KKK rally-- we can enjoy the results *together*.
So much hate. It's time it stopped.
You stressed plastic-- why?
For our protection. And to make sure none of the Anthrax flakes off the ink.
That stuff ain't cheap, you know.
Neither are lawyers. And believe me, you're going to need a good one.
Now tell me--
-- where is this rally?

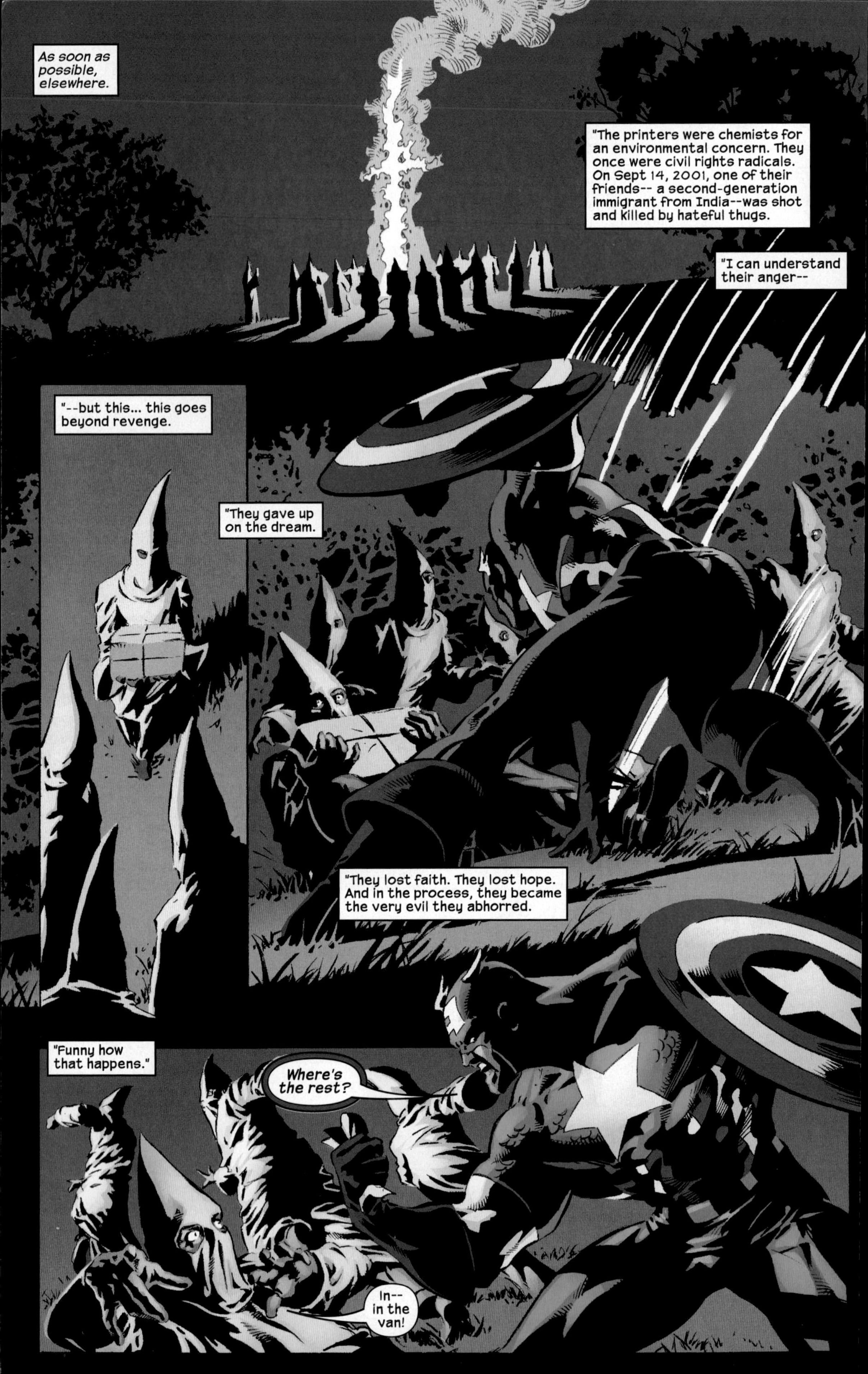
As soon as possible, elsewhere.
"The printers were chemists for an environmental concern. They once were civil rights radicals. On Sept 14, 2001, one of their friends-- a second-generation immigrant from India--was shot and killed by hateful thugs.
"I can understand their anger--
"--but this... this goes beyond revenge.
"They gave up on the dream.
"They lost faith. They lost hope. And in the process, they became the very evil they abhorred.
"Funny how that happens."
Where's the rest?
In-- in the van!

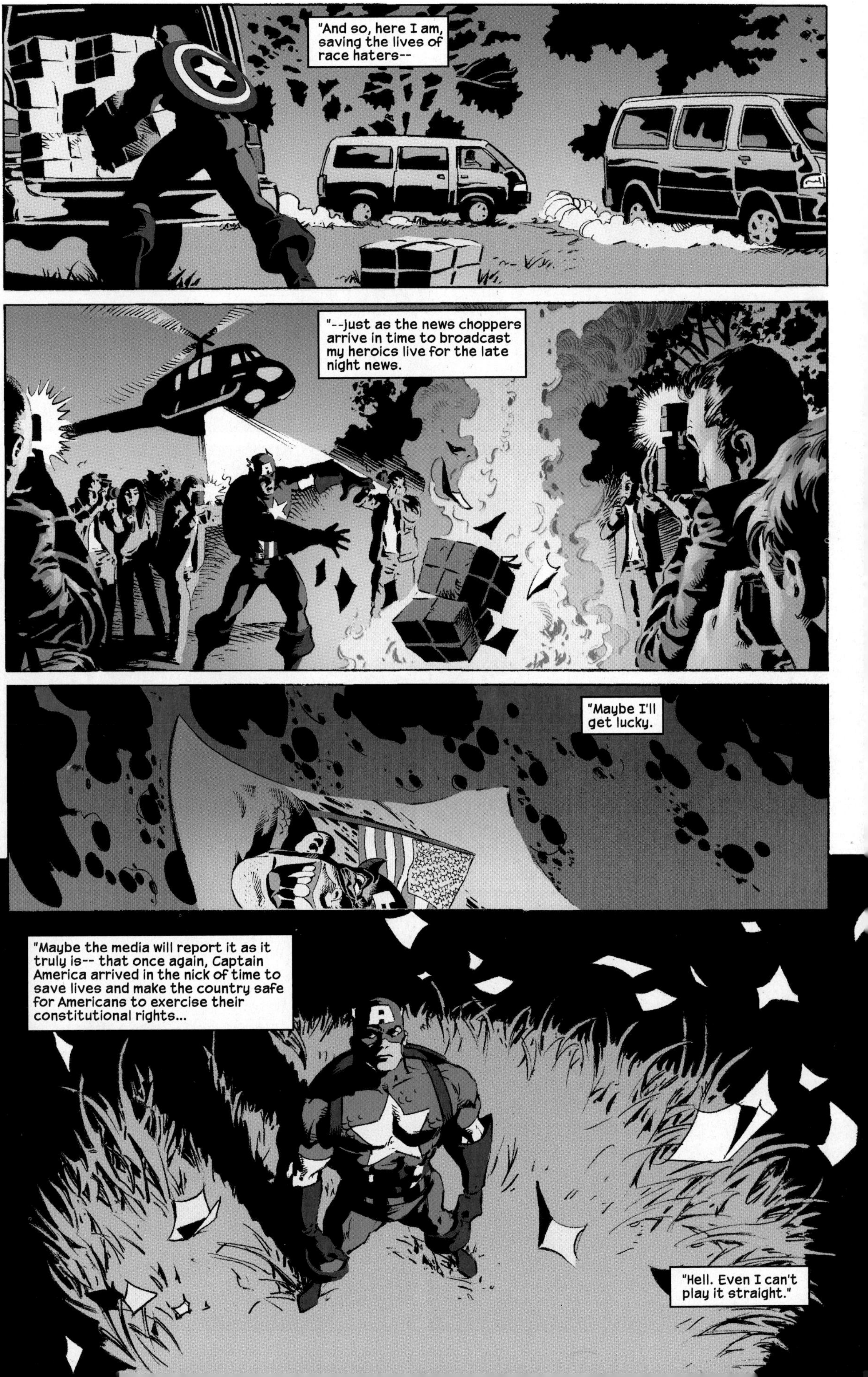
"And so, here I am, saving the lives of race haters--
"--just as the news choppers arrive in time to broadcast my heroics live for the late night news.
"Maybe I'll get lucky.
"Maybe the media will report it as it truly is-- that once again, Captain America arrived in the nick of time to save lives and make the country safe for Americans to exercise their constitutional rights...
"Hell. Even I can't play it straight."

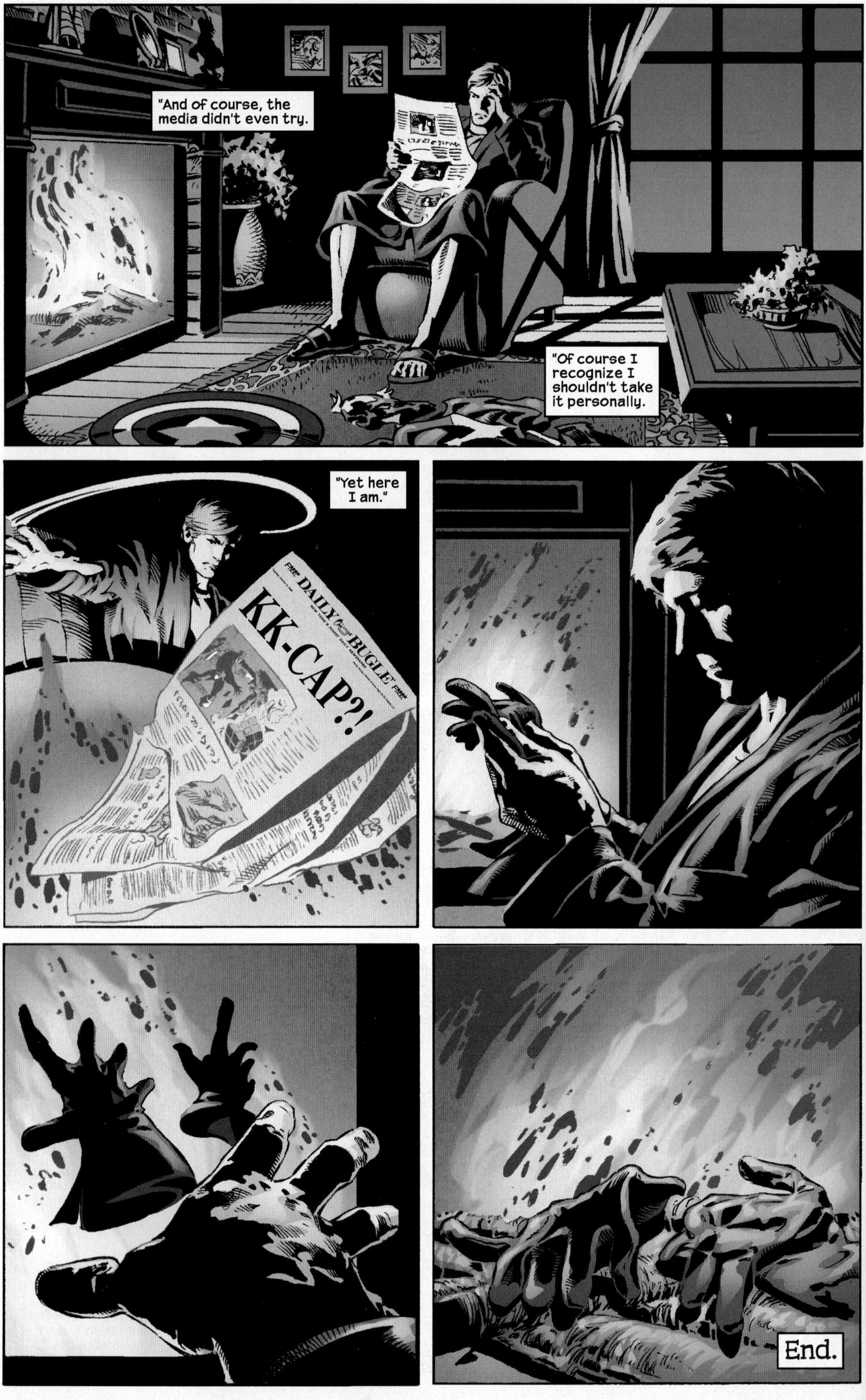
"And of course, the media didn't even try.
"Of course I recognize I shouldn't take it personally.
"Yet here I am."
DAILY BUGLE
KK-CAP?!
End.

SPECIAL BONUS! Re-printing the all-star backup stories from the landmark *Captain America #50 (2002)* and *Marvel Spotlight: Captain America Remembered.*

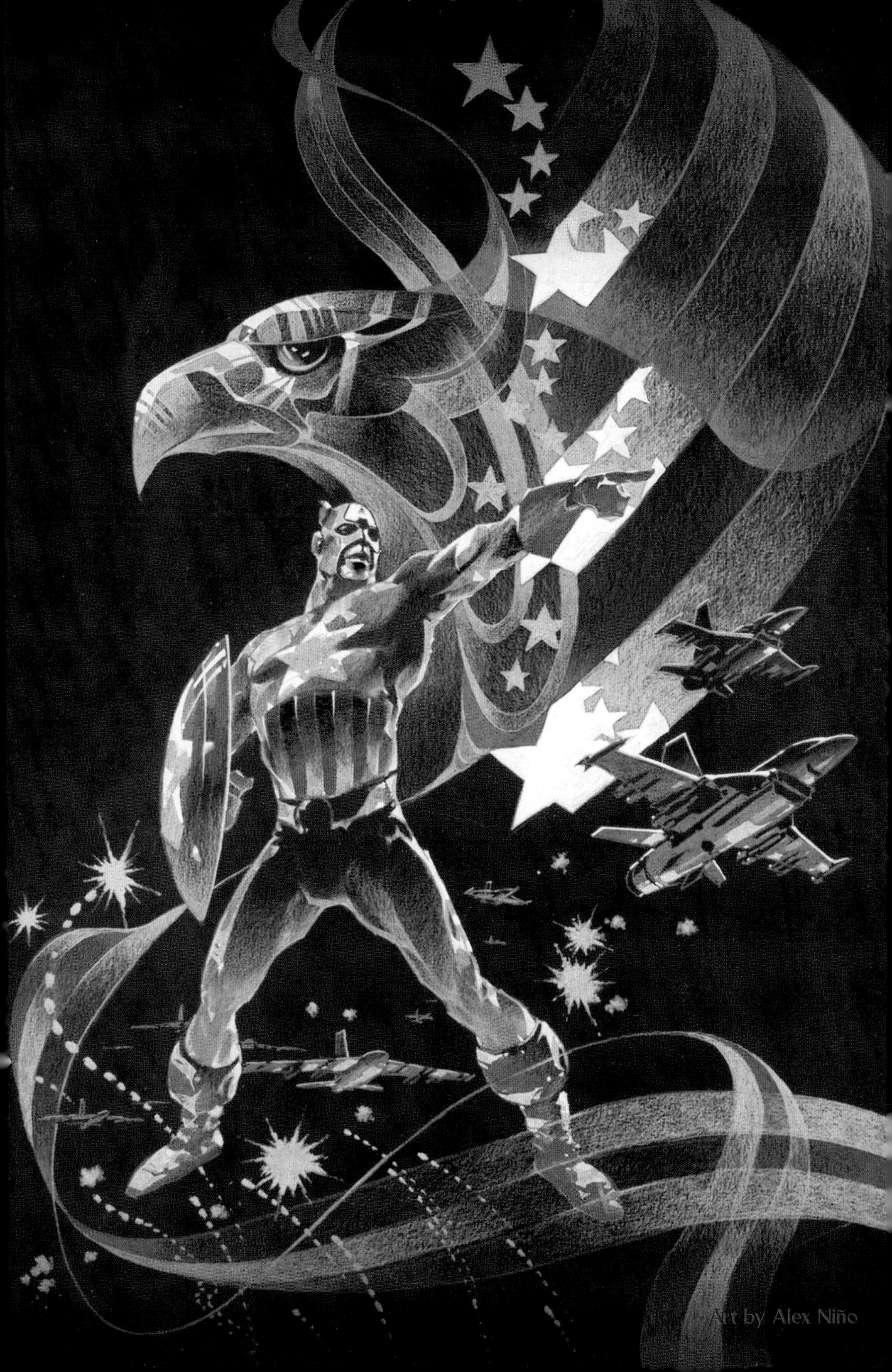

Art by Alex Niño

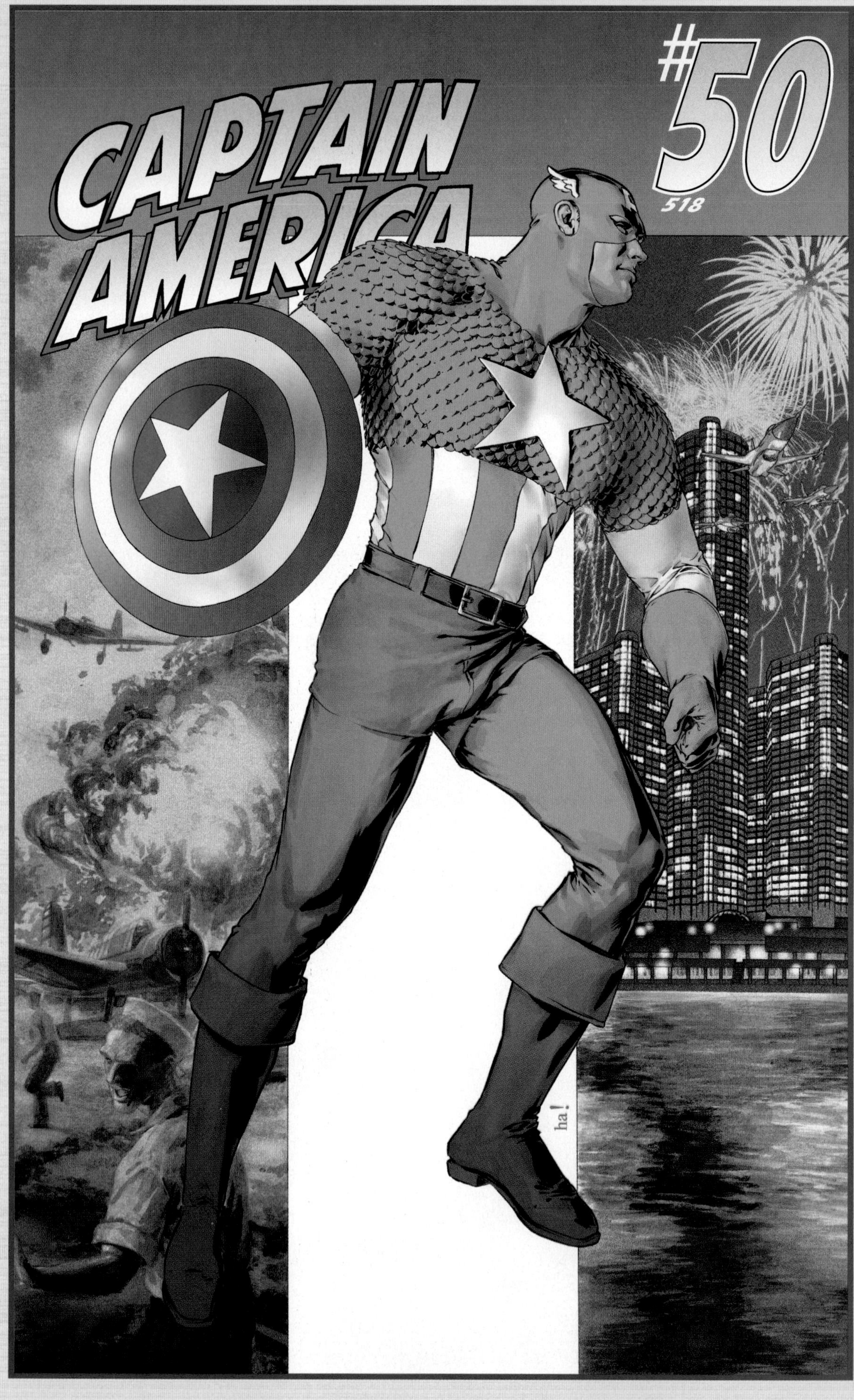
CAPTAIN AMERICA
#50
518
ha!

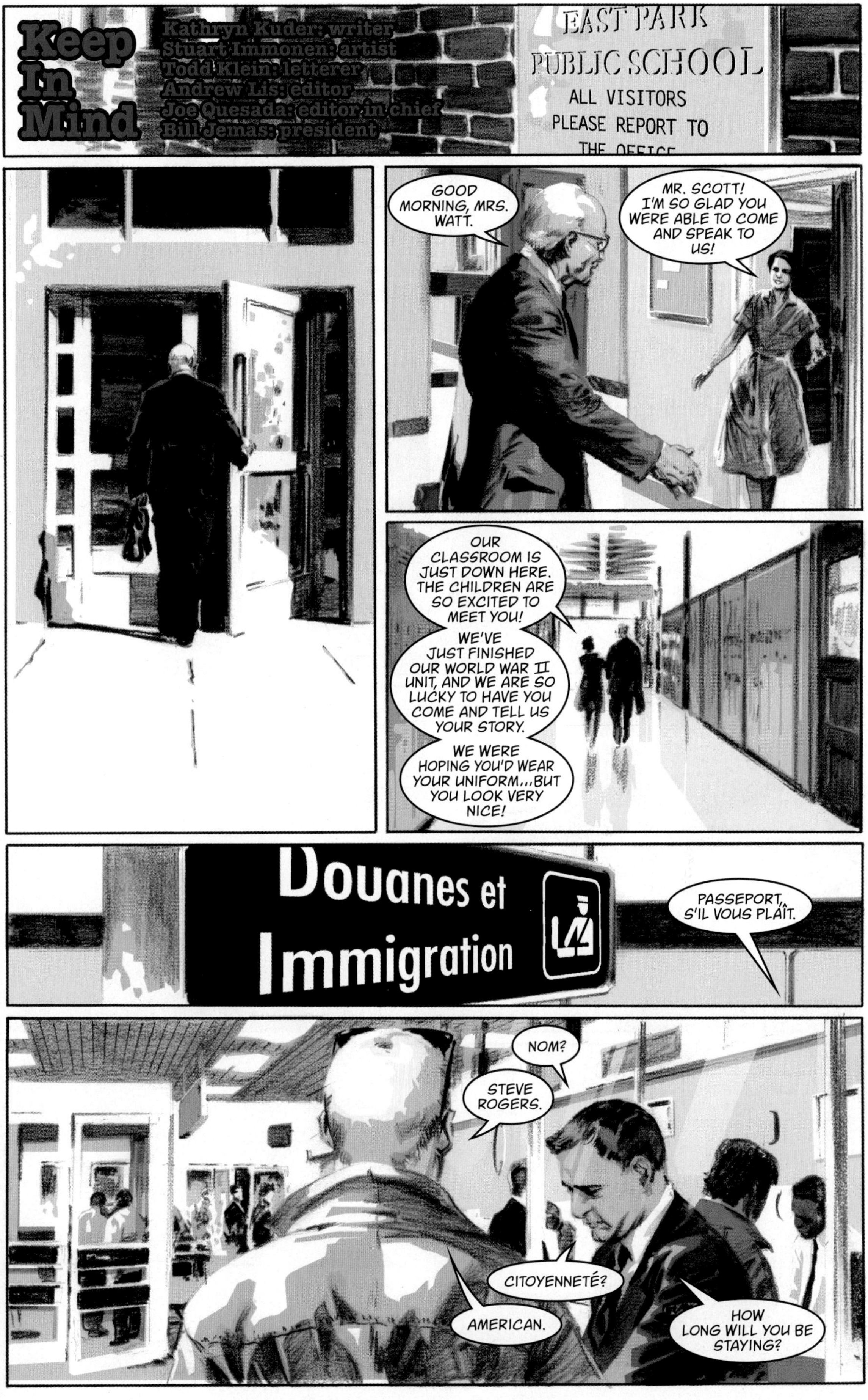
Keep In Mind
Kathryn Kuder: writer
Stuart Immonen: artist
Todd Klein: letterer
Andrew Lis: editor
Joe Quesada: editor in chief
Bill Jemas: president
EAST PARK PUBLIC SCHOOL
ALL VISITORS PLEASE REPORT TO THE OFFICE
GOOD MORNING, MRS. WATT.
MR. SCOTT! I'M SO GLAD YOU WERE ABLE TO COME AND SPEAK TO US!
OUR CLASSROOM IS JUST DOWN HERE. THE CHILDREN ARE SO EXCITED TO MEET YOU!
WE'VE JUST FINISHED OUR WORLD WAR II UNIT, AND WE ARE SO LUCKY TO HAVE YOU COME AND TELL US YOUR STORY.
WE WERE HOPING YOU'D WEAR YOUR UNIFORM...BUT YOU LOOK VERY NICE!
Douanes et Immigration
PASSEPORT, S'IL VOUS PLAÎT.
NOM?
STEVE ROGERS.
CITOYENNETÉ?
AMERICAN.
HOW LONG WILL YOU BE STAYING?

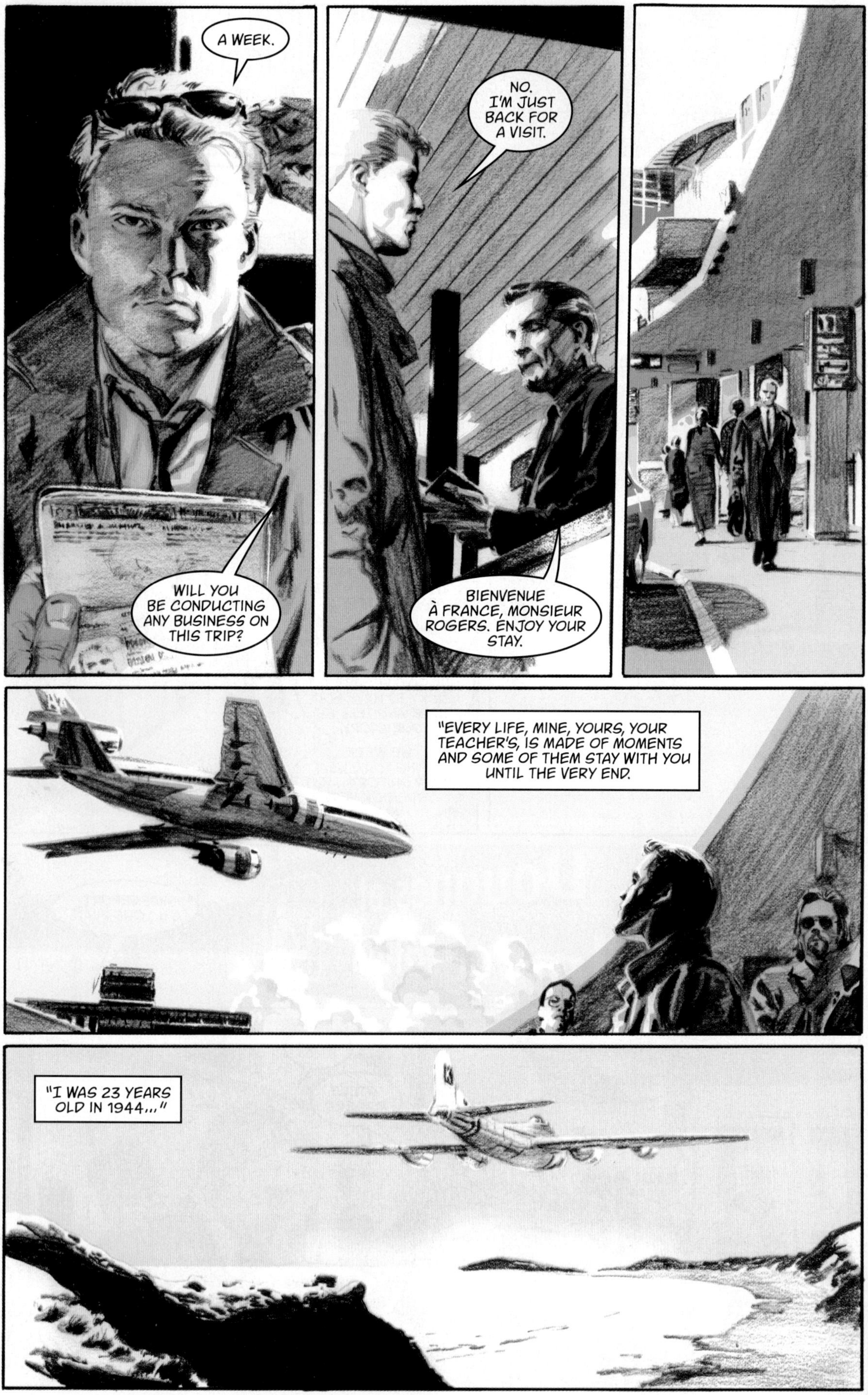
A WEEK.
WILL YOU BE CONDUCTING ANY BUSINESS ON THIS TRIP?
NO. I'M JUST BACK FOR A VISIT.
BIENVENUE À FRANCE, MONSIEUR ROGERS. ENJOY YOUR STAY.
"EVERY LIFE, MINE, YOURS, YOUR TEACHER'S, IS MADE OF MOMENTS AND SOME OF THEM STAY WITH YOU UNTIL THE VERY END.
"I WAS 23 YEARS OLD IN 1944..."

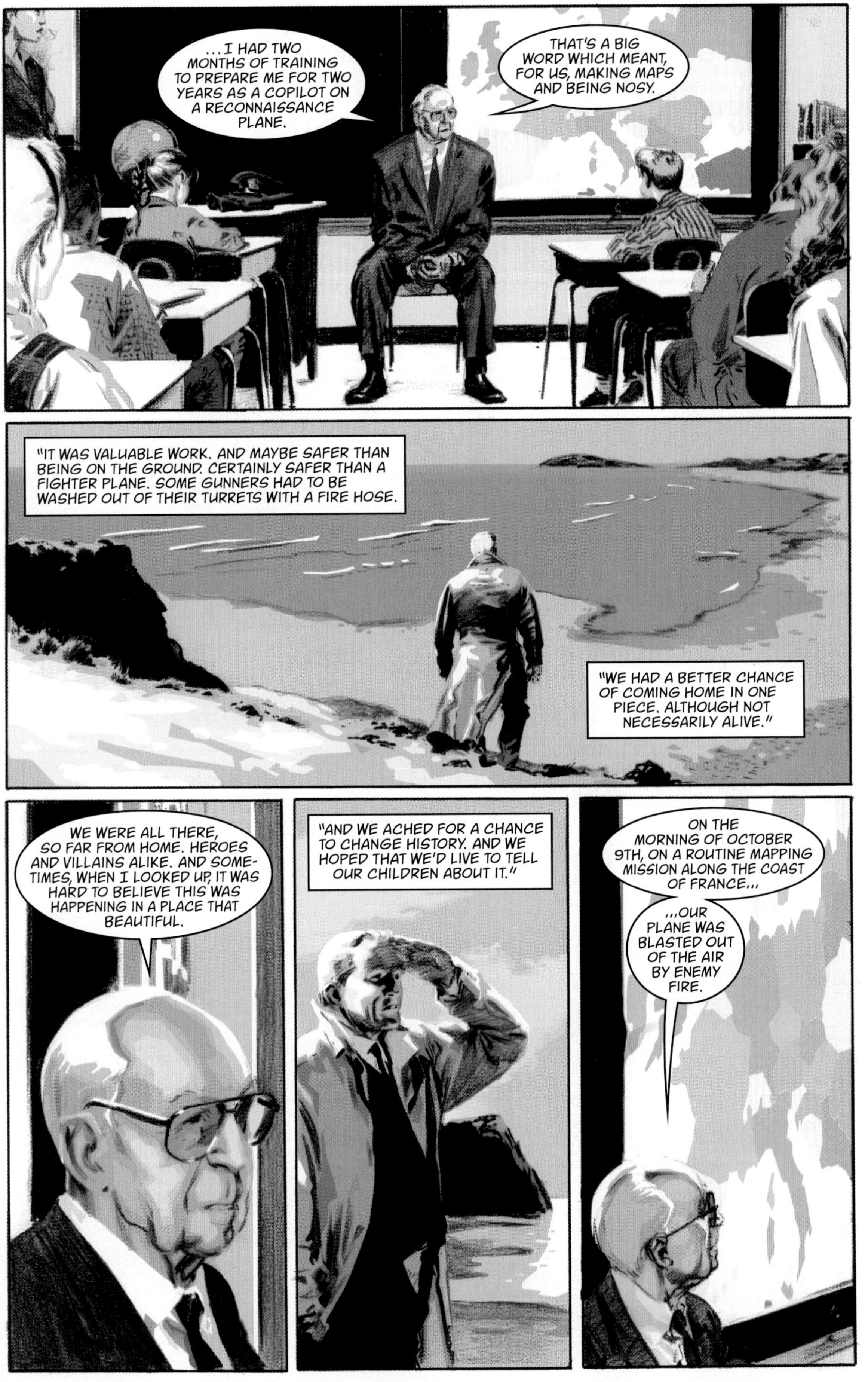
...I HAD TWO MONTHS OF TRAINING TO PREPARE ME FOR TWO YEARS AS A COPILOT ON A RECONNAISSANCE PLANE.
THAT'S A BIG WORD WHICH MEANT, FOR US, MAKING MAPS AND BEING NOSY.
"IT WAS VALUABLE WORK. AND MAYBE SAFER THAN BEING ON THE GROUND. CERTAINLY SAFER THAN A FIGHTER PLANE. SOME GUNNERS HAD TO BE WASHED OUT OF THEIR TURRETS WITH A FIRE HOSE.
"WE HAD A BETTER CHANCE OF COMING HOME IN ONE PIECE. ALTHOUGH NOT NECESSARILY ALIVE."
WE WERE ALL THERE, SO FAR FROM HOME. HEROES AND VILLAINS ALIKE. AND SOMETIMES, WHEN I LOOKED UP, IT WAS HARD TO BELIEVE THIS WAS HAPPENING IN A PLACE THAT BEAUTIFUL.
"AND WE ACHED FOR A CHANCE TO CHANGE HISTORY. AND WE HOPED THAT WE'D LIVE TO TELL OUR CHILDREN ABOUT IT."
ON THE MORNING OF OCTOBER 9TH, ON A ROUTINE MAPPING MISSION ALONG THE COAST OF FRANCE...
...OUR PLANE WAS BLASTED OUT OF THE AIR BY ENEMY FIRE.

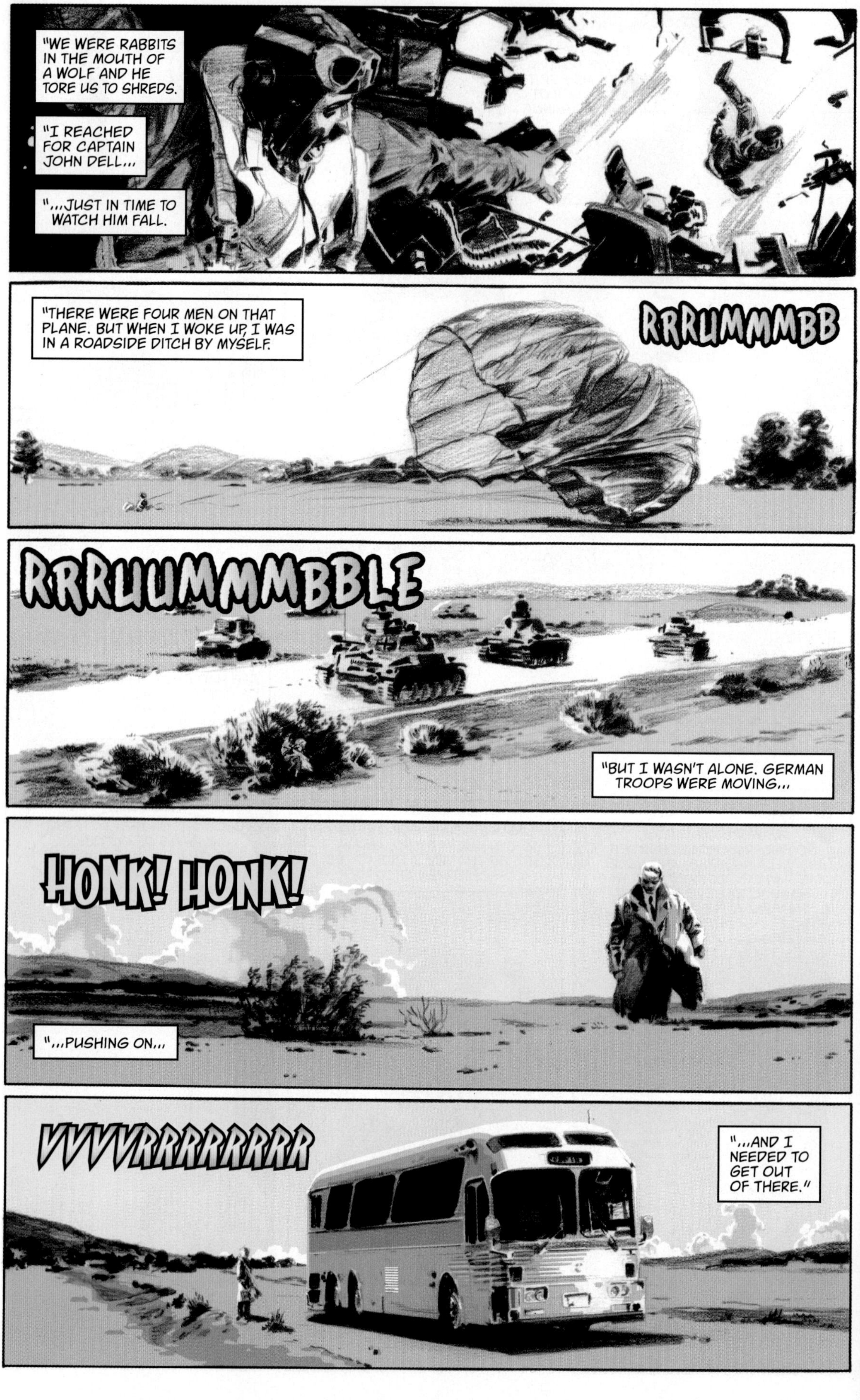
"WE WERE RABBITS IN THE MOUTH OF A WOLF AND HE TORE US TO SHREDS.
"I REACHED FOR CAPTAIN JOHN DELL...
"...JUST IN TIME TO WATCH HIM FALL.
"THERE WERE FOUR MEN ON THAT PLANE. BUT WHEN I WOKE UP, I WAS IN A ROADSIDE DITCH BY MYSELF.
RRRUMMMBB
RRRUUMMMMBBLE
"BUT I WASN'T ALONE. GERMAN TROOPS WERE MOVING...
HONK! HONK!
"...PUSHING ON...
VVVVRRRRRRRR
"...AND I NEEDED TO GET OUT OF THERE."

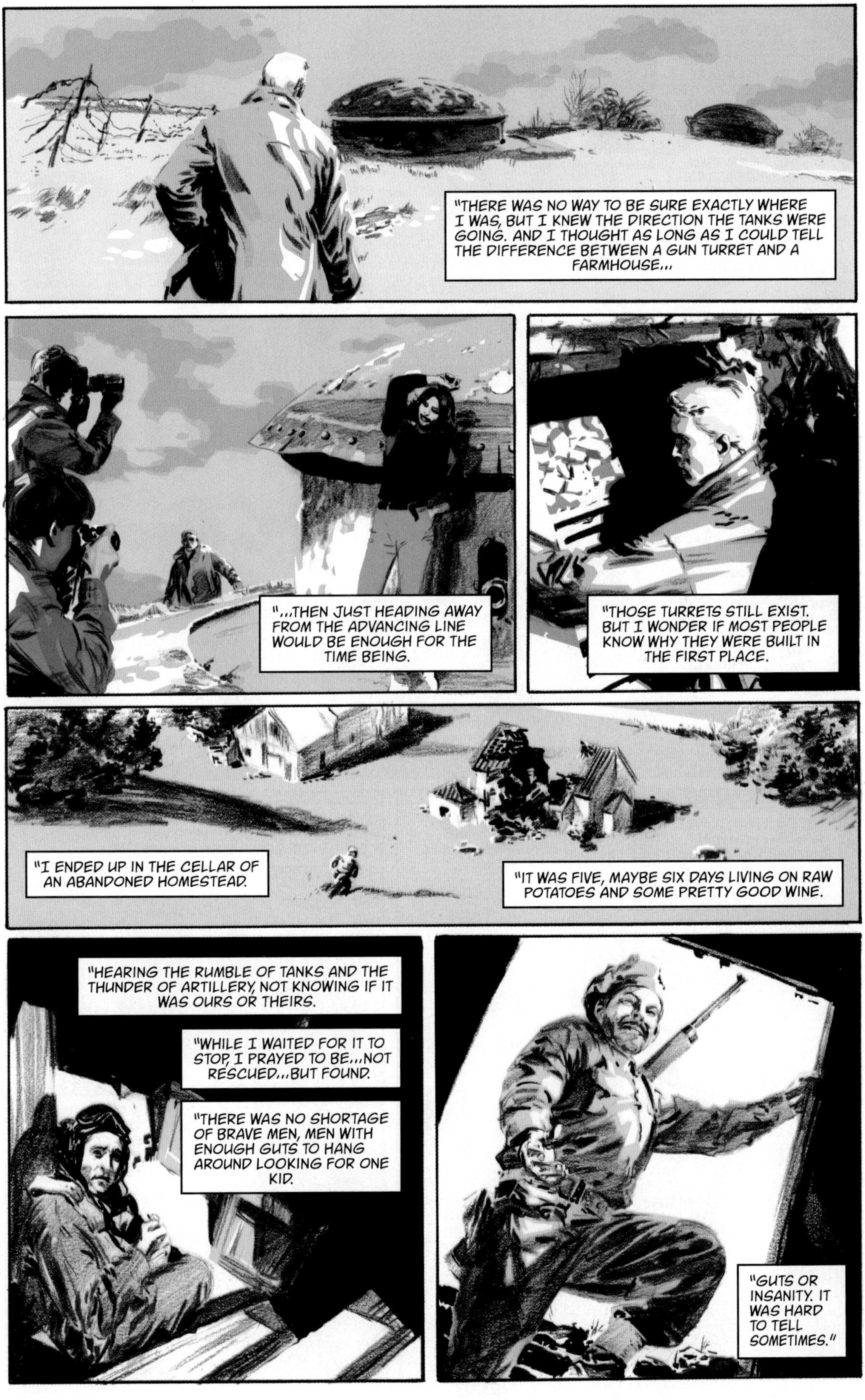
"THERE WAS NO WAY TO BE SURE EXACTLY WHERE I WAS, BUT I KNEW THE DIRECTION THE TANKS WERE GOING. AND I THOUGHT AS LONG AS I COULD TELL THE DIFFERENCE BETWEEN A GUN TURRET AND A FARMHOUSE...
"...THEN JUST HEADING AWAY FROM THE ADVANCING LINE WOULD BE ENOUGH FOR THE TIME BEING.
"THOSE TURRETS STILL EXIST. BUT I WONDER IF MOST PEOPLE KNOW WHY THEY WERE BUILT IN THE FIRST PLACE.
"I ENDED UP IN THE CELLAR OF AN ABANDONED HOMESTEAD.
"IT WAS FIVE, MAYBE SIX DAYS LIVING ON RAW POTATOES AND SOME PRETTY GOOD WINE.
"HEARING THE RUMBLE OF TANKS AND THE THUNDER OF ARTILLERY, NOT KNOWING IF IT WAS OURS OR THEIRS.
"WHILE I WAITED FOR IT TO STOP, I PRAYED TO BE...NOT RESCUED...BUT FOUND.
"THERE WAS NO SHORTAGE OF BRAVE MEN, MEN WITH ENOUGH GUTS TO HANG AROUND LOOKING FOR ONE KID.
"GUTS OR INSANITY. IT WAS HARD TO TELL SOMETIMES."

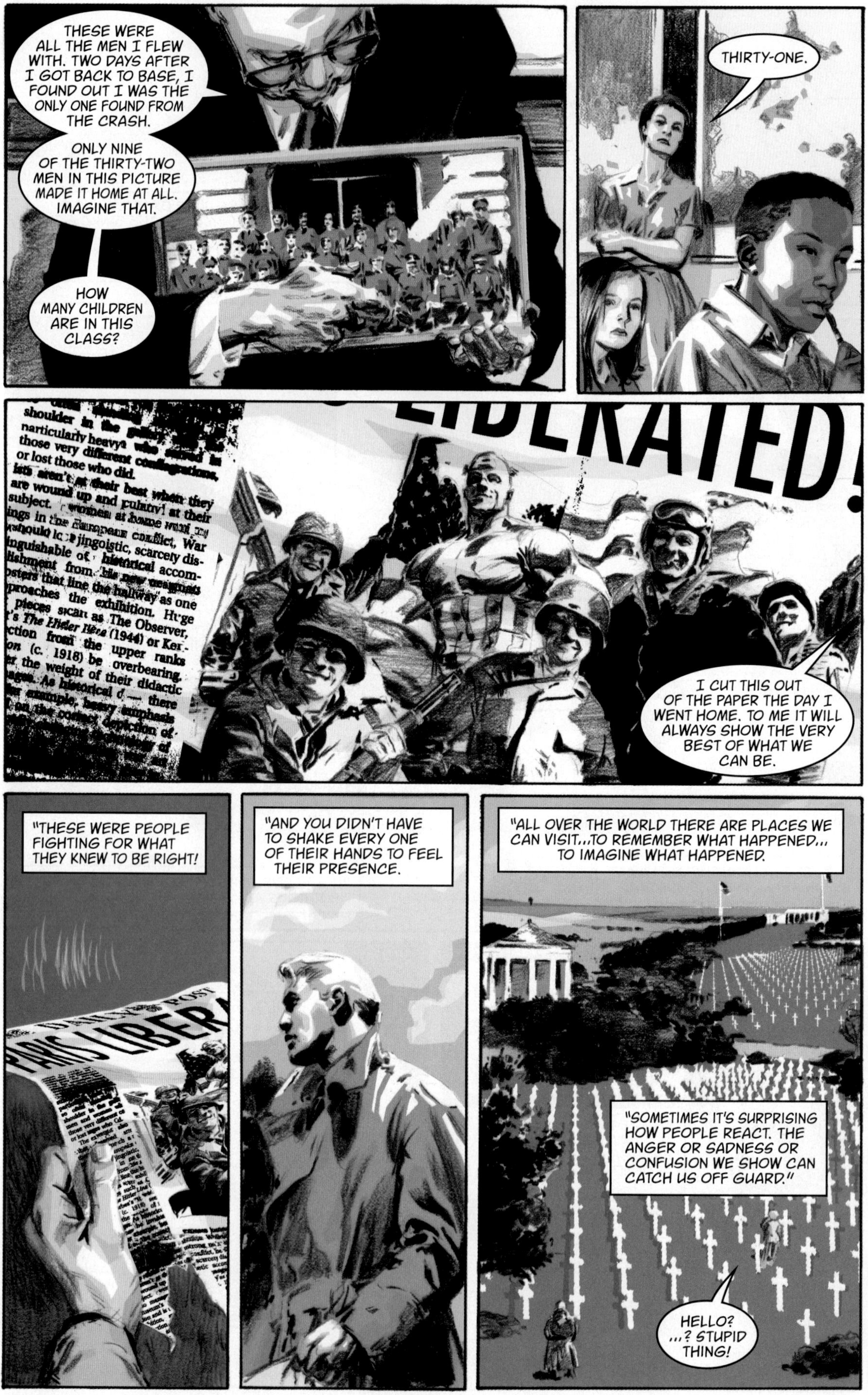
THESE WERE ALL THE MEN I FLEW WITH. TWO DAYS AFTER I GOT BACK TO BASE, I FOUND OUT I WAS THE ONLY ONE FOUND FROM THE CRASH.
ONLY NINE OF THE THIRTY-TWO MEN IN THIS PICTURE MADE IT HOME AT ALL. IMAGINE THAT.
HOW MANY CHILDREN ARE IN THIS CLASS?
THIRTY-ONE.
I CUT THIS OUT OF THE PAPER THE DAY I WENT HOME. TO ME IT WILL ALWAYS SHOW THE VERY BEST OF WHAT WE CAN BE.
"THESE WERE PEOPLE FIGHTING FOR WHAT THEY KNEW TO BE RIGHT!
"AND YOU DIDN'T HAVE TO SHAKE EVERY ONE OF THEIR HANDS TO FEEL THEIR PRESENCE.
"ALL OVER THE WORLD THERE ARE PLACES WE CAN VISIT...TO REMEMBER WHAT HAPPENED... TO IMAGINE WHAT HAPPENED.
"SOMETIMES IT'S SURPRISING HOW PEOPLE REACT. THE ANGER OR SADNESS OR CONFUSION WE SHOW CAN CATCH US OFF GUARD."
HELLO? ...? STUPID THING!

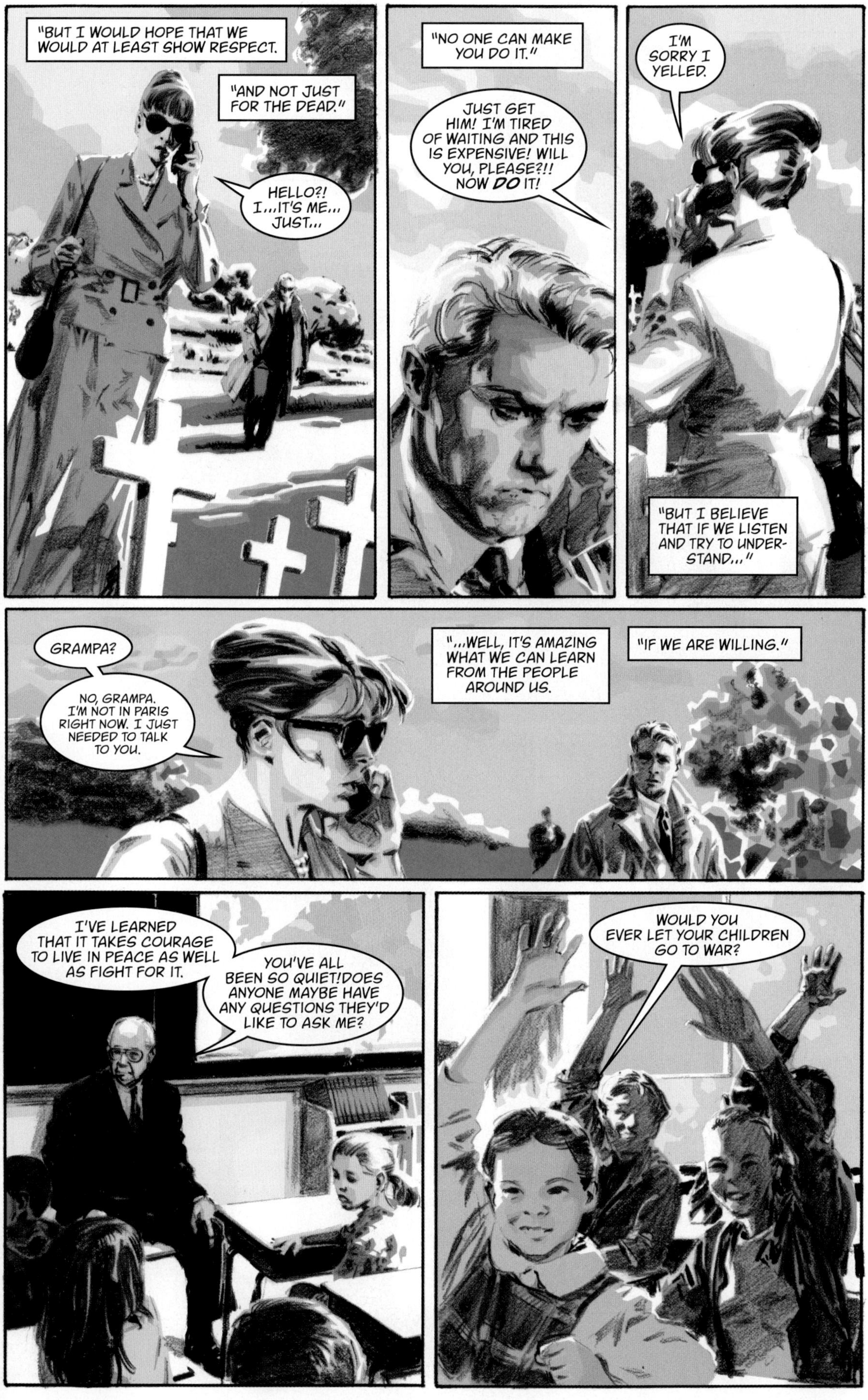
"BUT I WOULD HOPE THAT WE WOULD AT LEAST SHOW RESPECT.
"AND NOT JUST FOR THE DEAD."
HELLO?! I...IT'S ME... JUST...
"NO ONE CAN MAKE YOU DO IT."
JUST GET HIM! I'M TIRED OF WAITING AND THIS IS EXPENSIVE! WILL YOU, PLEASE?!! NOW DO IT!
I'M SORRY I YELLED.
"BUT I BELIEVE THAT IF WE LISTEN AND TRY TO UNDER-STAND..."
GRAMPA?
NO, GRAMPA. I'M NOT IN PARIS RIGHT NOW. I JUST NEEDED TO TALK TO YOU.
"...WELL, IT'S AMAZING WHAT WE CAN LEARN FROM THE PEOPLE AROUND US.
"IF WE ARE WILLING."
I'VE LEARNED THAT IT TAKES COURAGE TO LIVE IN PEACE AS WELL AS FIGHT FOR IT.
YOU'VE ALL BEEN SO QUIET!DOES ANYONE MAYBE HAVE ANY QUESTIONS THEY'D LIKE TO ASK ME?
WOULD YOU EVER LET YOUR CHILDREN GO TO WAR?

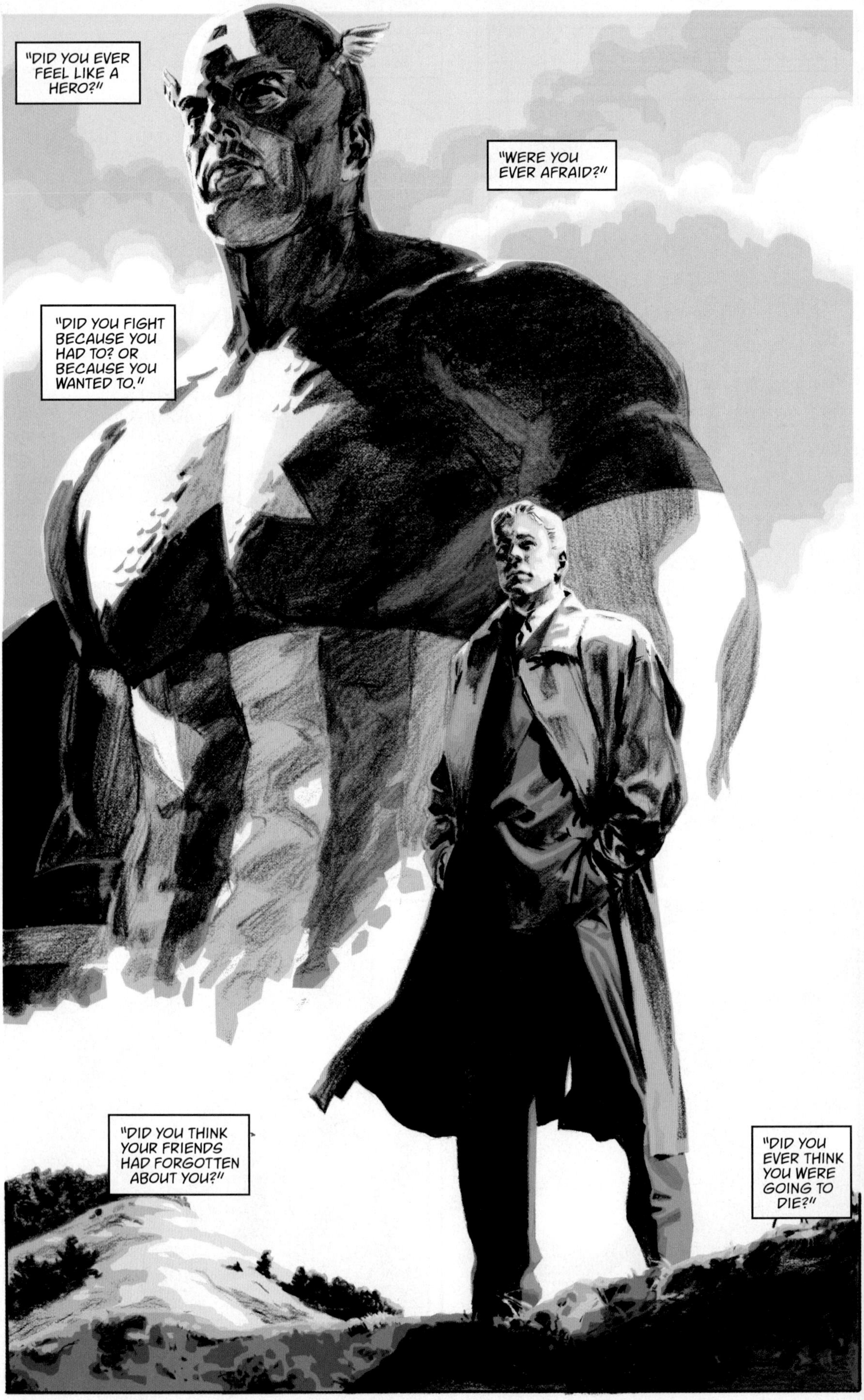
"DID YOU EVER FEEL LIKE A HERO?"
"WERE YOU EVER AFRAID?"
"DID YOU FIGHT BECAUSE YOU HAD TO? OR BECAUSE YOU WANTED TO."
"DID YOU THINK YOUR FRIENDS HAD FORGOTTEN ABOUT YOU?"
"DID YOU EVER THINK YOU WERE GOING TO DIE?"

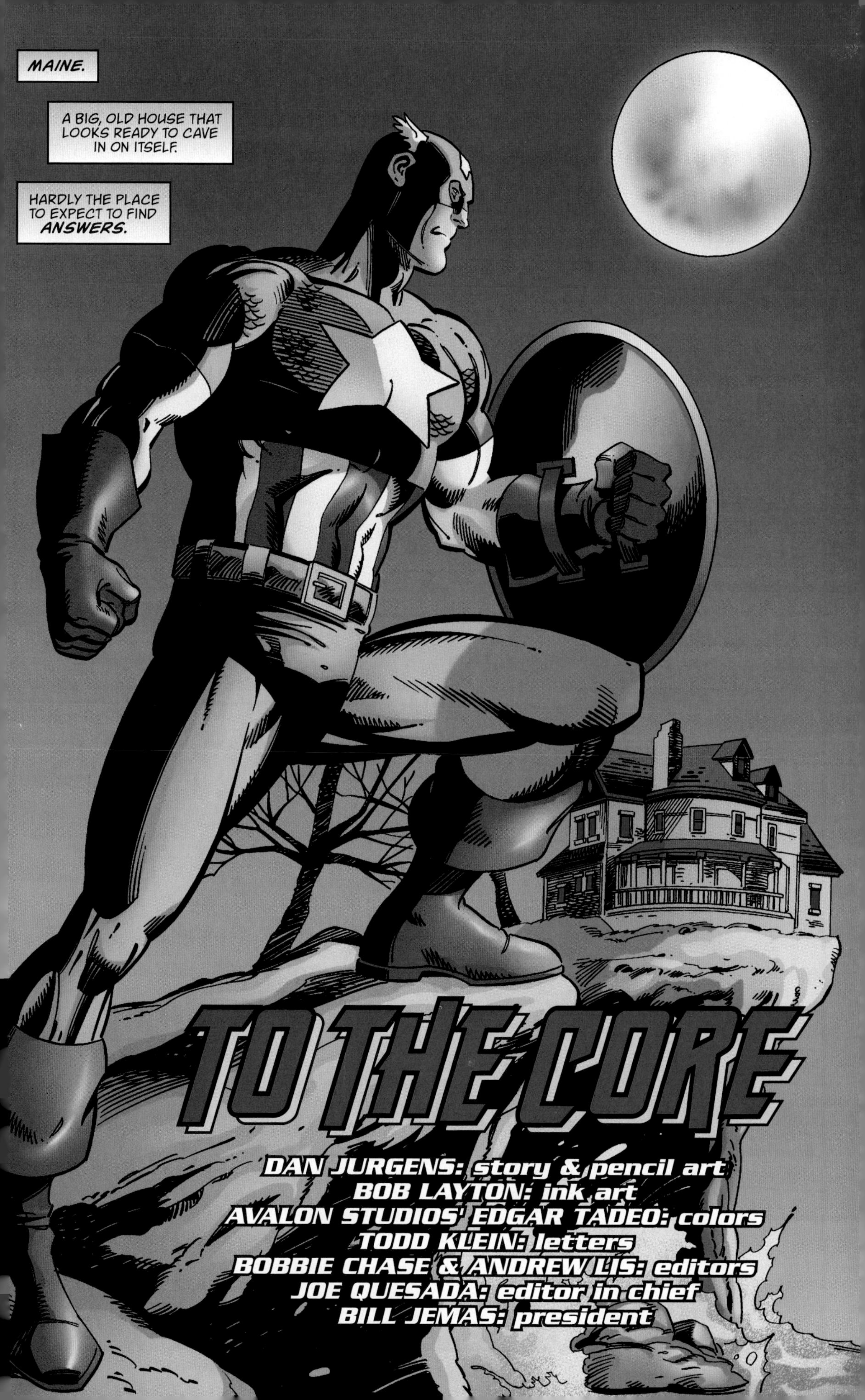
MAINE.
A BIG, OLD HOUSE THAT LOOKS READY TO CAVE IN ON ITSELF.
HARDLY THE PLACE TO EXPECT TO FIND ANSWERS.
TO THE CORE
DAN JURGENS: story & pencil art
BOB LAYTON: ink art
AVALON STUDIOS' EDGAR TADEO: colors
TODD KLEIN: letters
BOBBIE CHASE & ANDREW LIS: editors
JOE QUESADA: editor in chief
BILL JEMAS: president

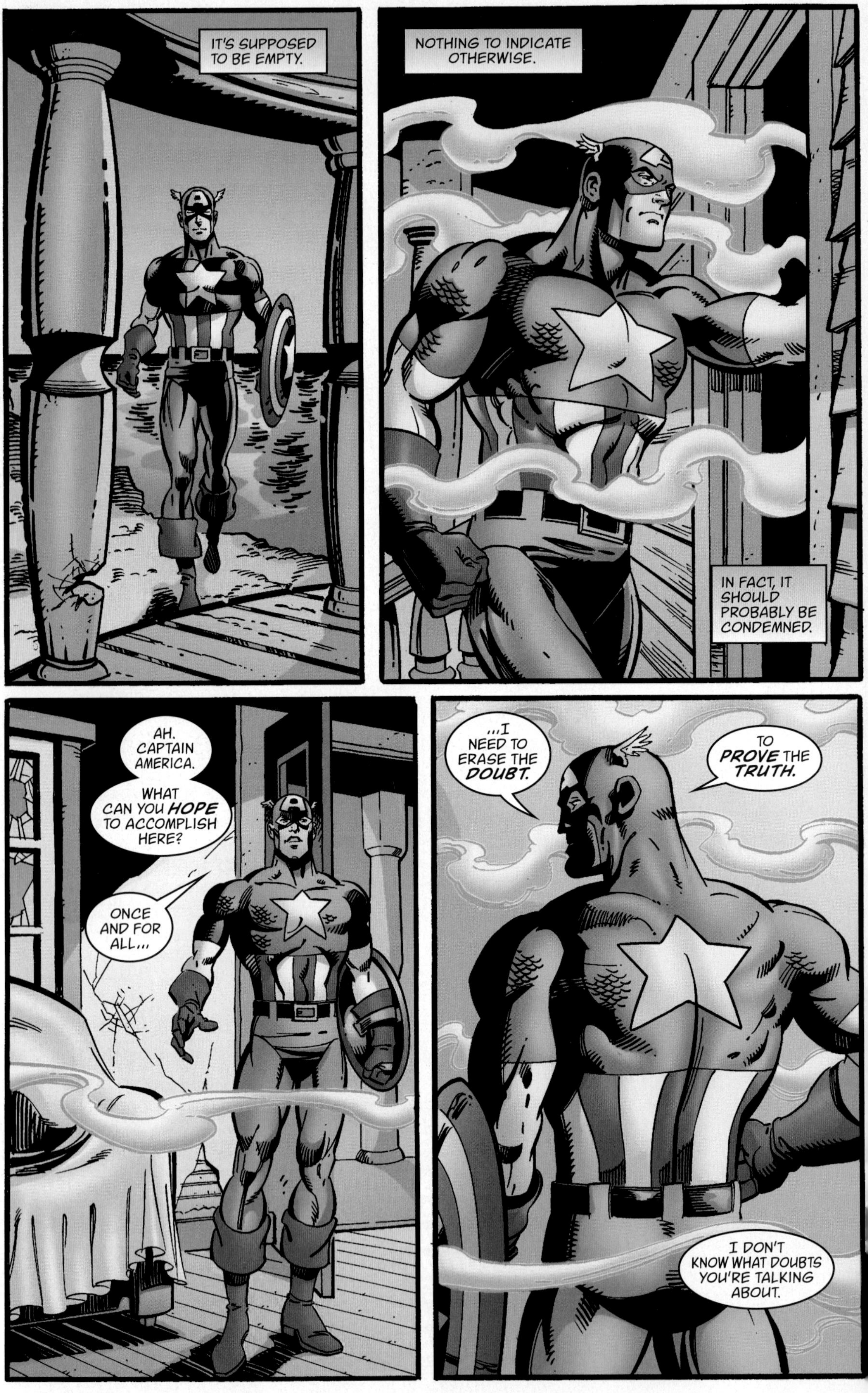
IT'S SUPPOSED TO BE EMPTY.
NOTHING TO INDICATE OTHERWISE.
IN FACT, IT SHOULD PROBABLY BE CONDEMNED.
AH. CAPTAIN AMERICA.
WHAT CAN YOU *HOPE* TO ACCOMPLISH HERE?
ONCE AND FOR ALL...
...I NEED TO ERASE THE *DOUBT.*
TO *PROVE* THE *TRUTH.*
I DON'T KNOW WHAT DOUBTS YOU'RE TALKING ABOUT.

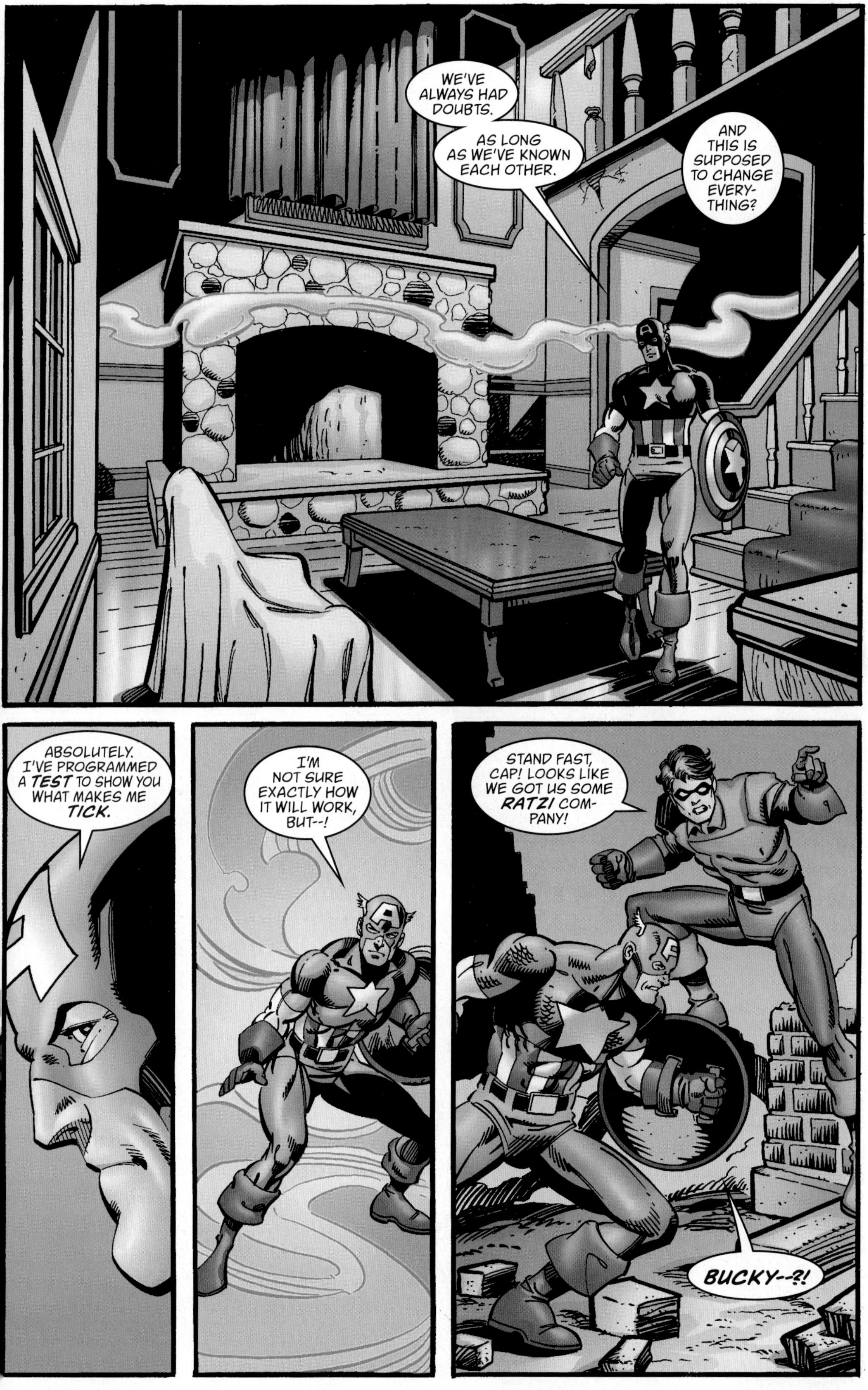
WE'VE ALWAYS HAD DOUBTS.
AS LONG AS WE'VE KNOWN EACH OTHER.
AND THIS IS SUPPOSED TO CHANGE EVERY-THING?
ABSOLUTELY. I'VE PROGRAMMED A TEST TO SHOW YOU WHAT MAKES ME TICK.
I'M NOT SURE EXACTLY HOW IT WILL WORK, BUT--!
STAND FAST, CAP! LOOKS LIKE WE GOT US SOME RATZI COM-PANY!
BUCKY--?!

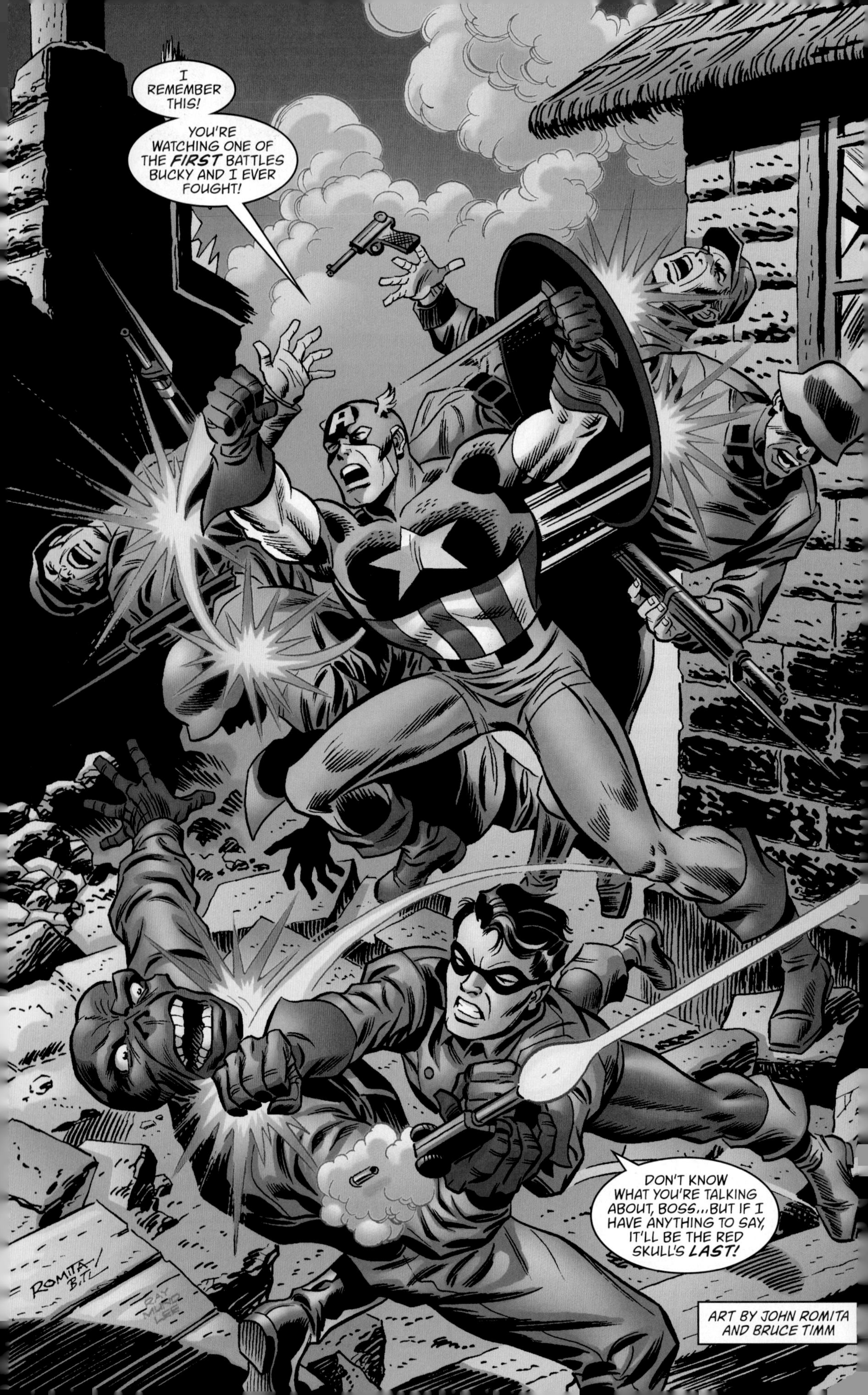
I REMEMBER THIS!
YOU'RE WATCHING ONE OF THE FIRST BATTLES BUCKY AND I EVER FOUGHT!
DON'T KNOW WHAT YOU'RE TALKING ABOUT, BOSS...BUT IF I HAVE ANYTHING TO SAY, IT'LL BE THE RED SKULL'S LAST!
ROMITA B.TL
ART BY JOHN ROMITA AND BRUCE TIMM

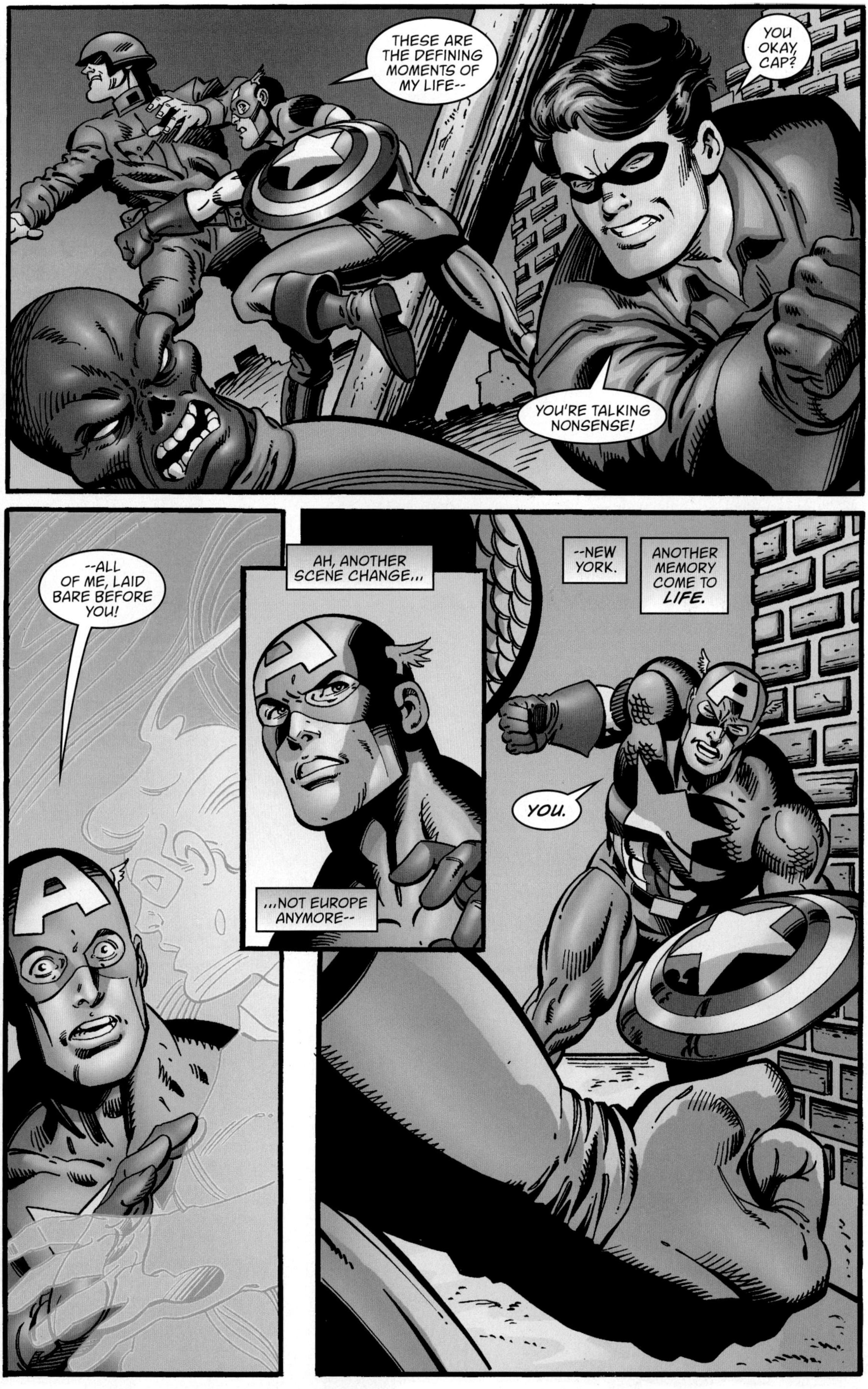
THESE ARE THE DEFINING MOMENTS OF MY LIFE--
YOU OKAY, CAP?
YOU'RE TALKING NONSENSE!
--ALL OF ME, LAID BARE BEFORE YOU!
AH, ANOTHER SCENE CHANGE...
...NOT EUROPE ANYMORE--
--NEW YORK.
ANOTHER MEMORY COME TO *LIFE*.
YOU.

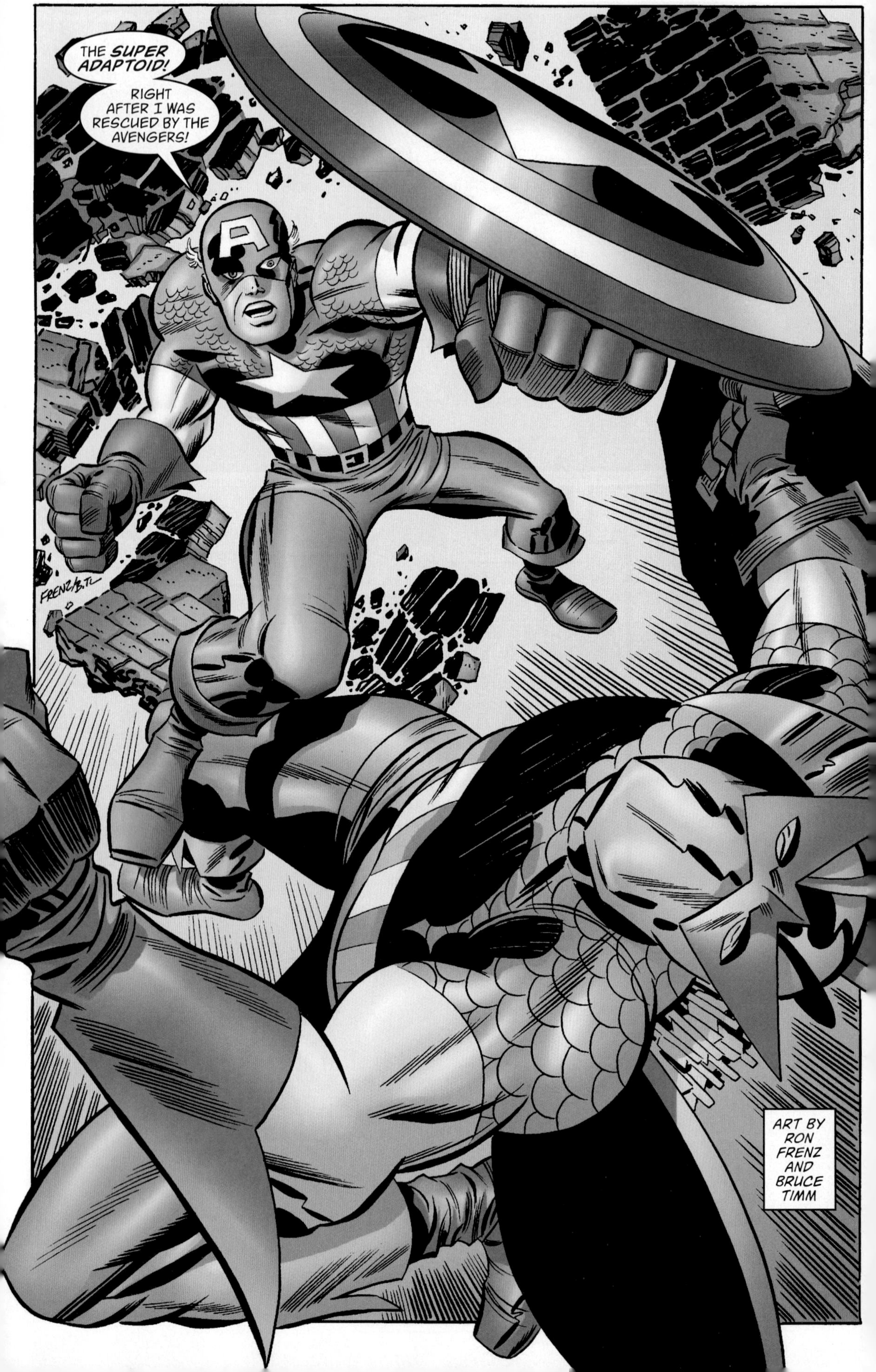
THE *SUPER ADAPTOID!*
RIGHT AFTER I WAS RESCUED BY THE AVENGERS!
FRENZ/B.T.
ART BY RON FRENZ AND BRUCE TIMM

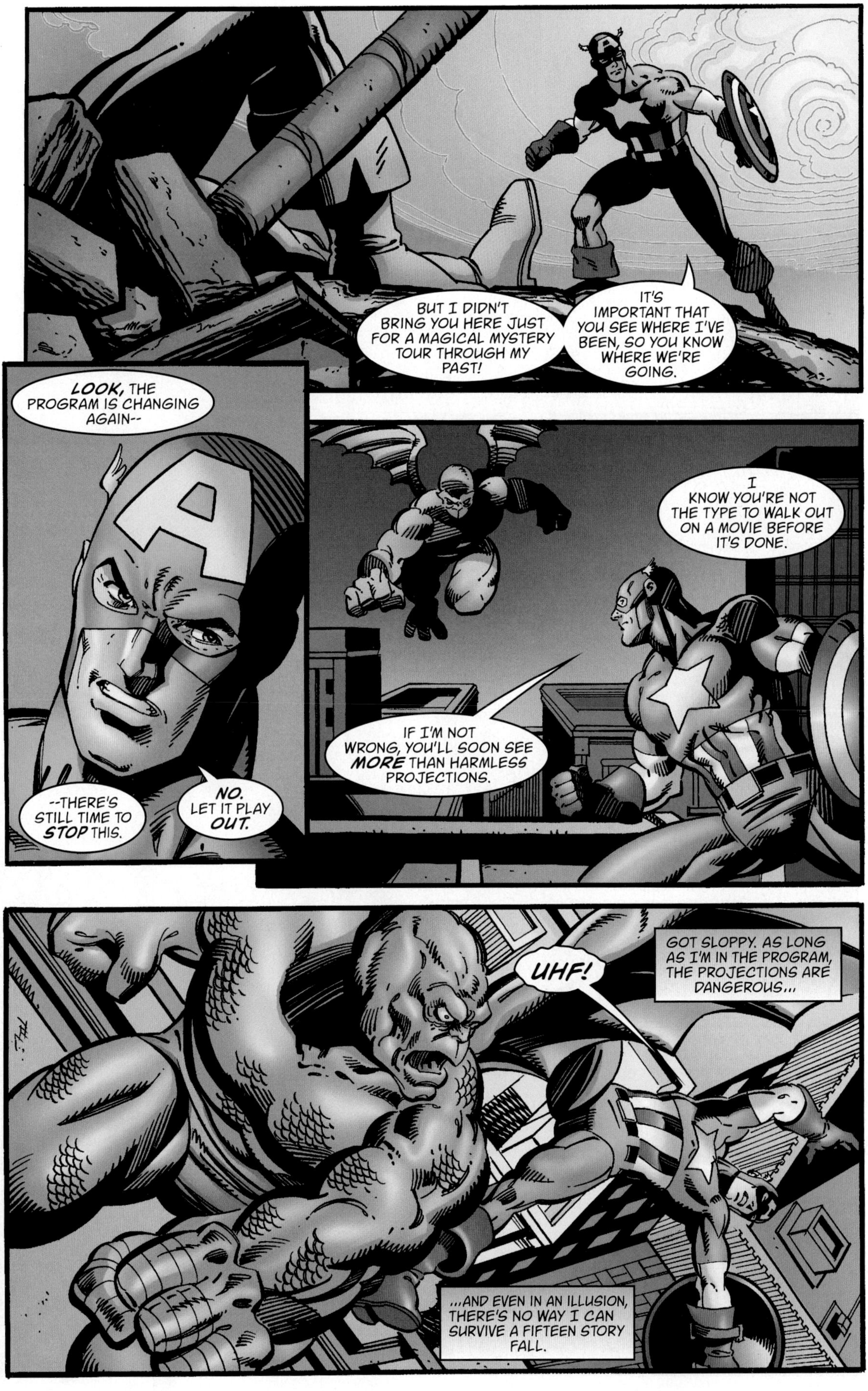
BUT I DIDN'T BRING YOU HERE JUST FOR A MAGICAL MYSTERY TOUR THROUGH MY PAST!
IT'S IMPORTANT THAT YOU SEE WHERE I'VE BEEN, SO YOU KNOW WHERE WE'RE GOING.
LOOK, THE PROGRAM IS CHANGING AGAIN--
--THERE'S STILL TIME TO STOP THIS.
NO. LET IT PLAY OUT.
I KNOW YOU'RE NOT THE TYPE TO WALK OUT ON A MOVIE BEFORE IT'S DONE.
IF I'M NOT WRONG, YOU'LL SOON SEE MORE THAN HARMLESS PROJECTIONS.
UHF!
GOT SLOPPY. AS LONG AS I'M IN THE PROGRAM, THE PROJECTIONS ARE DANGEROUS...
...AND EVEN IN AN ILLUSION, THERE'S NO WAY I CAN SURVIVE A FIFTEEN STORY FALL.

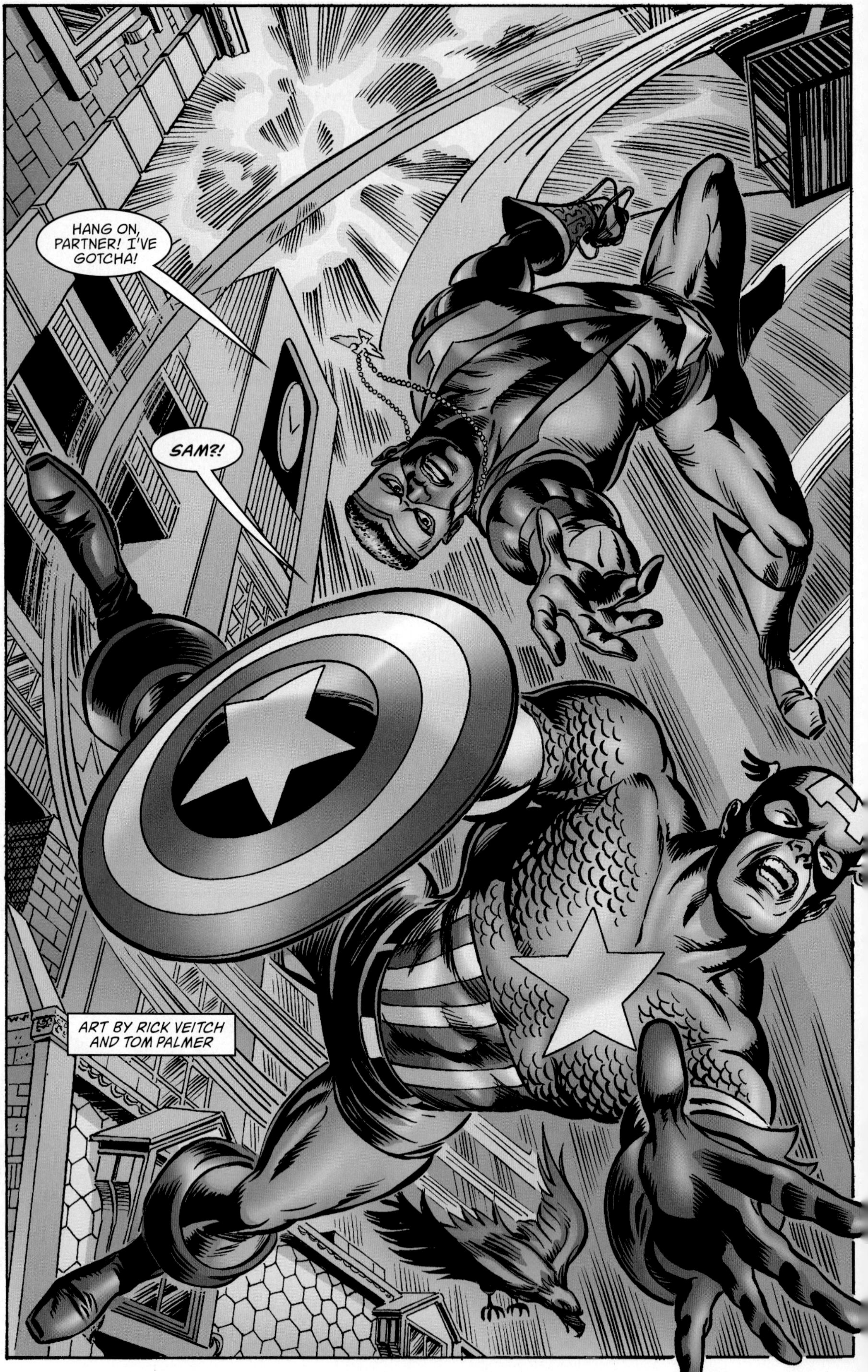
HANG ON, PARTNER! I'VE GOTCHA!
SAM?!
ART BY RICK VEITCH AND TOM PALMER

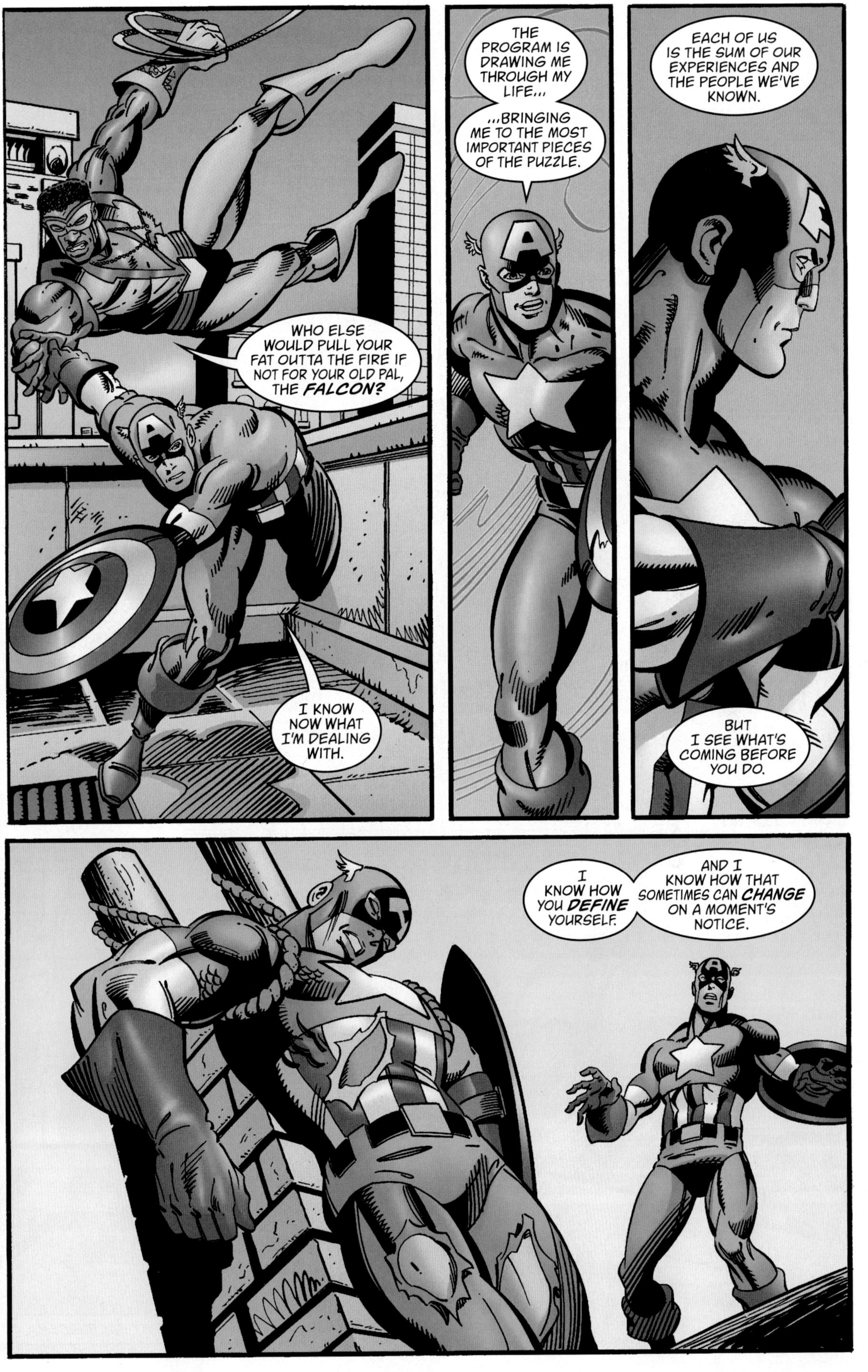
WHO ELSE WOULD PULL YOUR FAT OUTTA THE FIRE IF NOT FOR YOUR OLD PAL, THE FALCON?
I KNOW NOW WHAT I'M DEALING WITH.
THE PROGRAM IS DRAWING ME THROUGH MY LIFE...
...BRINGING ME TO THE MOST IMPORTANT PIECES OF THE PUZZLE.
EACH OF US IS THE SUM OF OUR EXPERIENCES AND THE PEOPLE WE'VE KNOWN.
BUT I SEE WHAT'S COMING BEFORE YOU DO.
I KNOW HOW YOU DEFINE YOURSELF.
AND I KNOW HOW THAT SOMETIMES CAN CHANGE ON A MOMENT'S NOTICE.

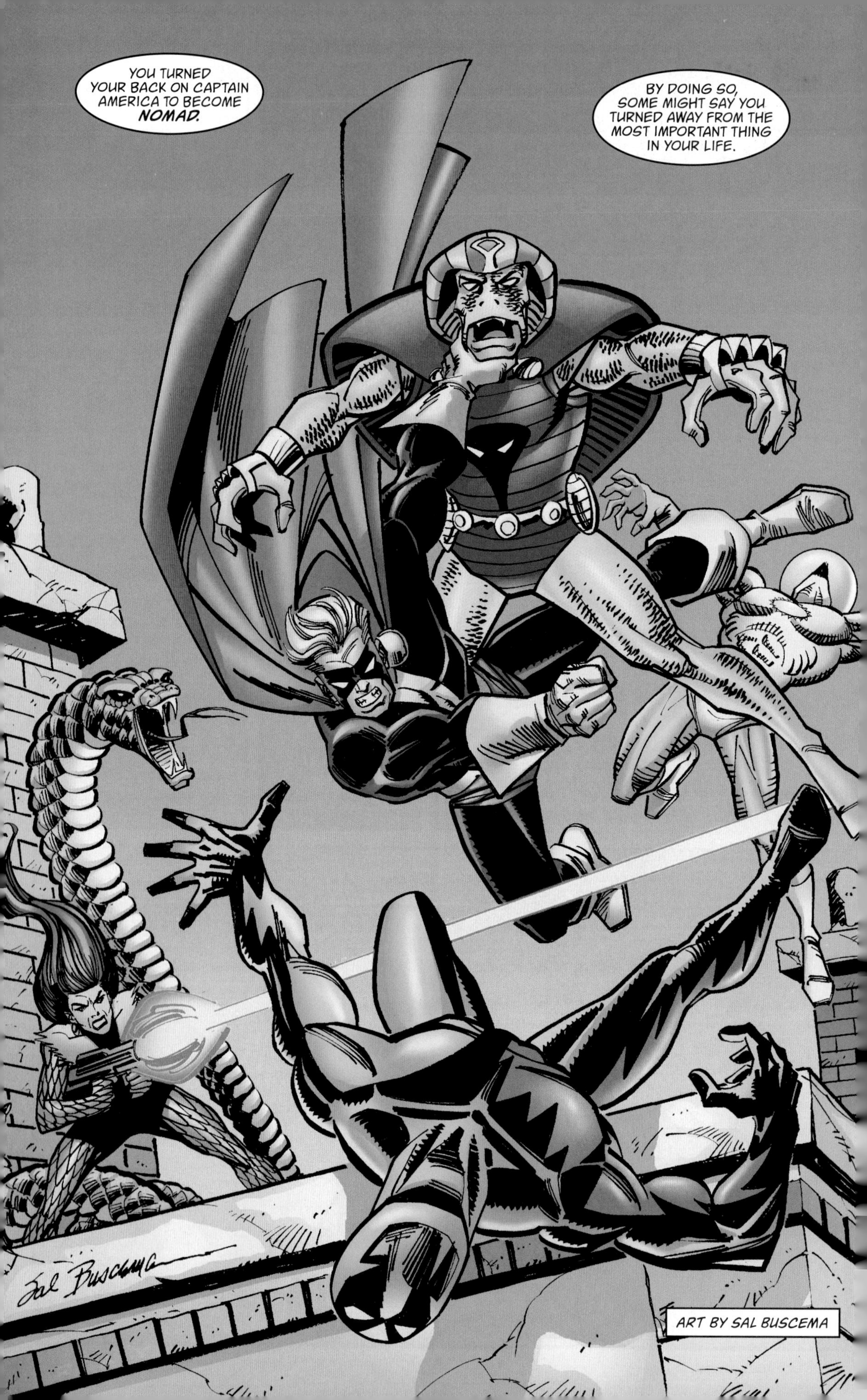
YOU TURNED YOUR BACK ON CAPTAIN AMERICA TO BECOME **NOMAD**.
BY DOING SO, SOME MIGHT SAY YOU TURNED AWAY FROM THE MOST IMPORTANT THING IN YOUR LIFE.
Sal Buscema
ART BY SAL BUSCEMA

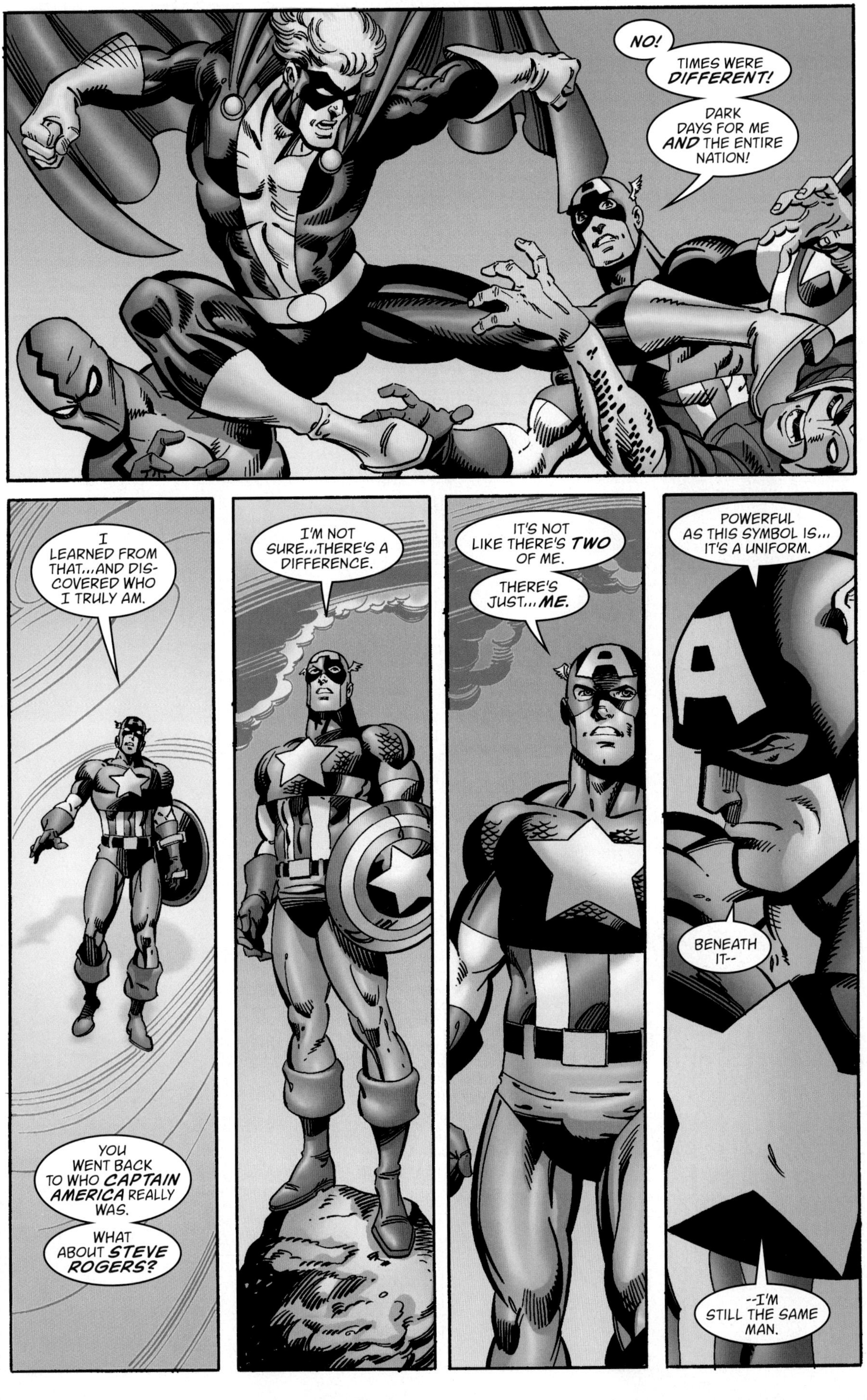
NO!
TIMES WERE DIFFERENT!
DARK DAYS FOR ME AND THE ENTIRE NATION!
I LEARNED FROM THAT...AND DISCOVERED WHO I TRULY AM.
YOU WENT BACK TO WHO CAPTAIN AMERICA REALLY WAS.
WHAT ABOUT STEVE ROGERS?
I'M NOT SURE...THERE'S A DIFFERENCE.
IT'S NOT LIKE THERE'S TWO OF ME.
THERE'S JUST...ME.
POWERFUL AS THIS SYMBOL IS... IT'S A UNIFORM.
BENEATH IT--
--I'M STILL THE SAME MAN.

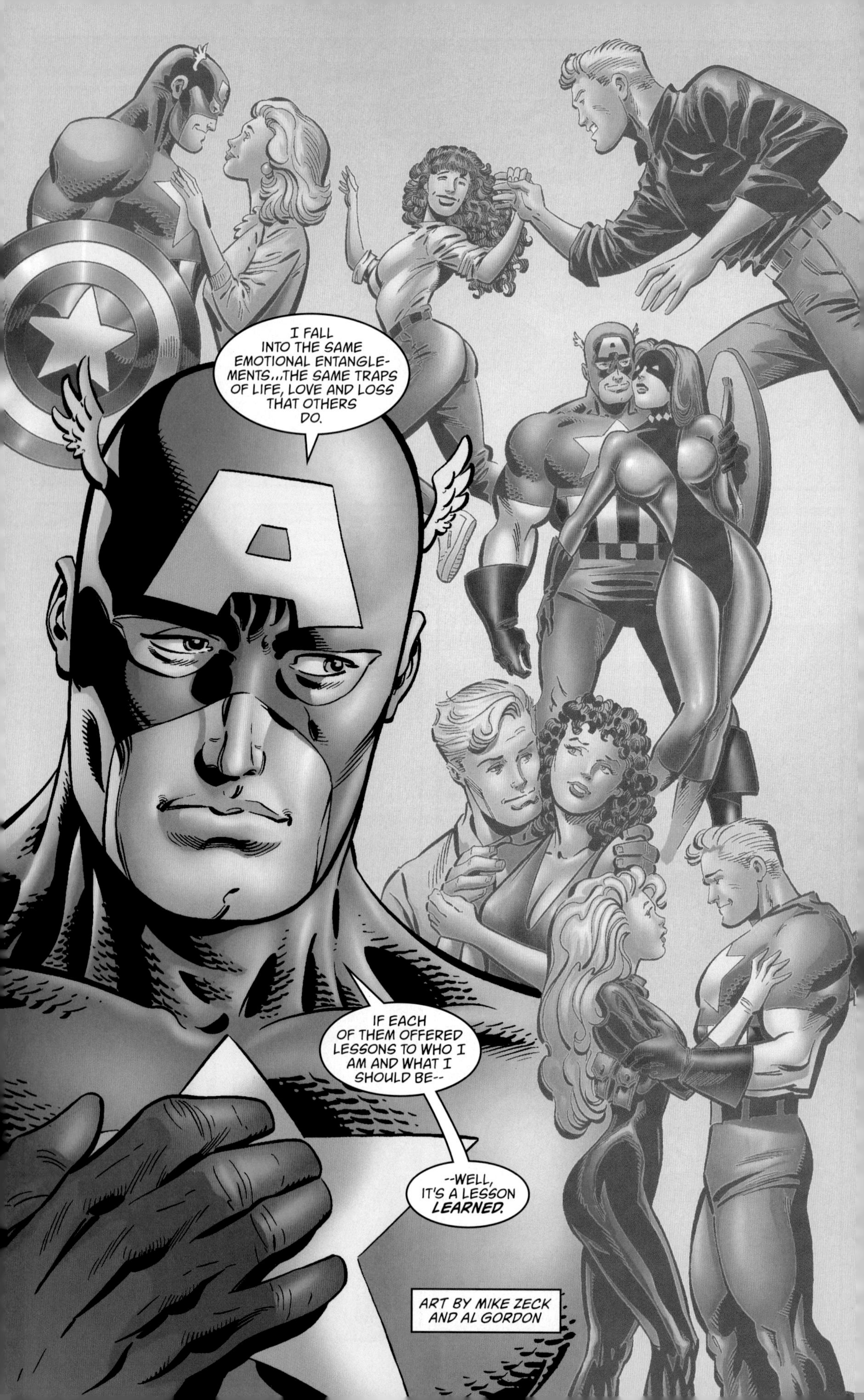
I FALL INTO THE SAME EMOTIONAL ENTANGLE-MENTS...THE SAME TRAPS OF LIFE, LOVE AND LOSS THAT OTHERS DO.
IF EACH OF THEM OFFERED LESSONS TO WHO I AM AND WHAT I SHOULD BE--
--WELL, IT'S A LESSON LEARNED.
ART BY MIKE ZECK AND AL GORDON

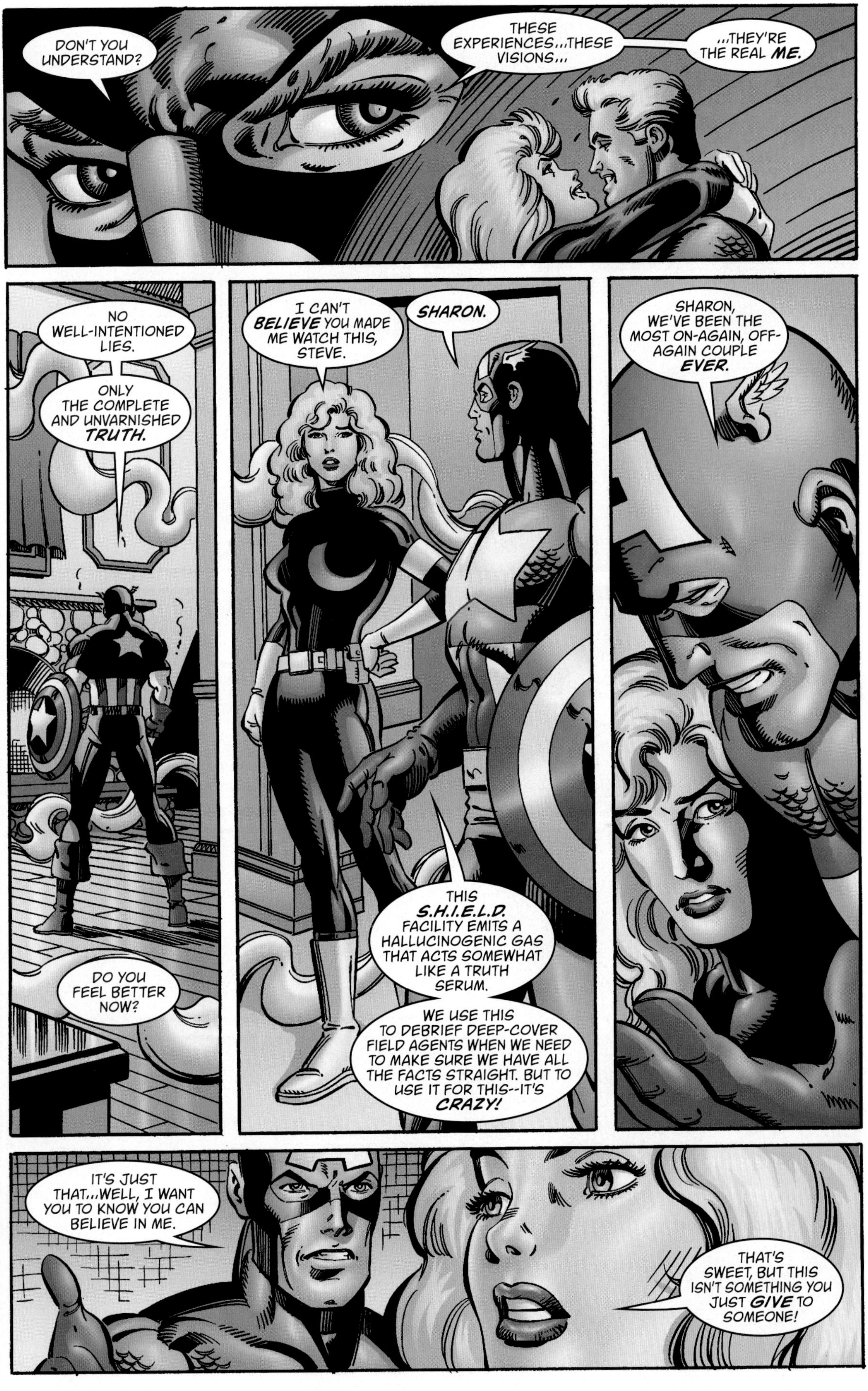
DON'T YOU UNDERSTAND?
THESE EXPERIENCES...THESE VISIONS...
...THEY'RE THE REAL ME.
NO WELL-INTENTIONED LIES.
ONLY THE COMPLETE AND UNVARNISHED TRUTH.
DO YOU FEEL BETTER NOW?
I CAN'T BELIEVE YOU MADE ME WATCH THIS, STEVE.
SHARON.
THIS S.H.I.E.L.D. FACILITY EMITS A HALLUCINOGENIC GAS THAT ACTS SOMEWHAT LIKE A TRUTH SERUM.
WE USE THIS TO DEBRIEF DEEP-COVER FIELD AGENTS WHEN WE NEED TO MAKE SURE WE HAVE ALL THE FACTS STRAIGHT. BUT TO USE IT FOR THIS--IT'S CRAZY!
SHARON, WE'VE BEEN THE MOST ON-AGAIN, OFF-AGAIN COUPLE EVER.
IT'S JUST THAT...WELL, I WANT YOU TO KNOW YOU CAN BELIEVE IN ME.
THAT'S SWEET, BUT THIS ISN'T SOMETHING YOU JUST GIVE TO SOMEONE!

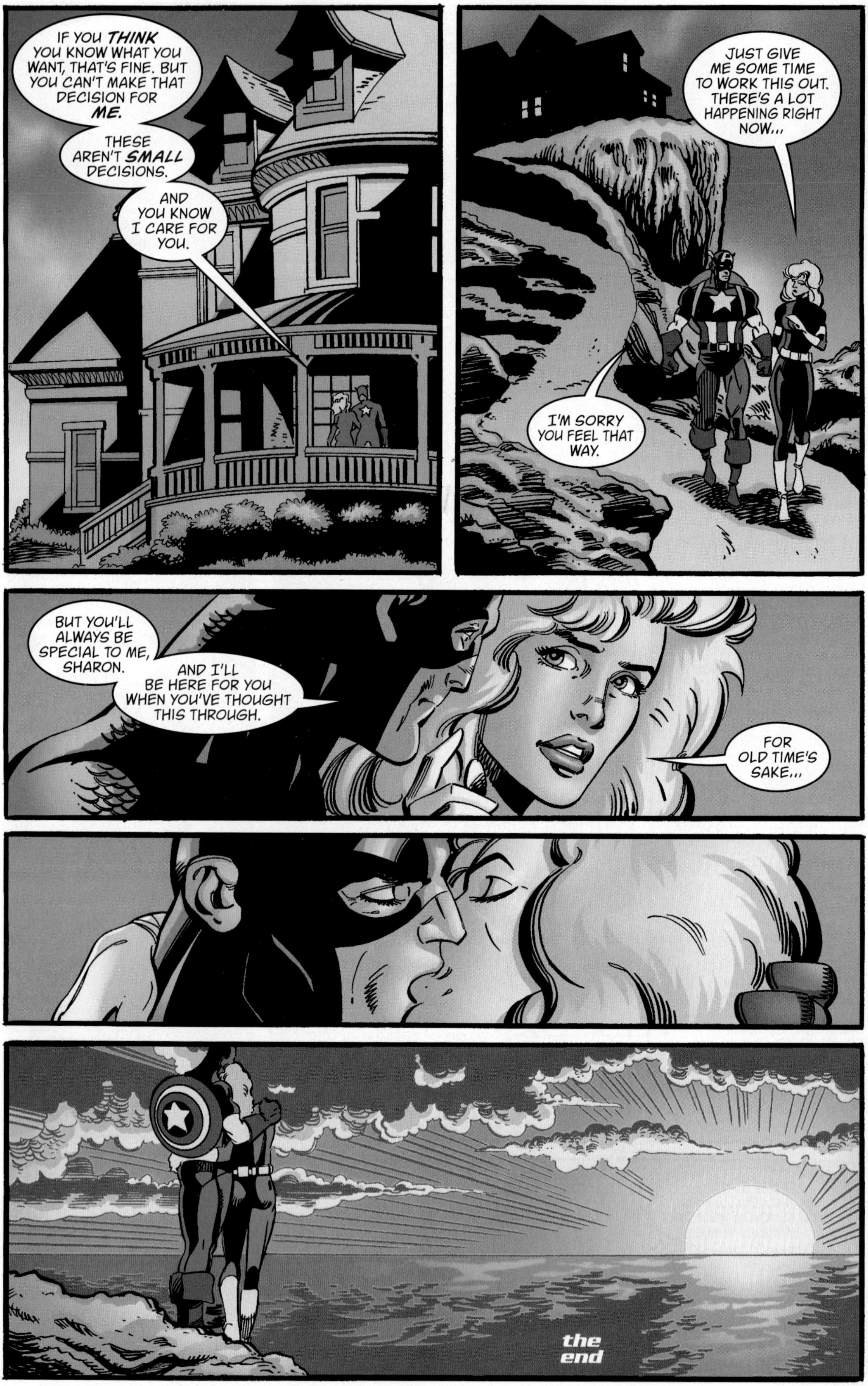
IF YOU THINK YOU KNOW WHAT YOU WANT, THAT'S FINE. BUT YOU CAN'T MAKE THAT DECISION FOR ME.
THESE AREN'T SMALL DECISIONS.
AND YOU KNOW I CARE FOR YOU.
JUST GIVE ME SOME TIME TO WORK THIS OUT. THERE'S A LOT HAPPENING RIGHT NOW...
I'M SORRY YOU FEEL THAT WAY.
BUT YOU'LL ALWAYS BE SPECIAL TO ME, SHARON.
AND I'LL BE HERE FOR YOU WHEN YOU'VE THOUGHT THIS THROUGH.
FOR OLD TIME'S SAKE...
the end

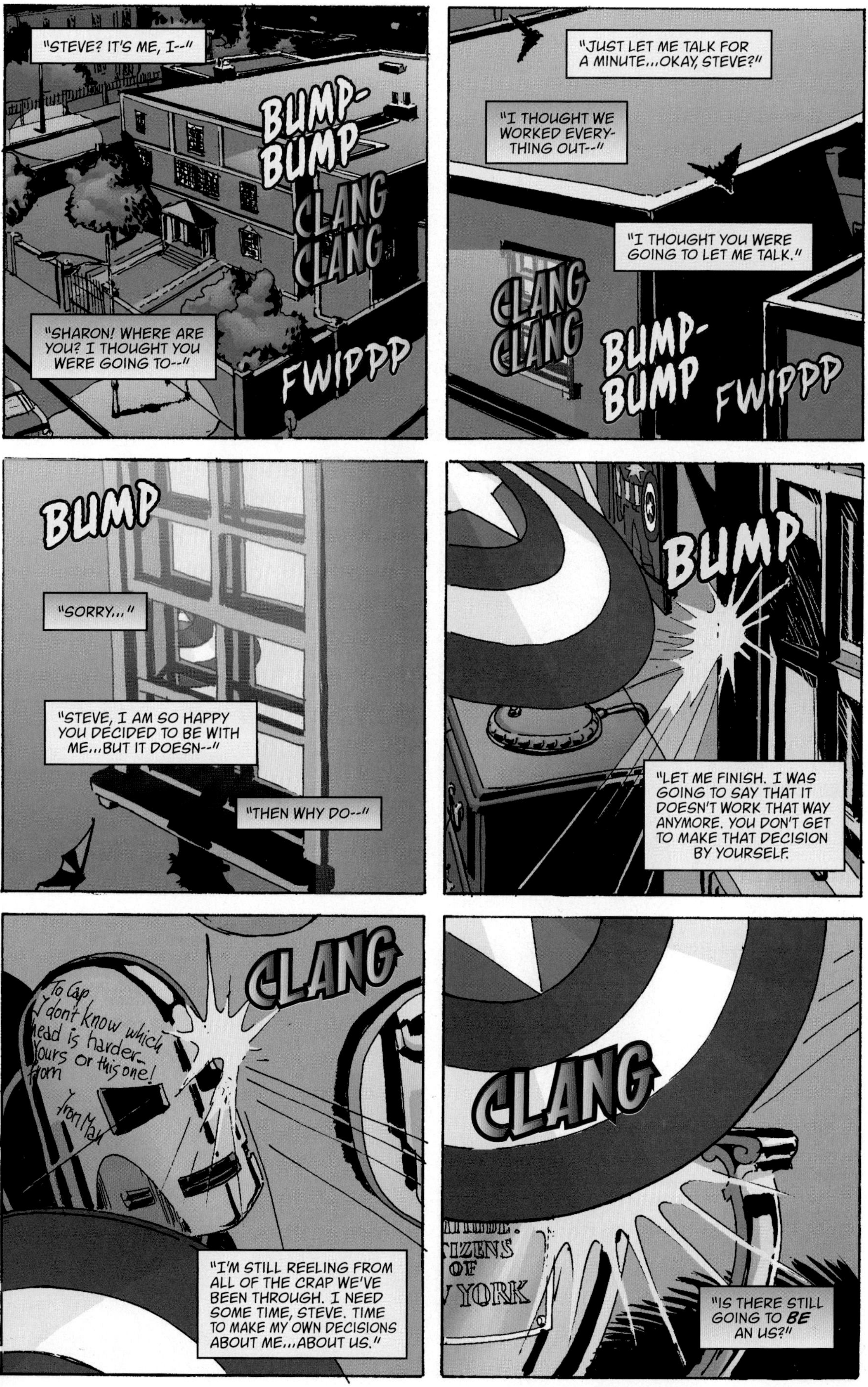
"STEVE? IT'S ME, I--"
BUMP-BUMP
CLANG CLANG
"SHARON! WHERE ARE YOU? I THOUGHT YOU WERE GOING TO--"
FWIPPP
"JUST LET ME TALK FOR A MINUTE...OKAY, STEVE?"
"I THOUGHT WE WORKED EVERY-THING OUT--"
"I THOUGHT YOU WERE GOING TO LET ME TALK."
CLANG CLANG
BUMP-BUMP
FWIPPP
BUMP
"SORRY..."
"STEVE, I AM SO HAPPY YOU DECIDED TO BE WITH ME...BUT IT DOESN--"
"THEN WHY DO--"
BUMP
"LET ME FINISH. I WAS GOING TO SAY THAT IT DOESN'T WORK THAT WAY ANYMORE. YOU DON'T GET TO MAKE THAT DECISION BY YOURSELF.
CLANG
To Cap I don't know which head is harder- Yours or this one! From Iron Man
"I'M STILL REELING FROM ALL OF THE CRAP WE'VE BEEN THROUGH. I NEED SOME TIME, STEVE. TIME TO MAKE MY OWN DECISIONS ABOUT ME...ABOUT US."
CLANG
"IS THERE STILL GOING TO *BE* AN US?"

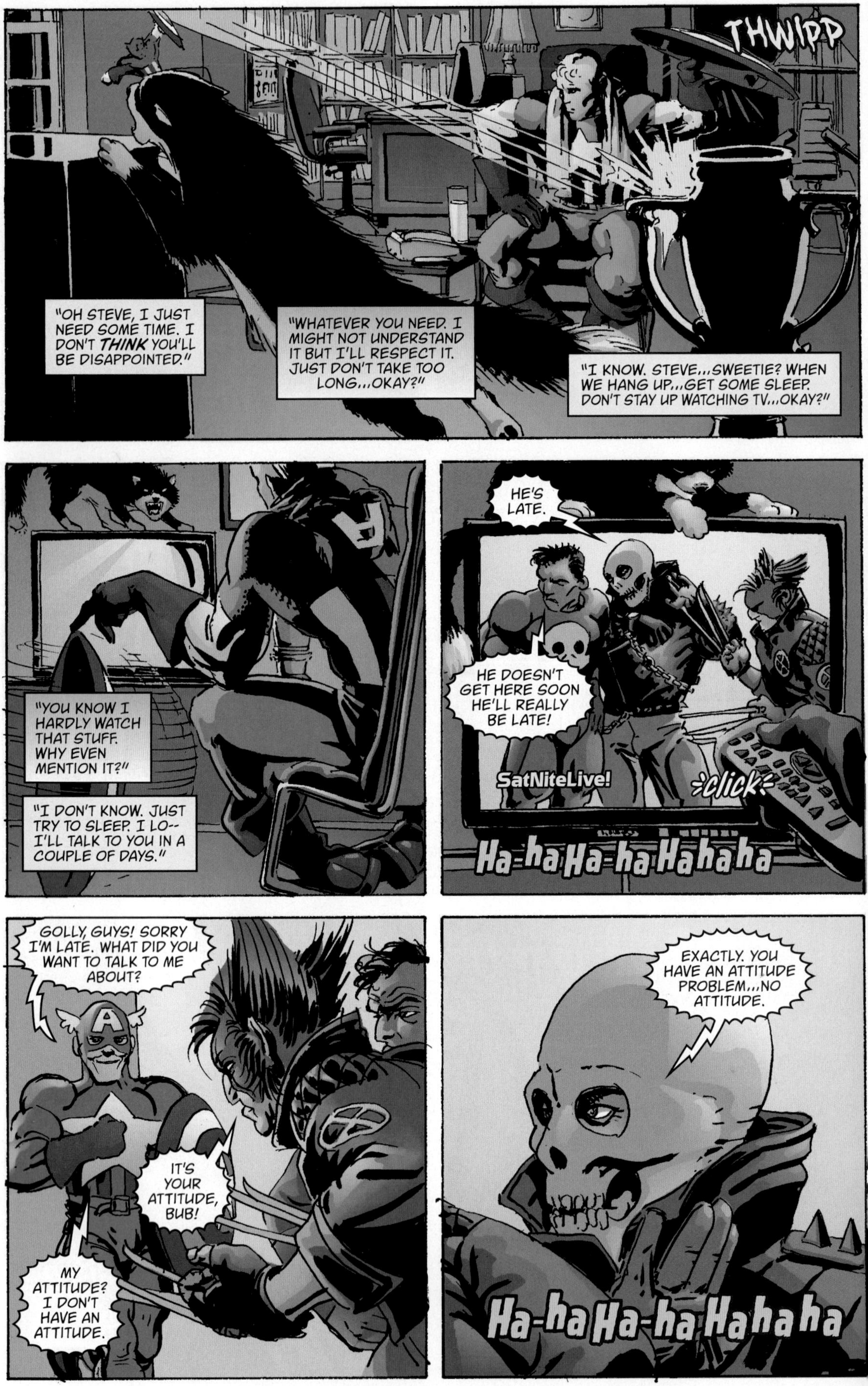
THWIPP
"OH STEVE, I JUST NEED SOME TIME. I DON'T THINK YOU'LL BE DISAPPOINTED."
"WHATEVER YOU NEED. I MIGHT NOT UNDERSTAND IT BUT I'LL RESPECT IT. JUST DON'T TAKE TOO LONG...OKAY?"
"I KNOW. STEVE...SWEETIE? WHEN WE HANG UP...GET SOME SLEEP. DON'T STAY UP WATCHING TV...OKAY?"
"YOU KNOW I HARDLY WATCH THAT STUFF. WHY EVEN MENTION IT?"
"I DON'T KNOW. JUST TRY TO SLEEP. I LO-- I'LL TALK TO YOU IN A COUPLE OF DAYS."
HE'S LATE.
HE DOESN'T GET HERE SOON HE'LL REALLY BE LATE!
SatNiteLive!
click
Ha-ha Ha-ha Hahaha
GOLLY, GUYS! SORRY I'M LATE. WHAT DID YOU WANT TO TALK TO ME ABOUT?
IT'S YOUR ATTITUDE, BUB!
MY ATTITUDE? I DON'T HAVE AN ATTITUDE.
EXACTLY. YOU HAVE AN ATTITUDE PROBLEM...NO ATTITUDE.
Ha-ha Ha-ha Hahaha

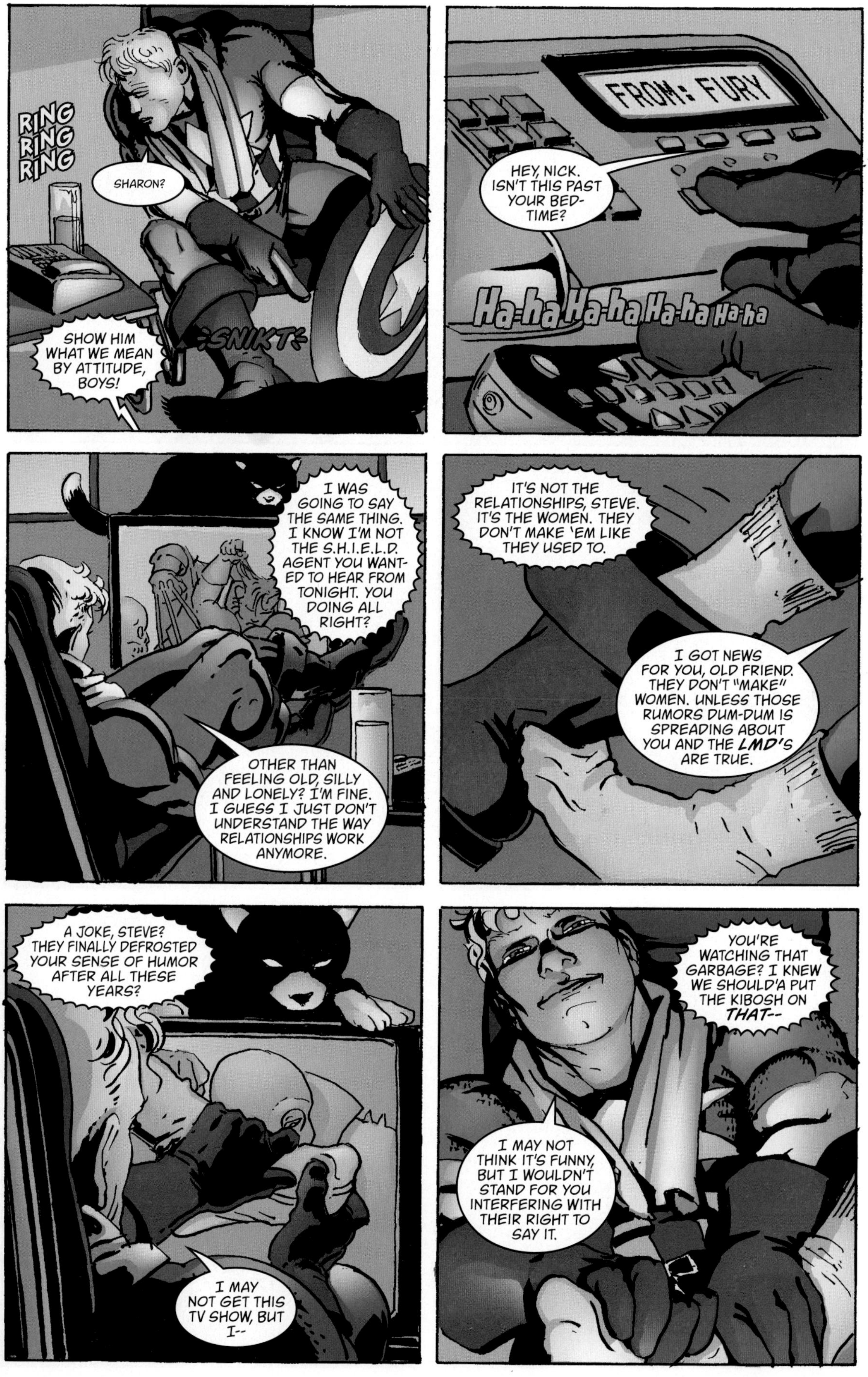
RING RING RING
SHARON?
SHOW HIM WHAT WE MEAN BY ATTITUDE, BOYS!
SNIKT
FROM: FURY
HEY, NICK. ISN'T THIS PAST YOUR BED-TIME?
Ha-ha Ha-ha Ha-ha Ha-ha
I WAS GOING TO SAY THE SAME THING. I KNOW I'M NOT THE S.H.I.E.L.D. AGENT YOU WANTED TO HEAR FROM TONIGHT. YOU DOING ALL RIGHT?
OTHER THAN FEELING OLD, SILLY AND LONELY? I'M FINE. I GUESS I JUST DON'T UNDERSTAND THE WAY RELATIONSHIPS WORK ANYMORE.
IT'S NOT THE RELATIONSHIPS, STEVE. IT'S THE WOMEN. THEY DON'T MAKE 'EM LIKE THEY USED TO.
I GOT NEWS FOR YOU, OLD FRIEND. THEY DON'T "MAKE" WOMEN. UNLESS THOSE RUMORS DUM-DUM IS SPREADING ABOUT YOU AND THE *LMD'S* ARE TRUE.
A JOKE, STEVE? THEY FINALLY DEFROSTED YOUR SENSE OF HUMOR AFTER ALL THESE YEARS?
I MAY NOT GET THIS TV SHOW, BUT I--
YOU'RE WATCHING THAT GARBAGE? I KNEW WE SHOULD'A PUT THE KIBOSH ON *THAT*--
I MAY NOT THINK IT'S FUNNY, BUT I WOULDN'T STAND FOR YOU INTERFERING WITH THEIR RIGHT TO SAY IT.

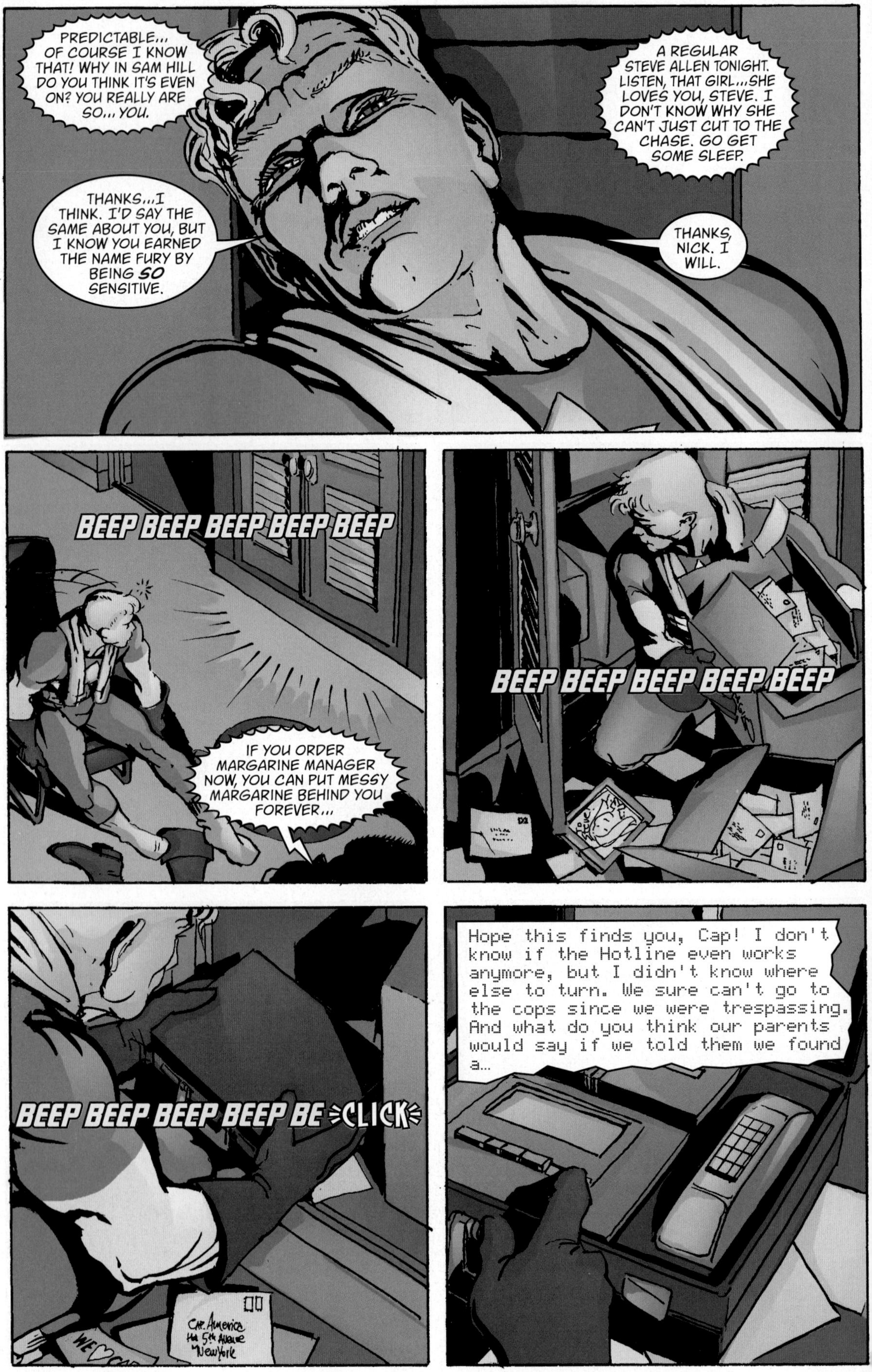
PREDICTABLE... OF COURSE I KNOW THAT! WHY IN SAM HILL DO YOU THINK IT'S EVEN ON? YOU REALLY ARE SO... YOU.
A REGULAR STEVE ALLEN TONIGHT. LISTEN, THAT GIRL... SHE LOVES YOU, STEVE. I DON'T KNOW WHY SHE CAN'T JUST CUT TO THE CHASE. GO GET SOME SLEEP.
THANKS... I THINK. I'D SAY THE SAME ABOUT YOU, BUT I KNOW YOU EARNED THE NAME FURY BY BEING SO SENSITIVE.
THANKS, NICK. I WILL.
BEEP BEEP BEEP BEEP BEEP
IF YOU ORDER MARGARINE MANAGER NOW, YOU CAN PUT MESSY MARGARINE BEHIND YOU FOREVER...
BEEP BEEP BEEP BEEP BEEP
BEEP BEEP BEEP BEEP BE CLICK
Hope this finds you, Cap! I don't know if the Hotline even works anymore, but I didn't know where else to turn. We sure can't go to the cops since we were trespassing. And what do you think our parents would say if we told them we found a...

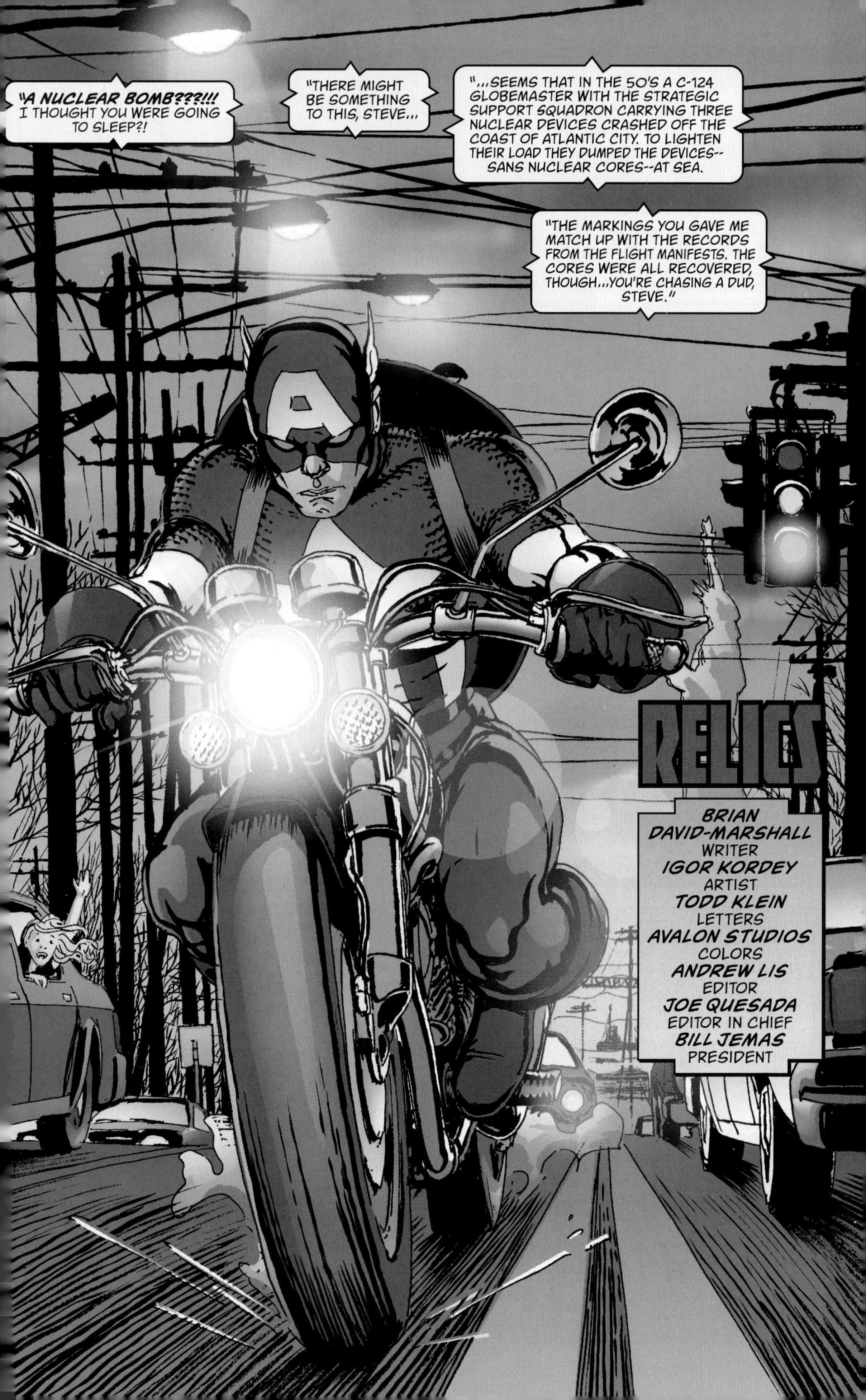
"A NUCLEAR BOMB???!!! I THOUGHT YOU WERE GOING TO SLEEP?!
"THERE MIGHT BE SOMETHING TO THIS, STEVE...
"...SEEMS THAT IN THE 50'S A C-124 GLOBEMASTER WITH THE STRATEGIC SUPPORT SQUADRON CARRYING THREE NUCLEAR DEVICES CRASHED OFF THE COAST OF ATLANTIC CITY. TO LIGHTEN THEIR LOAD THEY DUMPED THE DEVICES--SANS NUCLEAR CORES--AT SEA.
"THE MARKINGS YOU GAVE ME MATCH UP WITH THE RECORDS FROM THE FLIGHT MANIFESTS. THE CORES WERE ALL RECOVERED, THOUGH...YOU'RE CHASING A DUD, STEVE."
RELICS
BRIAN DAVID-MARSHALL WRITER
IGOR KORDEY ARTIST
TODD KLEIN LETTERS
AVALON STUDIOS COLORS
ANDREW LIS EDITOR
JOE QUESADA EDITOR IN CHIEF
BILL JEMAS PRESIDENT

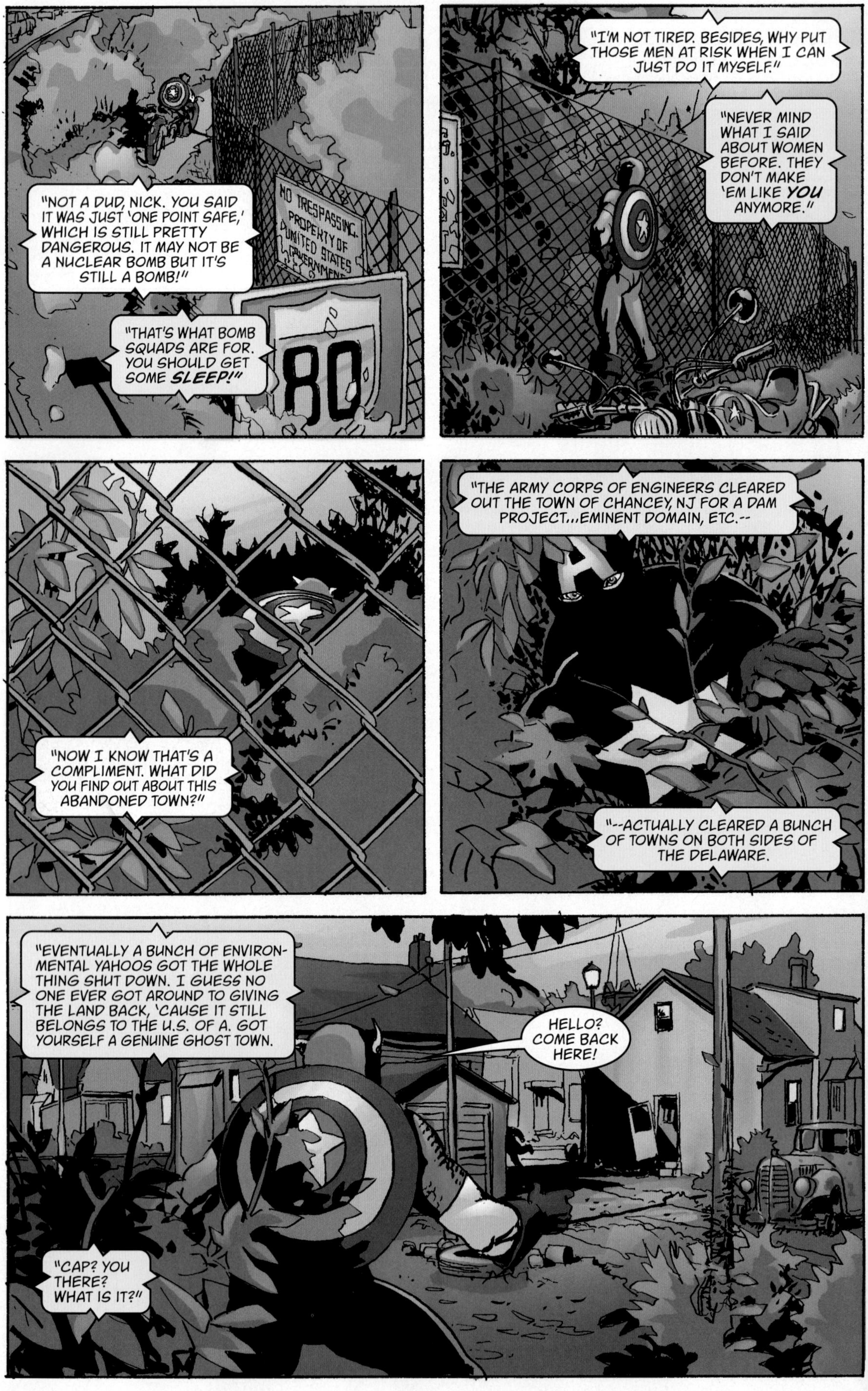
"NOT A DUD, NICK. YOU SAID IT WAS JUST 'ONE POINT SAFE,' WHICH IS STILL PRETTY DANGEROUS. IT MAY NOT BE A NUCLEAR BOMB BUT IT'S STILL A BOMB!"
NO TRESPASSING PROPERTY OF UNITED STATES GOVERNMENT
"THAT'S WHAT BOMB SQUADS ARE FOR. YOU SHOULD GET SOME SLEEP!"
80
"I'M NOT TIRED. BESIDES, WHY PUT THOSE MEN AT RISK WHEN I CAN JUST DO IT MYSELF."
"NEVER MIND WHAT I SAID ABOUT WOMEN BEFORE. THEY DON'T MAKE 'EM LIKE YOU ANYMORE."
"NOW I KNOW THAT'S A COMPLIMENT. WHAT DID YOU FIND OUT ABOUT THIS ABANDONED TOWN?"
"THE ARMY CORPS OF ENGINEERS CLEARED OUT THE TOWN OF CHANCEY, NJ FOR A DAM PROJECT...EMINENT DOMAIN, ETC.--
"--ACTUALLY CLEARED A BUNCH OF TOWNS ON BOTH SIDES OF THE DELAWARE.
"EVENTUALLY A BUNCH OF ENVIRONMENTAL YAHOOS GOT THE WHOLE THING SHUT DOWN. I GUESS NO ONE EVER GOT AROUND TO GIVING THE LAND BACK, 'CAUSE IT STILL BELONGS TO THE U.S. OF A. GOT YOURSELF A GENUINE GHOST TOWN.
HELLO? COME BACK HERE!
"CAP? YOU THERE? WHAT IS IT?"

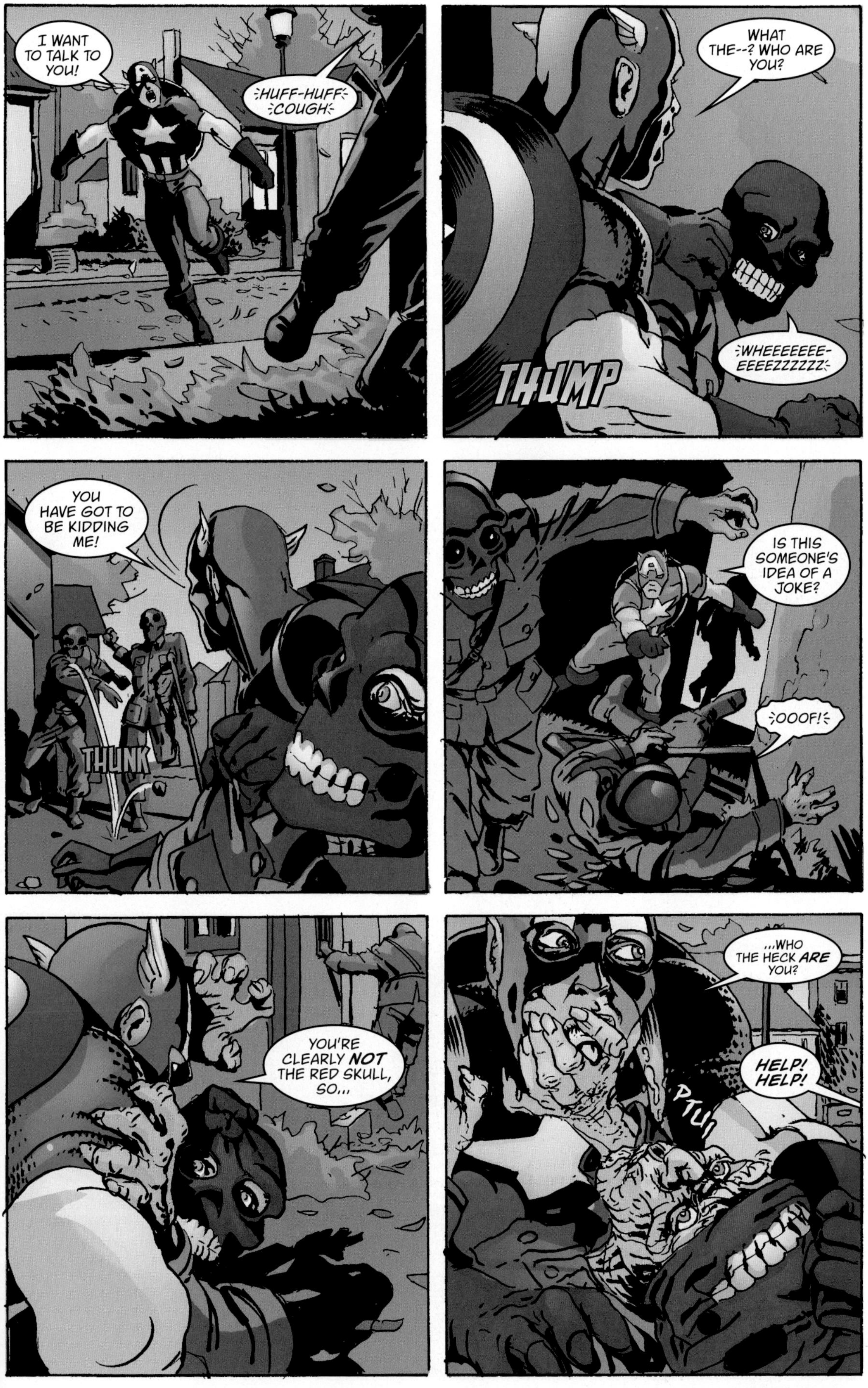
I WANT TO TALK TO YOU!
HUFF-HUFF COUGH
WHAT THE--? WHO ARE YOU?
WHEEEEEEE-EEEEZZZZZZ
THUMP
YOU HAVE GOT TO BE KIDDING ME!
THUNK
IS THIS SOMEONE'S IDEA OF A JOKE?
OOOF!
YOU'RE CLEARLY NOT THE RED SKULL, SO...
...WHO THE HECK ARE YOU?
HELP! HELP!
PTUI

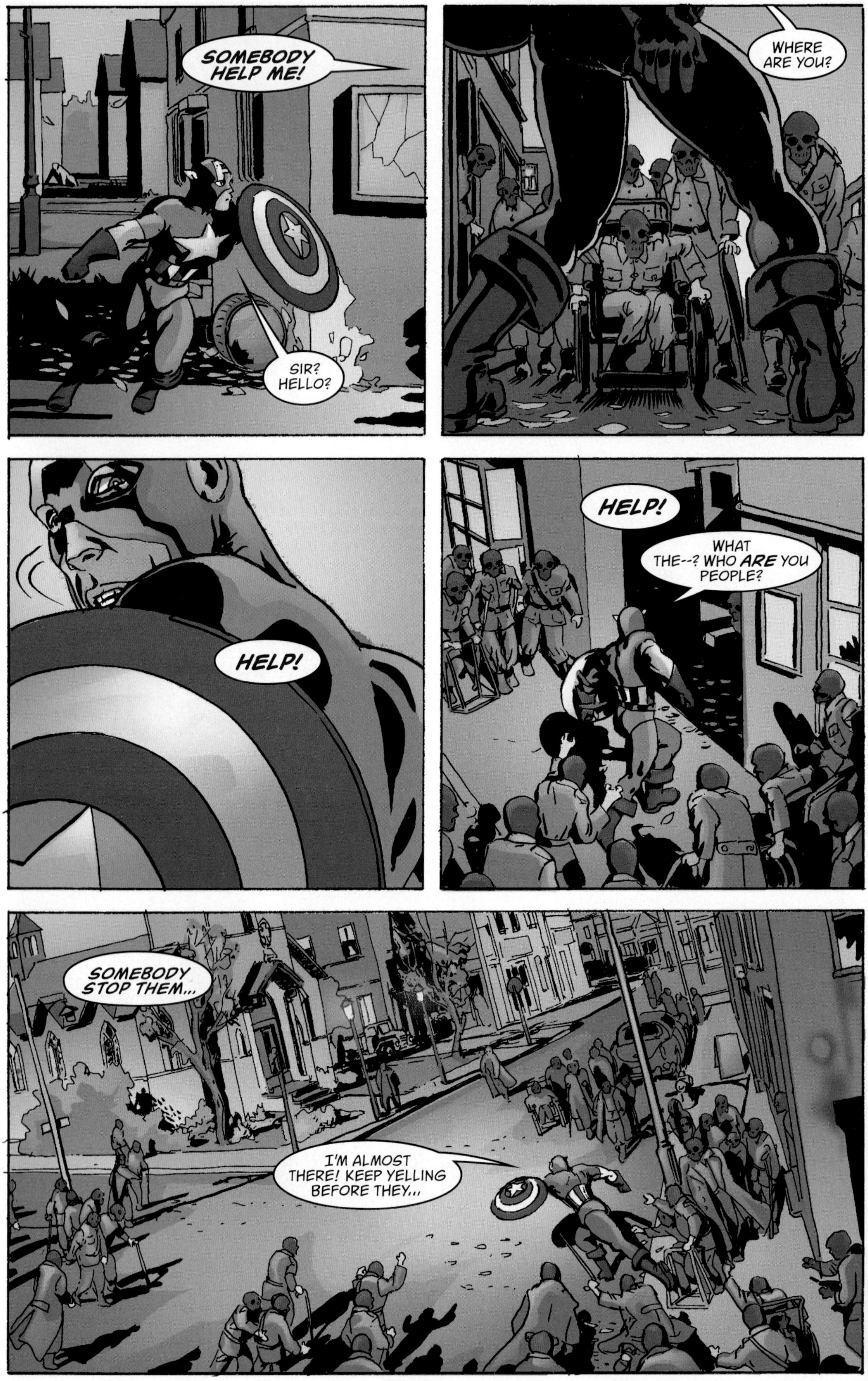
SOMEBODY HELP ME!
SIR? HELLO?
WHERE ARE YOU?
HELP!
HELP!
WHAT THE--? WHO ARE YOU PEOPLE?
SOMEBODY STOP THEM...
I'M ALMOST THERE! KEEP YELLING BEFORE THEY...

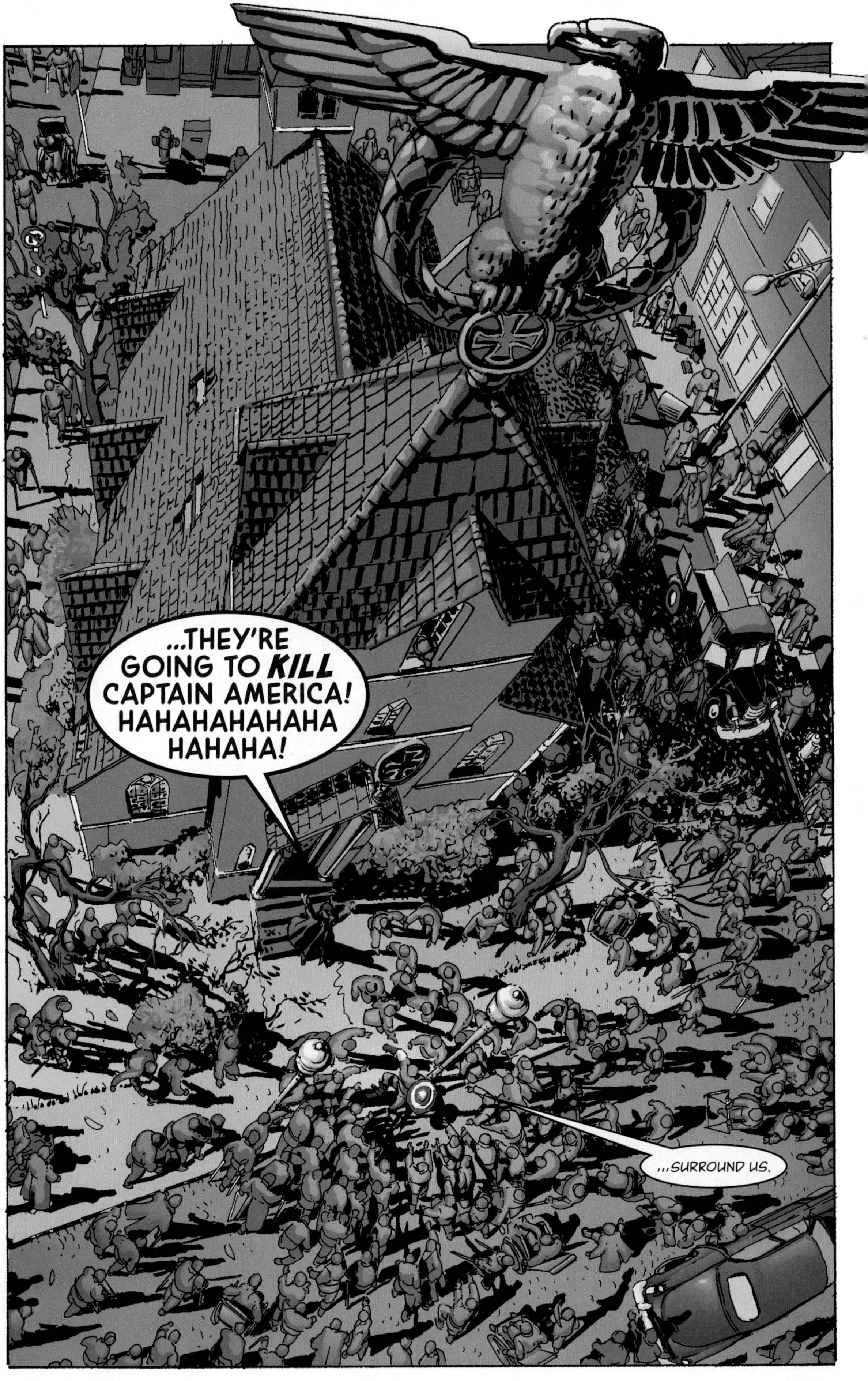
...THEY'RE GOING TO KILL CAPTAIN AMERICA! HAHAHAHAHAHA HAHAHA!
...SURROUND US.

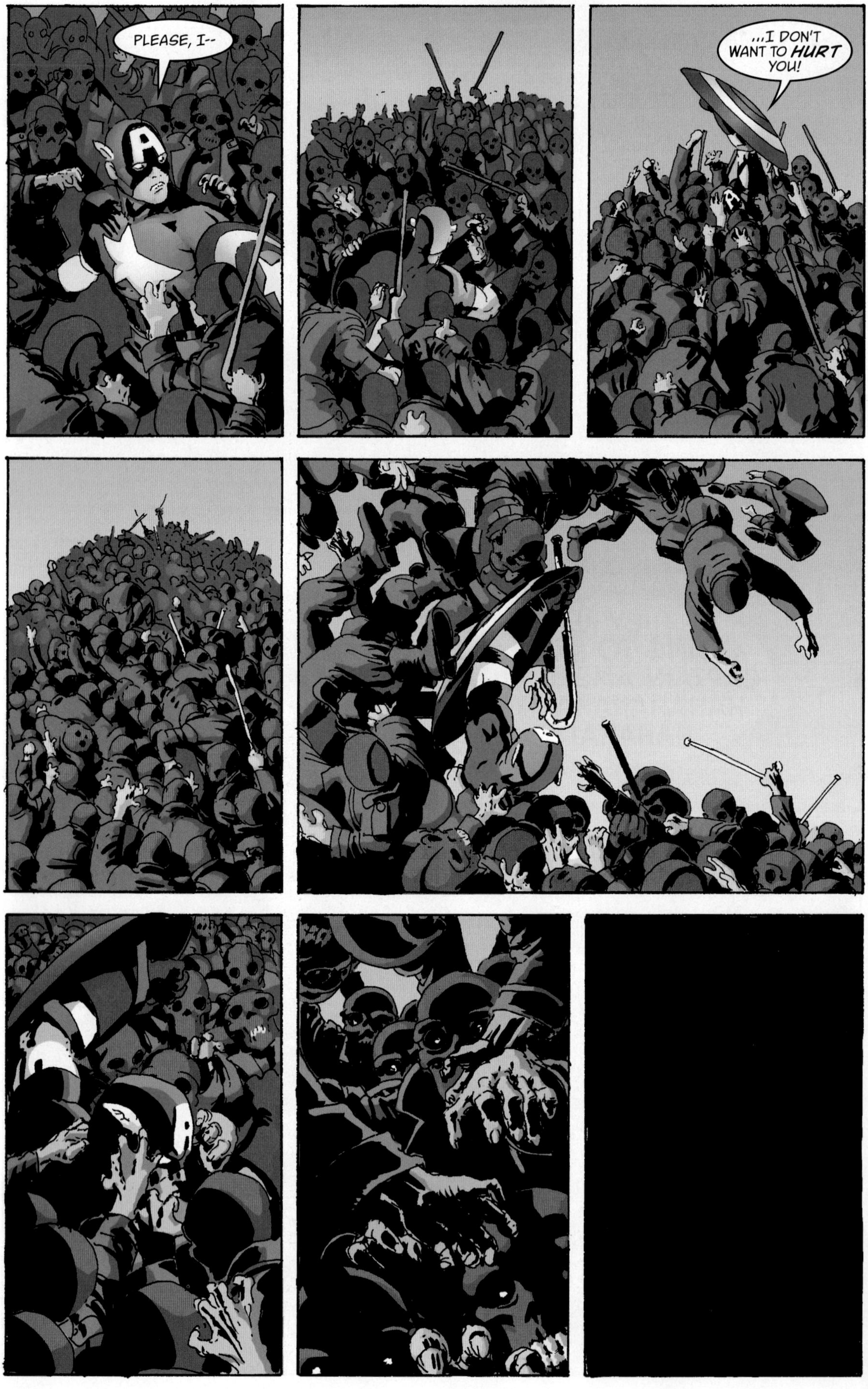
PLEASE, I--
...I DON'T WANT TO HURT YOU!

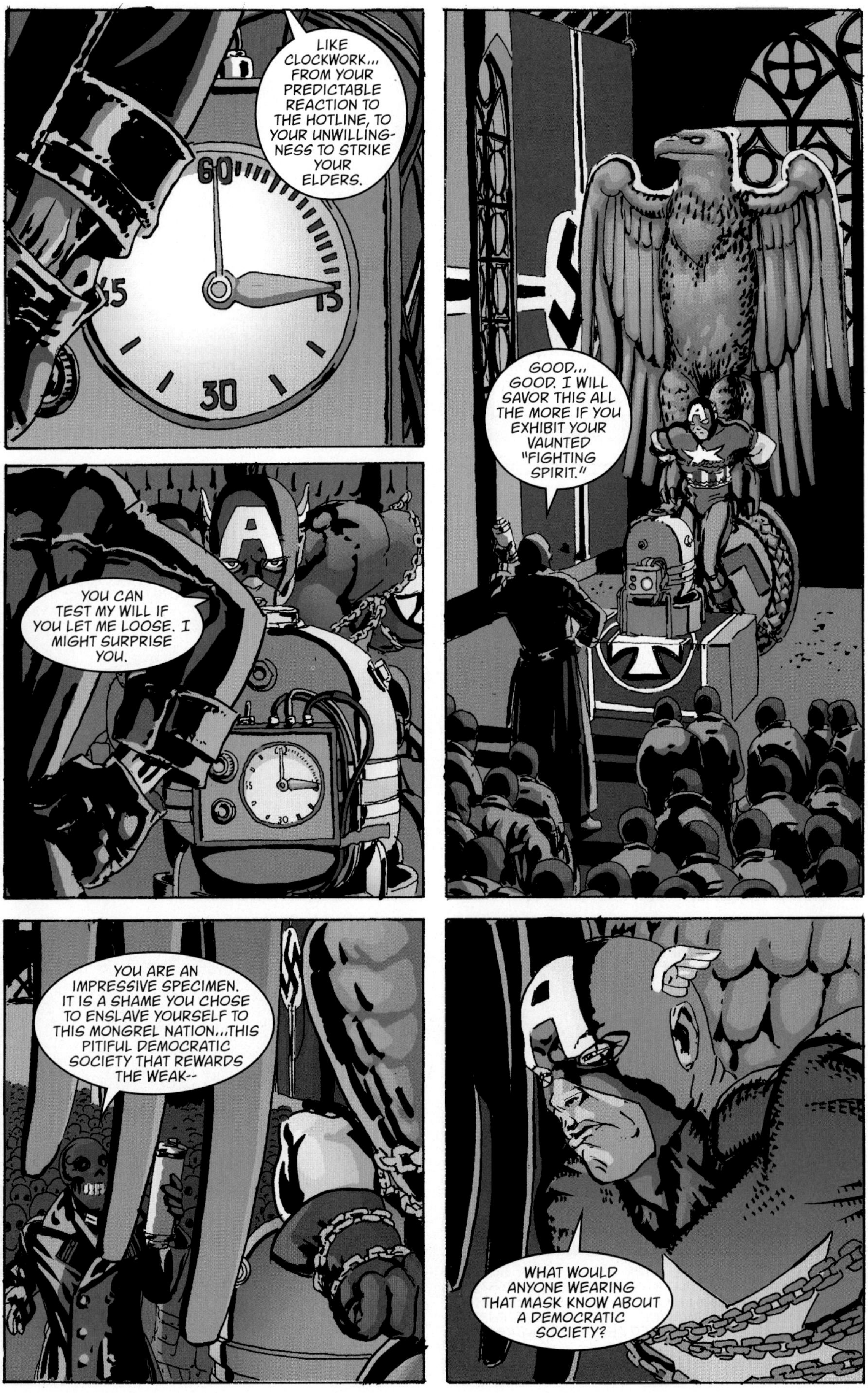
LIKE CLOCKWORK... FROM YOUR PREDICTABLE REACTION TO THE HOTLINE, TO YOUR UNWILLINGNESS TO STRIKE YOUR ELDERS.
60
45
15
30
YOU CAN TEST MY WILL IF YOU LET ME LOOSE. I MIGHT SURPRISE YOU.
GOOD... GOOD. I WILL SAVOR THIS ALL THE MORE IF YOU EXHIBIT YOUR VAUNTED "FIGHTING SPIRIT."
YOU ARE AN IMPRESSIVE SPECIMEN. IT IS A SHAME YOU CHOSE TO ENSLAVE YOURSELF TO THIS MONGREL NATION...THIS PITIFUL DEMOCRATIC SOCIETY THAT REWARDS THE WEAK--
WHAT WOULD ANYONE WEARING THAT MASK KNOW ABOUT A DEMOCRATIC SOCIETY?

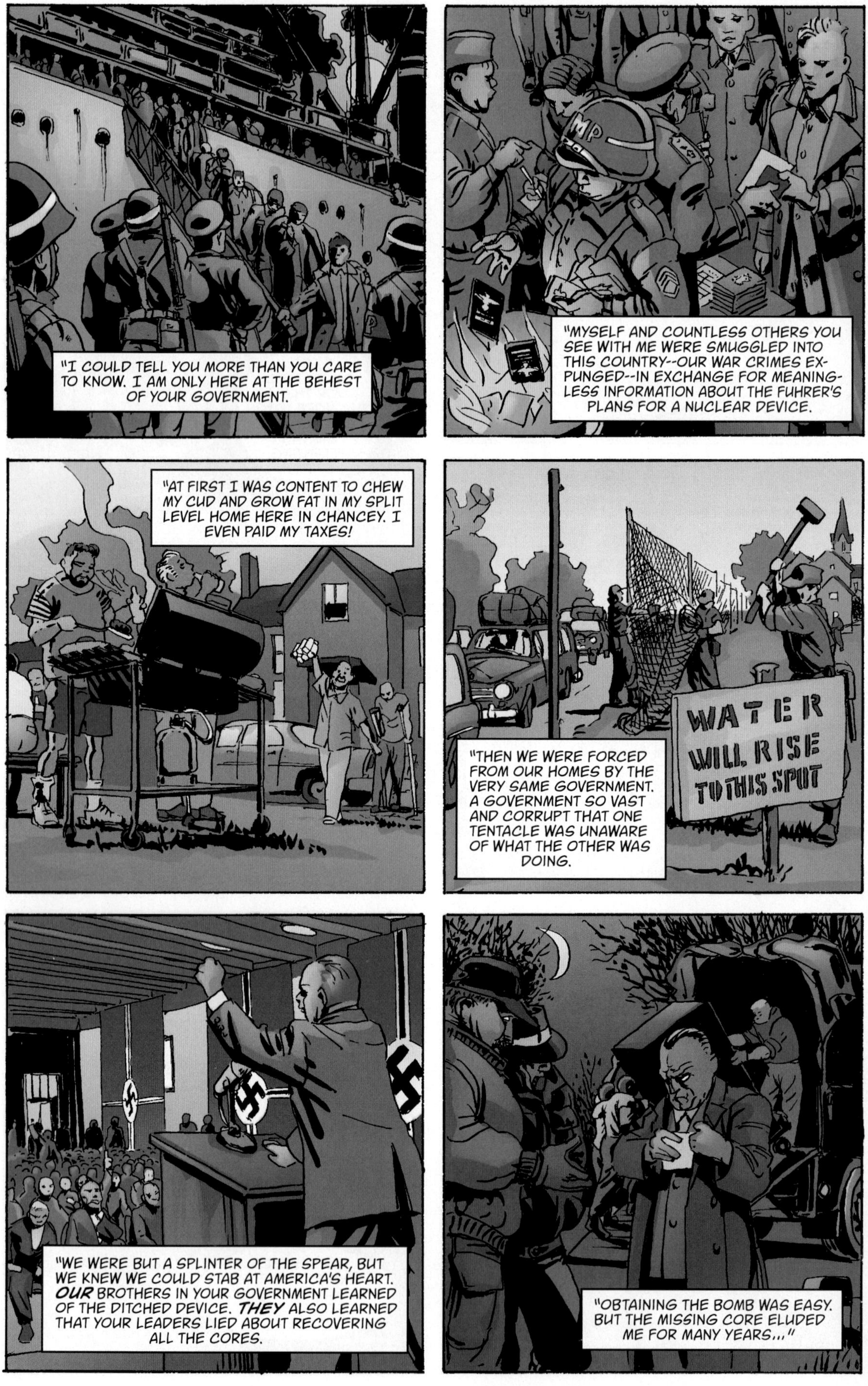
"I COULD TELL YOU MORE THAN YOU CARE TO KNOW. I AM ONLY HERE AT THE BEHEST OF YOUR GOVERNMENT.
"MYSELF AND COUNTLESS OTHERS YOU SEE WITH ME WERE SMUGGLED INTO THIS COUNTRY--OUR WAR CRIMES EXPUNGED--IN EXCHANGE FOR MEANINGLESS INFORMATION ABOUT THE FUHRER'S PLANS FOR A NUCLEAR DEVICE.
"AT FIRST I WAS CONTENT TO CHEW MY CUD AND GROW FAT IN MY SPLIT LEVEL HOME HERE IN CHANCEY. I EVEN PAID MY TAXES!
WATER WILL RISE TO THIS SPOT
"THEN WE WERE FORCED FROM OUR HOMES BY THE VERY SAME GOVERNMENT. A GOVERNMENT SO VAST AND CORRUPT THAT ONE TENTACLE WAS UNAWARE OF WHAT THE OTHER WAS DOING.
"WE WERE BUT A SPLINTER OF THE SPEAR, BUT WE KNEW WE COULD STAB AT AMERICA'S HEART. OUR BROTHERS IN YOUR GOVERNMENT LEARNED OF THE DITCHED DEVICE. THEY ALSO LEARNED THAT YOUR LEADERS LIED ABOUT RECOVERING ALL THE CORES.
"OBTAINING THE BOMB WAS EASY. BUT THE MISSING CORE ELUDED ME FOR MANY YEARS..."

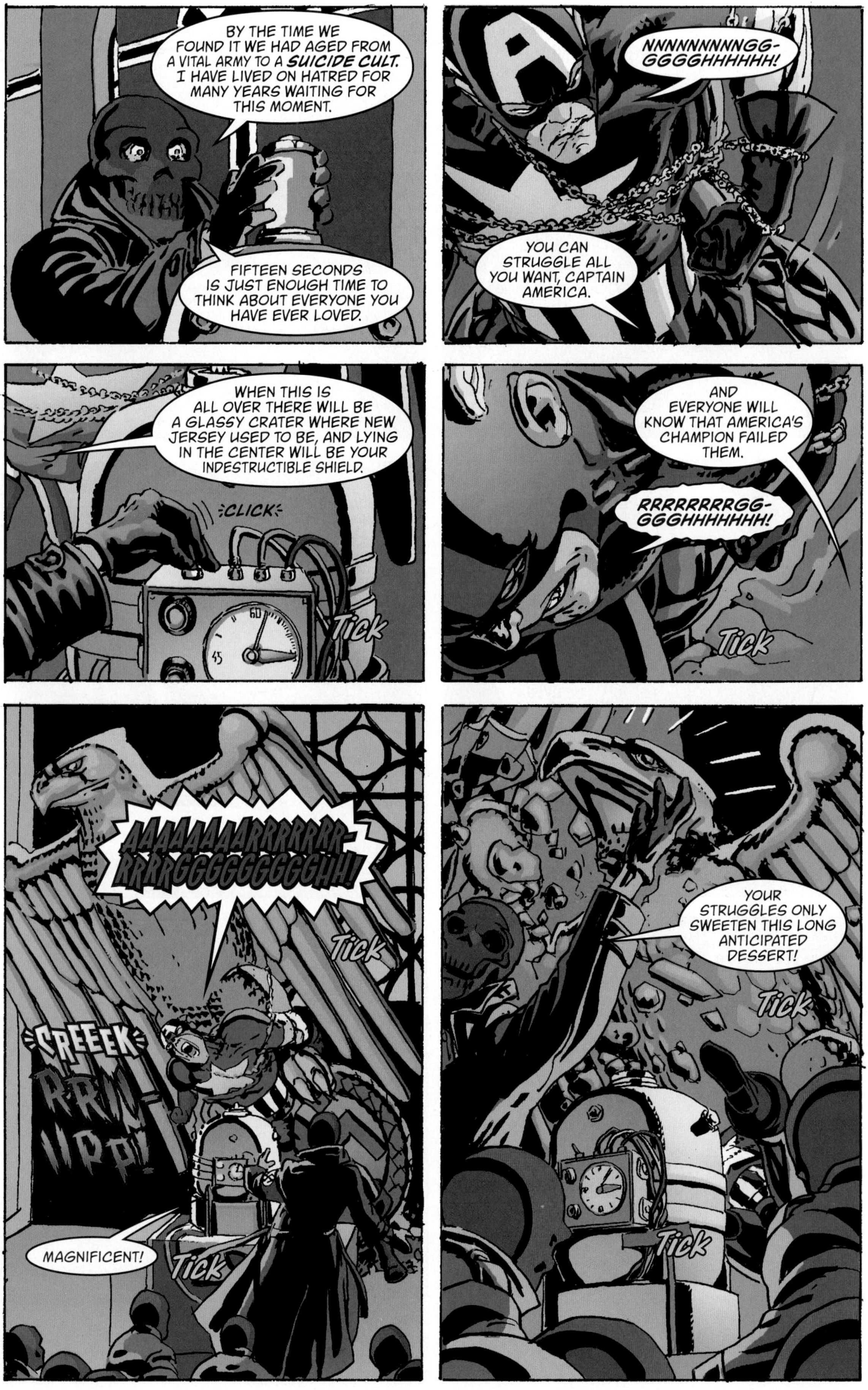
BY THE TIME WE FOUND IT WE HAD AGED FROM A VITAL ARMY TO A SUICIDE CULT. I HAVE LIVED ON HATRED FOR MANY YEARS WAITING FOR THIS MOMENT.
FIFTEEN SECONDS IS JUST ENOUGH TIME TO THINK ABOUT EVERYONE YOU HAVE EVER LOVED.
NNNNNNNNNGG-GGGGHHHHHH!
YOU CAN STRUGGLE ALL YOU WANT, CAPTAIN AMERICA.
WHEN THIS IS ALL OVER THERE WILL BE A GLASSY CRATER WHERE NEW JERSEY USED TO BE, AND LYING IN THE CENTER WILL BE YOUR INDESTRUCTIBLE SHIELD.
CLICK
Tick
AND EVERYONE WILL KNOW THAT AMERICA'S CHAMPION FAILED THEM.
RRRRRRRRGG-GGGHHHHHHH!
Tick
AAAAAAAARRRRRRR-RRRRGGGGGGGGGGHH!
Tick
CREEEK
RRIIIPPP!
MAGNIFICENT!
Tick
YOUR STRUGGLES ONLY SWEETEN THIS LONG ANTICIPATED DESSERT!
Tick
Tick

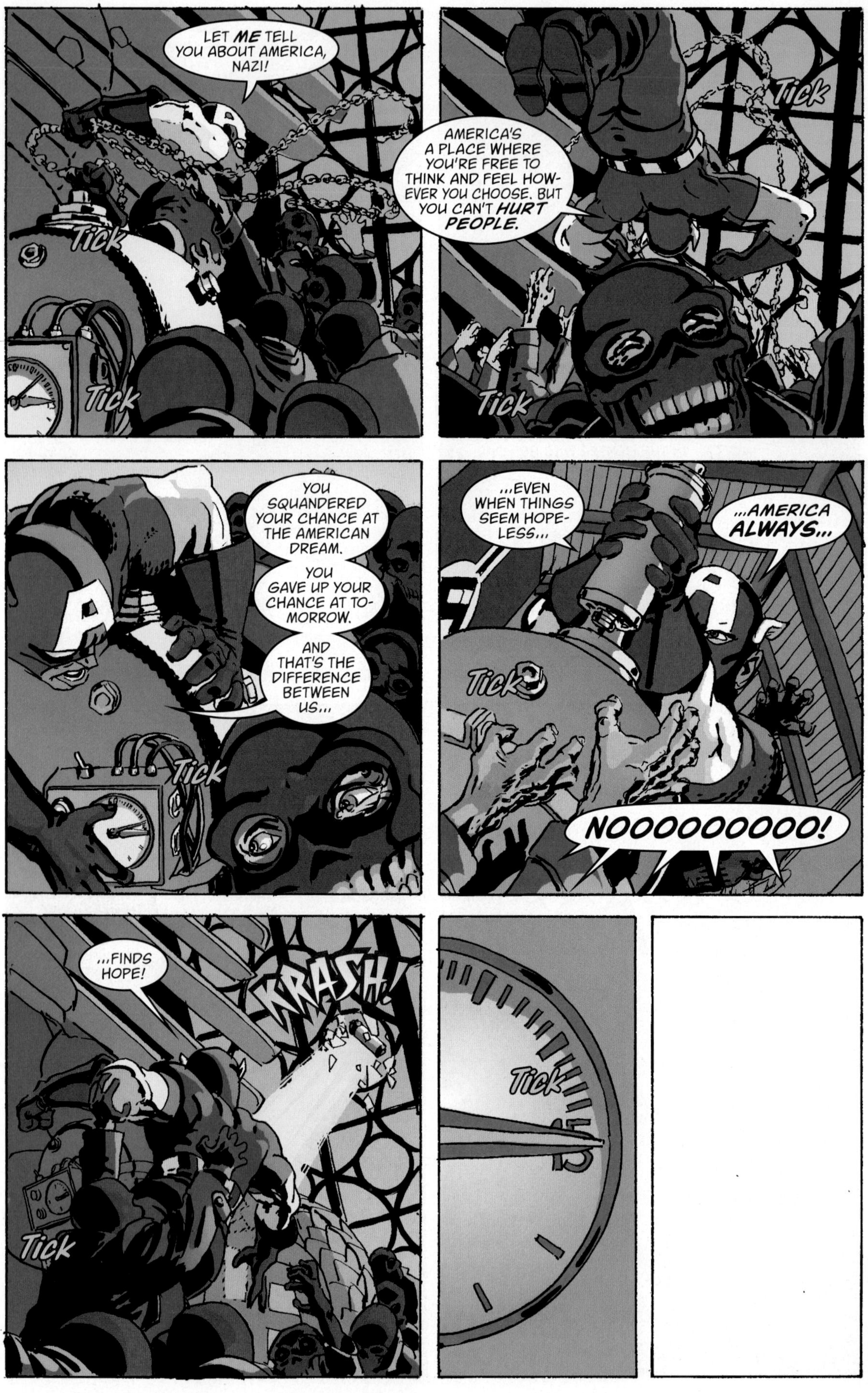
LET *ME* TELL YOU ABOUT AMERICA, NAZI!
Tick
Tick
Tick
AMERICA'S A PLACE WHERE YOU'RE FREE TO THINK AND FEEL HOW-EVER YOU CHOOSE. BUT YOU CAN'T ***HURT PEOPLE.***
Tick
YOU SQUANDERED YOUR CHANCE AT THE AMERICAN DREAM.
YOU GAVE UP YOUR CHANCE AT TO-MORROW.
AND THAT'S THE DIFFERENCE BETWEEN US...
Tick
...EVEN WHEN THINGS SEEM HOPE-LESS...
...AMERICA ***ALWAYS...***
Tick
NOOOOOOOOO!
...FINDS HOPE!
KRASH!
Tick
Tick
15

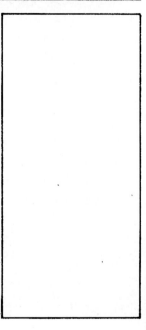

...NO SIR. ONLY THE BIKE... BUT THAT'S NOT SURPRISING IF HE WAS AT THE CENTER OF THE EXPLOSION. ANY IDEA YET ON WHAT HAP-PENED?

WHAT IN THE NAME OF SAM HILL DO YOU THINK? A GREAT MAN SAVED OUR HASH ONE MORE TIME.

TELL ME AGAIN, SON...

...ONLY THE BIKE? WHAT ABOUT THE SHIELD? DID YOU FIND THE SHIELD?

NO SIR, WE'RE STILL LOOKING--

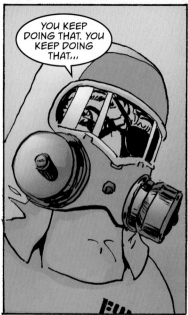

YOU KEEP DOING THAT. YOU KEEP DOING THAT...

ONE MORE TIME, OLD FRIEND...

...ONE MORE TIME.

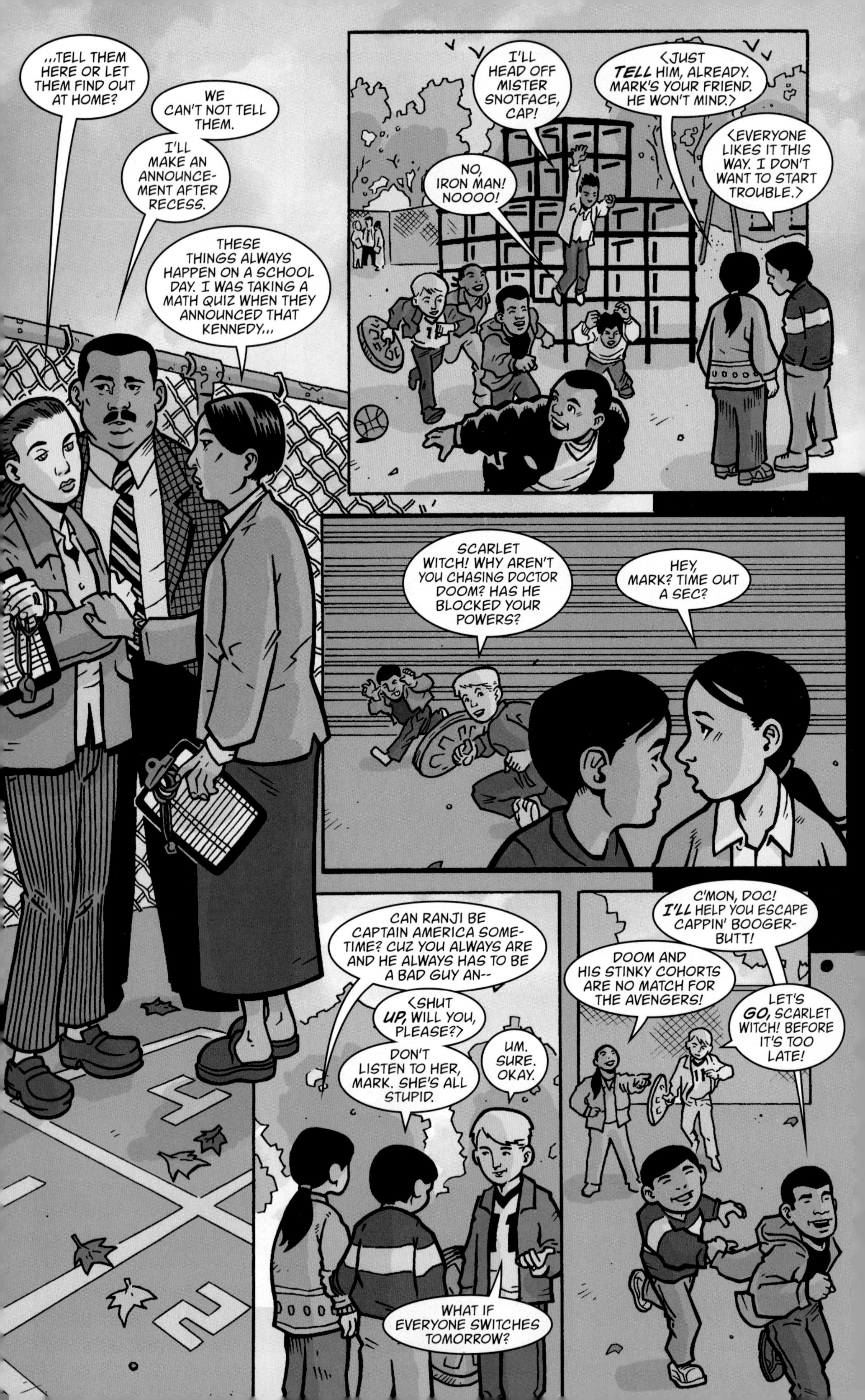
...TELL THEM HERE OR LET THEM FIND OUT AT HOME?
WE CAN'T NOT TELL THEM.
I'LL MAKE AN ANNOUNCEMENT AFTER RECESS.
THESE THINGS ALWAYS HAPPEN ON A SCHOOL DAY. I WAS TAKING A MATH QUIZ WHEN THEY ANNOUNCED THAT KENNEDY...
I'LL HEAD OFF MISTER SNOTFACE, CAP!
NO, IRON MAN! NOOOO!
<JUST **TELL** HIM, ALREADY. MARK'S YOUR FRIEND. HE WON'T MIND.>
<EVERYONE LIKES IT THIS WAY. I DON'T WANT TO START TROUBLE.>
SCARLET WITCH! WHY AREN'T YOU CHASING DOCTOR DOOM? HAS HE BLOCKED YOUR POWERS?
HEY, MARK? TIME OUT A SEC?
CAN RANJI BE CAPTAIN AMERICA SOMETIME? CUZ YOU ALWAYS ARE AND HE ALWAYS HAS TO BE A BAD GUY AN--
<SHUT **UP,** WILL YOU, PLEASE?>
DON'T LISTEN TO HER, MARK. SHE'S ALL STUPID.
UM. SURE. OKAY.
WHAT IF EVERYONE SWITCHES TOMORROW?
C'MON, DOC! **I'LL** HELP YOU ESCAPE CAPPIN' BOOGER-BUTT!
DOOM AND HIS STINKY COHORTS ARE NO MATCH FOR THE AVENGERS!
LET'S **GO,** SCARLET WITCH! BEFORE IT'S TOO LATE!

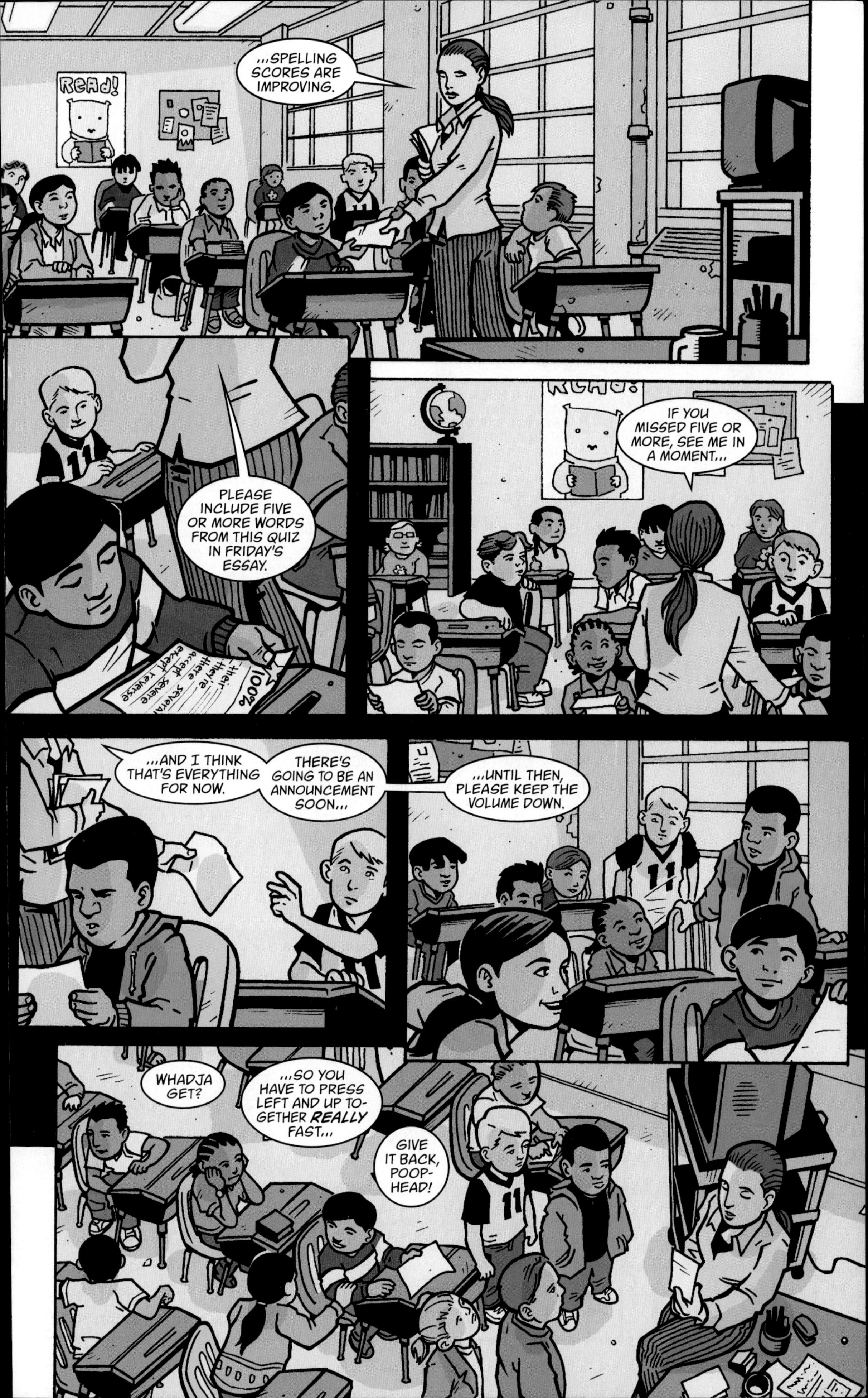
READ!
...SPELLING SCORES ARE IMPROVING.
PLEASE INCLUDE FIVE OR MORE WORDS FROM THIS QUIZ IN FRIDAY'S ESSAY.
IF YOU MISSED FIVE OR MORE, SEE ME IN A MOMENT...
...AND I THINK THAT'S EVERYTHING FOR NOW.
THERE'S GOING TO BE AN ANNOUNCEMENT SOON...
...UNTIL THEN, PLEASE KEEP THE VOLUME DOWN.
WHADJA GET?
...SO YOU HAVE TO PRESS LEFT AND UP TOGETHER REALLY FAST...
GIVE IT BACK, POOP-HEAD!

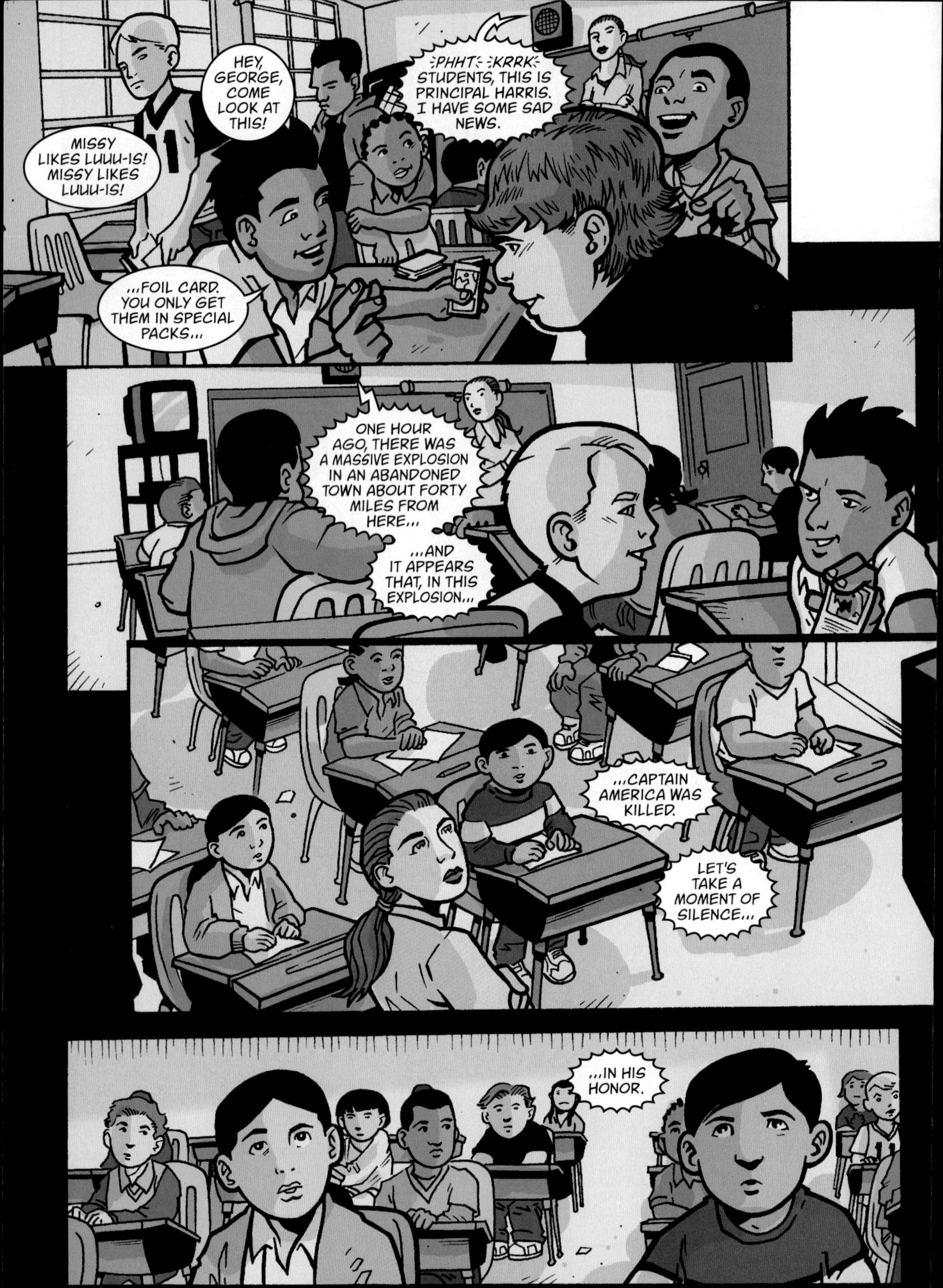
MISSY LIKES LUUU-IS! MISSY LIKES LUUU-IS!
HEY, GEORGE, COME LOOK AT THIS!
PHHT KRRK STUDENTS, THIS IS PRINCIPAL HARRIS. I HAVE SOME SAD NEWS.
...FOIL CARD. YOU ONLY GET THEM IN SPECIAL PACKS...
ONE HOUR AGO, THERE WAS A MASSIVE EXPLOSION IN AN ABANDONED TOWN ABOUT FORTY MILES FROM HERE...
...AND IT APPEARS THAT, IN THIS EXPLOSION...
...CAPTAIN AMERICA WAS KILLED.
LET'S TAKE A MOMENT OF SILENCE...
...IN HIS HONOR.

A MOMENT OF SILENCE

JEN VAN METER writer
BRIAN HURTT pencils
JIM MAHFOOD inks
AVALON STUDIOS colors
TODD KLEIN letters

ANDREW LIS editor
JOE QUESADA editor in chief
BILL JEMAS president

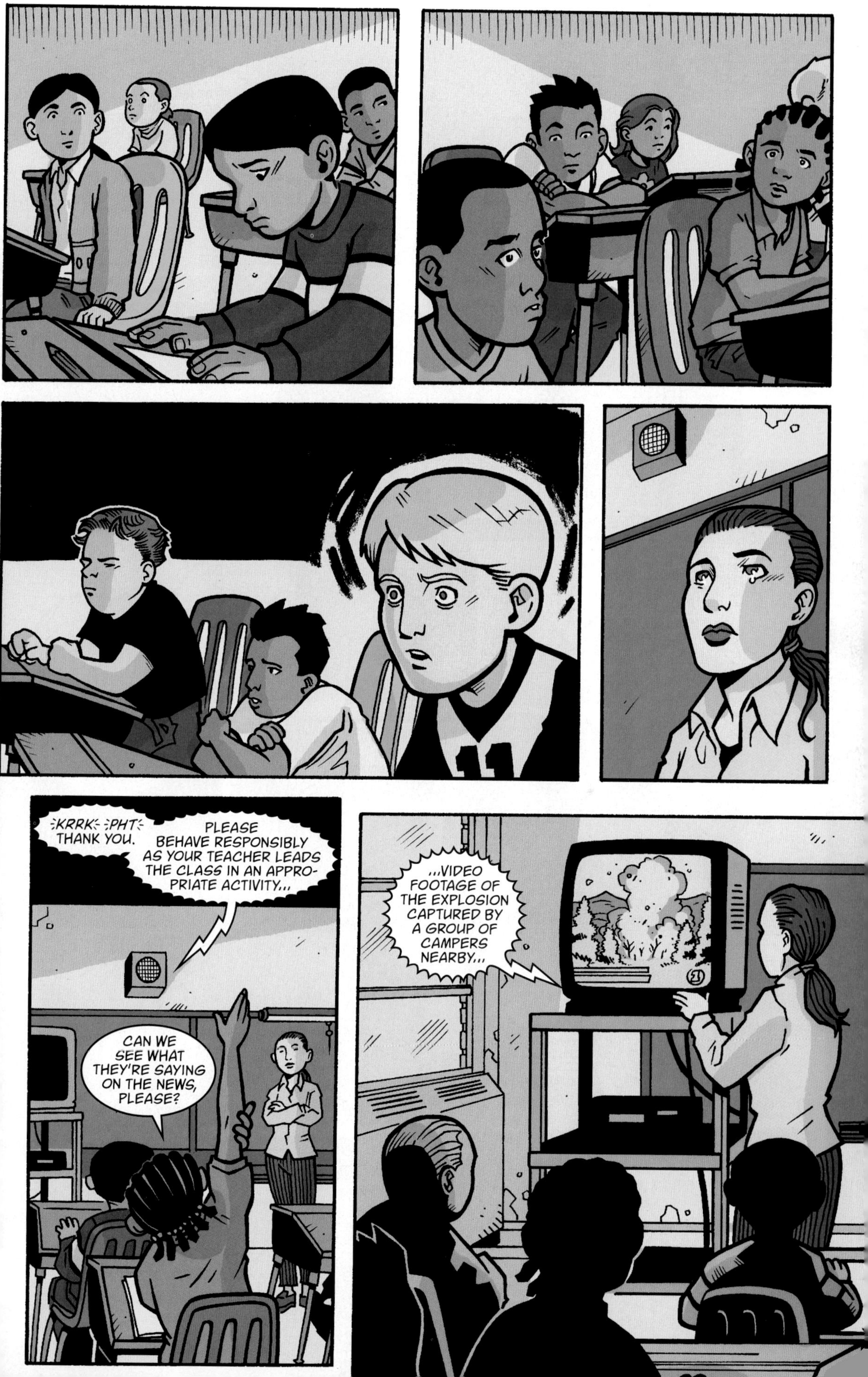

KRRK PHT THANK YOU.
PLEASE BEHAVE RESPONSIBLY AS YOUR TEACHER LEADS THE CLASS IN AN APPROPRIATE ACTIVITY...
CAN WE SEE WHAT THEY'RE SAYING ON THE NEWS, PLEASE?
...VIDEO FOOTAGE OF THE EXPLOSION CAPTURED BY A GROUP OF CAMPERS NEARBY...

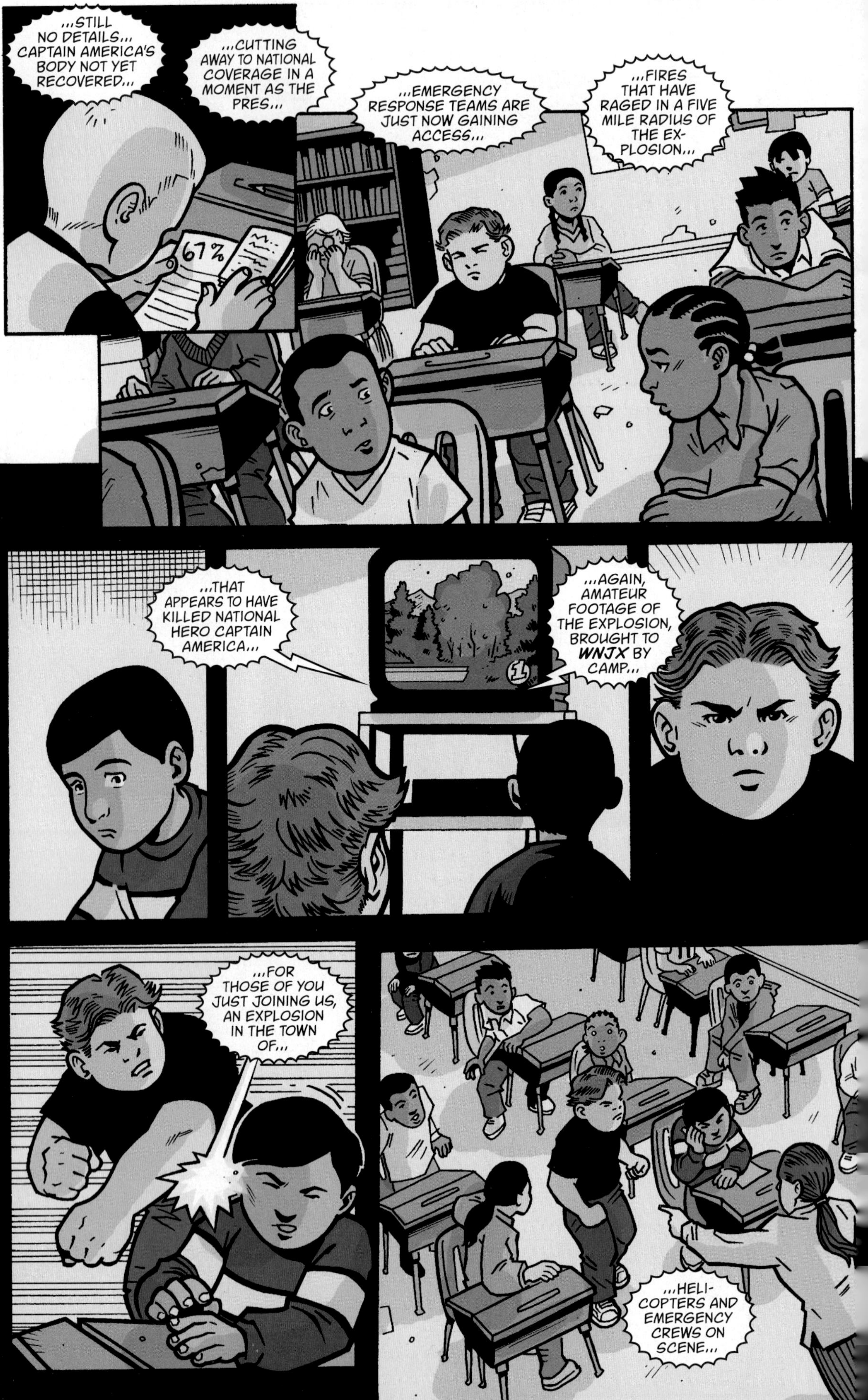
...STILL NO DETAILS... CAPTAIN AMERICA'S BODY NOT YET RECOVERED...
...CUTTING AWAY TO NATIONAL COVERAGE IN A MOMENT AS THE PRES...
67%
...EMERGENCY RESPONSE TEAMS ARE JUST NOW GAINING ACCESS...
...FIRES THAT HAVE RAGED IN A FIVE MILE RADIUS OF THE EX-PLOSION...
...THAT APPEARS TO HAVE KILLED NATIONAL HERO CAPTAIN AMERICA...
...AGAIN, AMATEUR FOOTAGE OF THE EXPLOSION, BROUGHT TO *WNJX* BY CAMP...
...FOR THOSE OF YOU JUST JOINING US, AN EXPLOSION IN THE TOWN OF...
...HELI-COPTERS AND EMERGENCY CREWS ON SCENE...

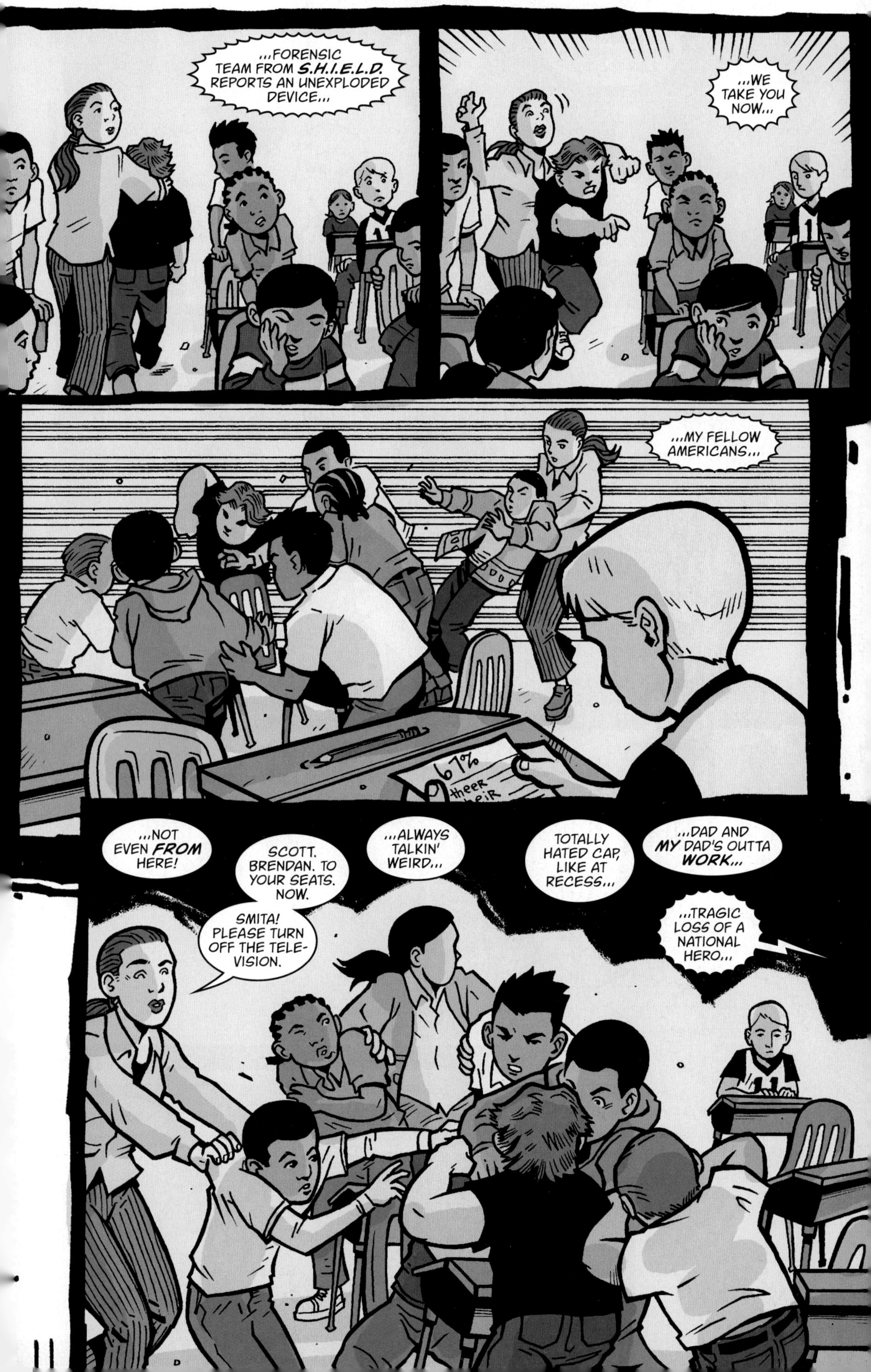
...FORENSIC TEAM FROM S.H.I.E.L.D. REPORTS AN UNEXPLODED DEVICE...
...WE TAKE YOU NOW...
...MY FELLOW AMERICANS...
67%
...NOT EVEN FROM HERE!
SCOTT. BRENDAN. TO YOUR SEATS. NOW.
SMITA! PLEASE TURN OFF THE TELE-VISION.
...ALWAYS TALKIN' WEIRD...
TOTALLY HATED CAP, LIKE AT RECESS...
...DAD AND MY DAD'S OUTTA WORK...
...TRAGIC LOSS OF A NATIONAL HERO...

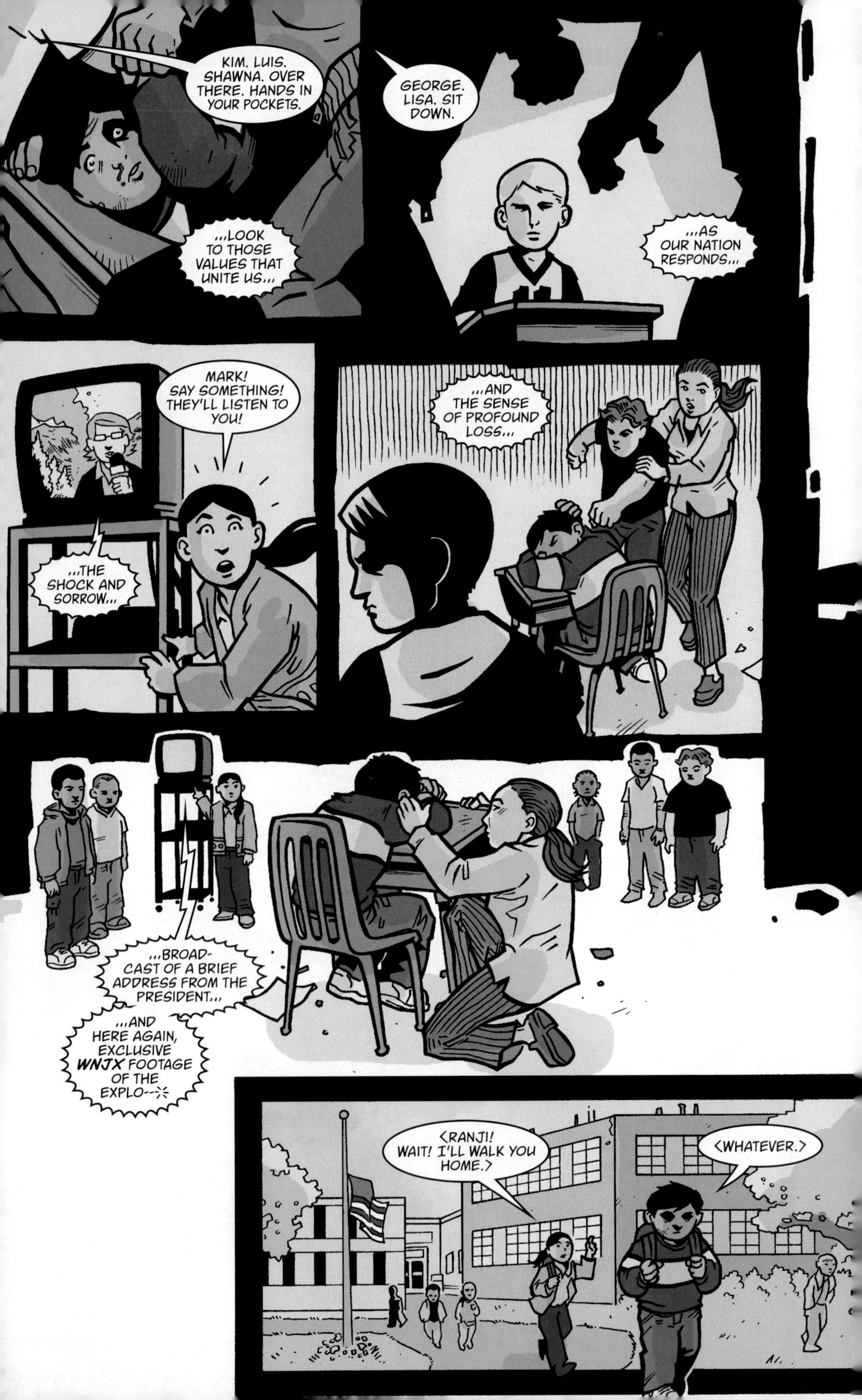
KIM. LUIS. SHAWNA. OVER THERE. HANDS IN YOUR POCKETS.
...LOOK TO THOSE VALUES THAT UNITE US...
GEORGE. LISA. SIT DOWN.
...AS OUR NATION RESPONDS...
MARK! SAY SOMETHING! THEY'LL LISTEN TO YOU!
...THE SHOCK AND SORROW...
...AND THE SENSE OF PROFOUND LOSS...
...BROAD-CAST OF A BRIEF ADDRESS FROM THE PRESIDENT...
...AND HERE AGAIN, EXCLUSIVE WNJX FOOTAGE OF THE EXPLO--
<RANJI! WAIT! I'LL WALK YOU HOME.>
<WHATEVER.>

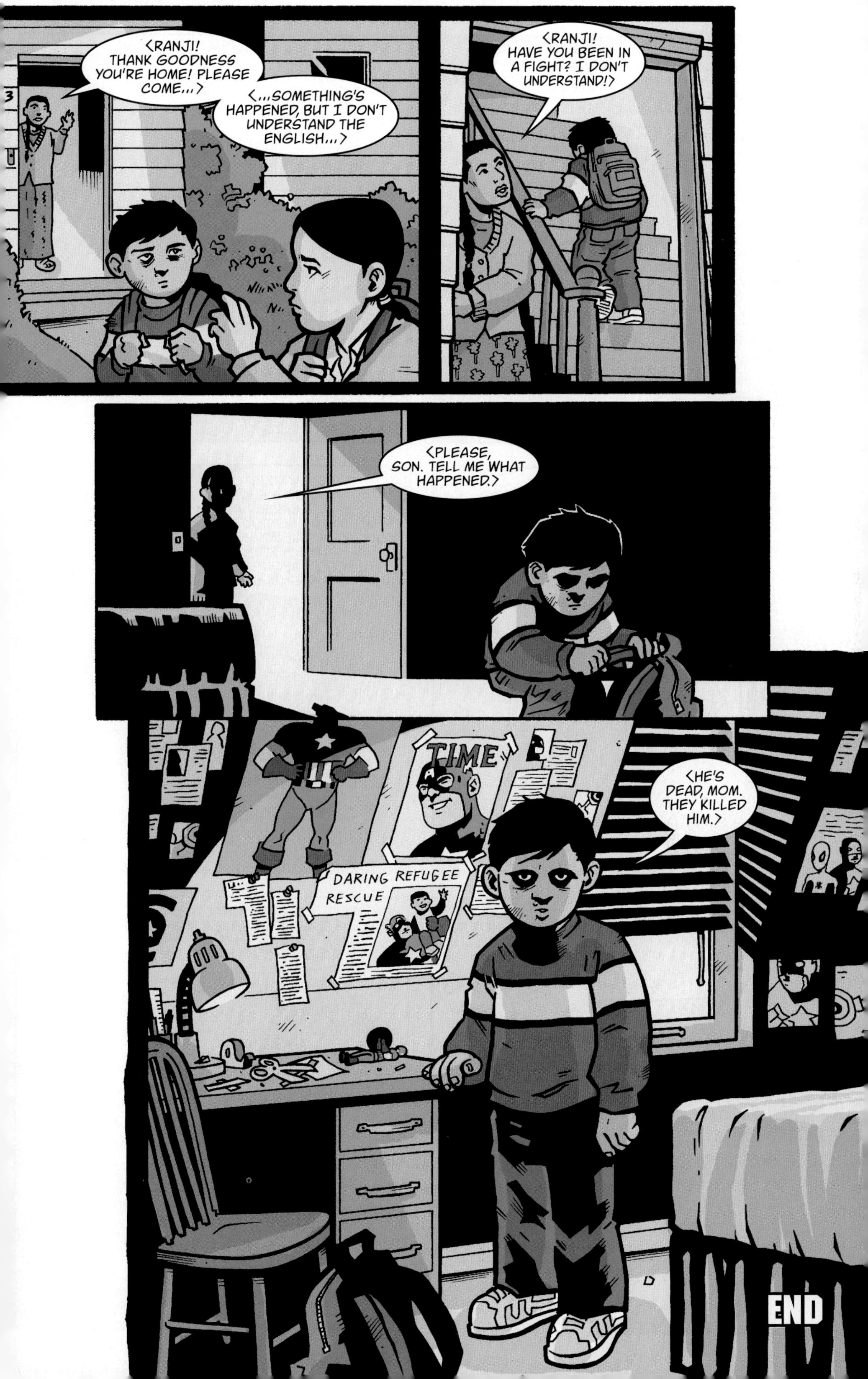

<RANJI! THANK GOODNESS YOU'RE HOME! PLEASE COME...>
<...SOMETHING'S HAPPENED, BUT I DON'T UNDERSTAND THE ENGLISH...>
<RANJI! HAVE YOU BEEN IN A FIGHT? I DON'T UNDERSTAND!>
<PLEASE, SON. TELL ME WHAT HAPPENED.>
TIME
DARING REFUGEE RESCUE
<HE'S DEAD, MOM. THEY KILLED HIM.>
END

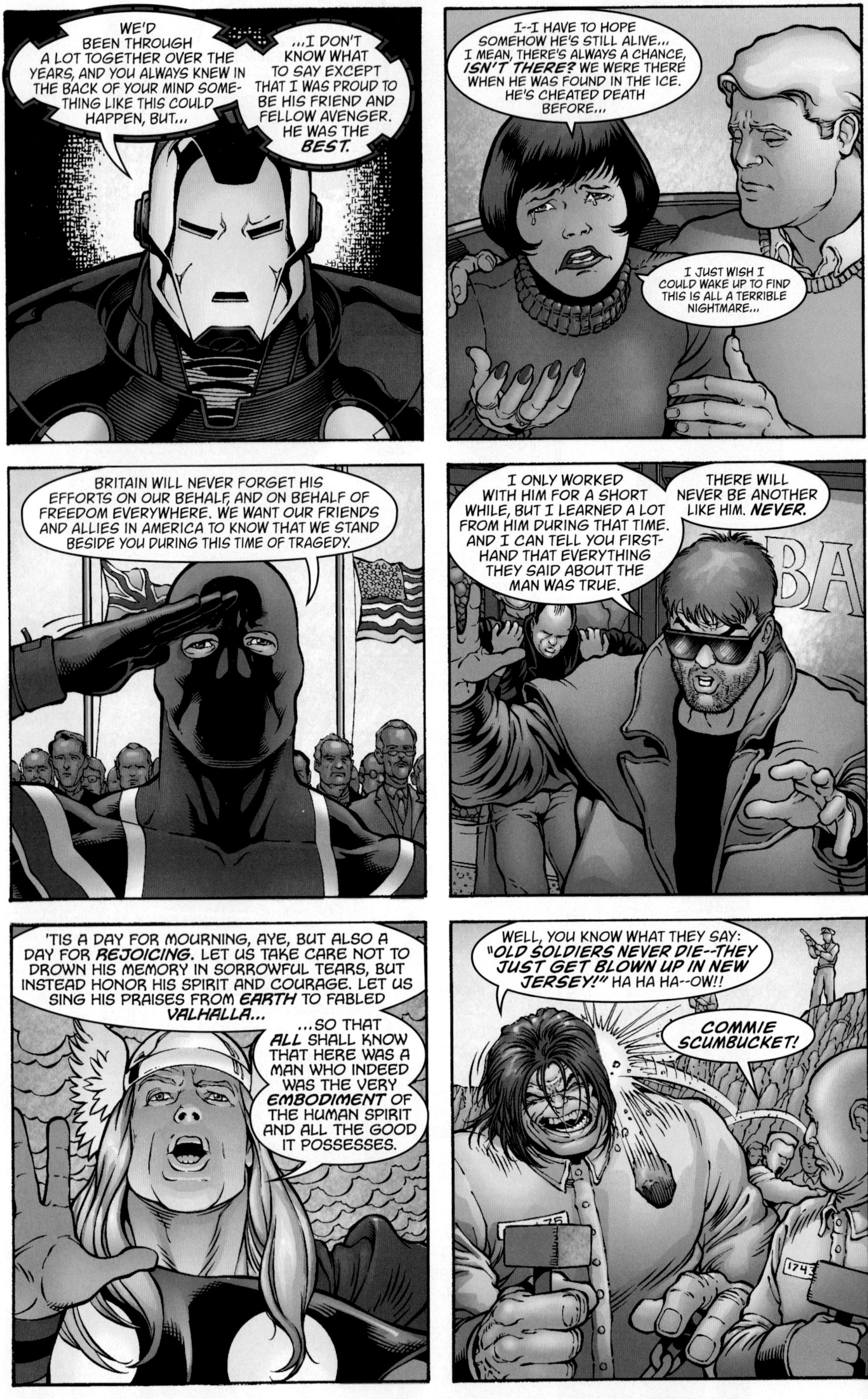
WE'D BEEN THROUGH A LOT TOGETHER OVER THE YEARS, AND YOU ALWAYS KNEW IN THE BACK OF YOUR MIND SOME-THING LIKE THIS COULD HAPPEN, BUT...
...I DON'T KNOW WHAT TO SAY EXCEPT THAT I WAS PROUD TO BE HIS FRIEND AND FELLOW AVENGER. HE WAS THE BEST.
I--I HAVE TO HOPE SOMEHOW HE'S STILL ALIVE... I MEAN, THERE'S ALWAYS A CHANCE, ISN'T THERE? WE WERE THERE WHEN HE WAS FOUND IN THE ICE. HE'S CHEATED DEATH BEFORE...
I JUST WISH I COULD WAKE UP TO FIND THIS IS ALL A TERRIBLE NIGHTMARE...
BRITAIN WILL NEVER FORGET HIS EFFORTS ON OUR BEHALF, AND ON BEHALF OF FREEDOM EVERYWHERE. WE WANT OUR FRIENDS AND ALLIES IN AMERICA TO KNOW THAT WE STAND BESIDE YOU DURING THIS TIME OF TRAGEDY.
I ONLY WORKED WITH HIM FOR A SHORT WHILE, BUT I LEARNED A LOT FROM HIM DURING THAT TIME. AND I CAN TELL YOU FIRST-HAND THAT EVERYTHING THEY SAID ABOUT THE MAN WAS TRUE.
THERE WILL NEVER BE ANOTHER LIKE HIM. NEVER.
'TIS A DAY FOR MOURNING, AYE, BUT ALSO A DAY FOR REJOICING. LET US TAKE CARE NOT TO DROWN HIS MEMORY IN SORROWFUL TEARS, BUT INSTEAD HONOR HIS SPIRIT AND COURAGE. LET US SING HIS PRAISES FROM EARTH TO FABLED VALHALLA...
...SO THAT ALL SHALL KNOW THAT HERE WAS A MAN WHO INDEED WAS THE VERY EMBODIMENT OF THE HUMAN SPIRIT AND ALL THE GOOD IT POSSESSES.
WELL, YOU KNOW WHAT THEY SAY: "OLD SOLDIERS NEVER DIE--THEY JUST GET BLOWN UP IN NEW JERSEY!" HA HA HA--OW!!
COMMIE SCUMBUCKET!

OF ALL THE SURFACE DWELLERS, TRULY HE WAS THE MOST DESERVING OF MY RESPECT.

FARE THEE WELL, CAPTAIN. FARE THEE WELL.

AS *A.I.M.* HAS DESTROYED *CAPTAIN AMERICA*, SO TOO SHALL WE TOPPLE HIS LEADERS! *TAKE WARNING!* SOON *ALL* WHO OPPOSE US WILL SHARE THE FATE OF THE SO-CALLED "DEFENDER OF LIBERTY!"

WE ALL SERVED ALONGSIDE HIM...AND ALTHOUGH THIS IS A SAD DAY FOR OUR COUNTRY AND OUR ARMED FORCES, IT IS OUR DUTY TO TAKE THE FLAG FROM HIM AND KEEP IT FLYING HIGH.

WE OWE HIM-- AND OURSELVES-- NOTHING LESS.

WHILE I'VE BEEN A BENEFACTOR OF THE AVENGERS FOR QUITE SOME TIME NOW, I CAN'T SAY I REALLY GOT TO KNOW THE MAN BEYOND HIS REPU- TATION.

NEEDLESS TO SAY, THE AVENGERS WILL WORK THROUGH THIS TIME OF CRISIS, AS WILL WE ALL.

I DON'T SEE WHAT THE *BIG DEAL* IS. I MEAN, I THOUGHT THAT GUY DIED *YEARS* AGO!

ANYWAY, I LIKE THAT *MUTANT* GUY, *WOLVERINE.* Y'KNOW, THE DUDE WITH THE *CLAWS?* NOW *THAT* GUY'S COOL!

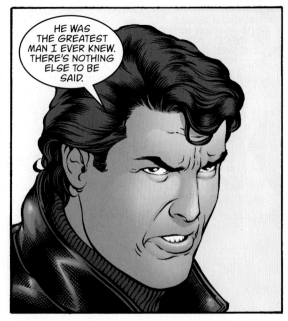

HE WAS THE GREATEST MAN I EVER KNEW. THERE'S NOTHING ELSE TO BE SAID.

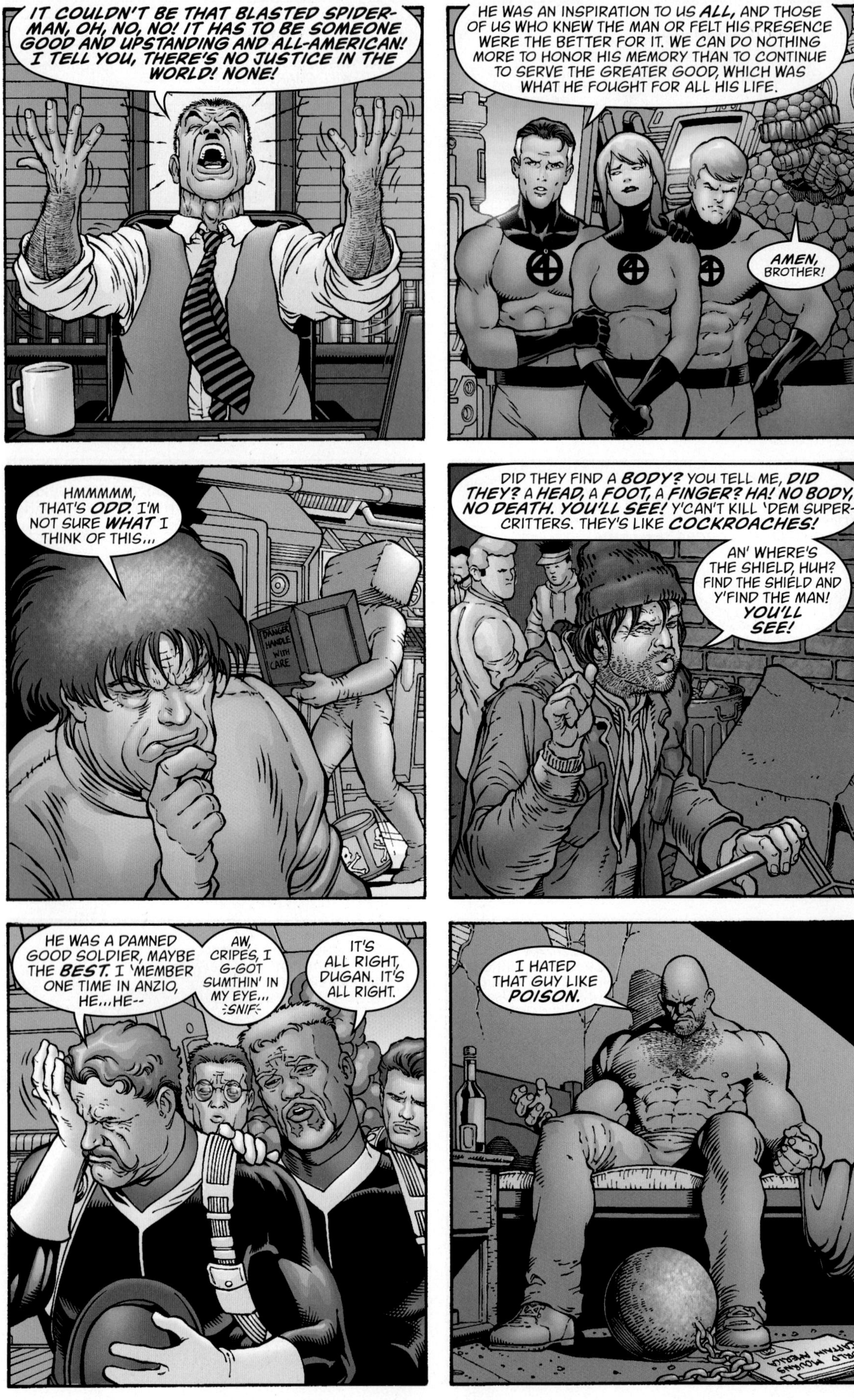
IT COULDN'T BE THAT BLASTED SPIDER-MAN, OH, NO, NO! IT HAS TO BE SOMEONE GOOD AND UPSTANDING AND ALL-AMERICAN! I TELL YOU, THERE'S NO JUSTICE IN THE WORLD! NONE!
HE WAS AN INSPIRATION TO US ALL, AND THOSE OF US WHO KNEW THE MAN OR FELT HIS PRESENCE WERE THE BETTER FOR IT. WE CAN DO NOTHING MORE TO HONOR HIS MEMORY THAN TO CONTINUE TO SERVE THE GREATER GOOD, WHICH WAS WHAT HE FOUGHT FOR ALL HIS LIFE.
AMEN, BROTHER!
HMMMMM, THAT'S ODD. I'M NOT SURE WHAT I THINK OF THIS...
DANGER HANDLE WITH CARE
DID THEY FIND A BODY? YOU TELL ME, DID THEY? A HEAD, A FOOT, A FINGER? HA! NO BODY, NO DEATH. YOU'LL SEE! Y'CAN'T KILL 'DEM SUPER-CRITTERS. THEY'S LIKE COCKROACHES!
AN' WHERE'S THE SHIELD, HUH? FIND THE SHIELD AND Y'FIND THE MAN! YOU'LL SEE!
HE WAS A DAMNED GOOD SOLDIER, MAYBE THE BEST. I 'MEMBER ONE TIME IN ANZIO, HE...HE--
AW, CRIPES, I G-GOT SUMTHIN' IN MY EYE... SNIF
IT'S ALL RIGHT, DUGAN. IT'S ALL RIGHT.
I HATED THAT GUY LIKE POISON.
WORLD MOURNS CAPTAIN AMERICA

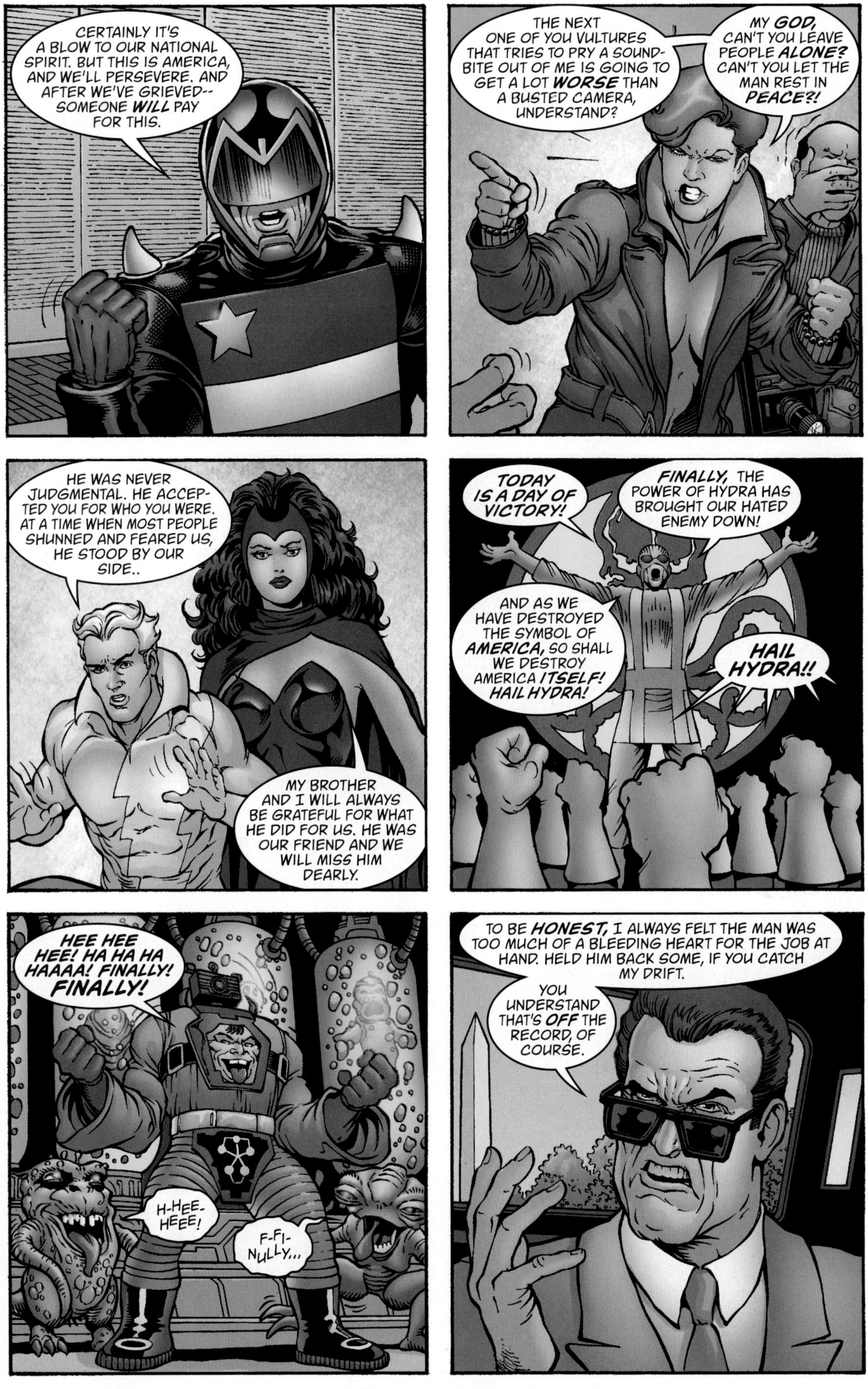
CERTAINLY IT'S A BLOW TO OUR NATIONAL SPIRIT. BUT THIS IS AMERICA, AND WE'LL PERSEVERE. AND AFTER WE'VE GRIEVED-- SOMEONE WILL PAY FOR THIS.
THE NEXT ONE OF YOU VULTURES THAT TRIES TO PRY A SOUND-BITE OUT OF ME IS GOING TO GET A LOT WORSE THAN A BUSTED CAMERA, UNDERSTAND?
MY GOD, CAN'T YOU LEAVE PEOPLE ALONE? CAN'T YOU LET THE MAN REST IN PEACE?!
HE WAS NEVER JUDGMENTAL. HE ACCEPTED YOU FOR WHO YOU WERE. AT A TIME WHEN MOST PEOPLE SHUNNED AND FEARED US, HE STOOD BY OUR SIDE..
MY BROTHER AND I WILL ALWAYS BE GRATEFUL FOR WHAT HE DID FOR US. HE WAS OUR FRIEND AND WE WILL MISS HIM DEARLY.
TODAY IS A DAY OF VICTORY!
FINALLY, THE POWER OF HYDRA HAS BROUGHT OUR HATED ENEMY DOWN!
AND AS WE HAVE DESTROYED THE SYMBOL OF AMERICA, SO SHALL WE DESTROY AMERICA ITSELF! HAIL HYDRA!
HAIL HYDRA!!
HEE HEE HEE! HA HA HA HAAAA! FINALLY! FINALLY!
H-HEE-HEEE!
F-FI-NULLY...
TO BE HONEST, I ALWAYS FELT THE MAN WAS TOO MUCH OF A BLEEDING HEART FOR THE JOB AT HAND. HELD HIM BACK SOME, IF YOU CATCH MY DRIFT.
YOU UNDERSTAND THAT'S OFF THE RECORD, OF COURSE.

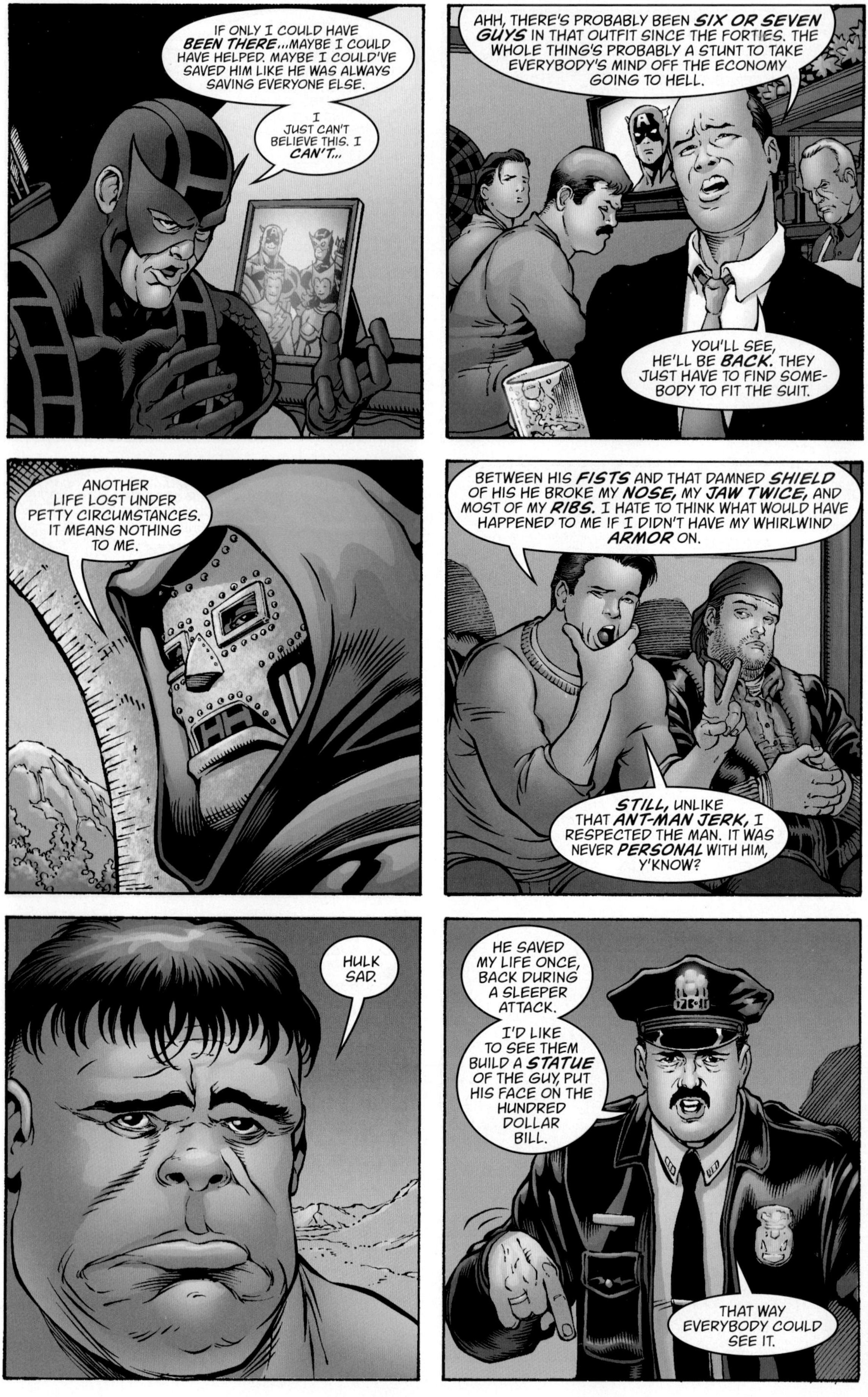
IF ONLY I COULD HAVE BEEN THERE... MAYBE I COULD HAVE HELPED. MAYBE I COULD'VE SAVED HIM LIKE HE WAS ALWAYS SAVING EVERYONE ELSE.
I JUST CAN'T BELIEVE THIS. I CAN'T...
AHH, THERE'S PROBABLY BEEN SIX OR SEVEN GUYS IN THAT OUTFIT SINCE THE FORTIES. THE WHOLE THING'S PROBABLY A STUNT TO TAKE EVERYBODY'S MIND OFF THE ECONOMY GOING TO HELL.
YOU'LL SEE, HE'LL BE BACK. THEY JUST HAVE TO FIND SOMEBODY TO FIT THE SUIT.
ANOTHER LIFE LOST UNDER PETTY CIRCUMSTANCES. IT MEANS NOTHING TO ME.
BETWEEN HIS FISTS AND THAT DAMNED SHIELD OF HIS HE BROKE MY NOSE, MY JAW TWICE, AND MOST OF MY RIBS. I HATE TO THINK WHAT WOULD HAVE HAPPENED TO ME IF I DIDN'T HAVE MY WHIRLWIND ARMOR ON.
STILL, UNLIKE THAT ANT-MAN JERK, I RESPECTED THE MAN. IT WAS NEVER PERSONAL WITH HIM, Y'KNOW?
HULK SAD.
HE SAVED MY LIFE ONCE, BACK DURING A SLEEPER ATTACK.
I'D LIKE TO SEE THEM BUILD A STATUE OF THE GUY, PUT HIS FACE ON THE HUNDRED DOLLAR BILL.
THAT WAY EVERYBODY COULD SEE IT.

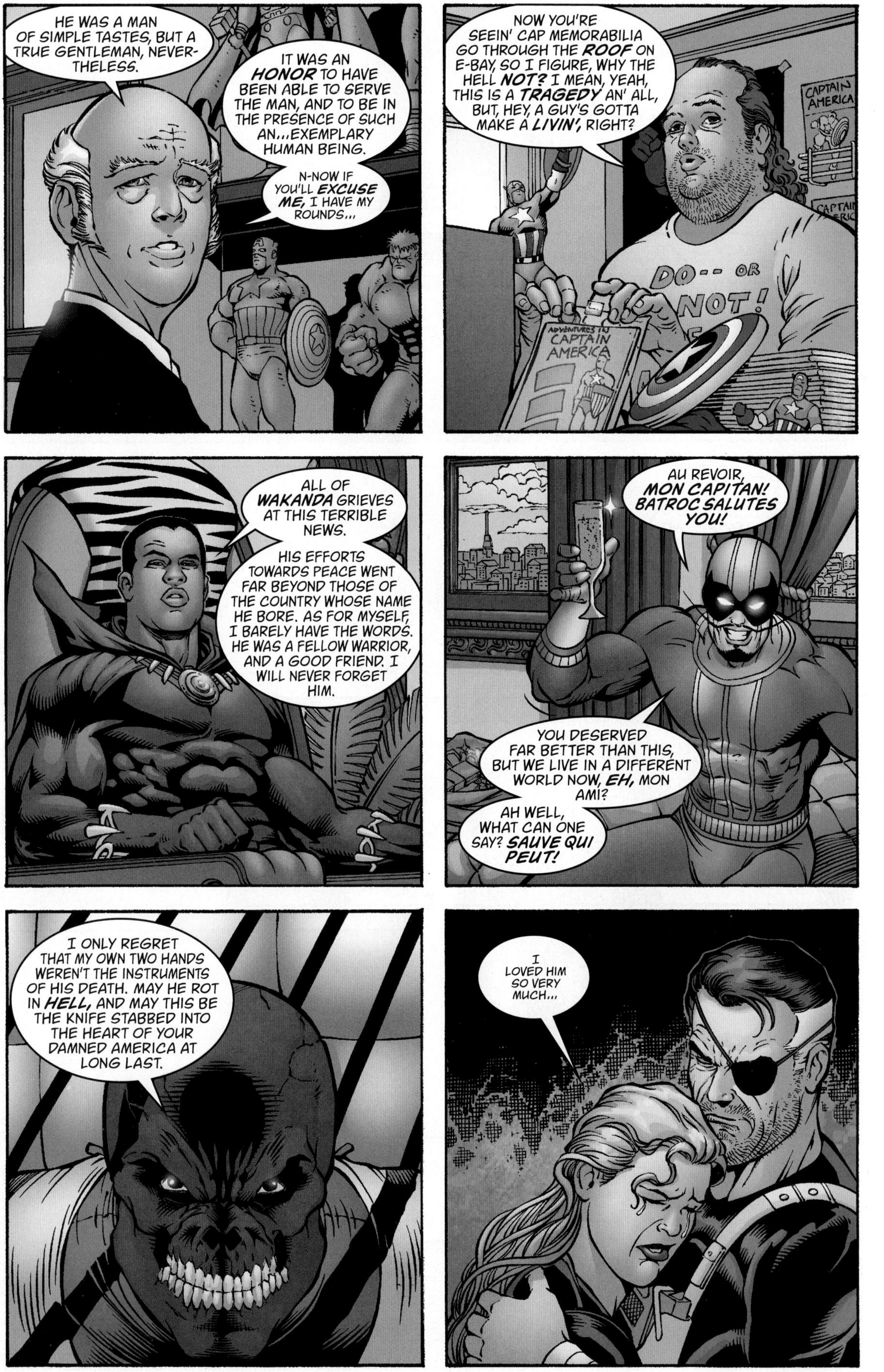
HE WAS A MAN OF SIMPLE TASTES, BUT A TRUE GENTLEMAN, NEVER-THELESS.
IT WAS AN HONOR TO HAVE BEEN ABLE TO SERVE THE MAN, AND TO BE IN THE PRESENCE OF SUCH AN...EXEMPLARY HUMAN BEING.
N-NOW IF YOU'LL EXCUSE ME, I HAVE MY ROUNDS...
NOW YOU'RE SEEIN' CAP MEMORABILIA GO THROUGH THE ROOF ON E-BAY, SO I FIGURE, WHY THE HELL NOT? I MEAN, YEAH, THIS IS A TRAGEDY AN' ALL, BUT, HEY, A GUY'S GOTTA MAKE A LIVIN', RIGHT?
CAPTAIN AMERICA
DO-- OR NOT!
ADVENTURES IN CAPTAIN AMERICA
ALL OF WAKANDA GRIEVES AT THIS TERRIBLE NEWS.
HIS EFFORTS TOWARDS PEACE WENT FAR BEYOND THOSE OF THE COUNTRY WHOSE NAME HE BORE. AS FOR MYSELF, I BARELY HAVE THE WORDS. HE WAS A FELLOW WARRIOR, AND A GOOD FRIEND. I WILL NEVER FORGET HIM.
AU REVOIR, MON CAPITAN! BATROC SALUTES YOU!
YOU DESERVED FAR BETTER THAN THIS, BUT WE LIVE IN A DIFFERENT WORLD NOW, EH, MON AMI?
AH WELL, WHAT CAN ONE SAY? SAUVE QUI PEUT!
I ONLY REGRET THAT MY OWN TWO HANDS WEREN'T THE INSTRUMENTS OF HIS DEATH. MAY HE ROT IN HELL, AND MAY THIS BE THE KNIFE STABBED INTO THE HEART OF YOUR DAMNED AMERICA AT LONG LAST.
I LOVED HIM SO VERY MUCH...

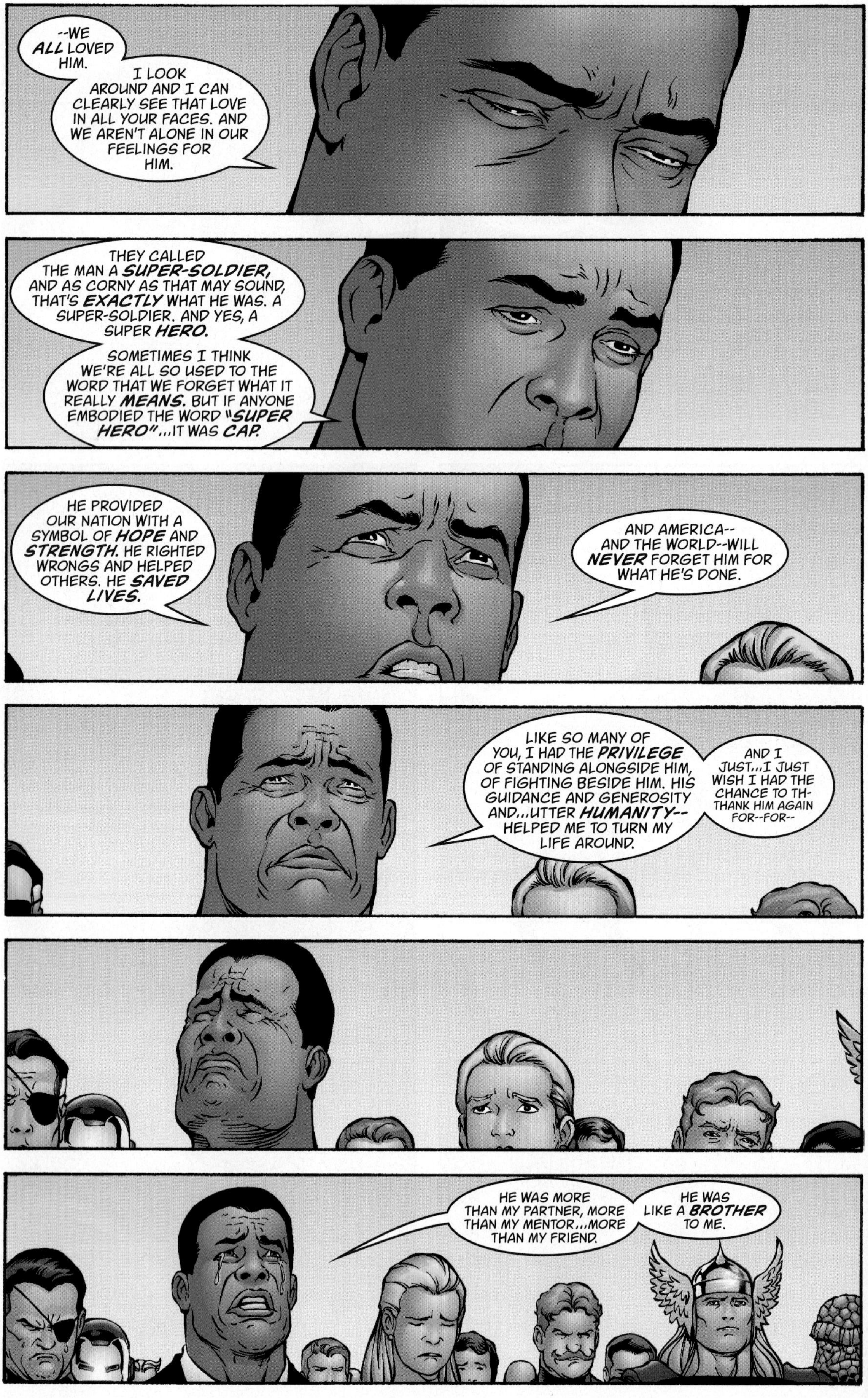
--WE ALL LOVED HIM.
I LOOK AROUND AND I CAN CLEARLY SEE THAT LOVE IN ALL YOUR FACES. AND WE AREN'T ALONE IN OUR FEELINGS FOR HIM.
THEY CALLED THE MAN A SUPER-SOLDIER, AND AS CORNY AS THAT MAY SOUND, THAT'S EXACTLY WHAT HE WAS. A SUPER-SOLDIER. AND YES, A SUPER HERO.
SOMETIMES I THINK WE'RE ALL SO USED TO THE WORD THAT WE FORGET WHAT IT REALLY MEANS. BUT IF ANYONE EMBODIED THE WORD "SUPER HERO"...IT WAS CAP.
HE PROVIDED OUR NATION WITH A SYMBOL OF HOPE AND STRENGTH. HE RIGHTED WRONGS AND HELPED OTHERS. HE SAVED LIVES.
AND AMERICA-- AND THE WORLD--WILL NEVER FORGET HIM FOR WHAT HE'S DONE.
LIKE SO MANY OF YOU, I HAD THE PRIVILEGE OF STANDING ALONGSIDE HIM, OF FIGHTING BESIDE HIM. HIS GUIDANCE AND GENEROSITY AND...UTTER HUMANITY-- HELPED ME TO TURN MY LIFE AROUND.
AND I JUST...I JUST WISH I HAD THE CHANCE TO TH-THANK HIM AGAIN FOR--FOR--
HE WAS MORE THAN MY PARTNER, MORE THAN MY MENTOR...MORE THAN MY FRIEND.
HE WAS LIKE A BROTHER TO ME.

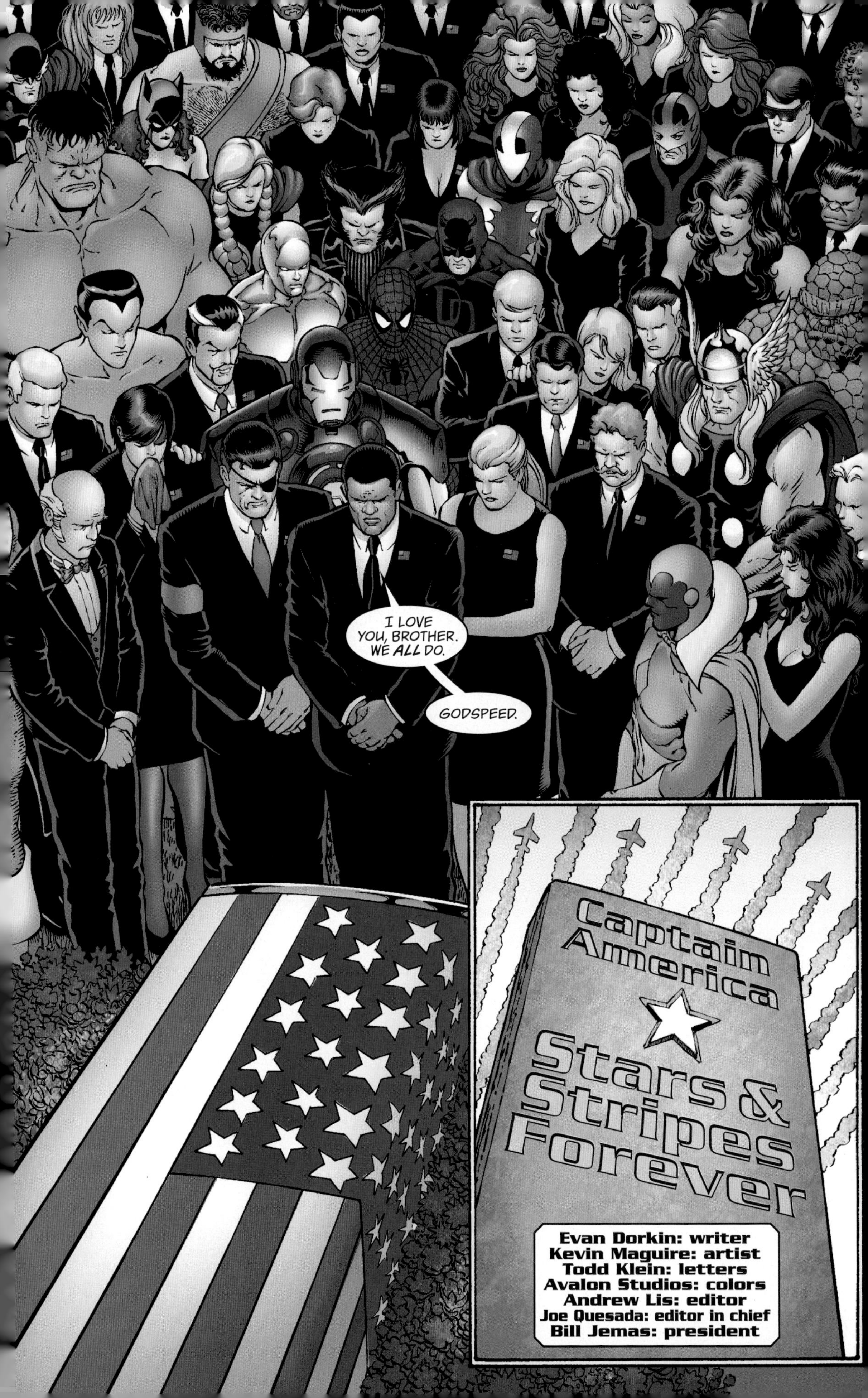
I LOVE YOU, BROTHER. WE ALL DO.
GODSPEED.
Captain America
Stars & Stripes Forever
Evan Dorkin: writer
Kevin Maguire: artist
Todd Klein: letters
Avalon Studios: colors
Andrew Lis: editor
Joe Quesada: editor in chief
Bill Jemas: president

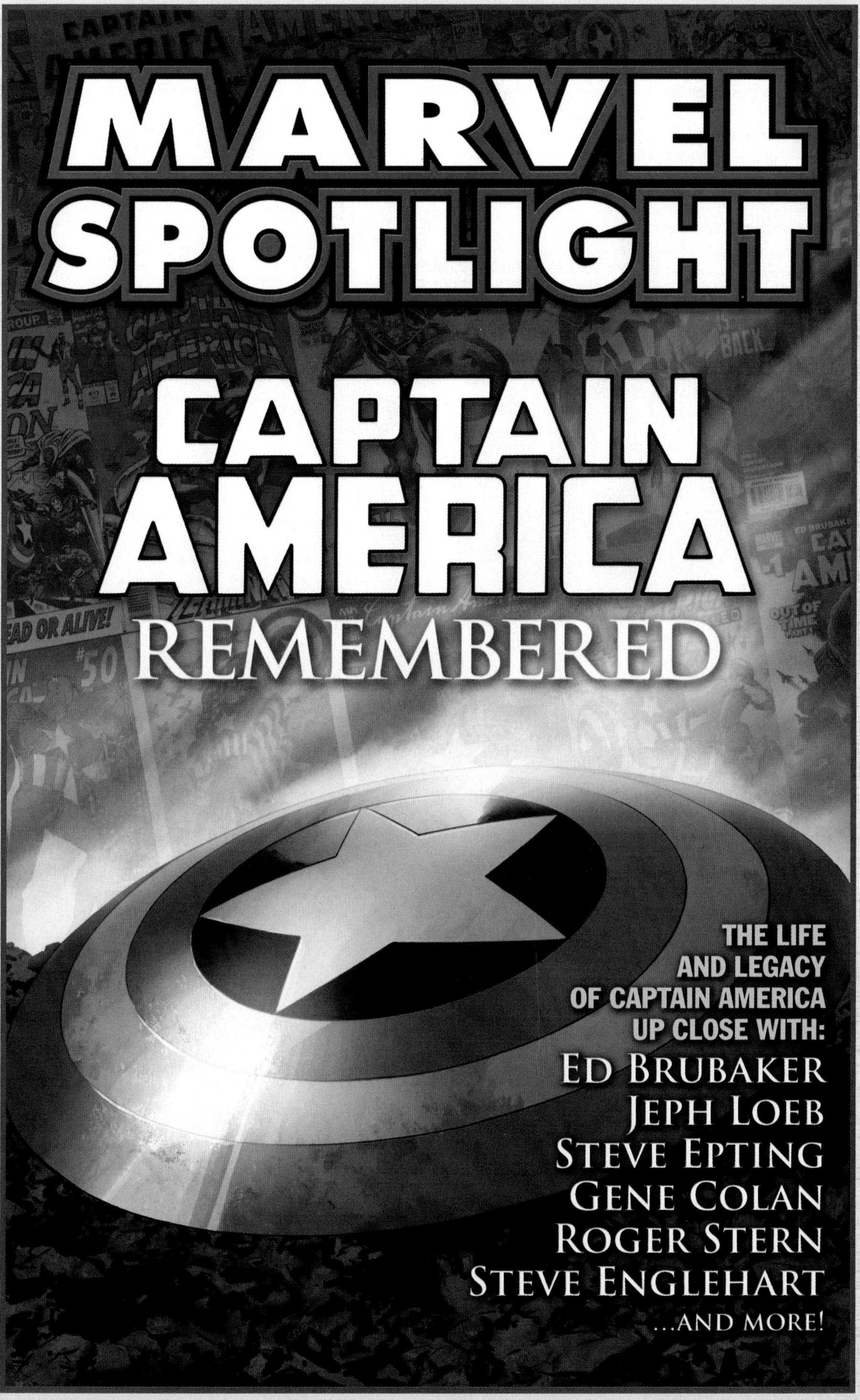
MARVEL SPOTLIGHT
CAPTAIN AMERICA
REMEMBERED
THE LIFE AND LEGACY OF CAPTAIN AMERICA UP CLOSE WITH:
ED BRUBAKER
JEPH LOEB
STEVE EPTING
GENE COLAN
ROGER STERN
STEVE ENGLEHART
...AND MORE!

PLUGGING IN THE SPOTLIGHT

Marvel Spotlight marks the solemn occasion of the death of Captain America with a special issue titled *Captain America Remembered*. There are too many highlights in Cap's 65-year career to cover in a single edition of *Spotlight*, but we've got some great coverage lined up in this issue with many of the top creators who have had a hand in telling some legendary, star-spangled tales!

I: The Front Page
An overview of Captain America through the decades!

II: The Man Who Killed Captain America
An instant classic, *Captain America #25* was the culmination of two years worth of definitive Cap stories by writer Ed Brubaker. Spotlight writer Dugan Trodglen's interview with Ed gets inside the Death of a Dream.

III: The Art of Captain America: Steve Epting
Ed's artistic partner, Steve sits with *Spotlight* to discuss the visual world he brings to life in the pages of *Captain America*!

IV: Bucky Lives, Winter Kills
Inside the modern classic *Winter Soldier: Winter Kills* one-shot by Ed Brubaker.

V: A Classic Cap Craftsman: Gene Colan
The Silver Age epoch of Captain America comics had some amazing talent behind the boards, but Gene Colan was one of the best! *Spotlight*'s John Rhett Thomas interviews Colan about his time drawing *Cap* and his approach to comic art, with some exclusive preview images of new Colan art for a yet to be published Cap story!!

VI: Cap In Crisis: Steve Englehart's Captain America
Spotlight writer Matt Adler caught up with iconic '70s writer Steve Englehart for his thoughts on writing Cap in the Me Decade…one of the most popular Cap runs ever!

VII: Remembering "Remembrance": Cap #247-255
Writer Roger Stern talks with *Spotlight*'s Dugan Trodglen about this classic run of comics best known as "War & Remembrance," a nine-issue run done in concert with legendary artist John Byrne.

VII: Death of a Dream: Jeph Loeb's Fallen Son
The Marvel Universe will never be the same after the death of Cap, and all-star writer Jeph Loeb talks with *Spotlight*'s Chris Arrant about *Fallen Son*, his new series of one-shots that carries the torch for Cap through the five stages of grief: Anger. Denial. Bargaining. Depression. And finally, acceptance.

CREDITS:

Head Writer/Coordinator:
John Rhett Thomas
Spotlight Bullpen Writers:
Matt Adler, Chris Arrant &
Dugan Trodglen
Editor: Jeff Youngquist
Associate Editors:
Jennifer Grünwald &
Mark D. Beazley
Assistant Editors:
Cory Levine & Michael Short
Vice President of Sales:
David Gabriel
Layout: BLAMMO! Content
& Design, Rommel & Regina
Alama and Jeff Walton
Editor in Chief: Joe Quesada
Publisher: Dan Buckley

Special thanks to Tom Brevoort,
Cory Sedlmeier, Doug Roberts
& David Postle

SPOTLIGHT ON CAPTAIN AMERICA

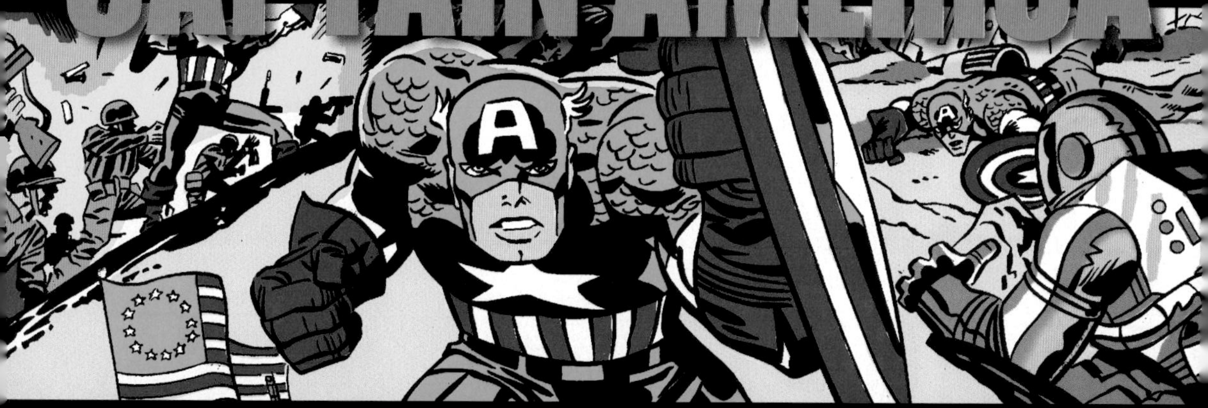

From the days when Cap was laying a hay maker on Hitler's jaw, to today, when the soldier has made his ultimate sacrifice, what Marvel fans are left with is a 65 year legacy of high adventure and super-heroics...Cap style! This overview of Cap's career in comics covers the origins of the Golden Age, the aborted Atlas Era revival, the triumphant return in Marvel's Silver Age, and on through the decades to today's pinnacle achievements by guys named Brubaker, Epting and Perkins!

COLLECT 'EM IN TRADE:

1940s-1950s:

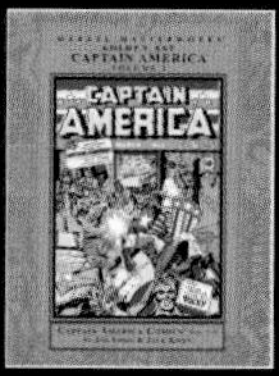
CAPTAIN AMERICA

GOLDEN AGE CAPTAIN AMERICA MASTERWORKS VOL. 1

GOLDEN AGE ALL-WINNERS MASTERWORKS VOL. 1-2

It was a time when America needed heroes – and Joe Simon and Jack Kirby delivered one! In the pages of these classic Masterworks, witness the birth of the Sentinel of Liberty, Captain America, as Marvel restores and reprints these priceless comics in deluxe hardcover editions!

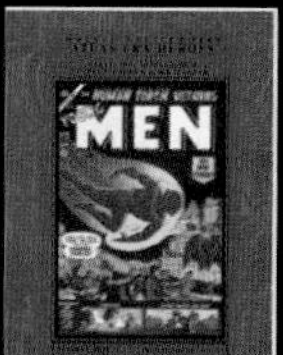
MEN

ATLAS ERA HEROES MASTERWORKS VOL. 1

In the mid-'50s, Stan Lee's Atlas line reintroduced the Timely era of heroes, including Human Torch, Sub-Mariner and Captain America. This time around, the identities of their foes had shifted from ruthless Nazis to Communist fifth columnists. Featuring some of the earliest work by John Romita, Sr., these are Cold War comic cult classics!

1960s:

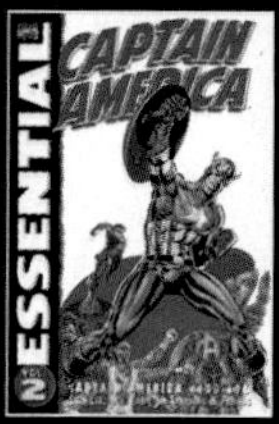
CAPTAIN AMERICA
ESSENTIAL

CAPTAIN AMERICA MASTERWORKS VOL. 1-3

ESSENTIAL CAPTAIN AMERICA VOL. 1-3

The Marvel Age of Comics was already in high gear when Stan Lee and Jack Kirby relaunched Cap solo tales in the pages of *Tales of Suspense*. You can get acquainted with Marvel's Man out of Time through either full-color Masterworks or black and white Essentials which take you on a journey through the entire '60s: Stan, Jack, Steranko, Romita, Colan...they're all here!

1970s:

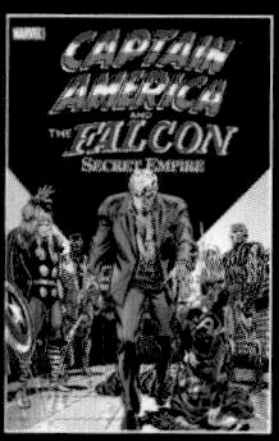
CAPTAIN AMERICA
AND THE FALCON
SECRET EMPIRE

SECRET EMPIRE TPB

NOMAD TPB

Two of Steve Englehart's most classic storylines available in full-color, classic trade paperbacks, featuring the coming of Nomad!

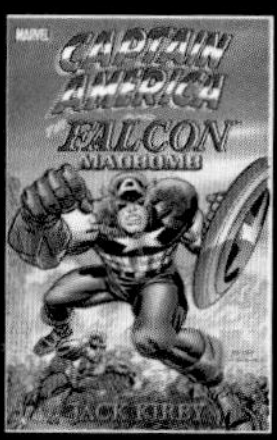
CAPTAIN AMERICA
AND THE FALCON
MADBOMB
JACK KIRBY

MADBOMB TPB

BICENTENNIAL BATTLES TPB

THE SWINE TPB

The return of the King! In the year of America's Bicentennial, Jack was back behind the drawing boards on the character he had created 35 years previously! These three color TPBs collect the entire run from *Cap #193-214*, plus *Annual #3-4* and the *Bicentennial Battles Treasury!*

1980s:

WAR & REMEMBRANCE TPB

Two words: Stern and Byrne! The legendary writer/artist team combine for a potent run that revives Cap's Invaders legacy!

1990s:

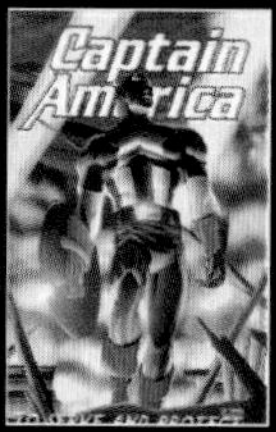
Captain America

HEROES REBORN: CAPTAIN AMERICA TPB

TO SERVE AND PROTECT TPB

Rob Liefeld's *Heroes Reborn* series sent Cap off to a pocket universe along with his Avengers teammates, and Mark Waid and Ron Garney's *Heroes Return* brought him back for a triumphant return! Both volumes are now in print and ready for your bookshelf!

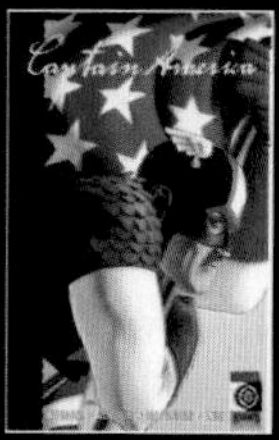
Captain America

THE NEW CENTURY:

VOL. 1: THE NEW DEAL

VOL. 2: THE EXTREMISTS

VOL. 3: ICE

VOL. 4: CAPTAIN AMERICA LIVES AGAIN

VOL. 5: HOMELAND

AVENGERS DISASSEMBLED: CAPTAIN AMERICA

Some of Marvel's top talents take on the Cap mythos in this complete reprinting in six volumes of "The New Deal" Cap, including John Cassaday, Robert Kirkman, Dave Gibbons, Trevor Hairsine and more!

BRUBAKER/EPTING/PERKINS:

The entire run of Ed Brubaker's Cap is now available in a range of TPBs and HCs, including:

Winter Soldier Vols. 1-2 HC/TPB

Red Menace Vols. 1-2 TPB

Civil War: Captain America TPB

Captain America by Ed Brubaker Omnibus Vol. 1 HC

the man who killed CAPTAIN AMERICA

Writer ED BRUBAKER, the man who brought life in a post-Disassembled world to the *Captain America* title, is also the man who has written the final chapter in the life of Steve Rogers.

By Dugan Trodglen

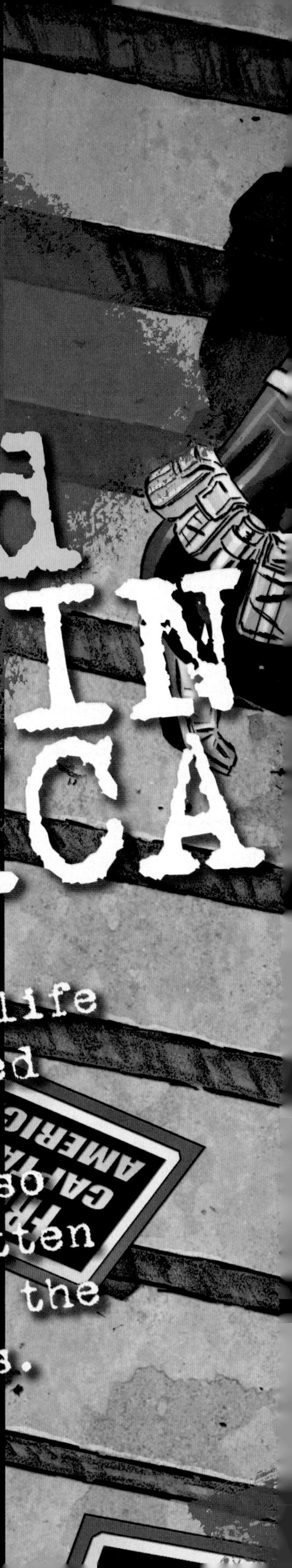

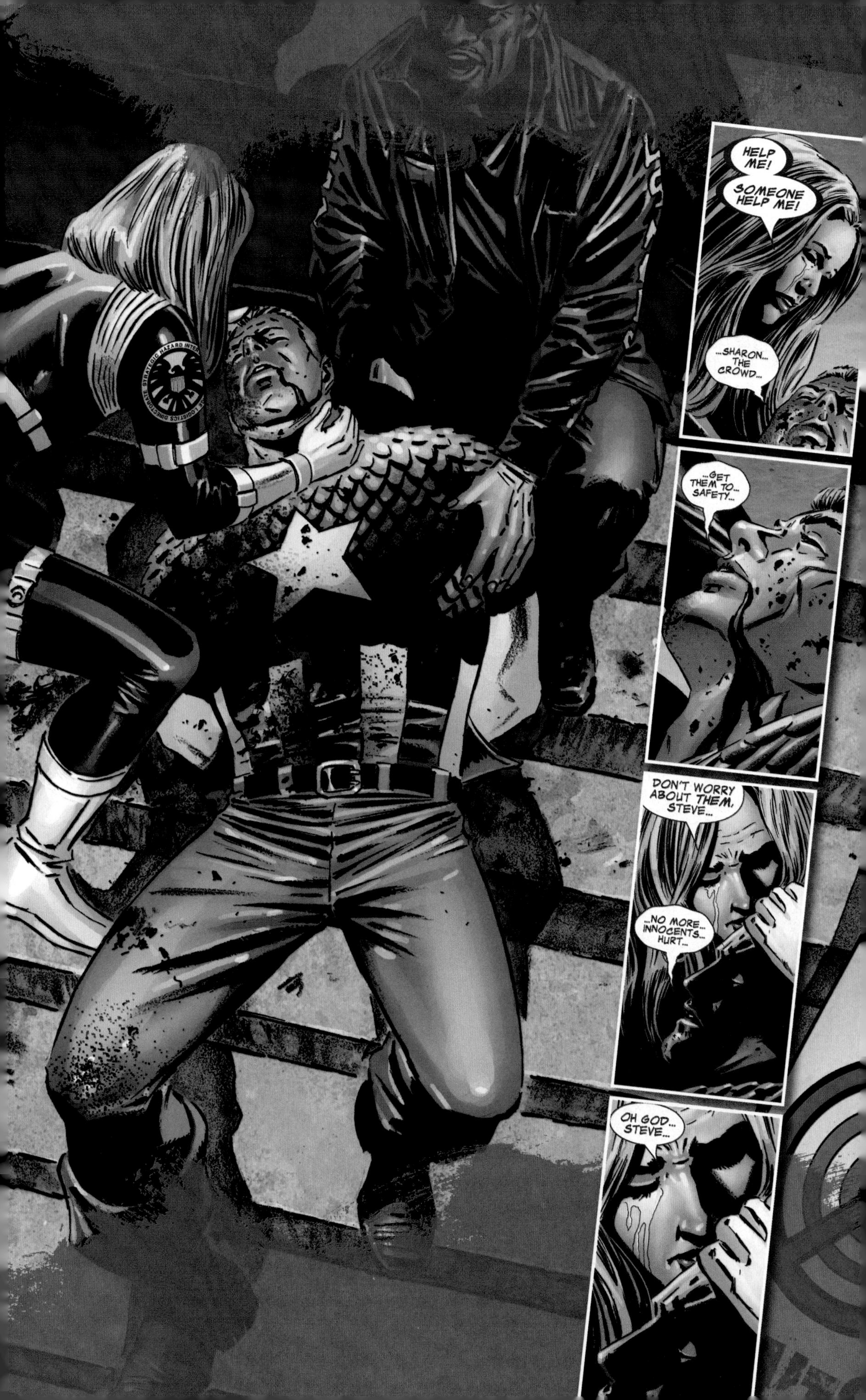
HELP ME!
SOMEONE HELP ME!
...SHARON... THE CROWD...
...GET THEM TO... SAFETY...
DON'T WORRY ABOUT THEM, STEVE...
...NO MORE... INNOCENTS... HURT...
OH GOD... STEVE...

When it was announced that the Avengers family of books (New Avengers, Cap, Iron Man) were getting revamped with new number one issues and A-list creative teams, the move that seemed like a perfect fit was Ed Brubaker being given the writing chores of Captain America. After displaying his skill at penning hard-boiled action in books like Batman, Gotham Central, and Sleeper, the newly Marvel-exclusive Brubaker seemed a great choice for a book that could lend itself to high adventure borne of espionage.

It turns out "great" may have been an underestimate.

Ed was only a few issues into his run before he was being declared one of the best Cap writers of all time. His run has been marked by breathtaking action, compelling plots, and emotionally stirring moments. Up until now, his defining achievement on the book was bringing back Cap's long-thought dead sidekick, Bucky. He turned that controversial move into something that even jaded old-timers had to admit was powerful storytelling. Well, that controversy is nothing compared to what Ed did to poor Steve Rogers in the pages of Captain America #25. That's right - he killed him! Marvel Spotlight talked to Ed about why he did it, the reaction from fans, and where on earth he can go from here.

SPOTLIGHT: Let's start with the attention Captain America's death received. This was the biggest story to come out of comics since the death of Superman. And with information moving at such an incredible volume and rate compared to ten-plus years ago, Cap's death arguably received even more attention than Superman's. As the writer of the story, what was your reaction to the mainstream media's coverage of the event, and the resulting sales?

ED: I was pretty overwhelmed by how much the media cared. I thought we'd get a couple of articles, and that we'd sell maybe a couple hundred thousand copies of the book at best. When the number of articles and news stories reached 700 the first day — that was kind of weird. Literally for two weeks after that, I don't think I did any work other than interviews with the media about Captain America. I was grateful when a weekend arrived, so I could get some work done. I did at least one interview a day for two weeks, and usually five or six.

SPOTLIGHT: Well, here's another one! (Laughter.) Going back editorially and creatively, how did the decision to kill Cap come about, including how it would dovetail with the Civil War event, and what was the reaction within Marvel?

ED: It's a really complicated story. It started in so many different ways that it's hard to pinpoint exactly when the idea came down. My memory of it is that I sort of floated it after we talked about a variety of things that could happen with Cap. I sort of said, "Why don't I do this; that'd be a big deal."

But early on, a few months before that, I was out at Marvel and Joe Quesada took me out to lunch. He was telling me about Civil War and the first broad strokes of it before I had been to any of the meetings about it. He said that they wanted to do something really big with Cap toward the end of the story — something huge would happen with Cap. He may have even mentioned the possibility that Cap would die or that this or that might happen. So I can't claim full credit for it, but the way the story was told and the way I integrated the ideas with my own ongoing Cap plot is something that goes back to January 2006. I started plotting out how to do this, and

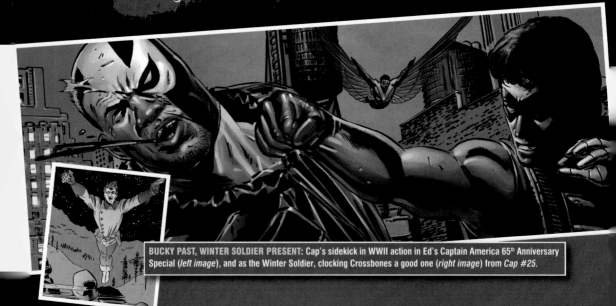

BUCKY PAST, WINTER SOLDIER PRESENT: Cap's sidekick in WWII action in Ed's Captain America 65th Anniversary Special (left image), and as the Winter Soldier, clocking Crossbones a good one (right image) from Cap #25.

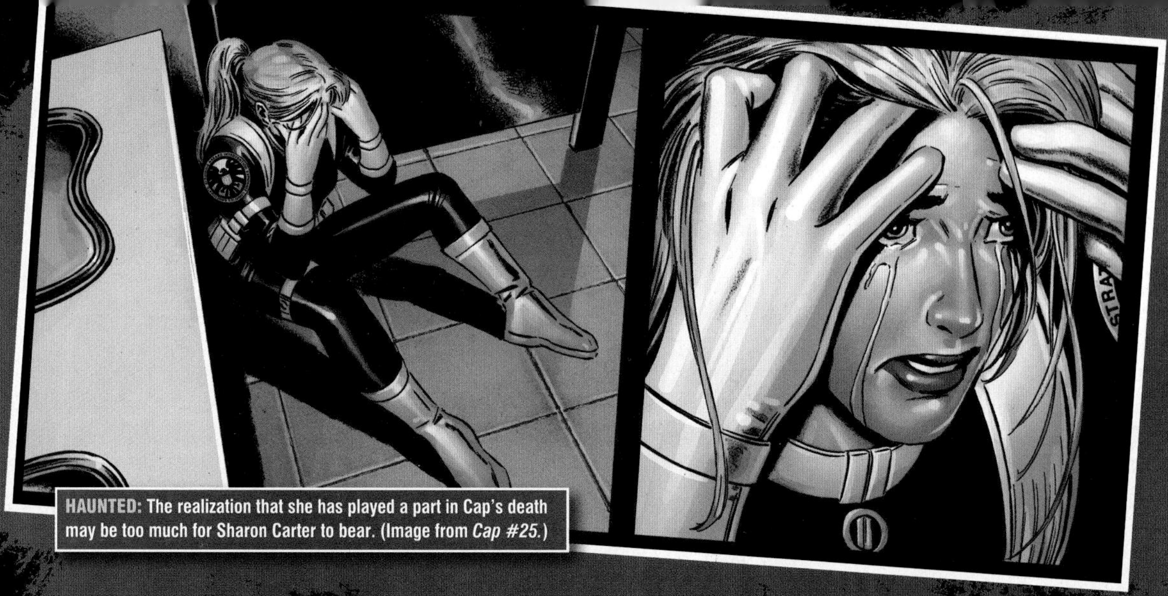

HAUNTED: The realization that she has played a part in Cap's death may be too much for Sharon Carter to bear. (Image from *Cap #25*.)

how to make it all work. I worked hard to make it a cool storyline and not just a stunt. To me it was never going to be a stunt.

I looked at *Civil War* and I looked at my options of what to do with Cap afterwards, and I thought the most interesting story to do with him would be to take Cap away from the Marvel Universe. There was an idea in one of the early *Civil War* outlines where it was suggested Cap would either go to jail or take off his costume and ride off on a motorcycle to find America. And I always thought, "Cap doesn't need to find America, America needs to find him." I don't think Cap is the one who's off the American path here. I don't think him not knowing about myspace or not caring about Paris Hilton makes him un-American. So I thought about how to write a story where America needs to find Captain America and for me that's where the whole idea went from being a stunt to being a story that's worth telling.

SPOTLIGHT: What about the specifics of Cap's death/murder? The sniper Crossbones followed by a mind-controlled Sharon Carter killing him?

ED: Well the Sharon thing was being set up in the book before I even heard about *Civil War*. I was moving things along with him and Sharon and preparing to reveal that she was under mind-control by Dr. Faustus. So there was already going to be some sort of Sharon betrayal. When the storyline got approved, I thought about it a lot. I knew the Red Skull had to ultimately be the one responsible, but I liked the idea off adding that twist to it of Sharon being the one who pulled the trigger. I knew that, no matter what, a lot of people were going to have his death spoiled, but almost no one had that extra twist spoiled. It makes it a much more character-driven story.

There was a moment when whether the death of Cap would happen in the *Civil War* book or in Cap's book was on the table. I can't recall exactly how that discussion went around. I remember I really wanted it to be in *Cap #25* from the moment that I first talked about doing it. I'm pretty sure Mark Millar didn't want to do it in *Civil War*, or maybe he was just being generous. It's hard to remember, but someone said we could have Steve surrender and as he's being led away in the crowd, Miriam Sharpe [the mother of one of the Stanford children killed at the beginning of *Civil War*] steps out with a gun and shoots him - and that's the death of Cap. In my gut, I felt that that's not a bad beat for *Civil War* but it's a terrible beat for Captain America. This is why I didn't care about the death of Superman: Superman was not killed by Lex Luthor. If Superman was killed by Lex Luthor, that would be a cool story. I knew that the Red Skull ultimately had to be responsible for killing Cap.

I also instinctively thought that Captain America is such an icon and the way American icons are killed is that they get assassinated. They don't die the way they're supposed to die; they die tragically. That was really what I was going for — making sure it played like an American tragedy.

SPOTLIGHT: One of the things that worked so well was that thousands of people who picked up the comic who hadn't in years all got a good story, and for those of us who had been reading the book regularly, this was a stunning continuation of an already compelling story; there was a lot there for regular Cap readers as well as the curious.

ED: It was definitely something I had in mind going in. I knew there would be at least a certain amount of people outside of comics who would hear about this and check it out, and I wanted to make it a book that anybody could just read and "get."

I think the nature of the story will have some benefit, too. I've been hearing from retailers who have people calling asking after the next issue who hadn't bought a comic in years until *Cap #25* and now they want the next issue.

SPOTLIGHT: So what can you tell us about the hotly anticipated next issue?

ED: Issue 26 is the wake. It's really cool. It's four or five scenes of the various wakes that are happening the night after Cap's funeral. So I jump ahead a week or two.

SPOTLIGHT: Without spoiling too much, what can we look for going forward in the book?

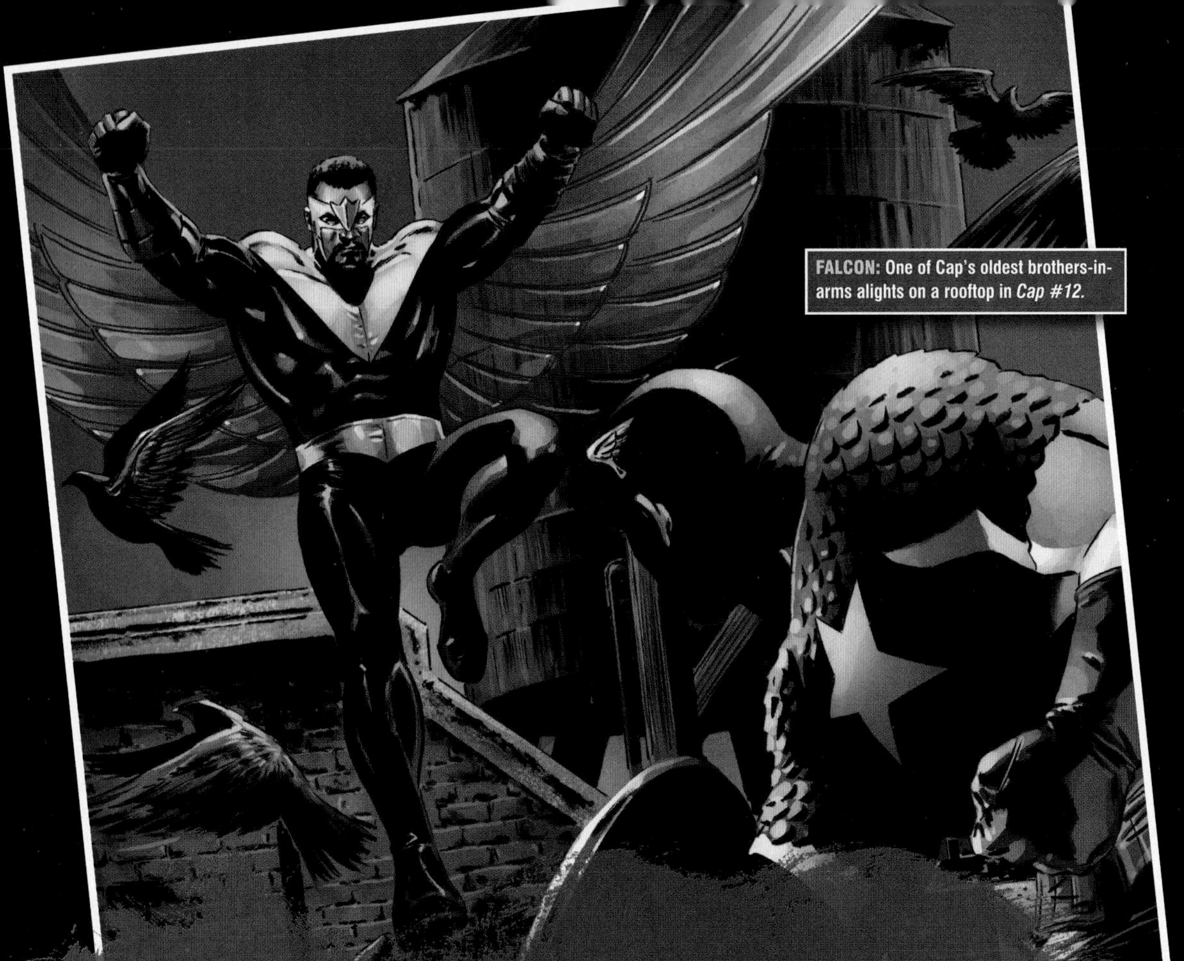

FALCON: One of Cap's oldest brothers-in-arms alights on a rooftop in *Cap #12*.

"I always thought, 'Cap doesn't need to find America, AMERICA NEEDS TO FIND HIM.'"

ED: Well...a lot! [*Laughter.*] We have a huge epic story about the death of Captain America and what that means to the supporting cast, what that means to America and what that means to the super hero and super-villain community. It becomes a story that swirls around the country as well as the cast having had their hearts torn out. There's a shockwave and each issue is another ripple of reaction. A lot of these characters get pitted against each other. Bucky is immediately not very happy with Tony Stark.

SPOTLIGHT: Speaking of that, let's go through the various cast members and their reactions and roles in the book, starting with Bucky Barnes, the Winter Soldier.

ED: Well, aside from being angry with Iron Man, he's already hated the Red Skull and now that's magnified. He obviously knows that Crossbones works for the Skull, so he's got some people that he's pretty unhappy with that he wants to deal with, so he's going off on his own, separated from Nick Fury. If anybody thought Bucky was mellowing out or was about to become a regular old super hero, the death of Cap is definitely the thing to push him right over that edge again.

SPOTLIGHT: How about poor Sharon Carter?

ED: Well, Sharon certainly has her own set of problems, obviously. You find out in *Cap #26* that she has a mental block. She's unable to tell anybody what she did.

SPOTLIGHT: Wow! You're mean to her!

ED: Yeah, yeah. But people will remember her. All people remember her for now is as a cute girl who once lit herself on fire.

She's in this really awful place with knowing what she did and knowing why she did it, but she can't tell anybody and can't act on it at all. She's doing what she can, though. She and the Falcon are sent out by Nick Fury to find the Winter Soldier when he goes underground. He goes off the grid again and they need to find him before he makes a bad situation even worse.

SPOTLIGHT: So what is the Falcon going through with the death of his old partner?

ED: I've been focusing more on him trying to be the rock for Sharon. One issue is largely from his point of view. He's one of the few heroes who operates in both worlds, having registered.

SPOTLIGHT: And Nick Fury is still going to be operating behind the scenes? Kind of a Charlie with Sharon and the Falcon being his "Angels" the way Bucky has been?

ED: Yeah. We see him a little bit, but he's kind of underground. Brian Michael Bendis has been building a story with him in *New Avengers* since *Secret War,* so I can't use Nick too much until then. But I have him where Brian needs him to be, which is underground, operating under his own agenda. He has his hand everywhere, but he's kind of trying to right the deck chairs on the Titanic at this point.

SPOTLIGHT: And Bucky was one of his main chess pieces, but he's lost him.

ED: Yes, and the way Bucky breaks away from him sort of screws up some of Fury's plans.

SPOTLIGHT: Moving on to the Red Skull, one of the cool things about his role in the story is that if you look at other iconic villains like Magneto or Dr. Doom, they have a kind of nobility and a respect for their nemeses. If Xavier were killed for instance, Magneto would probably mourn, and Doom would likely have mixed emotions about Richards dying. Not so with the Red Skull! It seems like he would feel nothing but glee at killing Captain America.

ED: I realized a little while ago that the Red Skull is the one major super-villain who is pretty much just straight up evil. He's not crazy; he's just evil. He's this nihilistic, anarchistic, fascist guy who brings out the worst aspects of all of those things. Magneto and Dr. Doom each have moments of redemption and each have a certain humanity that makes them who they are, but the Red Skull would happily fiddle while America burns.

SPOTLIGHT: And he is, I guess, the villain of the piece here?

ED: Oh, yeah. He has been since issue one. The Red Skull is moving his plot into place. Killing Cap was just the first step in the Red Skull's plan. There are a lot of pieces moving like a giant chess game. I feel it becoming more and more epic with each issue.

SPOTLIGHT: And Crossbones and the Red Skull's daughter, Sin, are major players as well?

ED: Well, Crossbones was captured in issue 25, so as a result Sin becomes the Skull's first lieutenant in the field. She recruits her own group of minions, which is the new Serpent Squad. So she has a storyline that's gonna get pretty intense. She's a trip — the Red Skull's even *more* evil daughter!

SPOTLIGHT: So the question everyone is asking is whether there will be a new Captain America and who it might be that will pick up the mantle. Without revealing an answer, is that something you'll be dealing with?

ED: Well, it's not anything you're gonna see anytime soon in the comic, I can tell you that. I do get asked about that a lot. Everyone assumes we're just aping the death of Superman and that we're going to have four different people become a different version of Cap, but no, we're not doing anything like that at all. I'm really happy with the story that we do have.

SPOTLIGHT: What did you think about Cap's position in *Civil War,* and how much input did you have there?

NEW FACE OF EVIL: She is the Red Skull's daughter, and her name is Sin! (Cover to *Cap #17.*)

ED: I didn't have any control over it, but I agreed with most of how Cap was portrayed during *Civil War*. Obviously I'm going to have some differences of opinion with anyone else's portrayal of Captain America just because I feel so proprietary about him. But I agree that Cap would have not been in favor of the registration act. I know it's a conceit of the story that they have to fight, but in my head I don't know if I see the story as this giant battle where people are killed so quickly, but that's the nature of the comic book event.

SPOTLIGHT: What are your favorite Captain America runs? Your favorite "takes" on Cap as a character?

ED: My favorite, favorite, favorite Captain America run is one of the shortest — the Steranko run. It can hardly be called a run, but I have it in one hardback book so I call it a run. That's my favorite three issues of Cap and most of what I do on the book owes a lot to those three issues, and my take on Cap is an extension of that. I was always disappointed to find out he only did three issues.

SPOTLIGHT: Those issues definitely have a "pulp" feel, which I know is something you value.

ED: I definitely look at what I do as pulp writing, and that's what makes me able to keep doing it and to keep trying to make it more fun and not just fall back into the clichés of the genre. But those Steranko issues are so different than the other Cap comics. Still, there's this depression to the character in those issues that is *so* Stan Lee. The opening scene for Steranko's first issue is Steve Rogers walking down the street and lighting a pipe, and somehow — though that's all he's doing — it's one of the saddest moments you've ever seen in anything ever. Cap became this hugely evocative character for me after that moment.

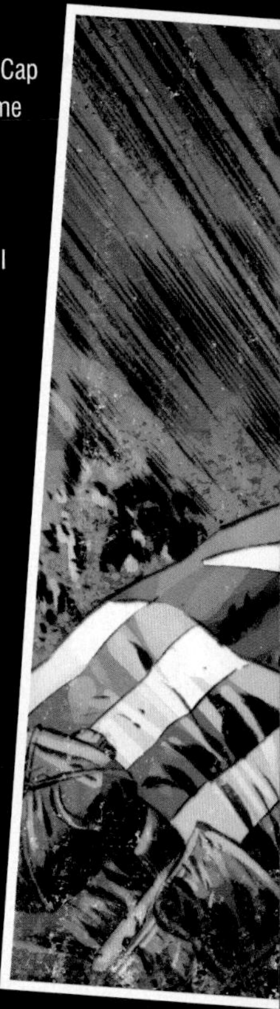

My other favorite run is probably the Steve Englehart/Sal Buscema run. That's the one I started on as a 4-5 year-old.

SPOTLIGHT: That's interesting. One could certainly enjoy that comic as a five-year-old, but there were a lot of adult themes that comics in general and Englehart's Cap specifically were dealing in.

ED: There really were some adult themes. He's making a lot of references to the modern world, which I didn't get. I still don't get all of them. When I read them recently, I thought, "Really? The Serpent Squad was a reference to the Symbionese Liberation Army?"

It was also probably the best art of Sal Buscema's career. There are a lot of things to say in favor of that run. I've reread it all in the last couple of years, and like most comics from the '70s, there are things about it that don't hold up.

The things that *do* hold up are the all the letters from Kurt Busiek in the letters column! [*Laughter.*] There were so many letters from Kurt back then it's just hysterical.

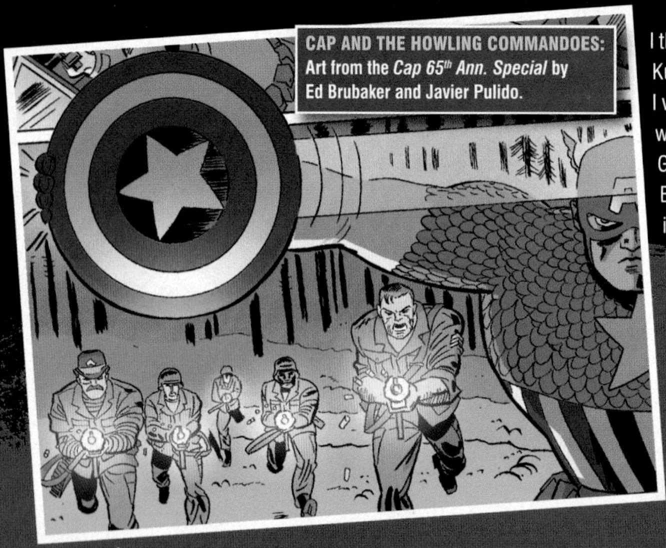

CAP AND THE HOWLING COMMANDOES: Art from the *Cap 65th Ann. Special* by Ed Brubaker and Javier Pulido.

I thought the Mark Waid run with Ron Garney and Andy Kubert was really good, too. I came to that late, when I was reading the whole Cap run in anticipation of writing the book. There are a couple of storylines in the Gruenwald run I like, especially the big "Super Patriot Becomes Cap" story that ends in *Cap #350*. I take issue with some of the depiction of Cap during that era because I think they took him too far away from the way Kirby and Steranko and those guys treated him when he first came back. He got taken from being this tough, bold soldier to this basic super hero.

SPOTLIGHT: It was very much a super hero comic at that time.

ED: Yeah. And that's fine. That's what comics were

"I was reading these comics and thinking, 'WHAT GOOD IS A SUPER SOLDIER WHO DOESN'T KILL THE ENEMY?'"

TIMELESS ENEMIES: Red Skull vs. Captain America, drawn by artist Mike Perkins in *Cap #15.*

then and that's the audience they were intended for, but I think saying that a guy who was created as a super soldier to fight in World War II never killed the enemy is weird. I was reading these comics and thinking, "How is this possible? What good is a super soldier who doesn't kill the enemy?" This was a war. That part bugged me. There was a scene in one issue where Cap can't reach his shield so he grabs a gun and shoots a terrorist and saves 35 people, and then he goes on TV and apologizes for it, for letting America down by killing someone. I thought, "Come on!" Then there was a story recently where there was a conspiracy that maybe America had put Cap in the ice because he found out we were gonna drop the atom bomb and he was going to stop them. When I read that before my run I said, "Okay, I'm just gonna pretend this story never existed." [*Laughter.*]

And not to slag off anybody, but I was definitely glad to be given the book and be given a free hand in how to portray the character and what direction to go in. I got a lot of flak for the first issue because there's a scene where Cap takes out some guys who were about to set off a dirty bomb on Coney Island, and one or two of them get killed. One of them jumps off a train, and Cap hits another in the head and puts him in a coma. It's brutal stuff. I talked to my editor Tom Brevoort and he said that I'd probably get some flak for the scene because later Sharon mentions the cost of the damage, and I thought about it and decided I wanted that. If you just have that scene and not have the scene where Sharon mentions the guy was in a coma or that the other one had died, then it just becomes like any other Marvel super hero fight scene. I really wanted to ground the book in the real world. Of course, it's not gonna be Al Qaeda, it's gonna be Hydra or AIM, but I wanted it to feel like the Steranko issues, or like *24*, so there had to be actual damage to people. I was glad to get the book at a time when I was given a really free hand to do that.

Whew! That makes me want to go and reread Ed's Cap run from the beginning! Thanks, Ed, for reminding us what has made the last two years of Captain America so thrilling. It sounds like the thrills aren't about to stop either, as despite the death of Steve Rogers, the story of Captain America continues monthly!

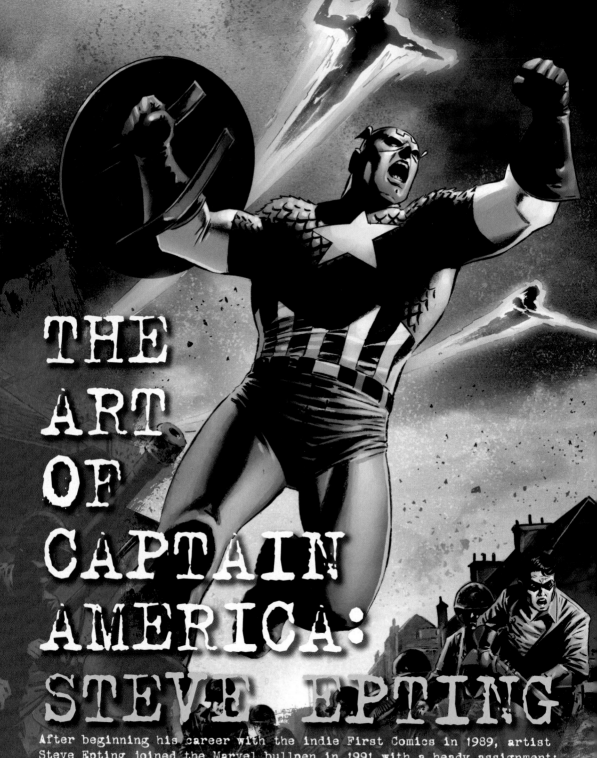

THE ART OF CAPTAIN AMERICA: STEVE EPTING

After beginning his career with the indie First Comics in 1989, artist Steve Epting joined the Marvel bullpen in 1991 with a heady assignment: drawing *Avengers*, one of Marvel's flagship titles. Now, nearly 20 years later, Steve is once again at the center of the Marvel Universe, joining writer Ed Brubaker in chronicling the adventures of the Avengers' heart and soul, Captain America. During *Civil War*, Cap hasn't had a higher profile since perhaps the days he was knocking Adolf Hitler's block off during World War II, and his death in the now timeless *Captain America #25* pushed his modern mainstream recognition through the roof. Spotlight's Dugan Trodglen continues his exploration of Brubaker and Epting's Cap in a chat with Steve about being an integral part of all of this action, both in and out of the pages of *Captain America*.

SPOTLIGHT: What a job — drawing the death of Steve Rogers! Did this feel like a big responsibility? What was it like drawing this particular scene?

STEVE: I didn't feel like it was a huge responsibility at the time, especially since I had no idea it was going to end up in the mainstream media all over the world, but it's probably a good thing that I didn't know because I would have second guessed myself and no doubt made it worse trying to get it just right. That said, I generally approach every scene the same — searching for the most effective way to not only convey what's happening, but to give it the subtlety or impact that it needs. Most of the time I just go with the image that immediately presents itself in my head, and that was the case here. Of course, some pages turn out better than others and this was one that was somewhat tricky to choreograph given that it was a very chaotic scene and included a panicking crowd. Hopefully everything is clear and dramatic and the art lives up to the importance of the scene.

SPOTLIGHT: What was your reaction to the incredible amount of mainstream news coverage, literally seeing your art on CNN for instance?

STEVE: The whole thing was very bizarre and unexpected. When I started seeing stories pop up all over the news I was amazed. I really had no idea this would happen. I started hoping that they wouldn't show panels where I had drawn some wonky face or something, but for the most part it was all very gratifying, and a little bit surreal.

SPOTLIGHT: Aside from the mainstream coverage *Civil War* and Cap's death received, what has it been like, as a comics professional, to be working in an era of huge events and a rapidly changing status quo?

STEVE: I think changing the status quo of the Marvel Universe definitely offers some exciting possibilities that wouldn't exist otherwise. We changed the status quo in Cap's book by bringing back Bucky, and *Civil War* has done something comparable to the Marvel U on an even greater scale. I'm really looking forward to what's coming up next, not just in our book, but across the board. Speaking strictly as a comics fan, this is a great time to be reading Marvel.

SPOTLIGHT: Bringing back Bucky as the Winter Soldier was, of course, a bold move. While the

fan reaction to the fallout of Steve Rogers' death has yet to play out, the Winter Soldier story has trounced fan skepticism and become very popular. What do you think accounts for the success of such a controversial move?

STEVE: One thing: Ed Brubaker. Believe me, I was just as skeptical when I learned that Bucky was coming back. I remember telling Ed after I read his outline for the first year that the fans were going to hate us. So yeah, I had my doubts, but I was a fan of Bru's work on *Gotham Central*, *Catwoman*, and *Sleeper*, so I had faith that he could pull it off. He really built the suspense and mystery along the course of the arc and did a great job of portraying the effect that all of this was having on Cap. All I had to do was draw it.

SPOTLIGHT: The domino mask is a nice nod to Bucky's original look. How did you come up with the Winter Soldier design?

STEVE: When Ed and I first discussed the design for the Winter Soldier, we started with the domino mask. That was the one thing we knew for sure was going to be part of the costume (well, that and the cybernetic arm). I drew up the first version and Ed, Tom, Joe Quesada and I went over it together. After a few tweaks and longer hair (credit to Joe for that one), the second version was approved. The tunic, with the two rows of snaps, is also intended as a nod to the double-breasted one that Bucky originally wore.

SPOTLIGHT: What can you tell us about Bucky Barnes going forward in this story? What about the rest of the supporting cast? I suppose they will play a larger role in these first issues after the death.

STEVE: I can't go too much into what happens next, but yes, the supporting cast — in particular Sharon Carter, Falcon and Winter Soldier — will be taking center stage for a bit.

SPOTLIGHT: When you returned to Marvel, was *Captain America* a book you had your eye on? Did you sign on to the title before or after you knew Ed Brubaker's plans?

WINTER SOLDIER: Epting's stirring character design for the new look Bucky!

STEVE: Frankly, I would love to have a chance at all of Marvel's characters eventually. Right around the time I was returning to Marvel, I believe *Captain America, Thor,* and *Iron Man* were all due to undergo creative team changes and I thought I may have a shot at getting assigned to one of them. I would have been thrilled with any of them, but I think Cap turned out to be a perfect fit for me. Tom couldn't tell me who the writer was when we first discussed Cap, because Ed was still exclusive with another company at the time. As soon as he was free, Tom sent me the outline for the first twelve issues, so yes, I knew that Bucky was coming back. I'll admit that made me a little nervous, but after working with Ed for a while, I realized we both had the same sensibilities about Cap and what we wanted the book to be like. I think we both are just trying to do the Captain America book that we always wanted to read, and hopefully the Cap fans out there are responding to it in a positive way.

SPOTLIGHT: You have drawn the best Red Skull in I don't know how long. Did a specific previous take inspire you?

STEVE: Thanks! When Tom told me that the Red Skull's head was an actual skull and not a mask, it really made it click. I've got a human skull model in my studio that I used for inspiration. After the Skull was assassinated and began residing in Lukin's brain, I turned to Kirby's original Red Skull design to portray Lukin when he puts the Skull mask on.

SPOTLIGHT: In an era of six-part stories, with the action scenes often giving way to what some folks refer to as "talky talky," Captain America has been especially action-packed. Is that the way you like it, or is it more difficult?

STEVE: Ed has struck a pretty good balance with the action scenes and the quieter stuff, and I think super hero comics, which are all about action, need the quieter scenes as a counterpoint. Cap's a great character to draw in action, especially tossing that shield around. It can sometimes be difficult choreographing complicated fight scenes, but it's always fun. The "talky" scenes are fun in a different way, because that's when your characters get to "act" through facial expressions, body language, etc…

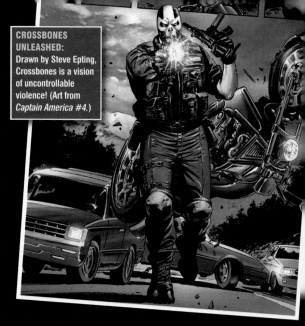

CROSSBONES UNLEASHED: Drawn by Steve Epting, Crossbones is a vision of uncontrollable violence! (Art from *Captain America #4.*)

SPOTLIGHT: Do you have any particular favorite scene you've done on Cap?

STEVE: It's hard to narrow it down to a favorite scene, but my favorite issue has been Captain America #14. After a yearlong build up, Cap and Bucky (or I guess I should say Winter Soldier) finally come face to face. I had been waiting to draw that since I first read Ed's outline. My answer to this question is definitely going to change though, because I know some of what's coming up and I'm pretty sure I'm going to have a new favorite in the future.

SPOTLIGHT: How is it working at Marvel now, particularly in this high-profile event, compared with your earlier run in the '90s?

STEVE: Well, obviously, Marvel and the comics industry as a whole are completely different now than they were in the early '90s. The only thing I worked on back then that was comparable to *Civil War* was the *Operation: Galactic Storm* crossover that ran through the Avengers titles, and though that was a massive event in the Avengers family of books, it was overshadowed by

"I had no idea it was going to end up in the mainstream media all over the world, but it's probably a good thing that I didn't know because I would have second guessed myself."

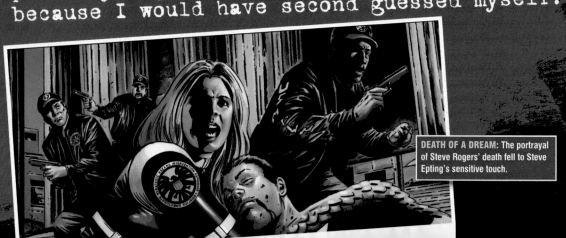

DEATH OF A DREAM: The portrayal of Steve Rogers' death fell to Steve Epting's sensitive touch.

the enormous interest in the new X-Men books and the launch of Image. *Avengers* was not a hot title in those days, so there was nowhere near the hype and attention that *Civil War* enjoys.

SPOTLIGHT: Do you have a favorite Cap moment from the *Civil War* series?

STEVE: There were a lot of great moments but the first thing that popped in my head was the scene in the first issue of Civil War where Cap escapes from S.H.I.E.L.D. surfing on the back of one of their jets. It's a great visual that just has stayed with me. Steve McNiven did a great job on that scene.

SPOTLIGHT: Who are your favorite Cap artists and why?

STEVE: Kirby, for literally defining the character. Kirby's Cap IS Cap. Steranko: Great design work. John Romita Sr.: I loved everything Romita drew and his short run is my favorite Cap art ever.

Sal Buscema: I read more of Sal's *Cap* issues than anyone else's back in the days before it was easy to get back issues. And Ron Garney, Andy Kubert, John Cassaday and Lee Weeks — some of the more recent artists who are phenomenally talented and have put a distinctive mark on the book in the modern era.

SPOTLIGHT: Your professional career dates back to 1989, and after just a couple of years, you were working for Marvel. How did you get your start?

STEVE: I graduated with a BFA in graphic design and had been doing that for a while when I read about a contest that First Comics was holding at the Atlanta Fantasy Fair. They were going to publish the best 6-page story as a back up in one of their books. I decided to enter just to see if there was any chance of getting into comics. I didn't know anyone in the business and had no idea how to go about trying to break in, so I figured this was worth a shot. Well, I arrived at the convention and was surprised to find out that nobody from First Comics knew anything about the contest. They had not authorized it and told the eight or nine people who entered that they would look at the entries, but that they would not be publishing anything. Another guy and I were declared the "winners" and First's art director met with us to discuss possibly doing some work for them. That's how I got my start, but I don't remember the other winner's name and I've often wondered who he was and if he went on to work in comics. Who knows, maybe he's reading this!

SPOTLIGHT: You sound pretty excited about drawing *Captain America*, not just the big stories you've already drawn but also about what's coming up. It must be gratifying that after nearly twenty years in the business, stories can still inspire you this much.

STEVE: For the most part, I've enjoyed all of the books I've worked on. Of course there were a few stinkers here and there, but that's bound to happen. *Captain America* is definitely one of the high points though, and it is great to know that something like this can still come along.

Thanks a lot, Steve, and keep up the great work in the pages of CAPTAIN AMERICA!

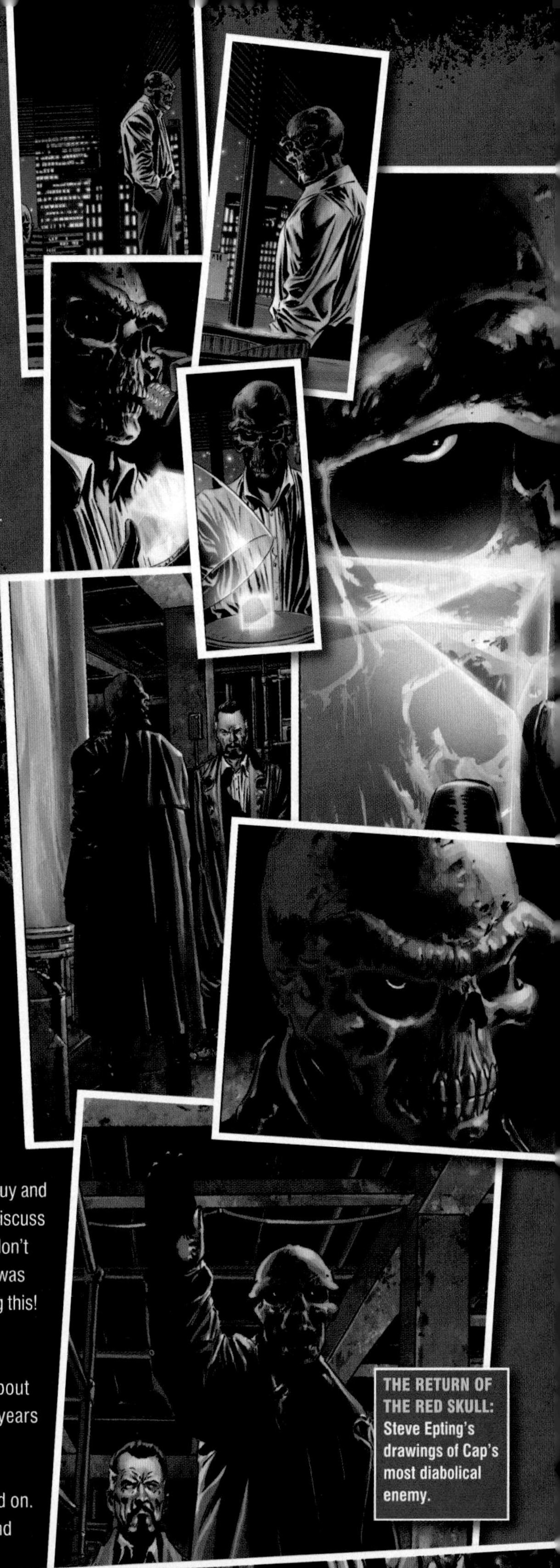

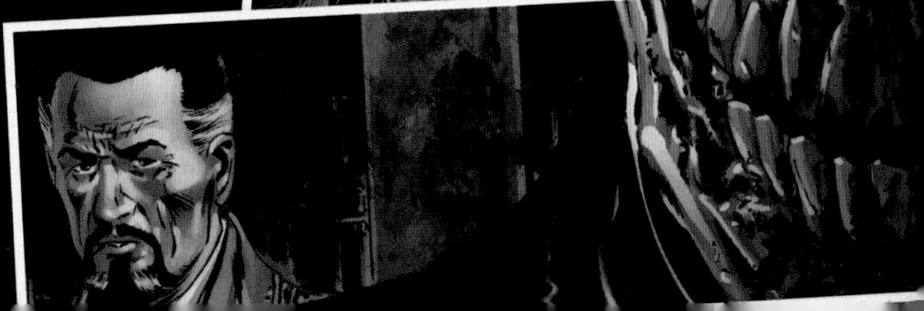

THE RETURN OF THE RED SKULL: Steve Epting's drawings of Cap's most diabolical enemy.

BUCKY LIVES,

Inside the one-shot *Civil War* special that co

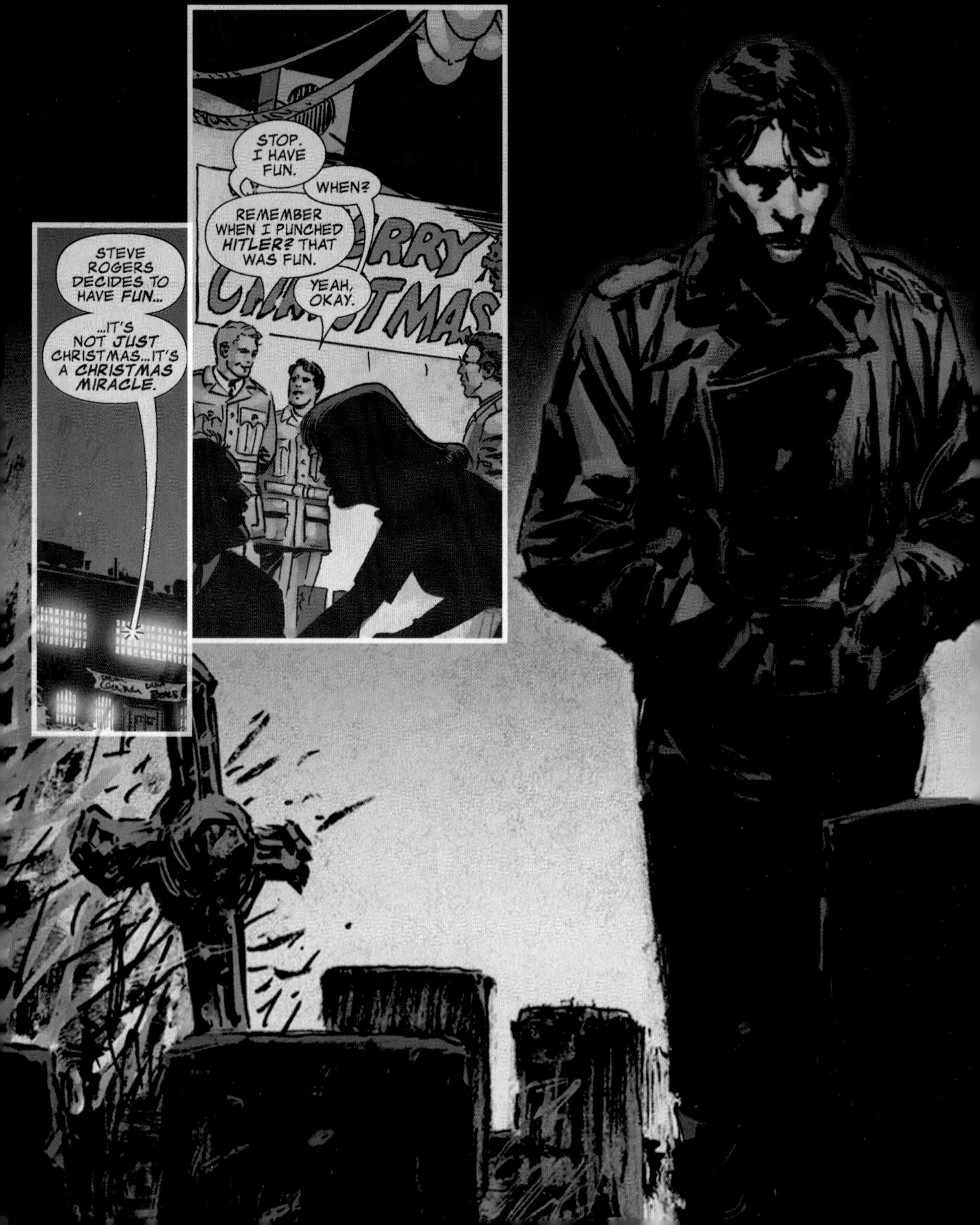

STEVE ROGERS DECIDES TO HAVE FUN...
...IT'S NOT JUST CHRISTMAS...IT'S A CHRISTMAS MIRACLE.
STOP. I HAVE FUN.
WHEN?
REMEMBER WHEN I PUNCHED HITLER? THAT WAS FUN.
YEAH, OKAY.

WINTER KILLS

...nects the dots on 65 years of Marvel history!

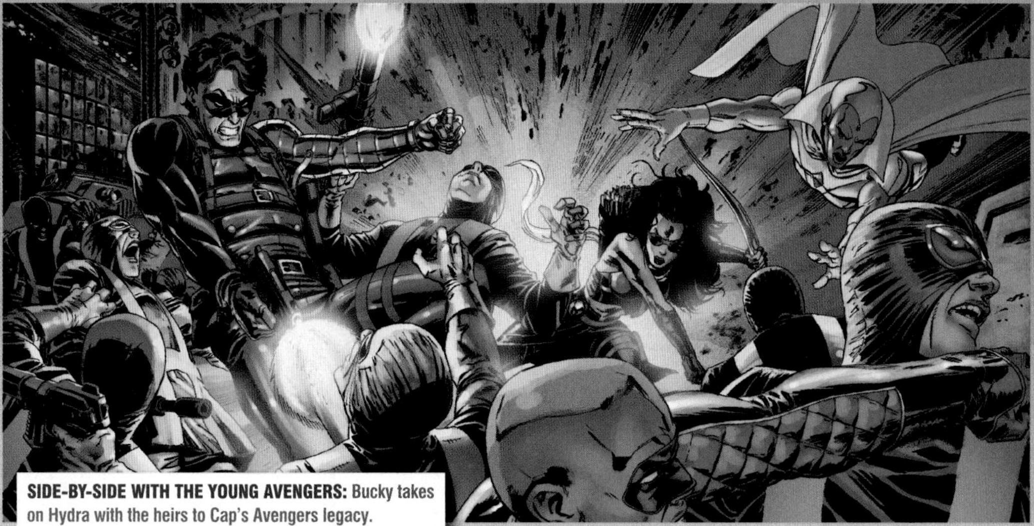

SIDE-BY-SIDE WITH THE YOUNG AVENGERS: Bucky takes on Hydra with the heirs to Cap's Avengers legacy.

ED BRUBAKER'S MOST DARING MOVE DURING HIS Captain America run was bringing Bucky Barnes back to the Marvel Universe (until the death of Cap, natch!) Long thought of as one of the "untouchable" deaths in the Marvel Universe, Bucky's return, while met with initial — and understandable — skepticism, was soon recognized as one of the great Marvel storylines of recent years. After breaking out of the brainwashing that had made him a killing machine for Soviet Russia, the Winter Soldier (as he was now called) has had a hard time adjusting to the modern world. Save for times he was unleashed on his assassination missions, his Soviet captors kept him in suspended animation, a stranger to his own free will. ★ Never has that been more on display than during the one-shot *Winter Soldier: Winter Kills*. Conceived as a tie-in to Civil War, the comic was soon recognized by many fans as an instant classic. The self-contained, double-sized story showcased Bucky's tough side in some swell action scenes alongside the Young Avengers, as well as providing some moving character moments, none more so than his first meeting with Namor since his return (at the grave of an old teammate; a scene that moistened the eyes of more than a few long-time Marvel readers). Marvel Spotlight was happy to talk to Ed about this powerful look at Bucky Barnes, the Winter Soldier.

SPOTLIGHT: First of all, that one-shot was maybe the best comic I read last year. [*Me too! — Ed.*]

ED: Thanks!

SPOTLIGHT: When it was announced, it was part of this group of comics that seemed designed to tide folks over while the main *Civil War* book was running late. The expectation was that it would be pretty cool, but when it came out, it seemed so much like a story that needed to be told regardless of it being a loose tie-in to *Civil War*, much less something to fill out the shipping schedule. What was the genesis of the comic?

ED: Really, it did come out of the Civil War delays. (*Laughter.*) I had wanted to do a Winter Soldier special but there was no way I was going to be able to do one because of my workload. But I knew the time was right to do one. And as it happened, with *Civil War's* delay, Cap's schedule got pushed back because of how they tied in, so I said, "Let me do a *Civil War* special if I don't have to write *Cap* this month." That was really convenient.

SPOTLIGHT: The reaction that I could see was pretty strong, especially

IT WAS AN HONOR, BUCKY.

FOR ALL OF US.

SALUTE TO A HERO: Bucky's sidekicks against Hydra show their respect.

him I couldn't believe that he wasn't writing the Marvel Universe J. Jonah Jameson. He's such a funny character to write. But he told me, "Yeah, but I've discovered that Prince Namor is just as fun to write," and as I was writing the *Winter Kills* story I realized that he really is one of the most fun characters of all time to write. He speaks in double negatives because he's pissed off at the surface world at all times.

SPOTLIGHT: Another great line from the issue is from Bucky. When he kills the Hydra agent, much to the shock of the Young Avengers, he says, "I killed a terrorist. Don't worry, there'll be two more to take his place."

ED: I like the idea of him grabbing Hawkeye's arrows and with one quick motion he kills the guy. They're shocked, but here's a guy who fought four years in World War II and he doesn't sit and cry over dead enemies who are trying to destroy the world.

SPOTLIGHT: And whether or not it's Ed Brubaker's point of view, it's a good comment from Bucky's on the real world we live in today.

ED: Yeah, exactly, that's who he is and how he sees things. At the same time, I like that those kids and he like each other. He goes on the mission with them and as they're fighting Hydra he's sort of judging them and thinking about what they need. And when they find out who he is they're thrilled to be working with Bucky.

SPOTLIGHT: Lee Weeks' work on that book was also extraordinary. I wish he were on a monthly book.

ED: Well, Lee doesn't draw that fast, and he's kind of picky, but I'd be happy to work with him on anything. I pushed really hard for him to work with [inker] Stefano Gaudiano. I remembered Lee Weeks from back when he was on *Daredevil* and I thought if he got an inker like Stefano who wouldn't make him look super slick that he'd be really happy, and lo and behold Lee never wants to be inked by anyone ever again.

Be sure and check out the Winter Soldier: Winter Kills one-shot as collected in the trade paperback CIVIL WAR: CAPTAIN AMERICA.

among long-time comic book readers. When you finished writing it, did it strike you as something really strong, or that would strike a chord?

ED: At first it didn't seem like there was much of a reaction, but I've since done appearances and conventions and I've signed a lot of copies of that and a lot of people told me it was one of their favorite comics of the year and things like that. I think it really hit with people. The fact is it barely has a plot. It's just Bucky on Christmas Eve feeling terrible about the modern world and thinking back to his last Christmas Eve, which was 1944. And while it was correctly pointed out that he and the Invaders should have been at the Battle of the Bulge, because they were special they got to fly into London for a quick holiday. For me, a lot of the plots I've done in Cap are just excuses to have people standing on a rooftop flashing back to a character moment from World War II.

SPOTLIGHT: That issue really shows Bucky's alienation from the modern world is even greater than Cap's was when he woke up.

WINTER SOLDIER: Cover to *Winter Kills* one-shot.

ED: Yeah, that's because a lot of what Bucky went through while Cap slept right through.

SPOTLIGHT: The reveal that Bucky and Namor were standing at Toro's grave was a real lump-in-the-throat moment, as was Namor's line about having had "the honor" of being present at Toro's heroic death.

ED: I really liked that scene. I knew eventually I'd have to do a story with Bucky and Namor in the modern world. It's funny — when I was doing one of my first issues of *Daredevil*, I called up Bendis and told

A CLASSIC CAP CRAFTSMAN:
GENE COLAN'S CAP

Comic art legend Gene Colan's heyday on Captain America was 1969-1971, but the singular artist is back for a little more in an upcoming annual with writer Ed Brubaker!

BY JOHN RHETT THOMAS

Ed Brubaker and his art team of Steve Epting and Mike Perkins have had a stellar run over the last two years on *Captain America*, with accolades coming from all sides of both the comics and mainstream press. But for the creative stable currently carrying the flag of Cap, perhaps no greater praise can come than when it is delivered by one of the giants who helped lay the groundwork for their success. So when word got back to Ed that no less than Gene "The Dean" Colan was keeping an eye on their achievements, it was a very special moment that linked two generations.

"I heard through Mike Perkins that he had met Gene at a convention," says Ed. "Apparently, Gene had come up and talked to him and complimented him on the work that we were doing on *Captain America*." A blessing from one of the all-time classic Cap artists is the kind of feedback that can really make a guy's day, and it made a little light bulb go off over Ed's head! "I thought, 'Gene Colan likes what we are doing! Let's get him to draw an annual or something!' I floated the idea out there, and several months later, Tom Brevoort calls me and tells me he has it all lined it up!"

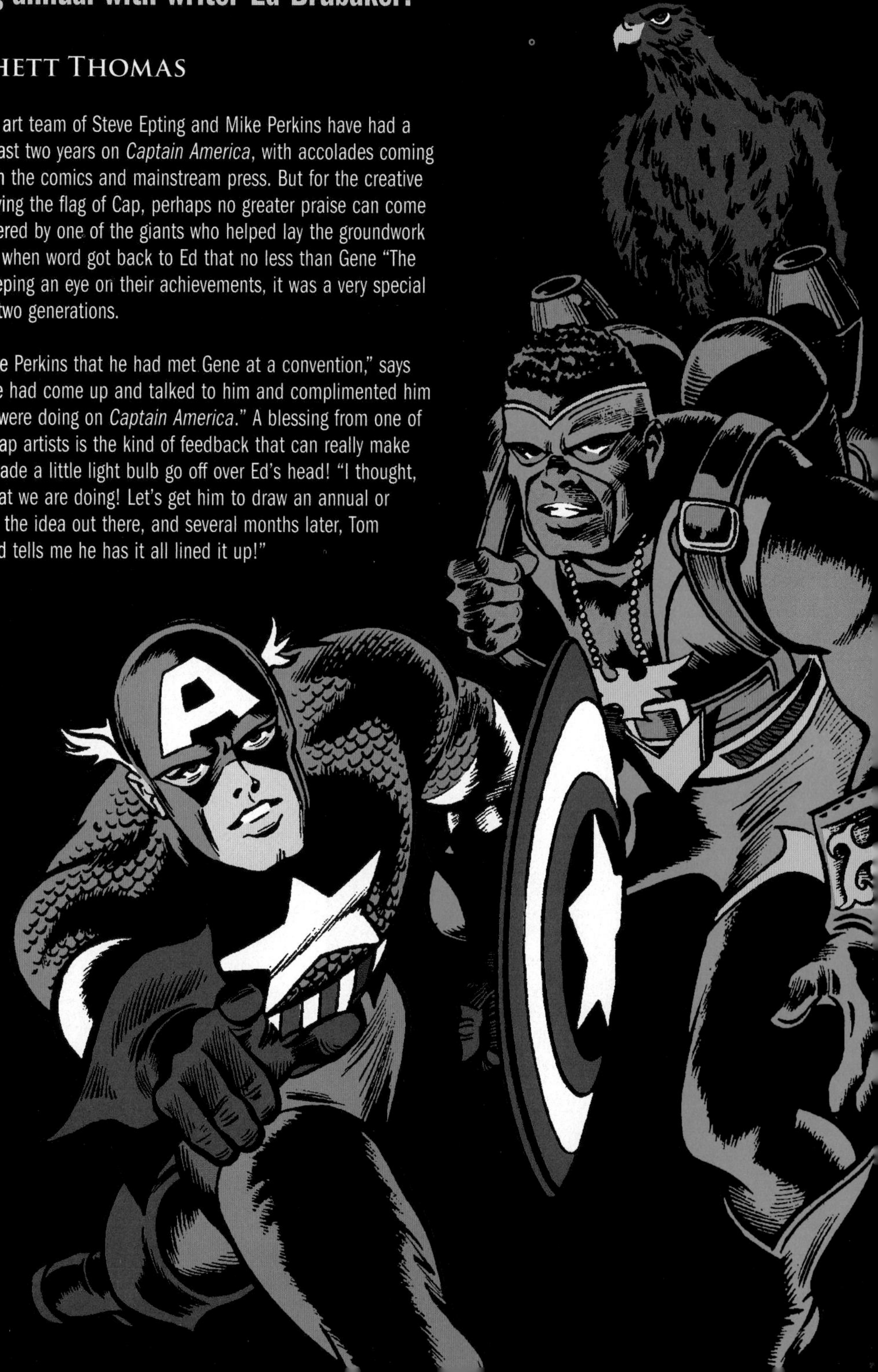

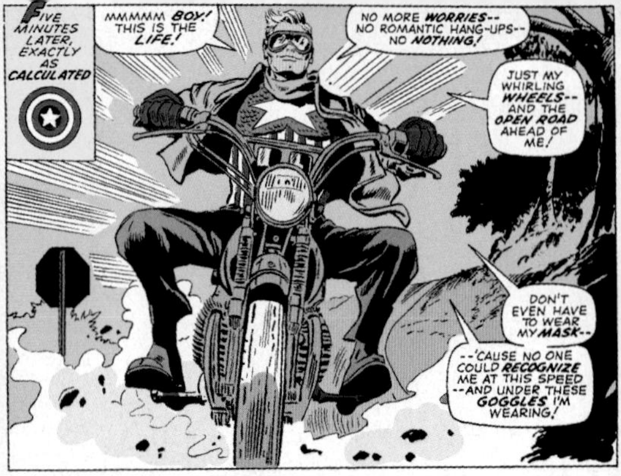
FIVE MINUTES LATER, EXACTLY AS CALCULATED
MMMMM BOY! THIS IS THE LIFE!
NO MORE WORRIES-- NO ROMANTIC HANG-UPS-- NO NOTHING!
JUST MY WHIRLING WHEELS-- AND THE OPEN ROAD AHEAD OF ME!
DON'T EVEN HAVE TO WEAR MY MASK--
--'CAUSE NO ONE COULD RECOGNIZE ME AT THIS SPEED --AND UNDER THESE GOGGLES I'M WEARING!

COLAN'S CAP: A little brighter than his more moody and darkly drawn work on *Daredevil* and *Doctor Strange*. (Art from *Cap #129*.)

Getting Gentleman Gene back in the saddle is certainly exciting news for Cap fans old and new, but caution must be extended. The annual is currently unscheduled, and Gene is definitely taking his time on delivering the finished pages. However, time hasn't dulled Gene's singular approach to comic book art. In fact, as a special bonus to tide you over until the finished product is ready to be solicited, *Marvel Spotlight* has an exclusive look at a couple pages of Gene's work (check out the gallery at the conclusion of this piece). We were all gung ho to talk with Gene about drawing Cap, his approach to art, and his work with Ed, and with that in mind, we are very happy to share with *Spotlight* readers the results of our special interview with a comic art legend, Mr. Gene Colan!

SPOTLIGHT: I spoke with Ed earlier today and he wanted to make sure I knew just how excited he is about working with you on this project.

GENE: I never expected it at all. It just came out of left field to do *Captain America*, but it's certainly an honor to be able to sit down and work on it again. It kinda brings back a lot of memories.

SPOTLIGHT: You drew the title for about two solid years, from 1969 to 1971.

GENE: Yeah, that's a long time. I forgot how long it's been!

SPOTLIGHT: What was your take on drawing Captain America back then during the late '60s?

GENE: It was an important book, and my intention from the very start was to try and get a book of my own to do. In those days, going back to the '40s, I was doing little things like short stories, crime stories, romance. I think it started out with Daredevil, and Captain America came in rather quickly after that. And then there's a big mix between Captain America and some of the other super heroes that I've done. *[Like Dr. Strange! – Ed.]*

But I enjoyed Captain America. He was already an important figure long before I got to him, and I had a great time doing it. To me it was like making a movie. I probably should have gone into the movie-making business, because I love film.

SPOTLIGHT: What was your impression of drawing Cap as opposed to what you brought to Daredevil and Dr. Strange? It seemed that in *Daredevil* you were developing the character to be at one with the dark shadows that were part of his world. And with *Dr. Strange*, you had all the mystical elements that came with the character. But with *Captain America*, you couldn't lean on those kinds of elements, because he was more of a straight-up, red white and blue super hero in broad daylight.

SPOTLIGHT: That's right, and I thought I was treating it that way. He didn't have the qualities that the others had in some respects. He was a wonderful figure to draw, full of action – maybe not so much on the dramatic side, as I know drama to be. But Daredevil would be more suitable for nighttime scenes and drama, due to the kind of character that he was, a guy dressed all in red with little horns on the top. So I could put him in any situation and have a good time with it. Dr. Strange...that one spoke for itself. But Captain America was all action, and I loved that. I enjoyed doing it.

SPOTLIGHT: You speak about your love of film. As a veteran artist who was around in Marvel's Silver Age heyday, what's your take on the similarities between film and comic story telling?

GENE: I looked upon it as having a chance to cast the characters myself, other than the super hero, because that was already established. Then the lighting! This would apply to any story that I would do: the lighting effects, the background...and I got it all from film.

In the earlier days – in the '40s certainly – all the films were black and white, which I loved doing and it was a great form to show dramatic stories and depict horror, because black and white is the most dramatic way to do it. The minute you put color into something, it takes away. I have a tendency to want to subdue that color and not play it up because it takes away from anything you might want to really say. I treated all those Captain America stories like I was making a film, and each panel represented the movie screen. That was the way I had fun doing it.

SPOTLIGHT: Do you recall doing the character design for the Falcon? He was a major character introduced while you were artist.

GENE: I don't remember if I did that design or not, or if it had been established before I got to it. I just can't remember. I doubt it, but I don't really know for sure.

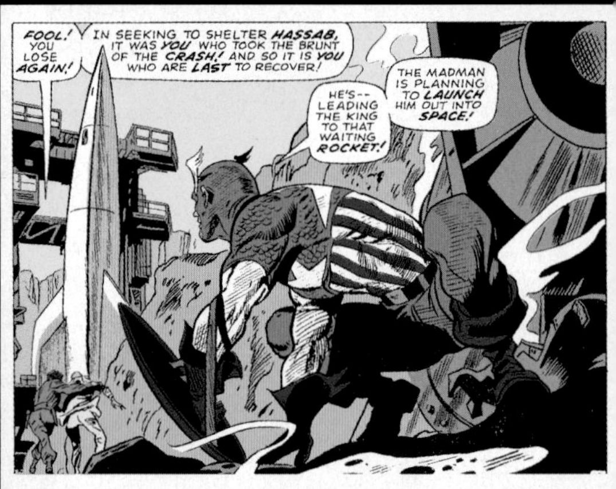
FOOL! YOU LOSE AGAIN!
IN SEEKING TO SHELTER HASSAB, IT WAS YOU WHO TOOK THE BRUNT OF THE CRASH! AND SO IT IS YOU WHO ARE LAST TO RECOVER!
HE'S-- LEADING THE KING TO THAT WAITING ROCKET!
THE MADMAN IS PLANNING TO LAUNCH HIM OUT INTO SPACE!

CAP ON THE CASE: Cap's muscular anatomy is showcased in Gene's dynamic figure drawings. (Art from *Cap #129*.)

SPOTLIGHT: Working with Ed Brubaker on this new annual, you've been getting pieces of scripts from him. How far along are you on the book now?

GENE: Not very far. I'm still continuing with it. I'm not a fast artist, I'm rather slow. I've always been slow. I'm a first class lint picker when it comes to drawing. *(Laughter.)* John Buscema, for instance, was very fast and so accurate! Everything he did, I admired. He was really a first-class artist.

SPOTLIGHT: Big John, eh? He was definitely a great peer of yours. Any other artists that you admire?

GENE: Milton Caniff, who did not work with Marvel, was my idol in doing art work. I loved the placement of his blacks! And of course Hal Foster, who did Prince Valiant, everything he drew was extremely accurate. I realized that it would be important to put accuracy in those books, and whatever I could get my hands on that I could use, I would file away.

SPOTLIGHT: Would you use photo reference and things like that?

GENE: Yes, a lot of photo reference. I had a file. I still do, but it's so ancient now. The edges of the reference pages look burnt and the color has changed, but the pages were just clippings of various looking characters, both men and women, in different poses. Like with a man: his front view, back view, side view. I would spin that character around and use that. And the more I did it, the more I wanted to do it. I really got into that photographic look. I tried to not do it so completely like the photograph that it looks like it came from a photograph. And I've done things without photographs. But I tend to go back to the photograph because it's authentic.

CAPT. AMERICA
15¢ 117
IND SEPT
APPROVED BY THE COMICS CODE AUTHORITY
CAPTAIN AMERICA
TM
THE COMING OF THE FALCON!
MARVEL COMICS GROUP

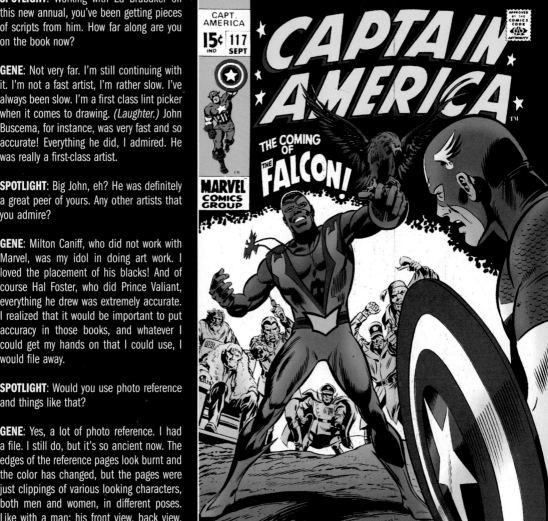

THE COMING OF THE FALCON! Gene was on hand to draw the first appearances of Sam Wilson, aka the Falcon! (Cover to *Cap #117*.)

If I'm looking for a piece of equipment and there's a photograph along with it, I kind of get drawn into it again. It's not just the equipment, it's the background. A lot of the war stories that I've done...for instance, I met John Severin who taught me to draw those guns like they were real, to put every nut and bolt into them. And he told me what books I should get on the subject, and of course I was very young and I listened to him. I've been doing it ever since that way.

SPOTLIGHT: I know that John Severin and Russ Heath have been used recently by Ed to draw some things in his *Iron Fist* book, so I think he has taken some real pleasure in getting new work from comic art veterans like yourself.

GENE: Ed has some first-class artists doing *Captain America* now!

SPOTLIGHT: Oh, definitely. What is your opinion of Steve Epting and Mike Perkins?

GENE: They're terrific, just terrific! I think they're headed for big things; these are probably very young guys now.

SPOTLIGHT: Do you see any elements of your style that they have pulled together?

GENE: I think that all artists, they copy and use. I don't mean the word 'copy,' but they use (older work) like a springboard. They use the artwork from other artists that they have a tendency to be attracted to, and they spring off onto their own. That's how I think a style is eventually established.

But these guys are terrific. It's like you are watching a film...all of it. The style is very consistent. It's not just the ability to draw – it's the ability to tell a good story. If you could do that! Now, some artists are not all that great, but boy they can tell a story. Then you got it made.

SPOTLIGHT: So far, what are some of the highlights of the experience working with Ed on the annual? Are there any particular things that you've been able to draw so far that you're really having fun with?

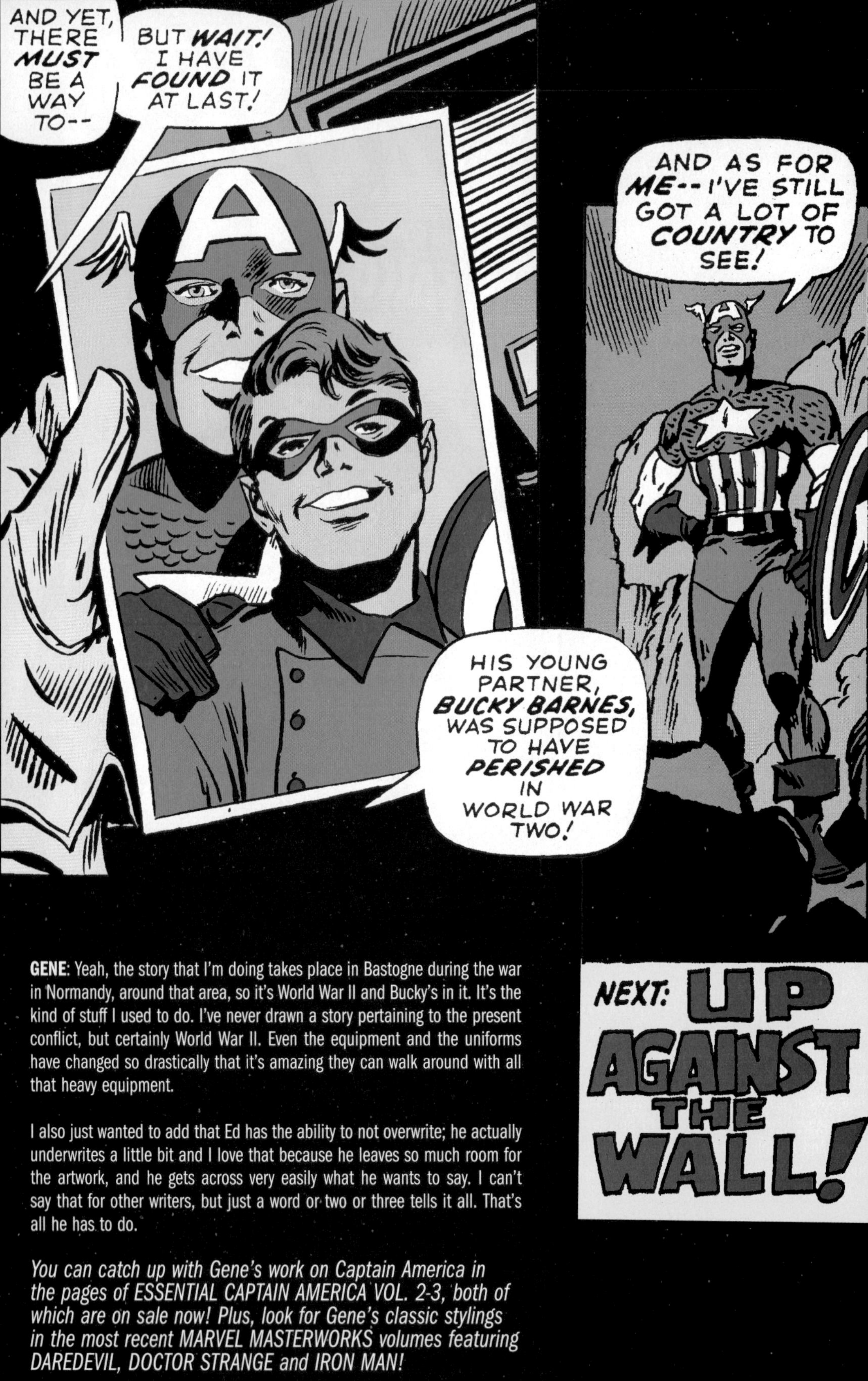
AND YET, THERE MUST BE A WAY TO--
BUT WAIT! I HAVE FOUND IT AT LAST!
HIS YOUNG PARTNER, BUCKY BARNES, WAS SUPPOSED TO HAVE PERISHED IN WORLD WAR TWO!
AND AS FOR ME--I'VE STILL GOT A LOT OF COUNTRY TO SEE!

GENE: Yeah, the story that I'm doing takes place in Bastogne during the war in Normandy, around that area, so it's World War II and Bucky's in it. It's the kind of stuff I used to do. I've never drawn a story pertaining to the present conflict, but certainly World War II. Even the equipment and the uniforms have changed so drastically that it's amazing they can walk around with all that heavy equipment.

I also just wanted to add that Ed has the ability to not overwrite; he actually underwrites a little bit and I love that because he leaves so much room for the artwork, and he gets across very easily what he wants to say. I can't say that for other writers, but just a word or two or three tells it all. That's all he has to do.

You can catch up with Gene's work on Captain America in the pages of ESSENTIAL CAPTAIN AMERICA VOL. 2-3, both of which are on sale now! Plus, look for Gene's classic stylings in the most recent MARVEL MASTERWORKS volumes featuring DAREDEVIL, DOCTOR STRANGE and IRON MAN!

NEXT: UP AGAINST THE WALL!

CAPTAIN AMERICA ANNUAL PREVIEW

Two pages of black and white pencil art from Gene Colan's collaboration with Ed Brubaker!

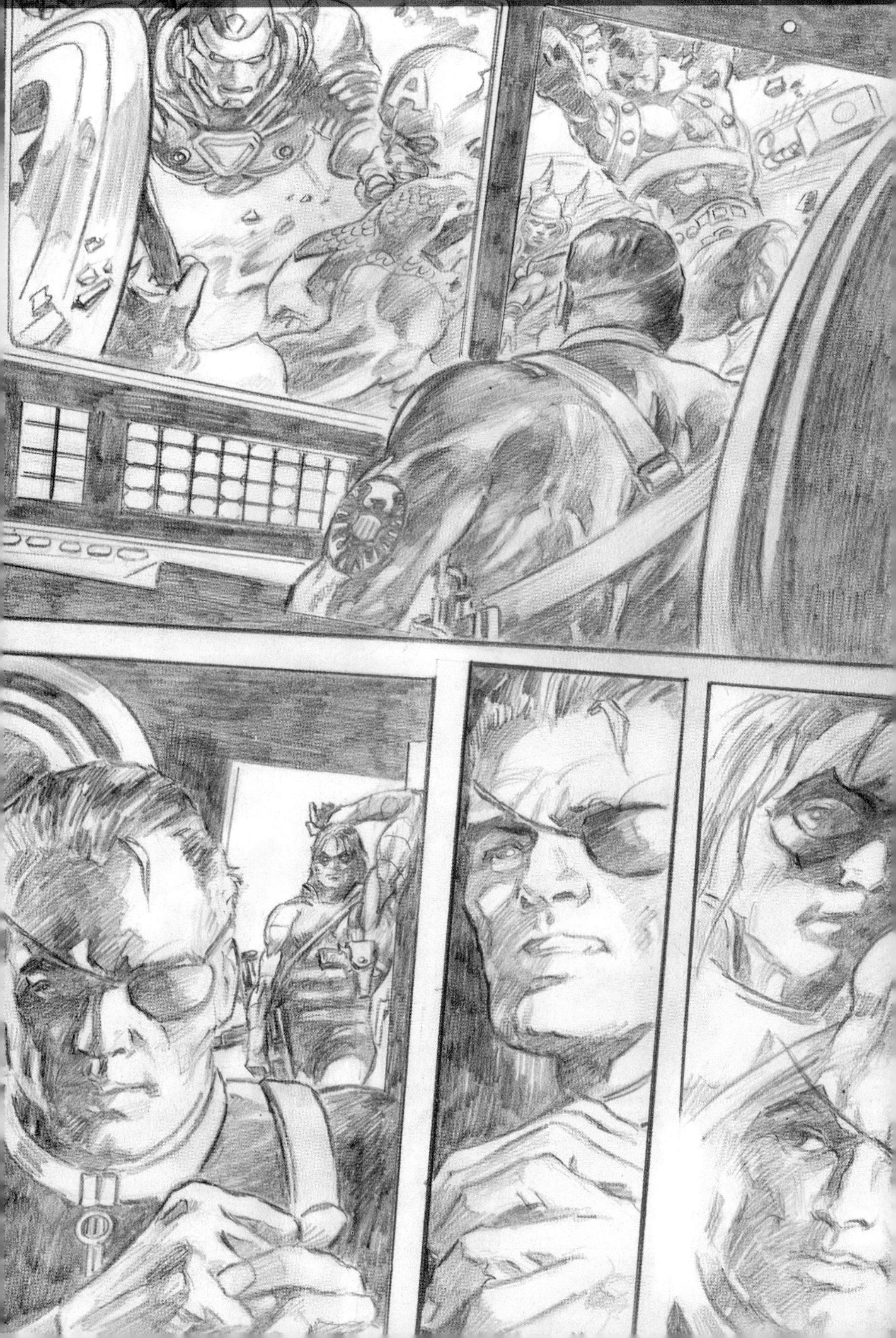

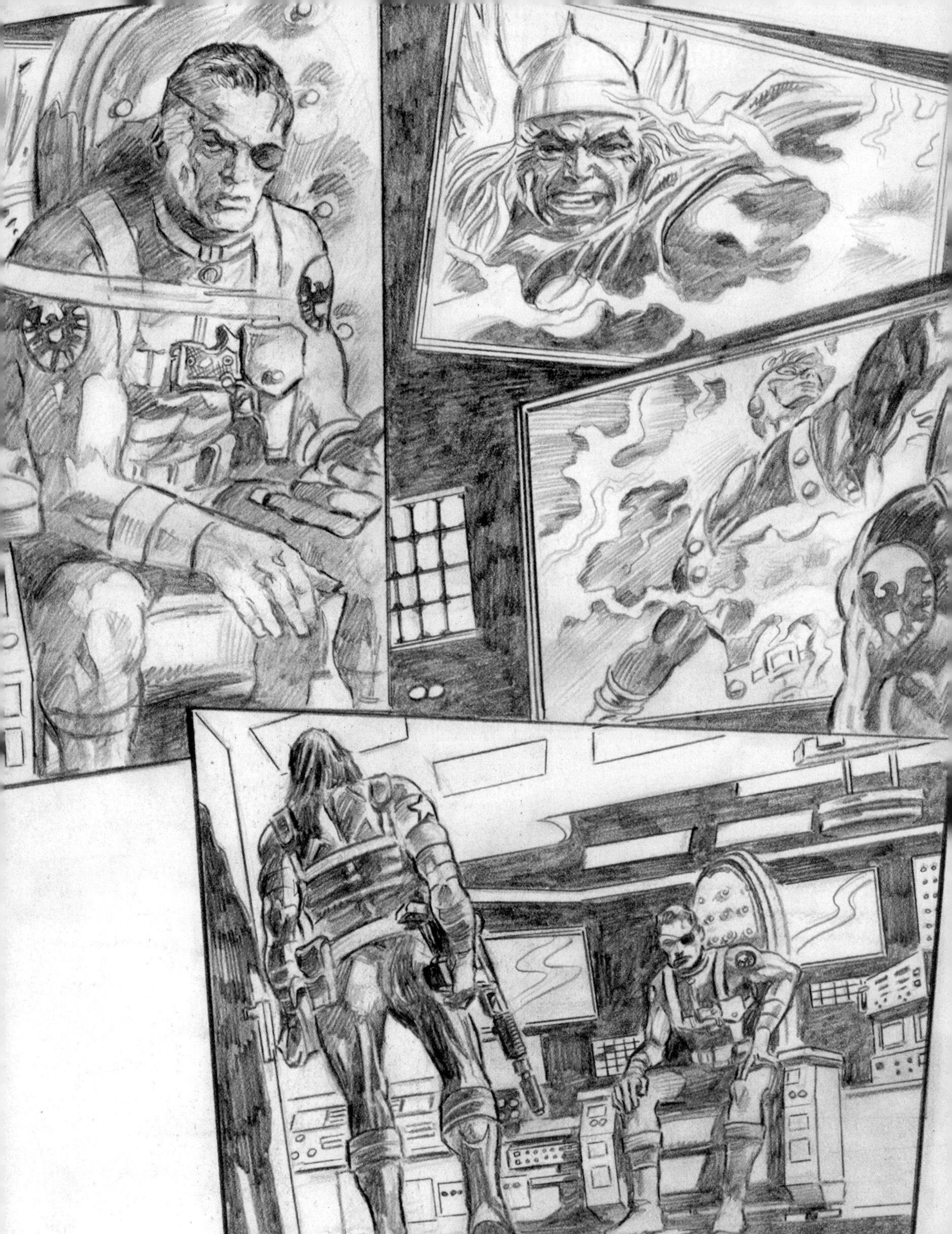

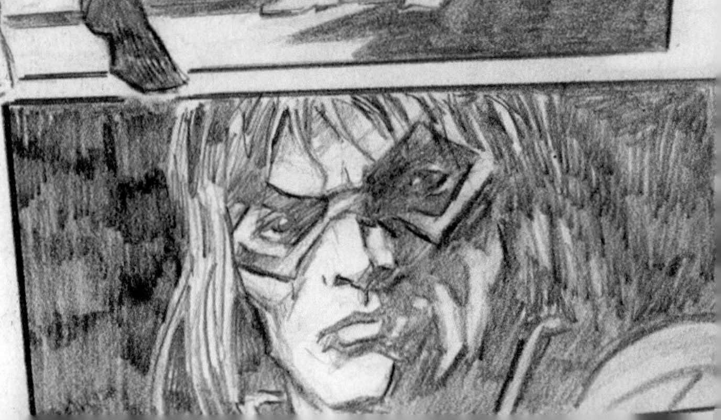

Keep an eye at Marvel.com and future issues of *Marvel Spotlight* for more information on the scheduling of Gene and Ed's modern masterwork!

CAPTAIN AMERICA REMEMBERED:

The Silver Age Revival: 1965-1970

Stan Lee • Jack Kirby • John Romita, Sr. • Gene Colan

Gene Colan closed out the '60s era of Cap in fine style, but he followed up a couple of timeless talents!

Jack "King" Kirby ushered in the Silver Age incarnation of Steve Rogers, Marvel's own Man Out of Time. Cap's first modern appearance, in a block of ice plucked from the icy waters of the North Atlantic *(Avengers #4)*, was quickly followed by his own monthly gig in the Tales of Suspense anthology, wherein he shared equal billing with Iron Man. When igniting this eminently successful revival, Stan didn't hesitate to imbed his Cap stories with the ultra-effective pathos of a hero haunted by a world he had known that had passed on, and the King was kicking it with the bombastic flash that he was perfecting as Stan's top man in the Marvel bullpen.

After an extended run in which Stan and Jack also reintroduced the classic villain Red Skull, the deadly Cosmic Cube, and a sidekick in the form of Rick Jones, the title's creative reins transferred over to Jim Steranko, a Silver Age stylist who helped redefine comic art expectations. One of his greatest Marvel triumphs was in the pages of *Captain America!* His run was oh-so brief *(Cap #110, 111, 113)*, but packed with high drama, proportion expanding page layouts, and Steranko's sultry, spy-oriented action.

These pinnacle achievements are available in their entirety in *Captain America Masterworks Vols. 1-3* and *Essential Captain America Vols. 1-2.*

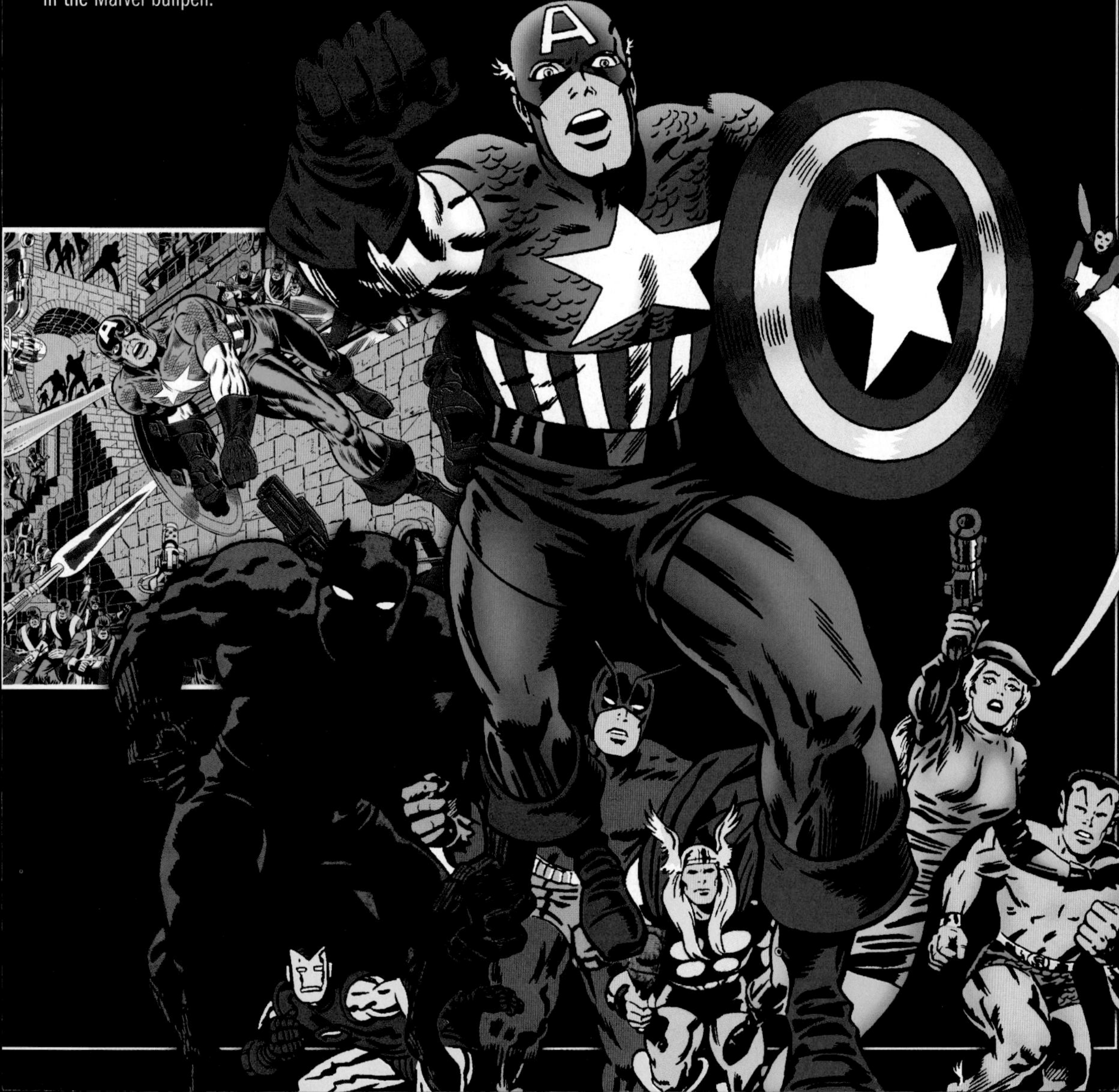

CAP IN CRISIS: STEVE ENGLEHART'S CAPTAIN AMERICA

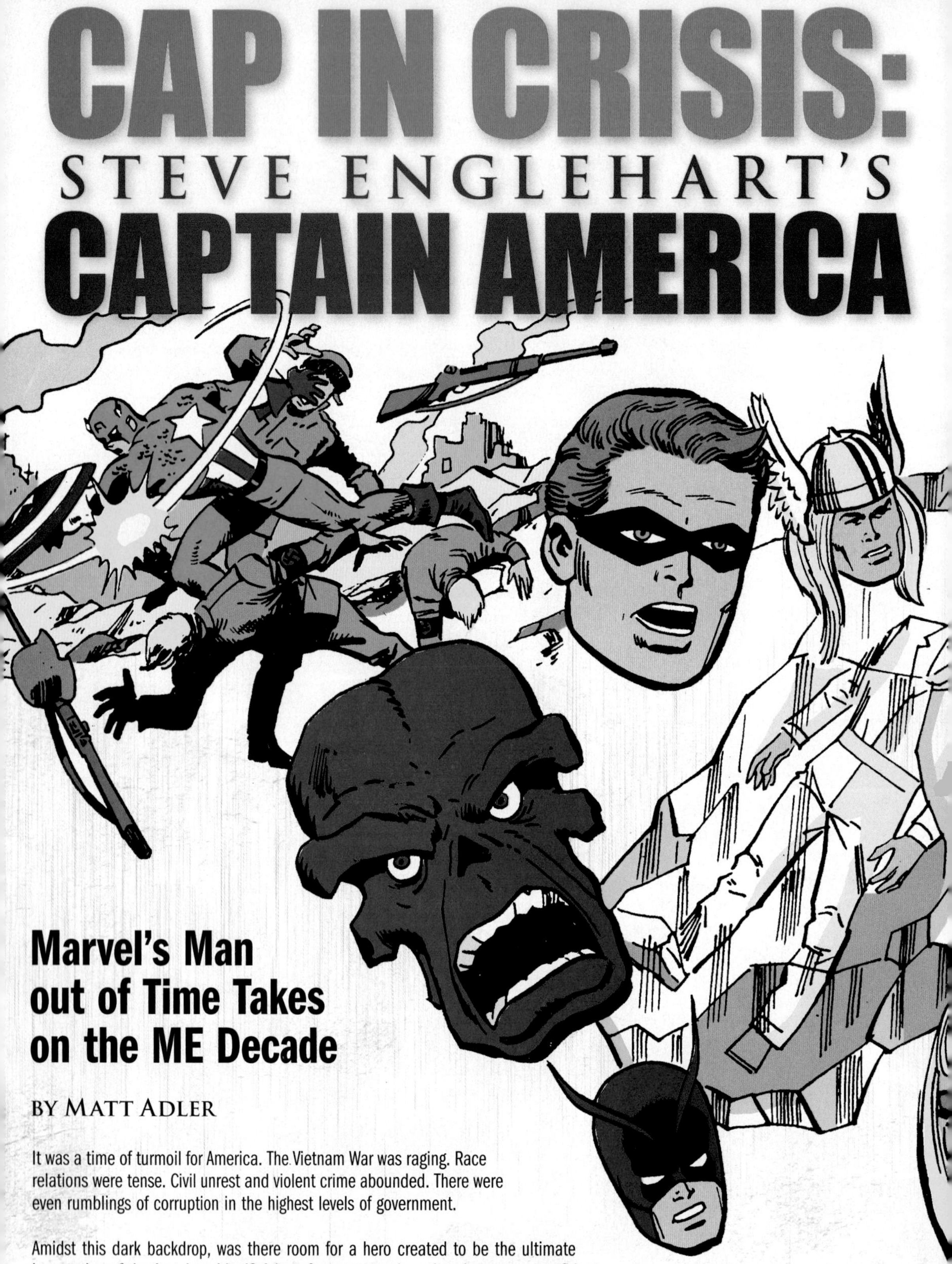

Marvel's Man out of Time Takes on the ME Decade

BY MATT ADLER

It was a time of turmoil for America. The Vietnam War was raging. Race relations were tense. Civil unrest and violent crime abounded. There were even rumblings of corruption in the highest levels of government.

Amidst this dark backdrop, was there room for a hero created to be the ultimate incarnation of the American ideal? A hero from an era where Americans were confident about the rightness of their cause and sure about the evil of the enemy they faced? That hero was Captain America, the Living Legend of World War II. He had been frozen in ice at the end of WWII, and revived in the early '60s, but by the Watergate era, the world was a much different place.

This was the world that *Marvel Comics* had to contend with in 1972, and reflective of this era, sales on Captain America's book were suffering. The public no longer seemed to have an appetite for the standard patriotic hero doing battle with unambiguous bad guys. Stan Lee had left the book a year earlier, and the writers who followed immediately after were unable to resolve this dilemma. Enter Steve Englehart. Steve was an up and coming writer at Marvel, and as he bluntly assesses it, "The book was failing, about to be reduced to bimonthly or even cancelled, so they gave it to the new guy."

Explaining his take on Cap, Steve says, "As far as Steve Rogers goes, he's a New Deal Democrat. He's a product of Roosevelt's rebuilding of the country's spirit, enhanced by World War II patriot spirit; he believes deeply in the ideals of America, the things they taught us all in school about why this is the greatest country on earth. Which is why, when the actual America falls short of that, his first reaction is to try to set things right."

This gelled with Steve's own background, though for him, the character comes first. "I've always followed current events, and I did and do have a 'fighting liberal' sort of philosophy. So, at that time, I was anti-war, anti-Watergate, and so pro-American ideals. But I'd point out that though that philosophy meshed pretty well with Cap, (a) I was a conscientious objector, having been in the Army and gotten out, writing a man born of war, and (b) I wrote a lot of other characters simultaneously, and have written a lot since, that had completely different philosophies (the Hulk, Silver Surfer, the Batman, the Joker, Atom Bob...). Point being, I write the character, not my philosophy."

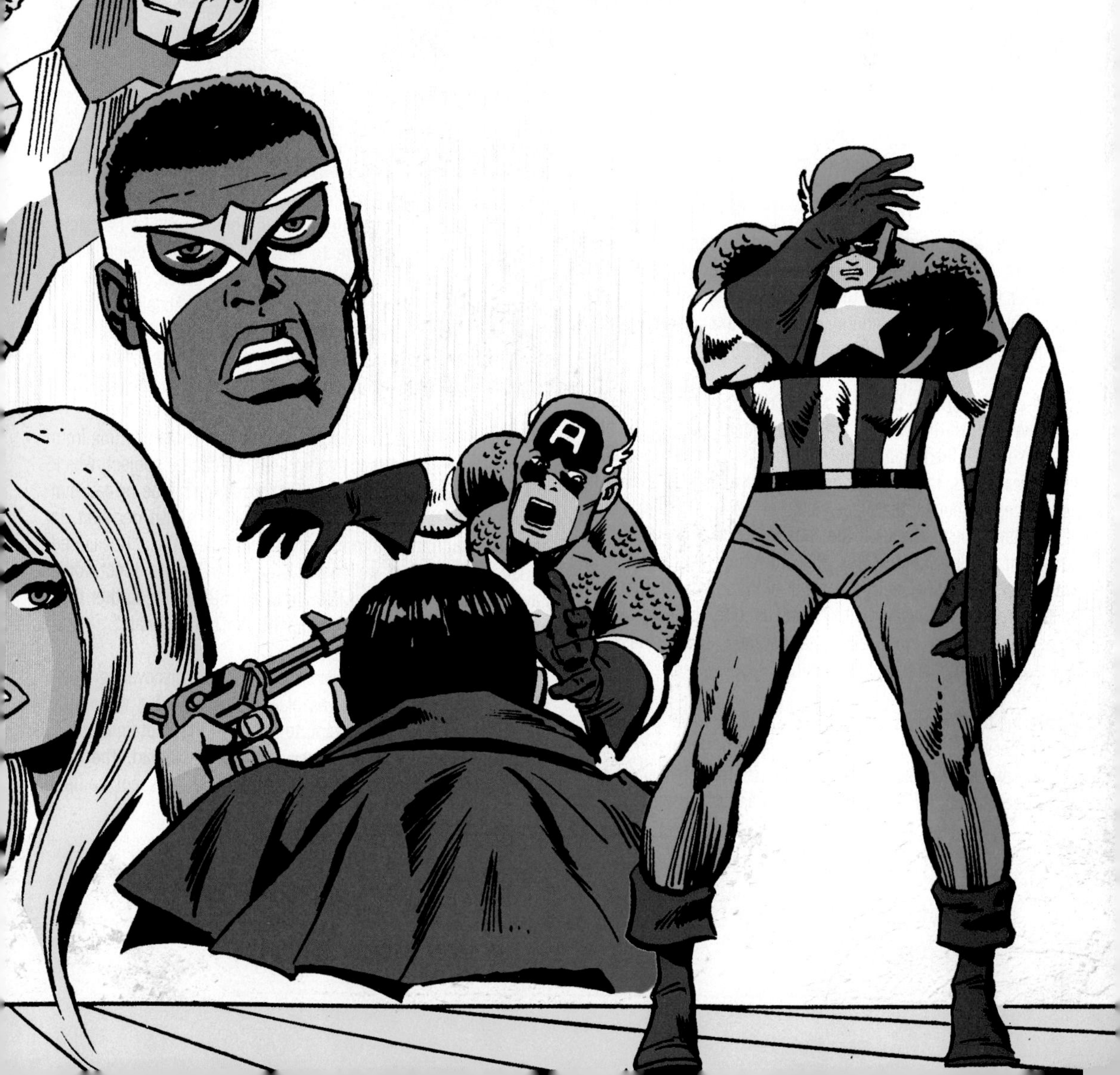

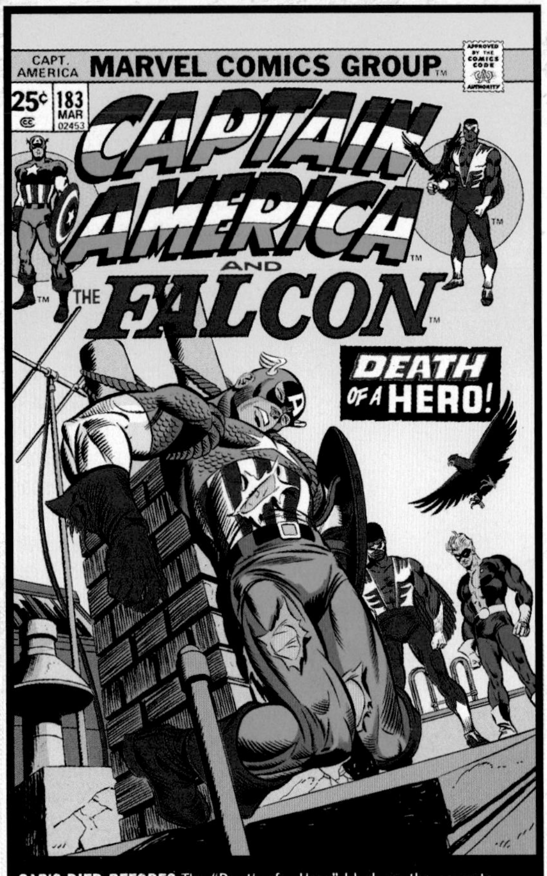
CAPT. AMERICA
MARVEL COMICS GROUP
25¢
183
MAR
02453
CAPTAIN AMERICA
AND
THE
FALCON
DEATH OF A HERO!

CAP'S DIED BEFORE? The "Death of a Hero" blurb on the cover to *Cap/Falcon #183* wasn't as legit as this year's Death of a Dream story in *Cap #25*.

But the philosophical divide in America was very much on display in Steve's first arc, when he tackled a bit of Captain America lore that went right to the heart of the character's philosophy. In the 1950s, there was a brief run of the *Captain America* comic where, in keeping with the spirit of the times, Captain America became a more aggressive, conservative, communist-fighting character. When the real Captain America made his return in the '60s, the appearance of the '50s Cap was left unexplained, until Steve came on the book. Steve made sure to do his research, explaining "I always read what's gone before me when I take over a series; I have a great respect for what the guys before me did, even if I'm going to go a different direction."

His story revealed that the '50s Cap had been groomed to replace Captain America when he disappeared at the end of WWII. The '50s Cap and his partner, a replacement for the original Bucky, started out with the goal to fight Communist spies and saboteurs, but due to imperfections in the process to simulate Cap's physical abilities, they began to grow more aggressive, and even paranoid, seeing threats to America where none existed. The government quickly realized they were out of control, and shut them down, placing them in suspended animation, until they were freed years later by a disgruntled government employee.

Newly awakened, they confronted the real Captain America and his partner the Falcon. Regarding the differences that underpinned this confrontation, Steve says, "In this case, the comics mirrored their eras; the late '30s-early '40s Cap was a liberal and the early '50s Cap was a conservative. The first one looked up to Roosevelt; the second looked up to McCarthy. That's about as fundamental as it gets." Thus, it was not only a physical battle, but a battle of ideologies in which Cap confronted the impostor with just how out of touch and extreme he had become, and in doing so, managed to defeat him.

In his next major storyline, Steve unveiled a conspiracy to take control of the U.S. government, plotted by a shadowy organization known as the Secret Empire. Using various pawns and agents, the Secret Empire sought to undermine Captain America, and portray him to the public as a villain and a traitor.

In the climactic finale of this arc, the Secret Empire attempts to take over the White House. When Captain America stops the plot, he chases their leader all the way into the Oval Office. Unmasking the mastermind, Captain America is shocked to find a face he recognizes. Although that face is never shown to the reader, it is clear through the dialogue that it is none other than the President of the United States, Richard Nixon, who at the time was embroiled in the real-life scandal of Watergate. Rather than face capture, the leader of the Secret Empire commits suicide right before Cap's eyes, leaving a horrified and disillusioned Steve Rogers to deal with the fallout.

Portraying the President of the United States, however unpopular, as a super-villain, was a bold move to take, but the open creative climate of Marvel allowed Steve to explore what might previously have been taboo. As Steve explains, "It was just absolutely clear to me that, during Watergate, Captain America, unlike Daredevil or Spider-Man, would have to react to what was going on in America. People at the time and since have asked, 'Did you get any editorial interference?,' and the answer is, 'Absolutely none.' Marvel encouraged pushing the envelope then, the Marvel U was completely connected to the world we all lived in, and there was no question in anyone's mind that it was the right thing to do."

Still, while Steve felt confident in the support he was getting from editorial, he realized that this was still a delicate subject, which led to his decision to not show Richard Nixon's face or call him by name. He makes clear this was purely his own decision, in order to avoid potential problems of public reaction. "I censored myself, and therefore, we'll never know if being more direct would have caused a reaction or not. I was definitely going farther than anyone ever had, and in the moment, that was my call."

Captain America's disillusionment upon discovering that the leader of his country was also the leader of a subversive conspiracy spurred his decision to abandon the Captain America mantle. He soon took up a new identity as Nomad, The Man Without a Country, but found that the public was not content

"AS FAR AS STEVE ROGERS GOES, HE'S A NEW DEAL DEMOCRAT. HE'S A PRODUCT OF ROOSEVELT'S REBUILDING OF THE COUNTRY'S SPIRIT..."

– WRITER STEVE ENGLEHART

without a Captain America. Several wannabes attempted to take up the red, white, and blue uniform, but all met with failure. One such attempt culminated in the tragic death of one of the would-be replacements, a young man named Roscoe, at the hands of the Red Skull. This prompted Cap to return to action, determined to take the Skull down.

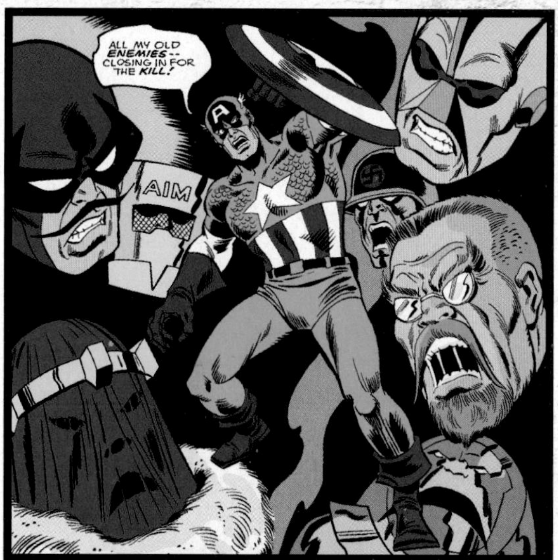
ALL MY OLD ENEMIES-- CLOSING IN FOR THE KILL!
AIM

ROGUES GALLERY REMEMBERED: Baron Zemo, Batroc, Doctor Faustus and more haunt the memory of Steve Rogers! (Image from *Cap/Falcon #185*.)

Throughout his run, Steve had used the Falcon's civilian status as an inner-city social worker to explore issues of race relations, and the divides within black culture. Explaining his motivation for these stories, Steve relates, "The '60s and '70s were a period of breakthroughs in race relations, with Martin Luther King, Jr. working one side of the street and Malcolm X and the Black Panthers working the other – and since I love reality, I was plugged into what was going on around me. I was young, single, liberal, and creative, in New York – I had plenty of experiences to draw from, and I wanted to do that drawing. But beyond all that, I also, as a comic book writer, had a rock-bottom conviction that the co-star of the book who was black should get as much attention as the co-star of the book who was white. It was called *Captain America And The Falcon*, after all."

So it was perhaps not surprising that Steve made the Falcon the centerpiece of his final arc on the book. Captain America and the Falcon pursued the Red Skull in the wake of Roscoe's death, and just when it seemed that Captain America would finally bring him to justice, the Red Skull turned the tables, ordering the Falcon to attack Captain America, and revealing in the process that the Skull had actually been behind the Falcon's origin, the first layers of which were introduced back in *Captain America #117* (1969).

Cap had originally met the Falcon when he was trapped on one of the Red Skull's hideaways known as Exile Island. At the time, the Falcon explained to Cap that he was a falcon trainer named Sam Wilson who, along with his bird Redwing, had been lured to Exile Island and became trapped there as well. Cap and the Falcon made their escape together, and subsequently became partners.

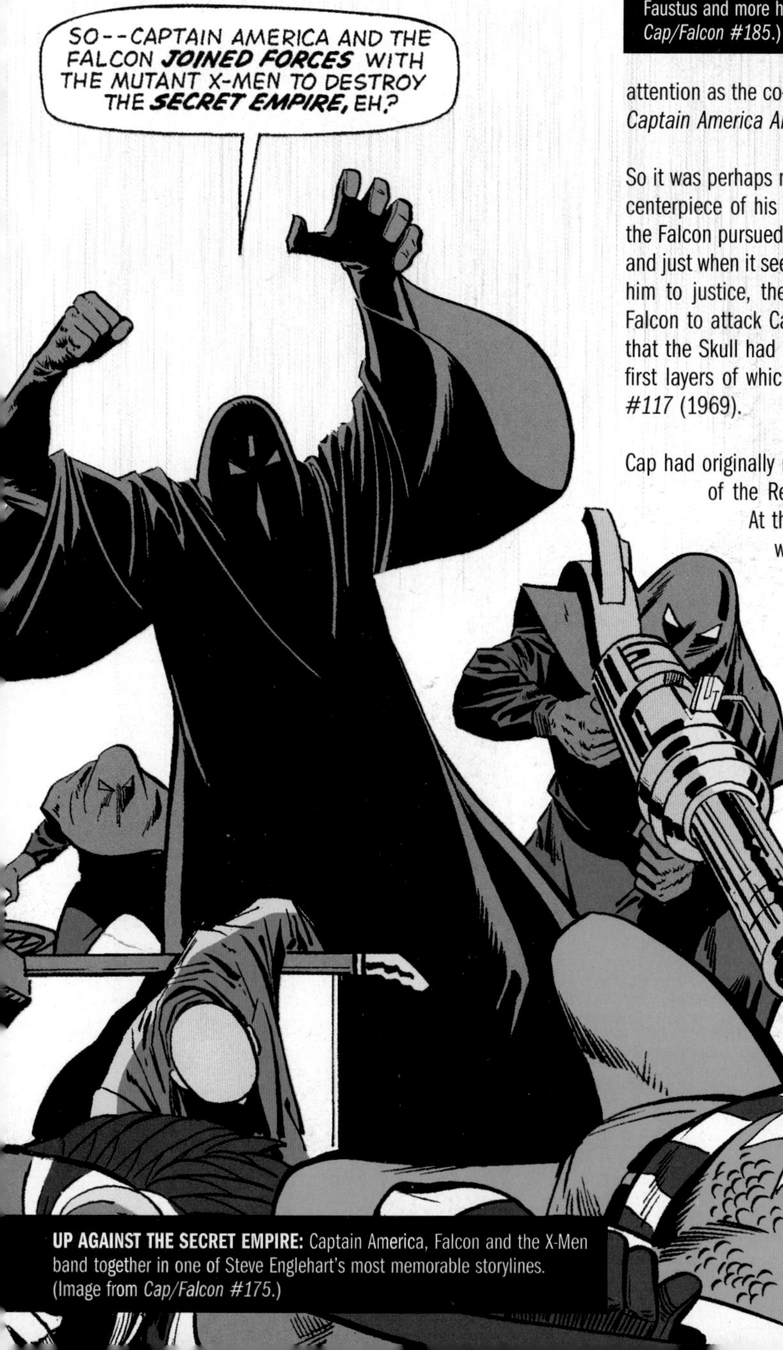
SO--CAPTAIN AMERICA AND THE FALCON JOINED FORCES WITH THE MUTANT X-MEN TO DESTROY THE SECRET EMPIRE, EH?

UP AGAINST THE SECRET EMPIRE: Captain America, Falcon and the X-Men band together in one of Steve Englehart's most memorable storylines. (Image from *Cap/Falcon #175*.)

CAPT. AMERICA
MARVEL COMICS GROUP
25¢ 186 JUNE 02453
CAPTAIN AMERICA AND THE FALCON
REVEALED AT LAST! THE TRUE FACTS BEHIND THE ORIGIN OF THE FALCON!
MY ALLY... MY ENEMY!
TODAY THE MOMENT I'VE WAITED FOR FINALLY COMES TO PASS!
TODAY THE FALCON SLAYS CAPTAIN AMERICA AT THE COMMAND OF THE RED SKULL!

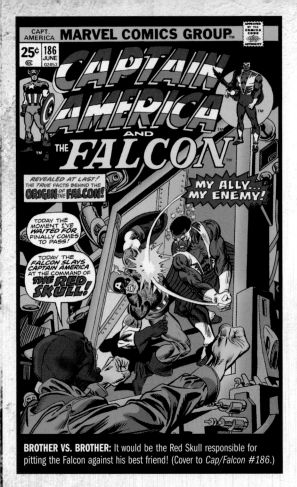

BROTHER VS. BROTHER: It would be the Red Skull responsible for pitting the Falcon against his best friend! (Cover to *Cap/Falcon #186*.)

"I CENSORED MYSELF, AND THEREFORE, WE'LL NEVER KNOW IF BEING MORE DIRECT WOULD HAVE CAUSED A REACTION OR NOT. I WAS DEFINITELY GOING FARTHER THAN ANYONE EVER HAD, AND IN THE MOMENT, THAT WAS MY CALL."

– ENGLEHART

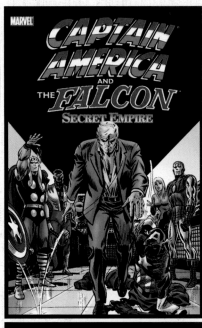

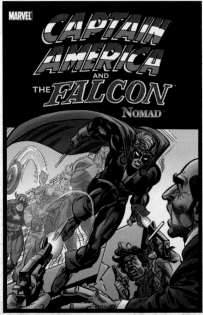

But Steve revealed that Sam had in actuality fallen into a life of crime in early adulthood, becoming a small-time hoodlum nicknamed "Snap" Wilson, and crashing on Exile Island during a smuggling mission. The Red Skull discovered him there and using the Cosmic Cube, brainwashed and implanted him with false memories, as well as granting him a psychic link with his falcon Redwing, and giving him subliminal orders to befriend Captain America, with the goal of one day turning the Falcon upon him.

Explaining the genesis of these revelations, Steve says, "Looking back at the Falcon just appearing on the Red Skull's island (in his first appearance), it seemed awfully damned pat. I thought it was an interesting angle to explore, and when I decided to leave the series, I thought it'd be a good starting point for the next writer, in the same way that Roy Thomas had handed me the '50s Cap idea when I was starting."

Indeed, that startling revelation would be Steve's final issue on the series, and it was up to other writers to deal with the fallout. To this day, Steve's run is remembered as one of the high points in the history of Captain America.

You can read this ground-breaking era in the CAPTAIN AMERICA AND THE FALCON: SECRET EMPIRE TPB, and the CAPTAIN AMERICA: NOMAD TPB. Don't miss them!

MARVEL
CAPTAIN AMERICA AND THE FALCON
SECRET EMPIRE

MARVEL
CAPTAIN AMERICA AND THE FALCON
NOMAD

REMEMBERING "REMEMBRANCE"

Stern & Byrne Take Their Turn With America's Fighting Legend

BY DUGAN TRODGLEN

Captain America has had its fair share of memorable runs, and occasionally the regard for a particular creative team is far greater than the time they spent on the book. Aside from the obvious example of Jim Steranko's too-brief tenure, the nine-issue run written by Roger Stern and drawn by John Byrne is considered an all-time Cap classic. During the run of *Captain America #247-255*, the pair managed to retell Cap's origin in a newly cohesive style, have Cap consider a run for president, introduce a love interest into the life of Steve Rogers, reintroduce some much-beloved Invaders characters, and have Cap face classic villains like Batroc, Mr. Hyde, and Baron Strucker. These nine issues were collected long ago in the trade paperback titled War & Remembrance, which Marvel is currently restoring and remastering for a new reprint due in July! *Spotlight* talked to Roger Stern about the enduring appeal of his run with all-star artist John Byrne.

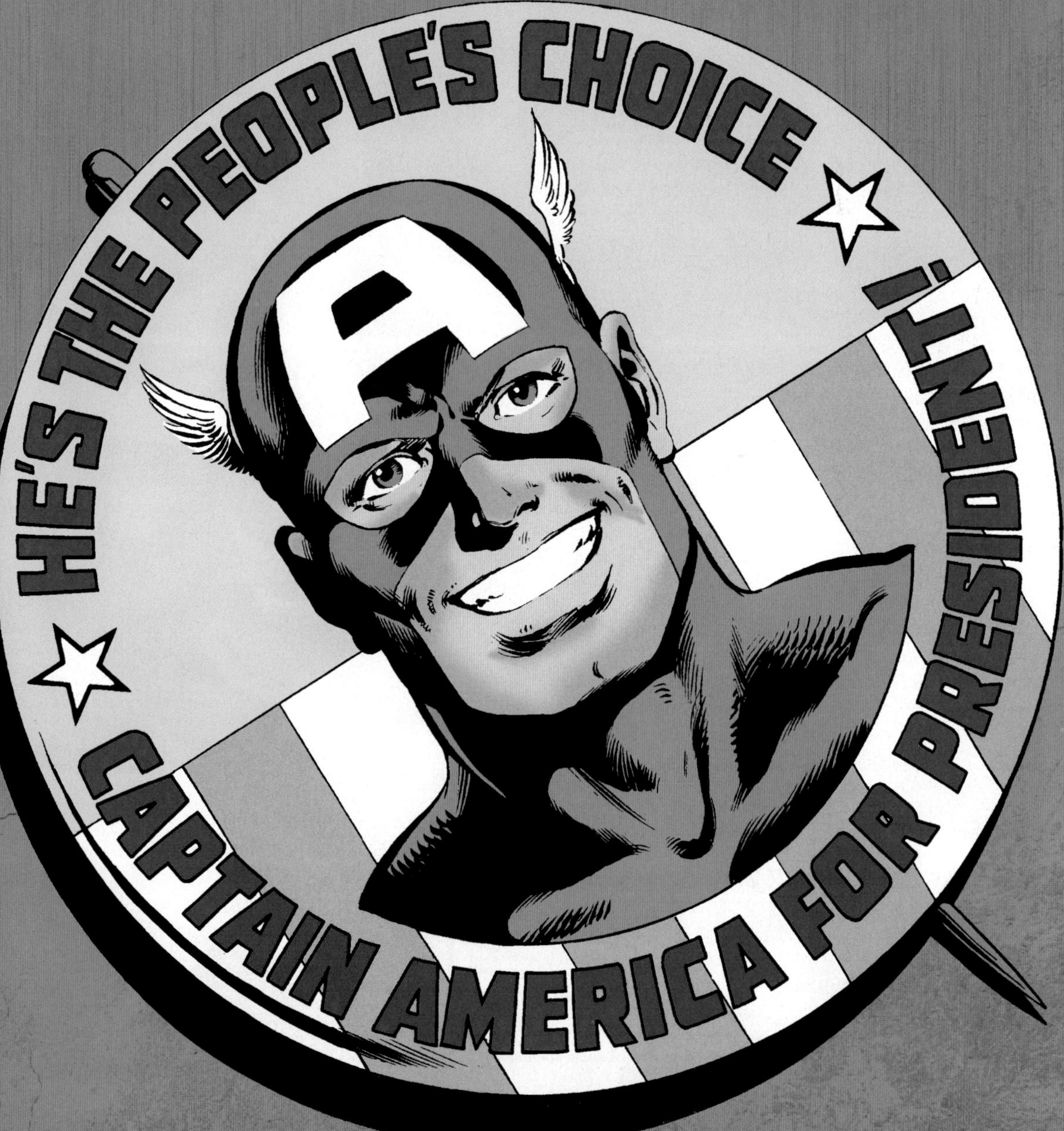

HE'S THE PEOPLE'S CHOICE
CAPTAIN AMERICA FOR PRESIDENT!

> ## "STEVE ROGERS IS A PATRIOT AND AN IDEALIST, BUT HE'S NO STARRY-EYED FOOL. AS HE GREW UP, HE SAW CORRUPTION, BIGOTRY, AND HYPOCRISY FIRST HAND."
>
> – WRITER ROGER STERN

SPOTLIGHT: In the introduction to the *War and Remembrance TPB* collection, you talk about heading to the bookstore to research the WWII era. Why was this important to you?

ROGER: I've always been big on researching the people I write about, and I felt that doubly important for as iconic a hero as Captain America. I'd read all of his adventures in *Avengers*, *Invaders*, and his own series — going all the way back through *Tales of Suspense* — many times over. But Captain America was a member of Brokaw's "Greatest Generation." Steve Rogers had been born during the boom years of the 1920s, had grown up during the Great Depression and FDR's New Deal, and fought his way across Europe during World War II. All of that made him what he was, far more than any treatment with Dr. Erskine's Super-Soldier formula. Those times defined his generation, just as the 1950s and '60s defined mine.

Now, I may be a Boomer, but I was also an only child until I was seven years old, so I always felt close to my parents' generation. Still, there was a lot more I wanted to know — that I needed to know — and my research helped me get inside Cap's head.

SPOTLIGHT: What did you learn that you applied to Cap?

ROGER: I mainly saw reinforcement for a lot of what I already knew. See, Steve Rogers is a patriot and an idealist, but he's no starry-eyed fool. As he grew up, he saw corruption, bigotry, and hypocrisy first hand — none of that is new or unique. You think Shock Radio was invented yesterday? From 1926 through 1940, an anti-Semitic bigot named Charles Coughlin had a huge following on radio. And even today, when people try to describe evil, they often invoke Hitler. Well, the young Steve Rogers would have seen the growth of the Nazi party and fascism; he would have seen the rise of Hitler and Mussolini. He saw the

Nazis marching into Czechoslovakia and Poland in newsreels and read about it in his daily newspaper, not in some dusty history book.

But Steve Rogers was also lucky enough to have a president who refused to use fear as a tool to manipulate the public. You've seen old news footage of Franklin Roosevelt's first inaugural address, we all have. Hey, Dave Letterman runs a clip at least once a week of FDR declaring that "the only thing we have to fear is, fear itself." But can you imagine what that speech meant to people? The country, the whole world was in terrible shape, but there was a president who inspired hope. And Steve Rogers heard that speech live on the radio. He drew inspiration from that, just

BARON BLOOD: A definitive moment in Cap history, perfectly told by Stern and Byrne. (Art from *Cap #253*.)

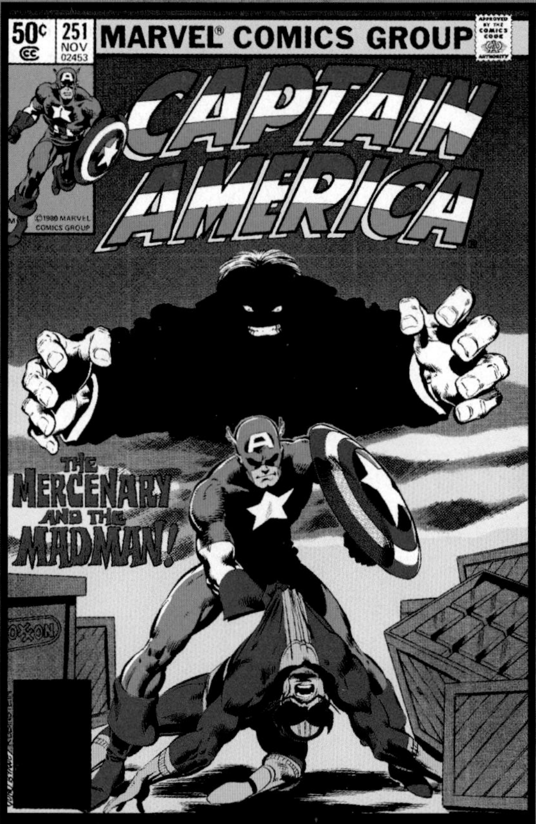
50¢
251
NOV
MARVEL® COMICS GROUP
CAPTAIN AMERICA
THE MERCENARY AND THE MADMAN!

CAP #251: Roger Stern and John Byrne pit Cap against the duo of Batroc and Mr. Hyde!

as millions of others did. And he saw the results the followed, saw people pulling together, working for the common good. And that stuck with him, all the days of his life. And that is why he is Captain America.

SPOTLIGHT: In your run, your plots balanced great action scenes with compelling character moments (not to mention continuity cleanup)! How did you manage this balance and how much did John Byrne contribute in terms of plot?

ROGER: Balancing action and character is really what comic book storytelling is all about. In fact, when you get right down to it, action can define character and vice versa. As to how I did it...well, I learned a lot of my craft from reading the masters: Stan Lee, Jack Kirby, and Steve Ditko. Of course, it helped that – midway through our run on *Captain America* – we were able to go from 17 to 22 pages. That gave us more room for everything.

But getting back to the plots, John and I were tossing ideas back and forth from the very beginning. (I used to joke that we spent so much time talking on the phone, our biggest fans were probably the Board of Directors of AT&T, back in the days of the one-and-only monolithic Telephone Company.) For example, our two-part story with Union Jack and Baron Blood grew out of a rough idea for an *Invaders/Avengers* story that John had come up with during the year or so that he was drawing – and I was editing – the *Avengers*. Together, we took that idea and turned it into a *Cap* story.

SPOTLIGHT: You had Cap considering an offer to run for president. Was this considered a risky story at the time by Marvel?

ROGER: No, not at all. After all, Howard the Duck had run for president just four years before. Why not Cap? *(Laughter.)*

Actually, when Don Perlin and Roger McKenzie were working on *Captain America*, and I was their editor, they'd wanted to have Cap run for president. But they'd also wanted to have Cap win the election and operate out of the White House for the next four years! And I thought that premise was just too far-fetched. Granted, there are people – far too many, really – who don't know who their congressman or senator are, but everybody knows who the president is. And no matter who won the next election, we would all know that the president wasn't really Captain America. You can only stretch the readers' suspension-of-disbelief so far. It was a fine idea for a What If? story (as Mike W. Barr later proved), but not for an ongoing Marvel Universe title.

A year or so after that, I wound up writing the book. John came into the city on one of his periodic visits, and we were having dinner after work with Jim Shooter and Ralph Macchio. Somewhere around the middle of the entrée, we started talking shop. Now, by that time, John and I already knew that we wanted to revisit Cap's origin for his 40th anniversary *(Cap #255)*, so we were tossing ideas around, trying to think of something special to do for *Captain America #250*.

I think it was over dessert that we realized that issue *#250* would be on sale in July – right around the time of the political conventions. Anyway, Jim suggested that we consider the "Cap for President" idea. I was still skeptical at first. After all, I really didn't think that Cap was the type who would be interested in running for office. But then, Jim said that should be the whole point of the story – that we should make it about who Cap is and why he wouldn't run. John and I looked at each other, and it was as if two cartoon light bulbs suddenly went off over our heads! *(Laughter.)*

From there on the story just fell together. We'd taken the premise in a totally different direction from the one Don and Mac had suggested, but I still felt beholden to let them both know what we were doing. And I made sure that they were credited with the idea on letters page in *Cap #250*.

SPOTLIGHT: The highlight of your run has to be the Baron Blood story featuring the return not only of the horrific vampire but also Union Jack in his first contemporary Marvel appearance. What made you want to revisit Cap's Invaders roots?

ROGER: As I said, it had all started with John's idea for an *Avengers* story. You must understand: he and I had both grown up in a world that had largely been defined by World War II. John especially. As a boy in England, he grew up among family for whom the Blitz still felt like yesterday. And we were both big fans of the great art that Frank Robbins had drawn for Roy Thomas on the Invaders. Sadly, that book had been discontinued a little over a year before. So we thought it was high time that Cap looked in on his old allies.

Plus, when we were working on *Cap*, the Second World War was already starting to slip into the realm of "ancient history" as far as our younger readers were concerned. If we were going to visit Lord Falsworth, we had to do it before he died of old age.

SPOTLIGHT: You introduced the third Union Jack, and gave him the interesting spin of not being part of the elite family lineage. Instead, he came from a more working class background, something that has been an important part of his character ever since.

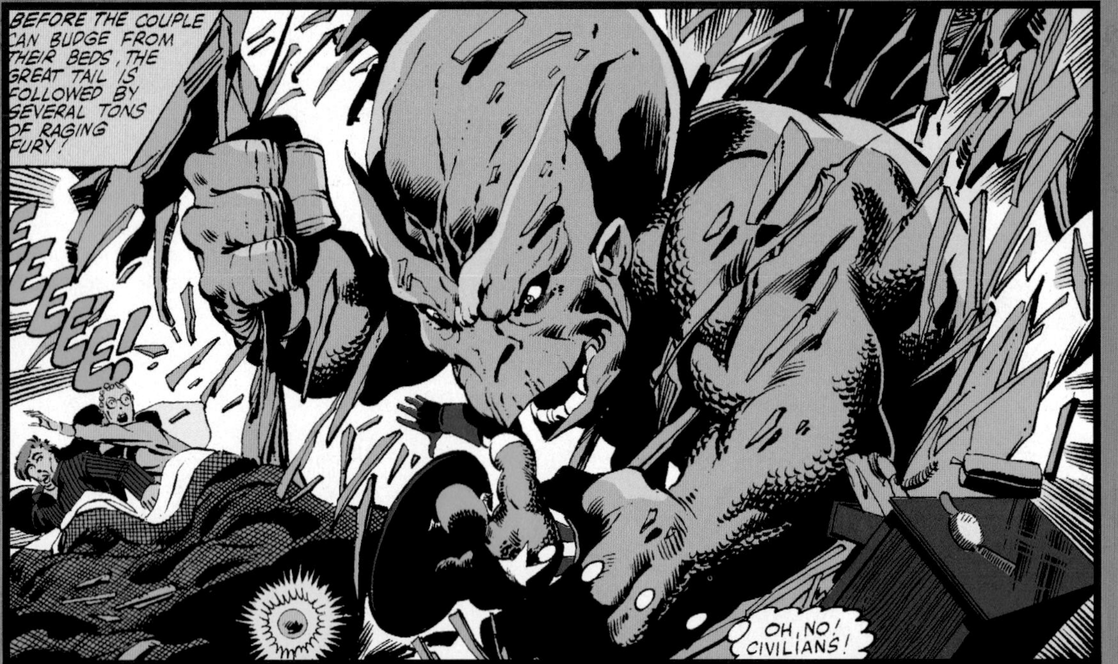
BEFORE THE COUPLE CAN BUDGE FROM THEIR BEDS, THE GREAT TAIL IS FOLLOWED BY SEVERAL TONS OF RAGING FURY!
OH, NO! CIVILIANS!

CAP vs. **THE DRAGON MAN:** Sensational art by John Byrne depicts the violent rampage of Dragon Man! (Art from *Cap #248.*)

ROGER: Our new Union Jack was at least partially inspired by John Lennon's song, "Working Class Hero." The British members of the Invaders had mostly been of the nobility, but it was the common man who did most of England's fighting and dying. There's a verse from Rudyard Kipling's poem Tommy that sums it up:

We aren't no thin red 'eroes, nor we aren't no blackguards too,
But single men in barricks, most remarkable like you;
An' if sometimes our conduck isn't all your fancy paints,
Why, single men in barricks don't grow into plaster saints;
While it's Tommy this, an' Tommy that, an' "Tommy, fall be'ind,"
But it's "Please to walk in front, sir," when there's trouble in the wind...

I just thought it was about time that a commoner became the archetypical British super-hero.

SPOTLIGHT: How does it feel to have Joey Chapman still going, even stronger than ever? Is he still largely the character as you conceived him?

ROGER: Well, we really never got to do too much with Joey other than in that one story. I haven't seen any of his contemporary appearances, but it's nice to learn that he's still around.

SPOTLIGHT: Bernie Rosenthal was another character you created who had legs (so to speak). Why did you give Steve Rogers a love interest, particularly one who was a "civilian"?

ROGER: Hey, Steve needed a little romance in his life. Since the Avengers had revived him, the only love in his life had been S.H.I.E.L.D. Agent Sharon Carter, and when we started on the book, she was dead.

I thought that if Steve Rogers was going to have a life out of costume, he needed a smart, down-to-earth sweetheart – someone who wasn't a secret agent or another super hero. And that was Bernie.

The thing that I really liked about their relationship was that while Bernie and Steve were about the same "age" physiologically, culturally they had a May-December romance.

SPOTLIGHT: You and John Byrne celebrated the 40th anniversary of *Captain America* by retelling his first adventure, streamlining his origin in the process. It was obviously a kick, but did this feel like a big responsibility?

ROGER: I don't think that what we did was a streamlining so much as it was a case of finally putting all the ducks in a row – taking all the versions of Cap's origin and bringing them together. We were just the latest guys to carry the torch, doing our best to be faithful to the hero that Joe Simon and Jack Kirby had created all those years before. That issue has been reprinted a number of times since, so I guess we did all right. And it was all great fun, especially the part where I got to write dialogue for Franklin Delano Roosevelt.

SPOTLIGHT: Your run was short but well remembered. Does that realization take some of the sting out of leaving the book before you wanted to?

ROGER: Looking back, we're probably fortunate in that we weren't on the book long enough to overstay our welcome. *(Laughter.)*

Here it is, well over 25 years since we made those comics, and people are still asking me to autograph them. It's a great feeling. And it's very nice seeing these stories back in print again.

As we go to press, the reissue of CAPTAIN AMERICA: WAR AND REMEMBRANCE TPB is due to hit store shelves on July 5, merely the day after the celebration of America's independence! A lot of great moments were packed in Stern & Byrne's great run, so make sure to check out this commemorative reprint volume and find out for yourself! Thanks to Roger Stern for talking to us about his time writing Captain America.

CAPTAIN AMERICA REMEMBERED:

1985-1995

Mark Gruenwald

Quick question: Who wrote *Captain America* the longest? Was it Simon and Kirby? Stan Lee? Steve Englehart? All great writers and vital contributors to the *Captain America* mythos to be sure, but the answer to this question is Mark Gruenwald. Mark was a writer and editor for Marvel Comics from 1978 until his untimely death in 1996 at the age of 43. And in that time, he made a tremendous contribution to the lore of *Captain America*, writing the series for eleven years from 1985 to 1995!

During his epic run, Mark lined up a bunch of fun, exciting, dramatic, and at times controversial, storylines back to back. Chief among these from his early years on the title was the Scourge arc *(Cap #318-320)*, in which a mystery vigilante launches a wave of serial killings aimed at depopulating Marvel's stable of lame super-villians. (This was a story element that the Handbook savvy Gruenwald attacked with particular gusto!) Also, Mark delivered a poignant storyline that had Captain America adopt the new ID of The Captain rather than submit to what he felt was unwarranted government control over his life. This narrative also introduced fan-favorite John Walker, who took the identity of Captain America for a short time before ultimately yielding it back to Cap so he could take on his new role as USAgent! (Raid those back issue bins for *Cap #332-350!*)

Other highlights of Mark's tenure included the introduction of the villainous Crossbones, the femme fatale Diamondback, the epic Bloodstone Saga story arc, the seminal Cap/Wolverine team-up in *Cap Annual #8*, and, honestly, too many other milestone moments to mention in the space alloted. *[Hey, how about we do a big Gruenwald feature for our next Cap Spotlight? – Ed.]* After eleven years, Mark's run on *Captain America* came to a close. Tragically, a year later, he passed away. But to this day, the characters and concepts he created continue to shape the Marvel Universe and Captain America.

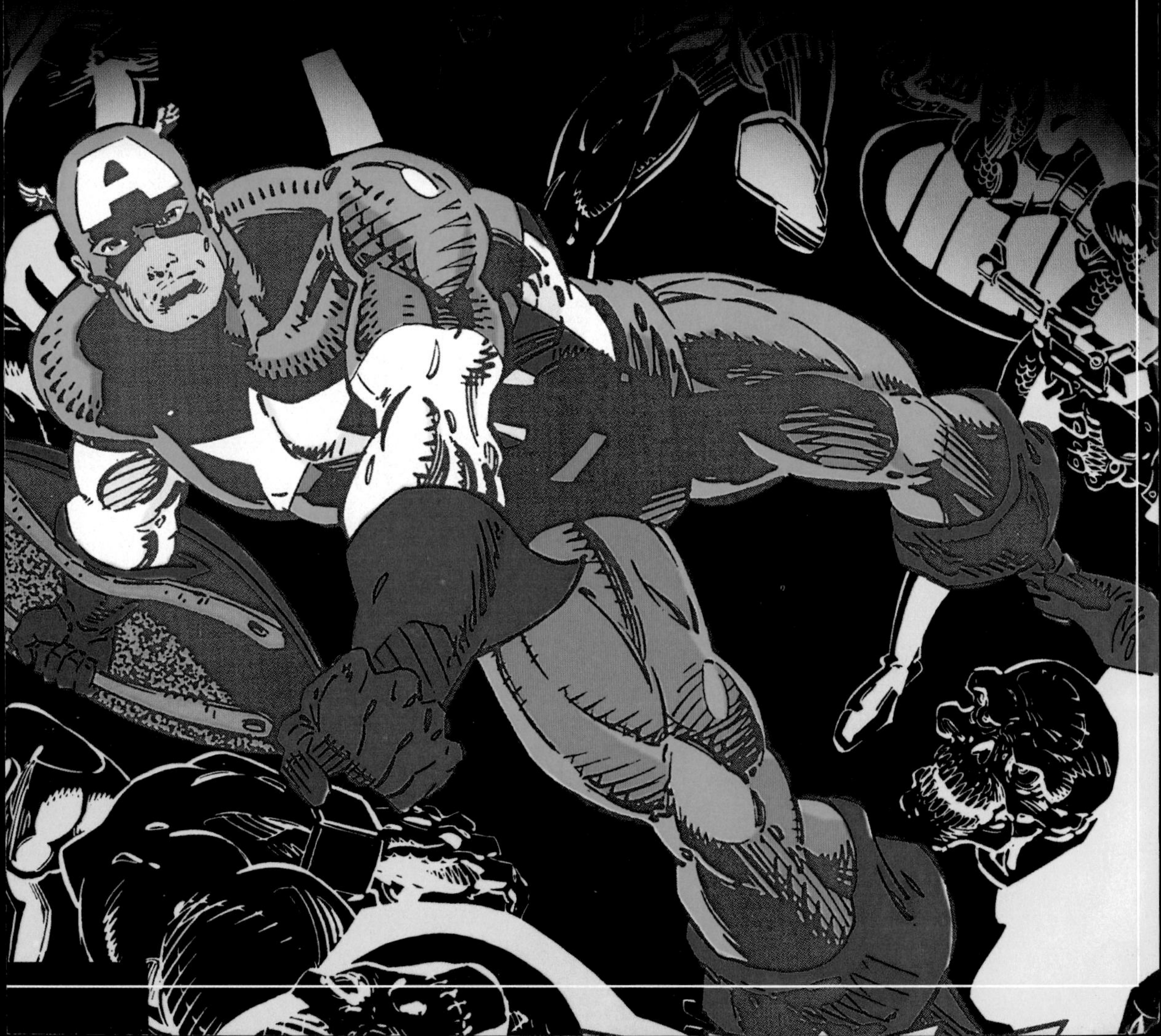

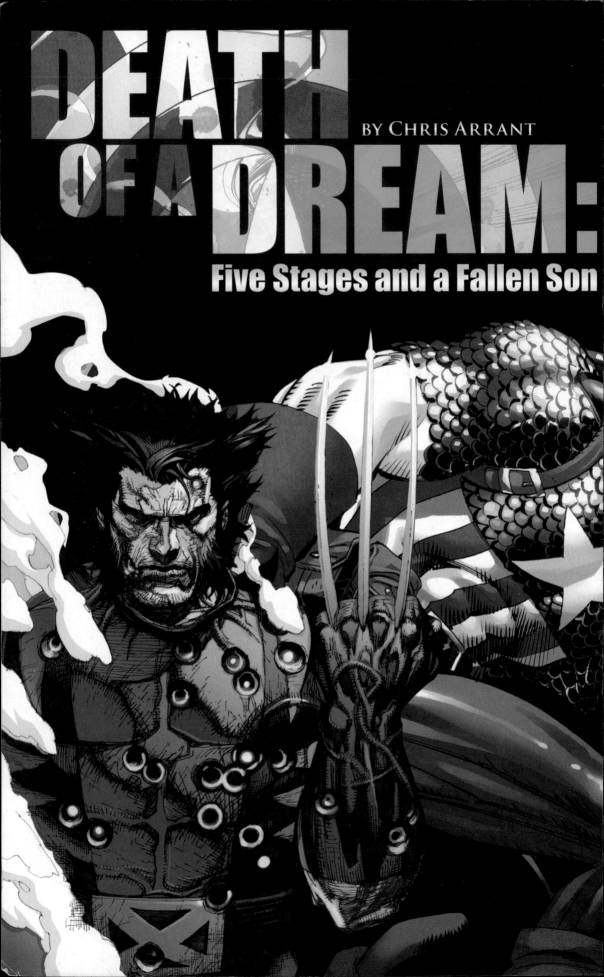

DEATH OF A DREAM:

BY CHRIS ARRANT

Five Stages and a Fallen Son

Writer Jeph Loeb and a stable of superstar artists mark the reaction of the Marvel Universe to death of its Fallen Son.

The news of Captain America's death hit comics fans, and hit them hard. Regardless of their thoughts on the issue, it was something that was felt across the community. And writer Jeph Loeb is no different.

Loeb first learned of the plans of what would become *Captain America #25* in the fall of 2006, at a writers summit hosted by Marvel. It is at these summits that writers and editors brainstorm the overarching elements in the Marvel Universe in the coming months and years, and it was here that the bombshell was dropped to Loeb. An admitted Captain America fan, Loeb has written the *Star-Spangled Avenger* on several occasions, including a brief run on the title itself in 1996. Although a veteran writer of both comics and film, the news of Captain America's impending death hit Loeb hard as a fan.

That kinetic blow quickly propelled Loeb's mind into gear and blurted out an opportunity to erect a monument, a moment of silence, and a chance for the Marvel Universe to react. What it became is *Fallen Son: The Death of Captain America*, a five-issue series of one-shots that found Loeb teamed with the some of the preeminent artists of today. Each issue corresponds to a stage of what the psychological community has dubbed "The Five Stages of Grief": denial, anger, bargaining, depression, and acceptance. It is a process by which people deal with grief and tragedy, and one Loeb knows all too well.

This limited series marks the first of many major events that Loeb is scripting as part of his new exclusive agreement with Marvel, including extended runs on Wolverine and The Ultimates. While comics have been a major part of Loeb's life since his first published work in 1991, he still finds time to keep a day job in the busy world of Hollywood, acting as Co-Executive Producer and a writer for the NBC hit drama *Heroes*.

Loeb knows heroes, and in Fallen Son he comes to terms with perhaps the most American hero of them all.

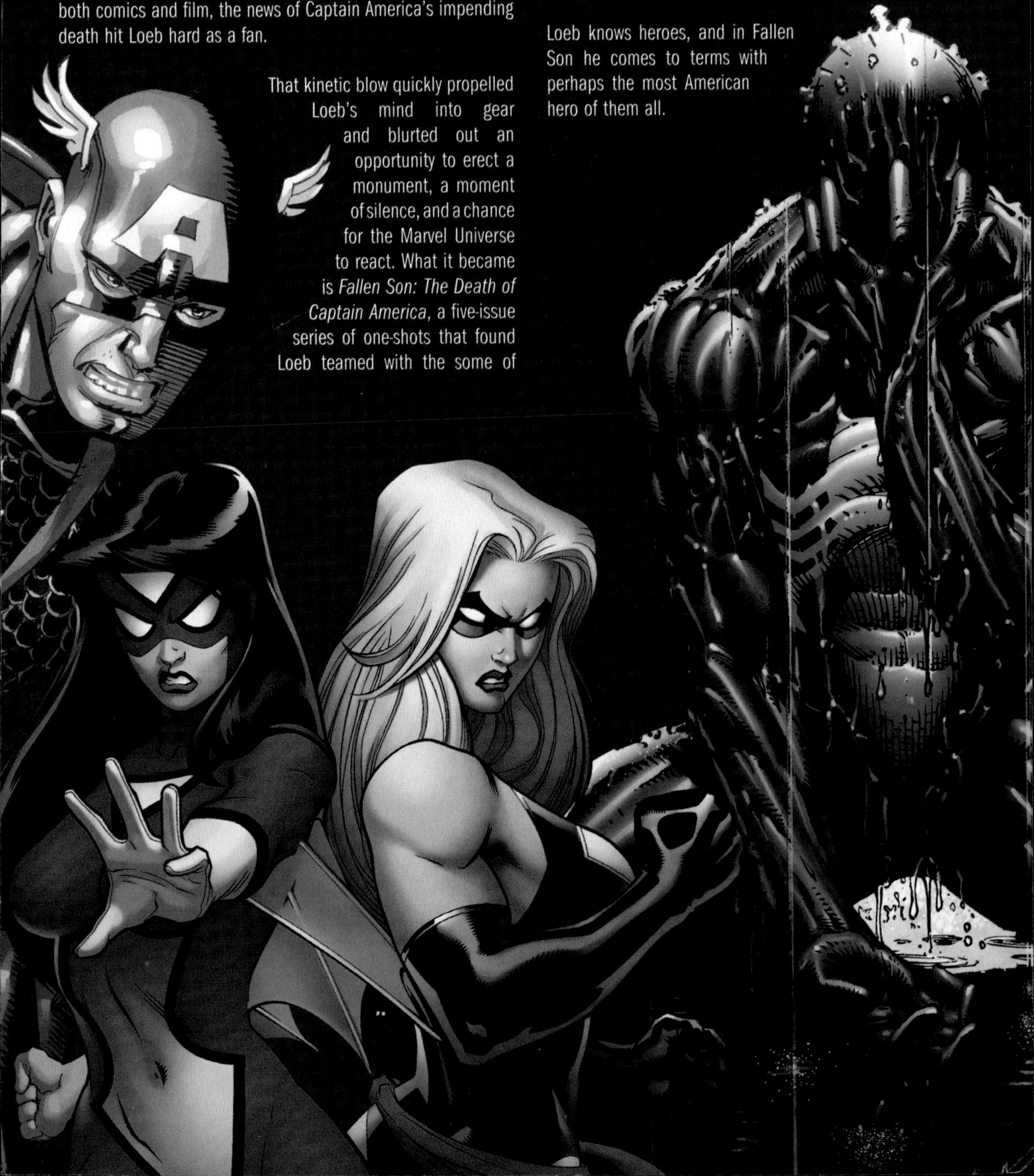

SPOTLIGHT: Jeph, how were you originally informed that Steve Rogers would be dying...and what was your initial gut reaction to it?

JEPH: I was surprised. Not that we were doing it, but I had somehow missed that we were doing it. That's what happens when you miss a creative retreat! But, once I was brought up to speed, I thought it was going to be huge. Lead story on Nightly News, Joe Quesada going back on Steven Colbert, that sort of thing... And what'dya know!

SPOTLIGHT: Well we do know, and we've seen. The idea of Captain America's death was first floated at Marvel during a writer's summit. Why did this story idea grab you so firmly out of the gate?

JEPH: Some of that is I'm a huge Captain America fan. He's the closest thing the Marvel Universe has to Superman and still he's very much not Superman. But, I like that "man out of time" part of his character. So, being able to be part of this is something I very much wanted.

Secondly, on a more personal nature, I unfortunately have too intimate a knowledge of grief and the process of losing a son *[Jeph lost his 17-year old son Sam Loeb in 2005 to cancer – Ed.]* and hopefully, I can bring some of that to this project.

SPOTLIGHT: The Fallen Son mini-series walks the characters of the Marvel Universe – and the reader – through the five stages of grief, an idea brought into the conversation by J. Michael Straczynski. Why is this so appropriate in the aftermath of Steve Rogers' assassination?

JEPH: Isn't it enough that JMS said that's what it should be?! *(Laughter.)* It is a very clear, clean way to express what is happening to the Marvel heroes. Not just for me as a writer, but for the readers, too. Big concepts, high emotional impact.

SPOTLIGHT: The title of the series is *Fallen Son* – with Captain America being denoted as the 'son'; so who is he the son of?

JEPH: Of us all. When we send "our boys" out to war, it's all of us. Cap fought for all of us throughout his entire career. So, he's like our son. Again the echoes of my own personal loss were part of calling it that, too.

SPOTLIGHT: What does Captain America as a character mean to you?

JEPH: Well, again, using the Superman metaphor in that Superman inspires us to be the best human being we can be; Cap is much more about thinking in real world terms. He's a soldier. He's a hero. He's actively trying to inspire others to believe what JFK said about not asking what your country can do for you, but what you can do for your country. Given where we are in the world today, that's a hard concept for most people, and Cap's death is all the more tragic in that we need him now more than ever to show us the way.

SPOTLIGHT: How is Captain America different from other heroes?

JEPH: He was created to be a living symbol. By wearing the flag, he separates himself from the others in that he has a name and purpose that is about country and heritage and loyalty. Most heroes are trying to do their job and if that job inspires, so be it. But Cap was saddled with that responsibility from his origin.

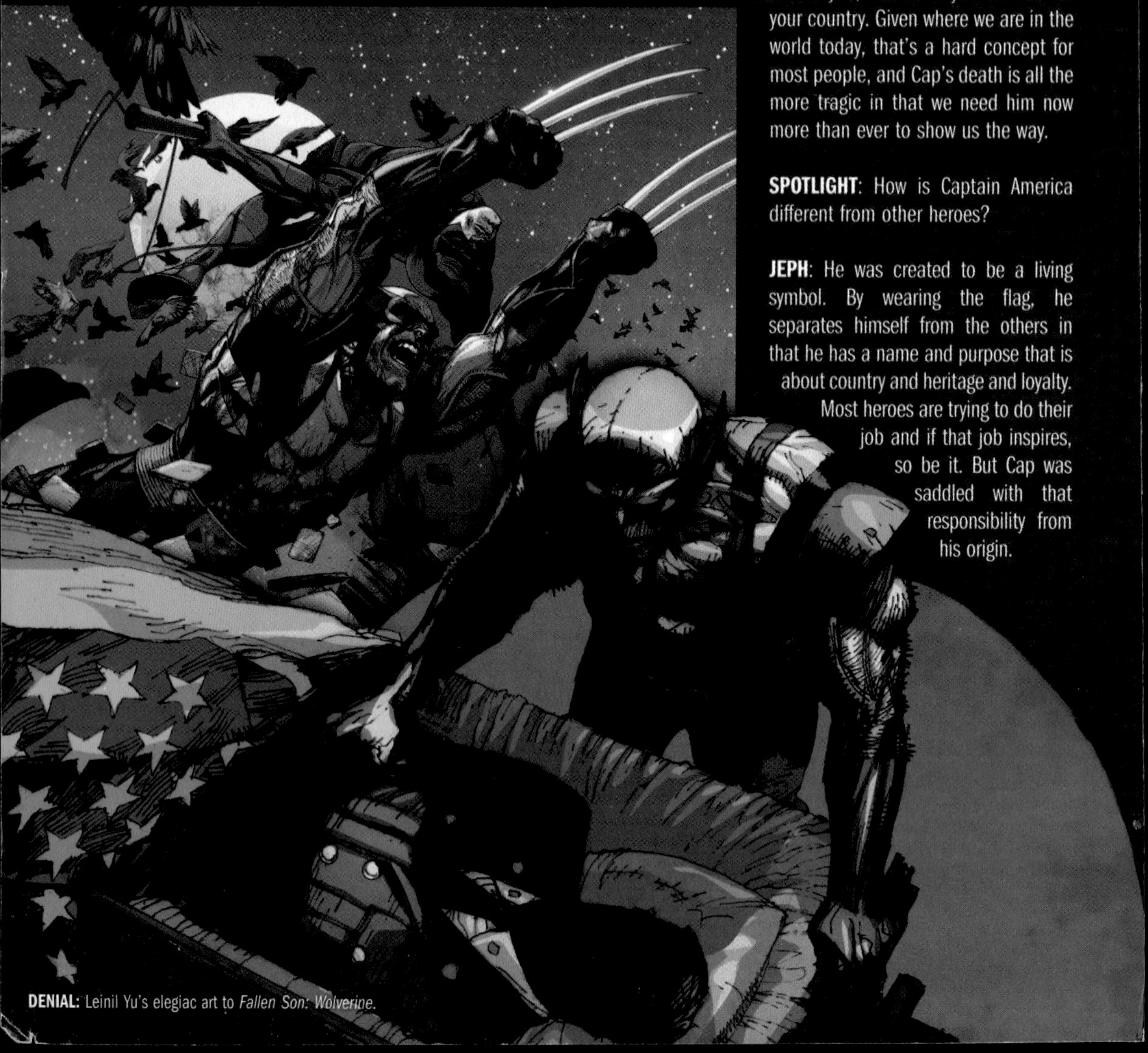

DENIAL: Leinil Yu's elegiac art to *Fallen Son: Wolverine*.

SPOTLIGHT: How did you go about pairing up the stages with the featured characters of each issue?

JEPH: They just felt right for each stage. I can't really explain it but once J. Michael Straczynski uttered the words "we should use the five stages of grief as the structure" I had it all. I literally could see the comics on the stands.

Weird, I know. But, I'm weird!

SPOTLIGHT: Fallen Son leads off with Wolverine and the theme of 'Denial.' Wolverine's an interesting choice: as someone who has denied death's grip countless times with his healing factor yet had many friends and lovers die around him, Logan has a lot of experience with it.

First off, seeing as how Wolverine has fought beside Captain America back in the '40s through to the modern day, what's Logan's take on his friendship with Steve Rogers?

JEPH: Logan isn't going to wear that "take" right out there on his sleeve. He's, in his own way, in denial. He wants to see the body; he wants to talk to the assassin, to Tony Stark. It's all a sign of his love for Steve, but he keeps that in check.

SPOTLIGHT: Why is Logan the perfect character to embody the denial and doubt in the death of Captain America?

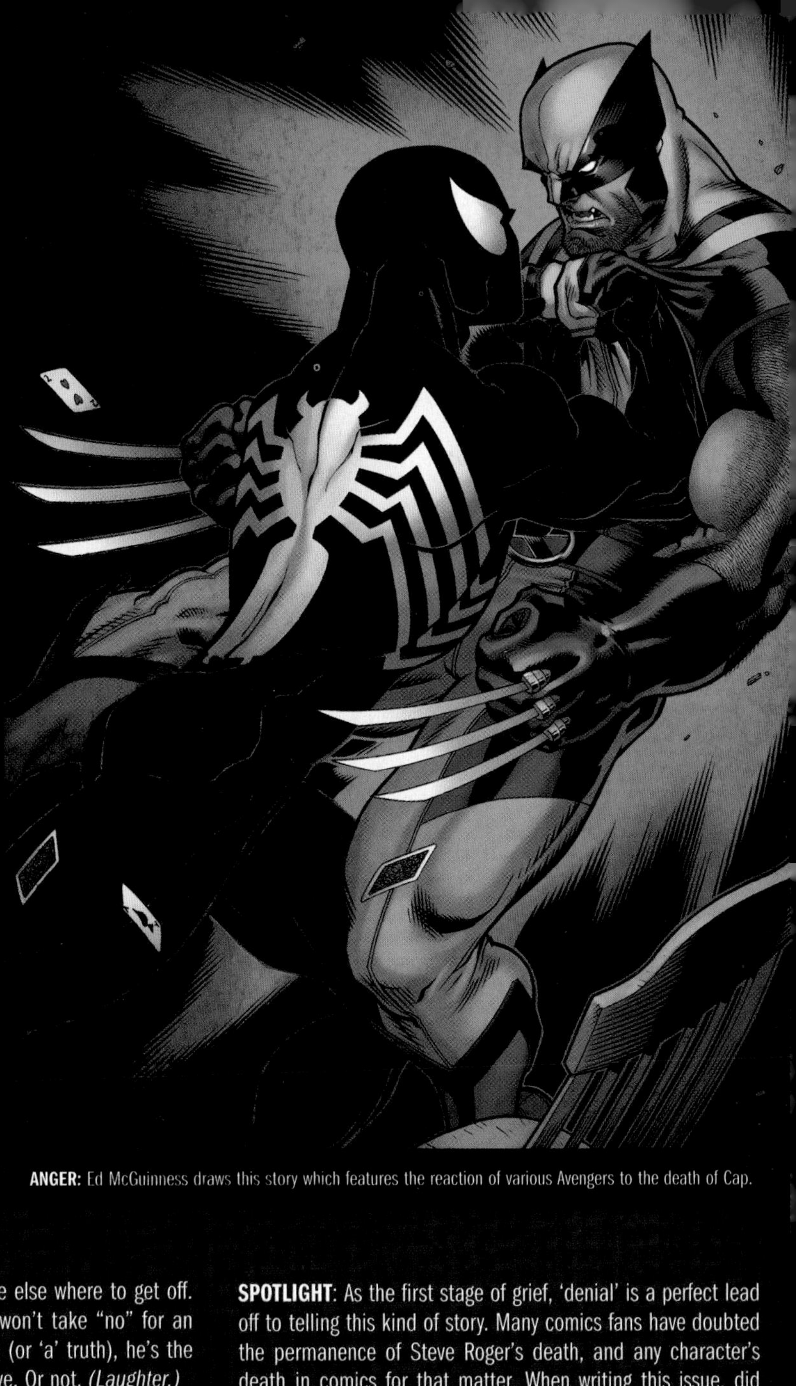

ANGER: Ed McGuinness draws this story which features the reaction of various Avengers to the death of Cap.

JEPH: He has the stones to tell everyone else where to get off. You need a guy doing the digging who won't take "no" for an answer. And when he finds out the truth (or 'a' truth), he's the guy who everybody else is going to believe. Or not. *(Laughter.)*

SPOTLIGHT: Wolverine's taking his doubts and trying to find out the truth, and he's enlisted some help from other heroes including Daredevil. With Logan being such a loner, why does he bring in some extra hands?

JEPH: It's not a simple thing. This is a massive investigation and could be a massive conspiracy. For everyone he has asked to join him he has a reason. Logan has thought this through.

SPOTLIGHT: As the first stage of grief, 'denial' is a perfect lead off to telling this kind of story. Many comics fans have doubted the permanence of Steve Roger's death, and any character's death in comics for that matter. When writing this issue, did you have the intention of allowing readers to come to terms with this?

JEPH: Moi? *(Laughter.)*

SPOTLIGHT: Pleading the fifth on that one, let's move on. Collaborating with you on the Wolverine issue is Leinil Yu. Why was he the first person on your dream list of artists to illustrate the story?

"LEINIL, FOR ME, HAS BEEN THE FIRST ORIGINAL VOICE ON THAT CHARACTER IN A VERY LONG TIME."

– WRITER JEPH LOEB, ON ARTIST LEINIL YU'S WOLVERINE

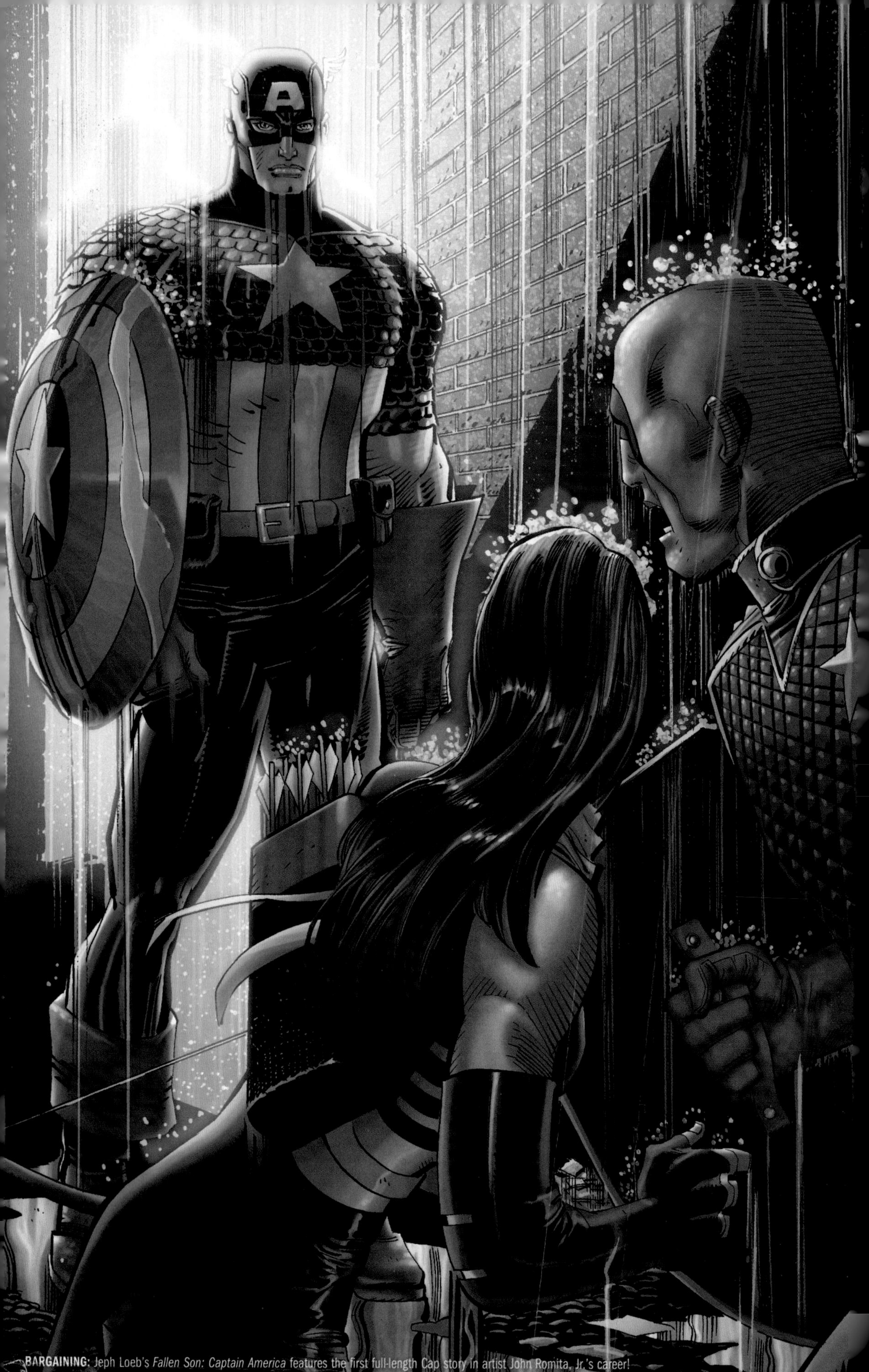

BARGAINING: Jeph Loeb's *Fallen Son: Captain America* features the first full-length Cap story in artist John Romita, Jr.'s career!

JEPH: I've said elsewhere that with all due respect to everyone who has worked on the character since (and there have been some fantastic people – yo, Humberto Ramos!) Leinil, for me, has been the first original voice on that character in a very long time. If we were going to finally get to work together (aside from a five page story in *Fantastic Four #50*), I wanted him to be on the character that broke him out from the pack. He rocks.

By the way, check out Simone Bianchi's work on *Wolverine #50-55* (currently in stores) where he is showing me the future of Wolverine's next great artists, today!

SPOTLIGHT: Which happens to be written by you, Mr. Loeb! Back to the subject at hand, the second issue of *Fallen Son* deals with Anger, and is told from the perspective of the Avengers – both Mighty and New. Why are they the ones to embody anger, and what do they do in the issue?

JEPH: They were his friends. And speaking from a certain amount of experience (again, unfortunately), Steve's friends are the ones who will have the most immediate – and in many ways the loudest response. Since Brian Michael Bendis was clever enough to split the team in two, I was able to craft a story where both teams could have separate stories dealing with the same heartbreaking issue. The Mighty Avengers go kick the crap out some poor super-villain who never knew what was coming while the New Avengers...play poker. Yep. Just like they used to – only it gets equally ugly by the end of that story as well. The stories are told side-by-side. It was fun figuring that out.

SPOTLIGHT: Illustrating this issue is your long-time collaborator Ed McGuiness, who is also working with you with on a top secret Marvel project. Why did his name drop into your head as the must-have to draw this issue?

JEPH: The story required someone who could draw two huge casts. Ed McGuiness and I have had fun and he's terrific at doing just that on our *Superman/Batman* run. Since the idea of splitting the story in two and running both of them side-by-side was something that worked quite well on *Superman/Batman*, it seemed like the right fit. And Ed knocked it out of the park.

SPOTLIGHT: The third issue, a centerpiece, is dealing with 'Bargaining' and is advertised as being from Captain America's perspective *[This interview was conducted prior to the release of Fallen Son: Captain America – Ed.]*. Is this told in a flashback, or an after-life moment, or how?

JEPH: Ah, that would be telling. But, let's just say that Cap plays a significant role!

SPOTLIGHT: The theme is 'bargaining'. Who is doing the bargaining, and what are they bargaining for?

JEPH: Well, again, I don't want to tip it. But, it does deal with the question of who died here. Is it Steve Rogers or Captain America? And depending on your point of view, does Captain America have to die?

SPOTLIGHT: It's been said that this issue will deal somewhat with the casting of a new Captain America. Can you speak to this at all, or how you handle it?

JEPH: It gets addressed head-on. There are some folks who think that Cap is a uniform (think about it, "Captain" is a rank in the army)! and the right man can replace Steve. That's an interesting place to begin.

SPOTLIGHT: Although a comic art veteran, this is John Romita Jr.'s first time doing a Captain America story. Can you tell us of some specific aspects of JRJR's work that made him ideal for this issue?

JEPH: I always thought JRJR would tell a very compelling story with this character. His visual style lends itself to that acrobatic kind of character (think Daredevil and Spider-Man) but he also is a superb storyteller (think...oh, anything! *(Laughter.)*)

So, when I started talking about this story, I couldn't get JRJR's visuals out of my head. He, without knowing it, told me how to tell the story. And it shows on every page!!!

SPOTLIGHT: Spider-Man deals with Captain America's passing in his own way – 'Depression' – in the fourth issue. What is Spider-Man's take on Captain America?

JEPH: It's funny because they never were particularly close – but when you "idolize" someone (and I think that's a little strong) it's hard to get close to them. But, Peter Parker is doing the same job as Steve was doing, and if Cap can die – jeez, Captain America can die?! – how is Spidey supposed to do that job and not feel like...well, depressed?

SPOTLIGHT: And why is Peter taking it so especially hard?

JEPH: I feel like Peter's life has been marked by death. It began with Uncle Ben. He's an orphan to begin with. Harry. Captain Stacy. And, of course, Gwen. As a hero, your career is often judged by the lives you save. Peter will always think of himself as someone who will be judged by the lives he lost...

SPOTLIGHT: Illustrating this one is the dynamic David Finch. Spider-Man's always been a unique character, even within the Marvel Universe. Why was getting Finch in this a no-brainer?

JEPH: Uh...because he draws the most bitchen Spider-Man ever and when you put Dave Finch in a graveyard and have it raining it looks like the most awesome thing in the world. But, don't let me influence you, judge for yourself! *(Laughter.)*

DEPRESSION: Black and white uncolored David Finch art from *Fallen Son: Spider-Man!*

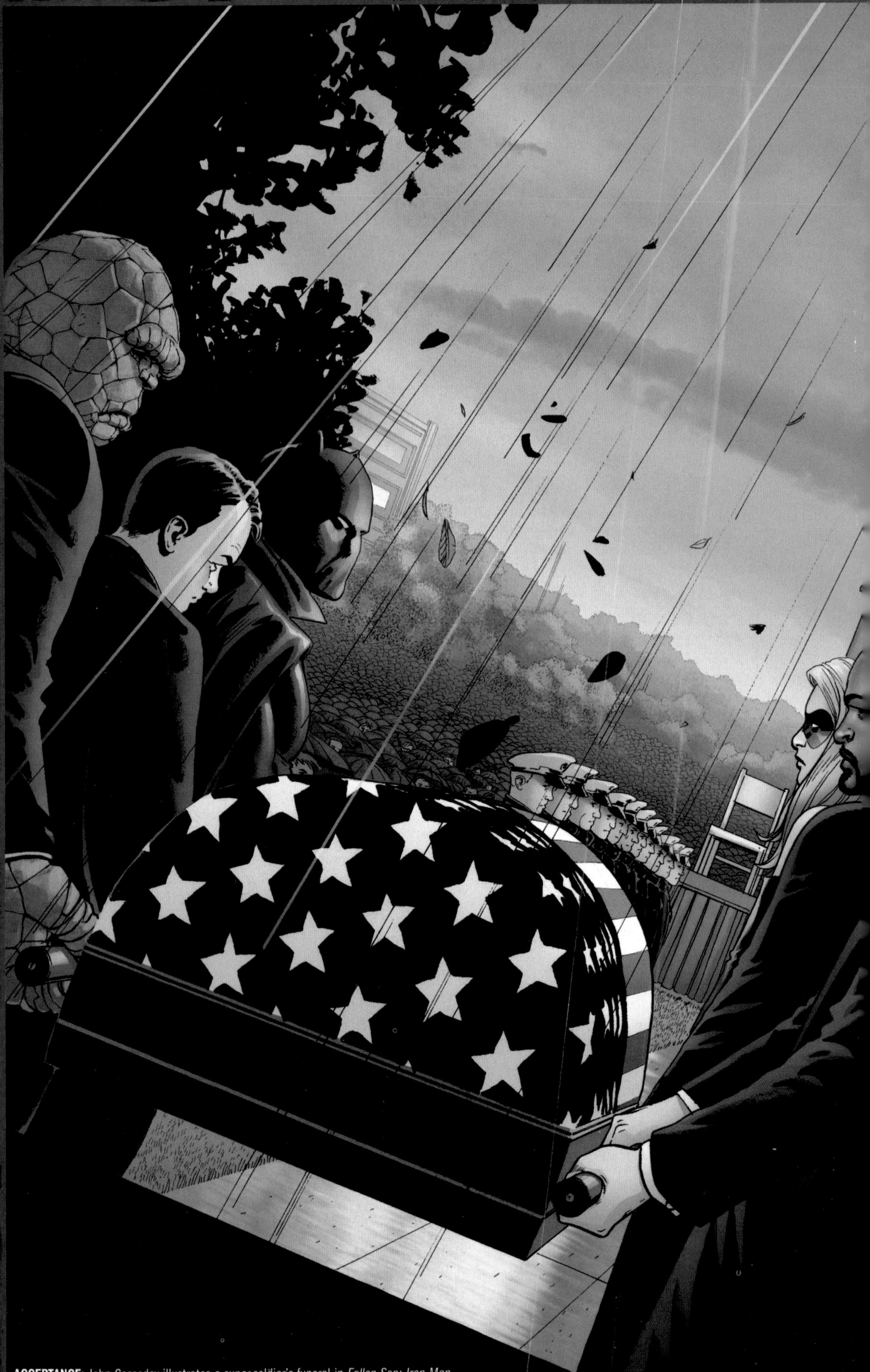

ACCEPTANCE: John Cassaday illustrates a super-soldier's funeral in *Fallen Son: Iron Man.*

"THE STYLE AND STRUCTURE OF THE TALE ARE AS IMPORTANT AS THE STORY ITSELF WHEN YOU WORK WITH CASS. HE'S IN A LEAGUE OF HIS OWN WHEN IT COMES TO CAP."

– LOEB, ON ARTIST JOHN CASSADAY

SPOTLIGHT: Rounding out the series is Iron Man's perspective, and the theme of 'Acceptance'. Tony Stark's take on the post-Civil War events have been documented to some extent in *Civil War: The Confession* – so can you tell us what new ground you're covering in this issue?

JEPH: Acceptance isn't restricted to Tony – he happens to be the one who I focused the story on. And whether or not he can actually accept any of this is different from his confession. This one was definitely the hardest for that reason...(I'm) very much looking forward to that reaction.

SPOTLIGHT: Illustrating this story is someone who has been called the definitive Captain America artist of the modern age: John Cassaday. John has been on record a number of times talking about the innate closeness he feels with the character of Captain America. Does this work into your plans to make this last issue 'special'?

JEPH: Totally. And he and I have had many conversations on this subject. The style and structure of the tale are as important as the story itself when you work with Cass. He's in a league of his own when it comes to Cap.

SPOTLIGHT: Speaking more to the artistic side of this equation, you've always been known as a writer who has been able to work with a plethora of the most high-profile artists in the business. To what would you attribute this opportunity?

JEPH: Luck?! I don't know. I like them. I want them to be able to showcase their illustrations in the boldest way possible. Some of that is I've been a filmmaker and a screenwriter longer that anything – it's actually the only "real" job I've ever had and that's a very "words into pictures" way of thinking. So, it's on me, in me.

SPOTLIGHT: Before we wrap things up here Jeph, is there anything you wanted to stress to the readers about the Fallen Son limited one-shots?

JEPH: I just want to add that we haven't talked a lot about how there's a tissue thread of continuity through the books. They aren't just a series of one-shots – there IS a story that's being told throughout. Folks who have read the scripts said they were surprised (and delighted) by that – and that was something editors Tom Brevoort and Bill Rosemann and I talked about in the very early stages of this. So, by way of example, when Wolverine is running around in Denial, that story is referred to and dealt with in Anger as well. I hope the readers enjoy finding that out along the way. I wanted to tell a story that show how the Marvel Universe is all connected and death is a way that connects us that is very sad, but also very much something that we all share.

The Fallen Son: The Death of Captain America Premiere Hardcover *that collects the five* Fallen Son *one-shots (Wolverine, Avengers, Captain America, Spider-Man, and Iron Man) is in stores now!*

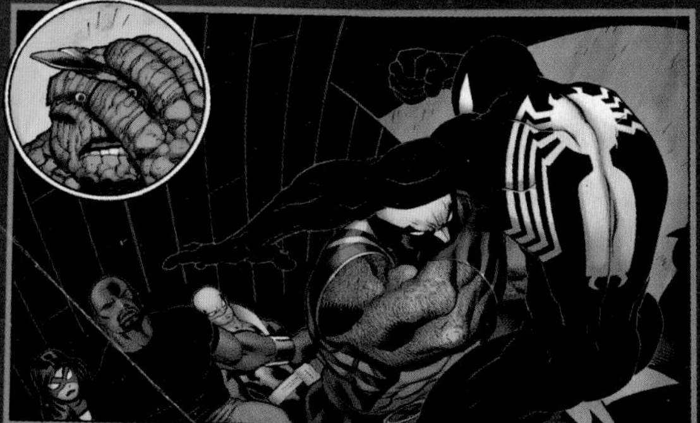

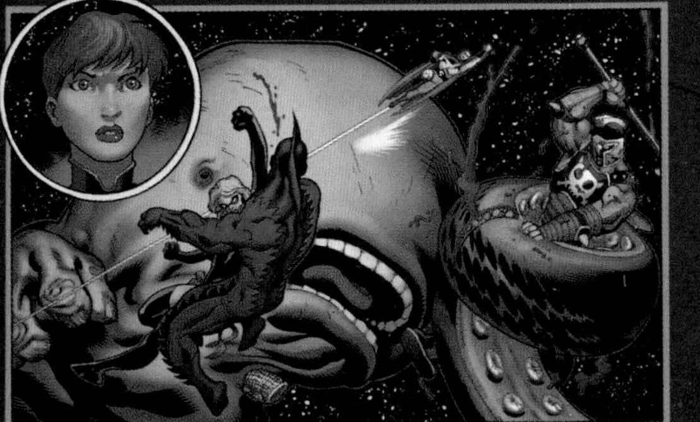

MIGHTY MCGUINNESS: Both teams of Avengers are in fine hands with artist Ed McGuinness in *Fallen Son: Avengers*.

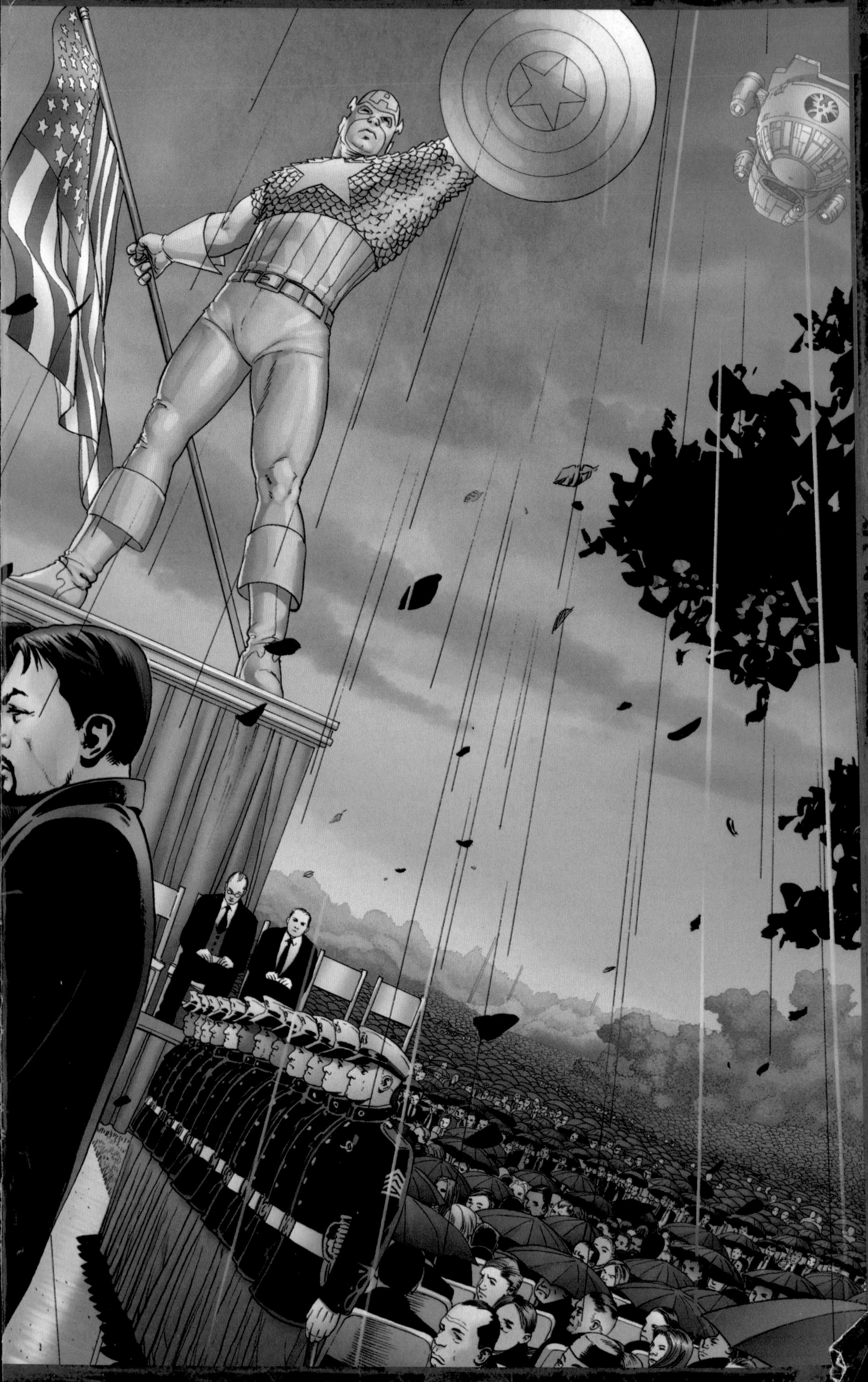

But it was a victory bought at a terrible price. In the war's final days, my young partner was killed in a Nazi trap.

And so I "died" once more.

Decades later my ice-bound body was recovered by superstitious tribesmen, and ultimately resurrected by a new generation of modern-day heroes.

Shielded by my body's advanced physiology, I was thrown into a near-death coma.

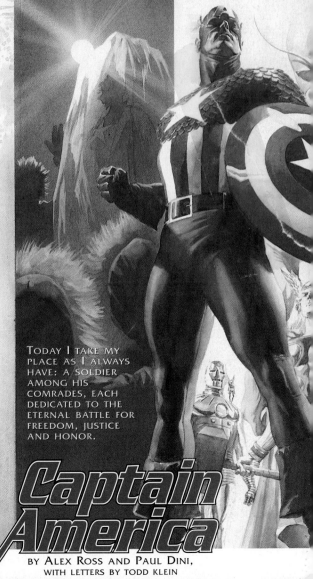

Today I take my place as I always have: a soldier among his comrades, each dedicated to the eternal battle for freedom, justice and honor.

Captain America

by Alex Ross and Paul Dini,
with letters by Todd Klein

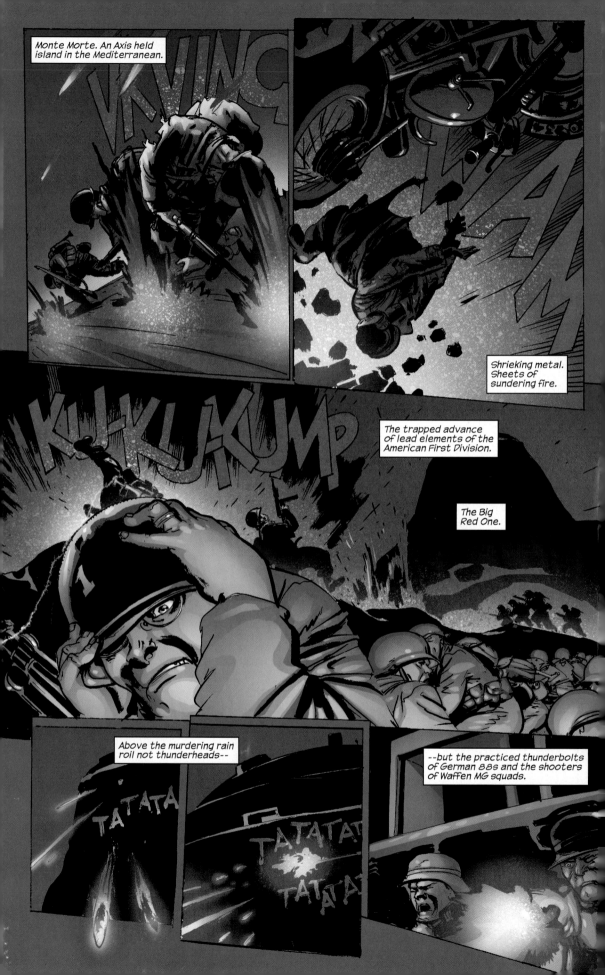

Monte Morte. An Axis held island in the Mediterranean.

Shrieking metal. Sheets of sundering fire.

The trapped advance of lead elements of the American First Division.

The Big Red One.

Above the murdering rain roil not thunderheads--

--but the practiced thunderbolts of German 88s and the shooters of Waffen MG squads.

VN VINC

KLITH KLIA KUMP

TATATA

TATATAT

TAT AT AT

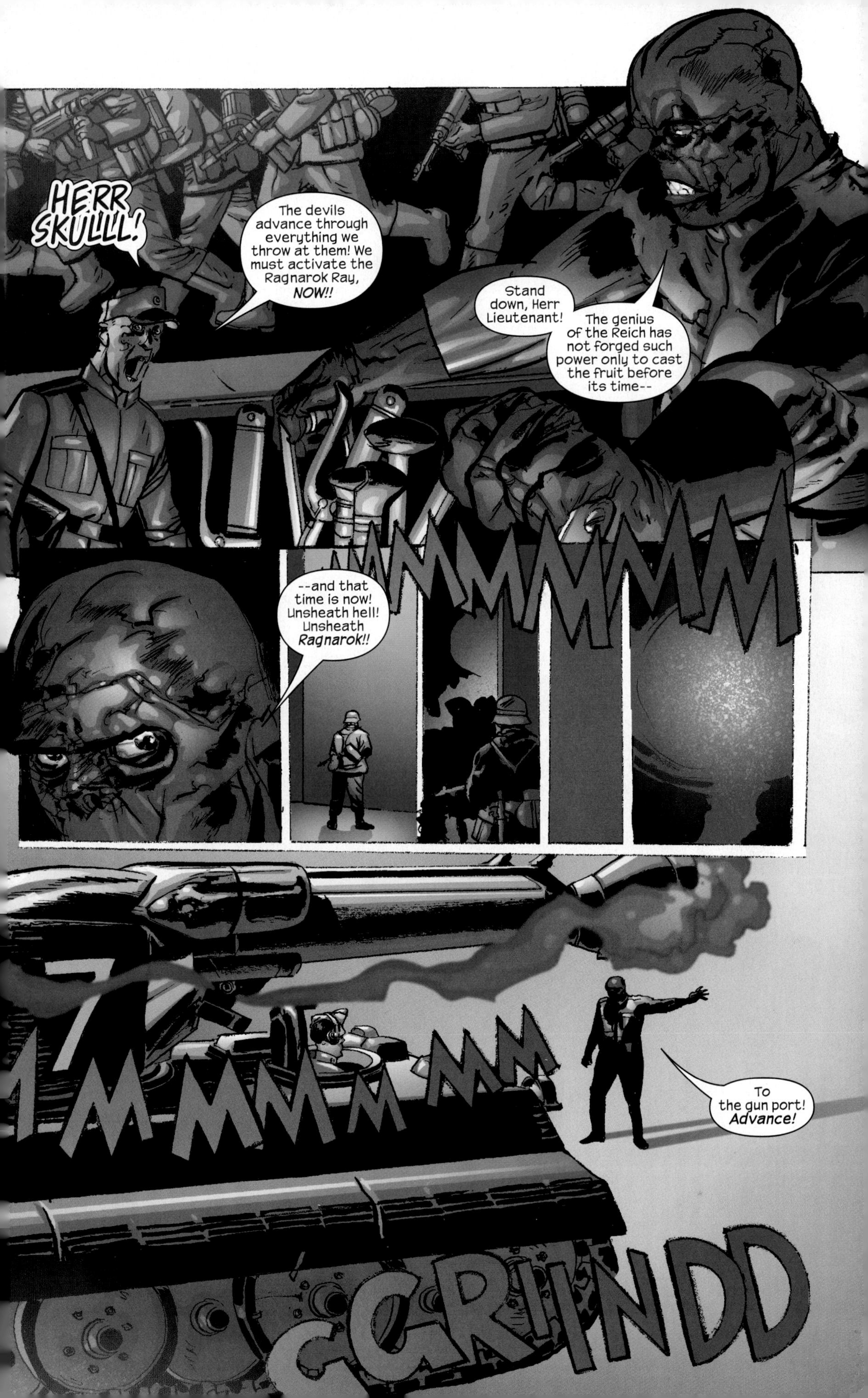
HERR SKULLL!
The devils advance through everything we throw at them! We must activate the Ragnarok Ray, NOW!!
Stand down, Herr Lieutenant!
The genius of the Reich has not forged such power only to cast the fruit before its time--
MMMMMMM
--and that time is now! Unsheath hell! Unsheath Ragnarok!!
MMMMMM
To the gun port! Advance!
GRIINDD

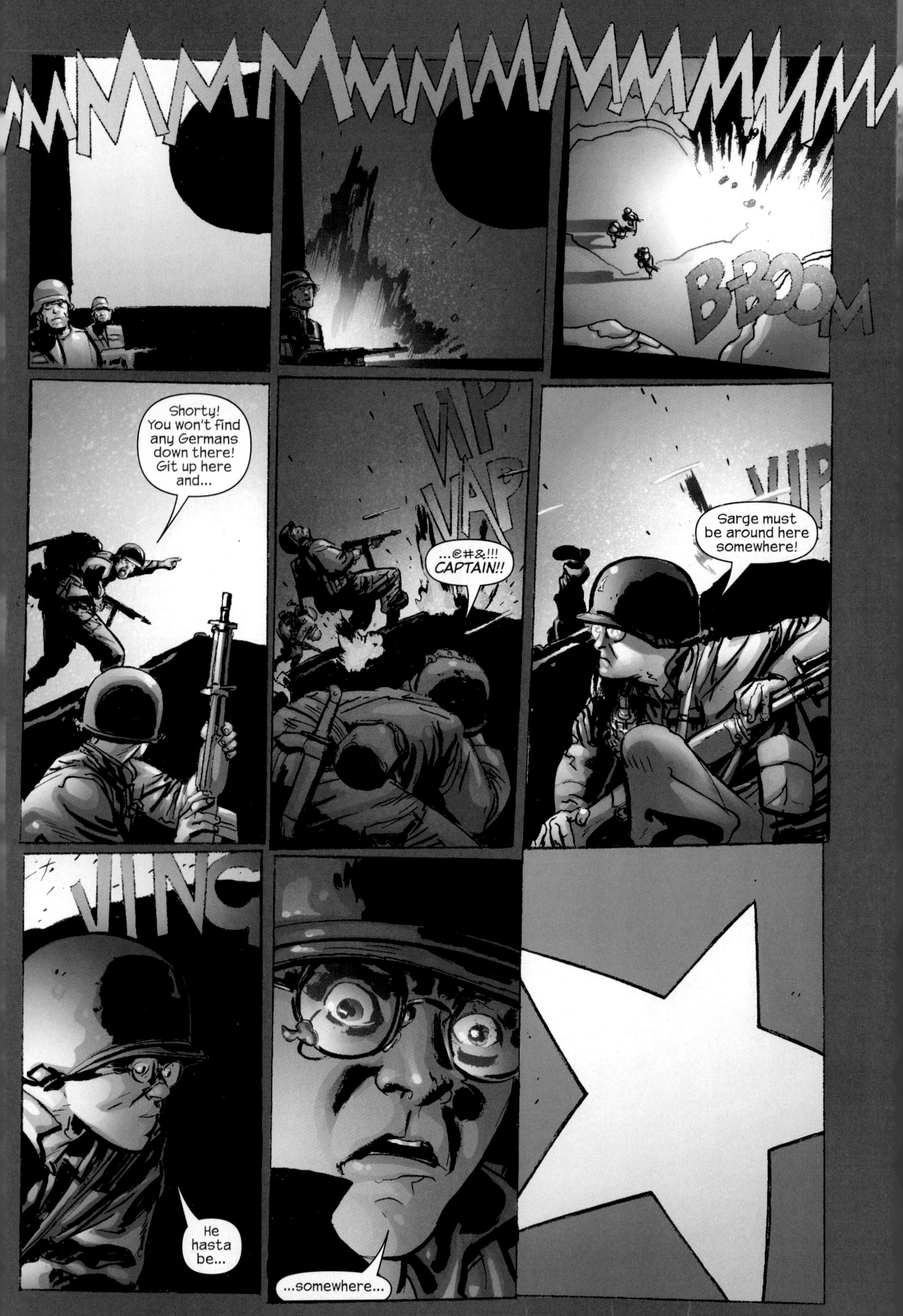
MMMMMMMMMMMMMMMM
B-BOOM
Shorty! You won't find any Germans down there! Git up here and...
VIP
VAP
...@#&!!! CAPTAIN!!
VIP
Sarge must be around here somewhere!
VING
He hasta be...
...somewhere...

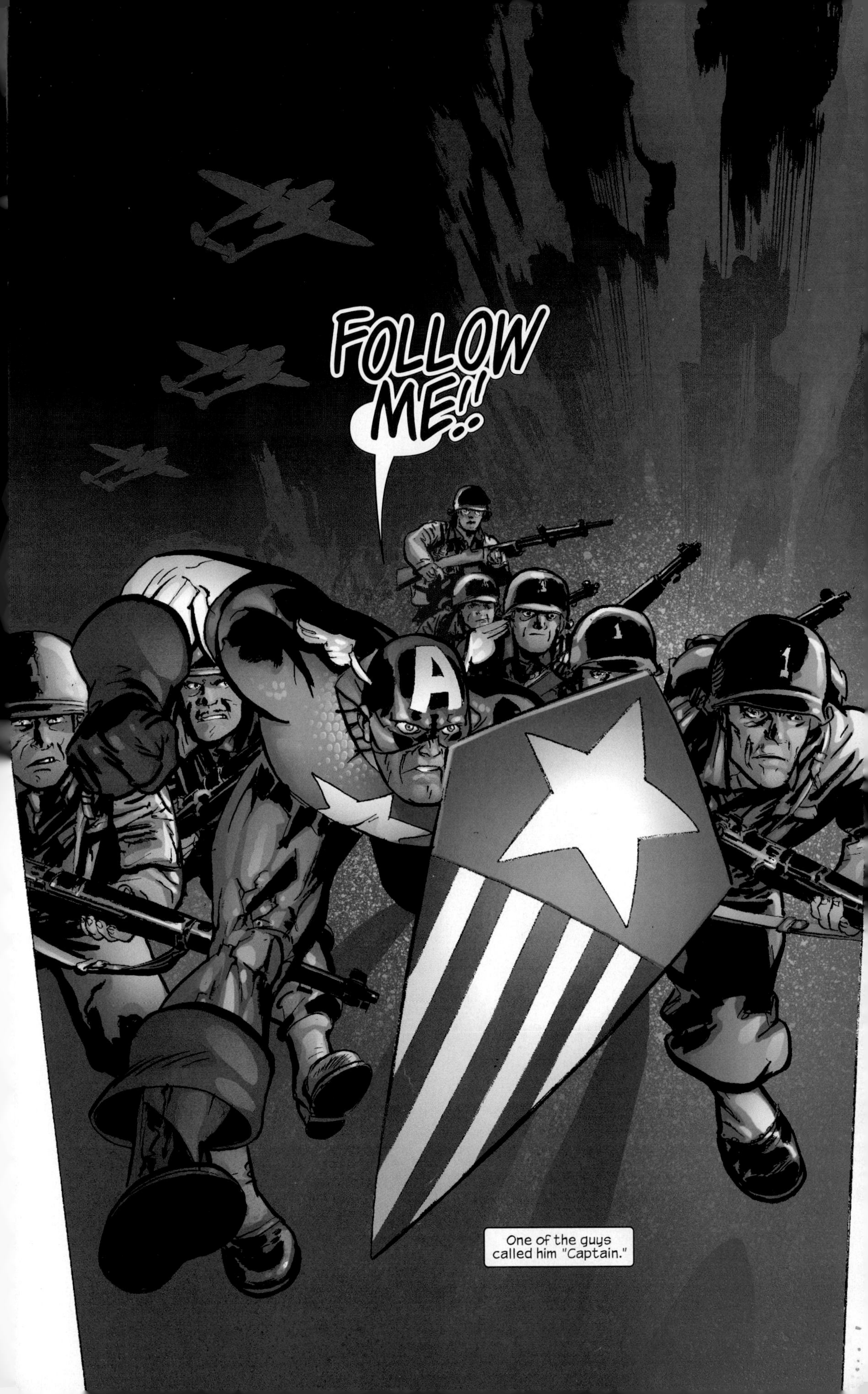
FOLLOW ME!!
One of the guys called him "Captain."

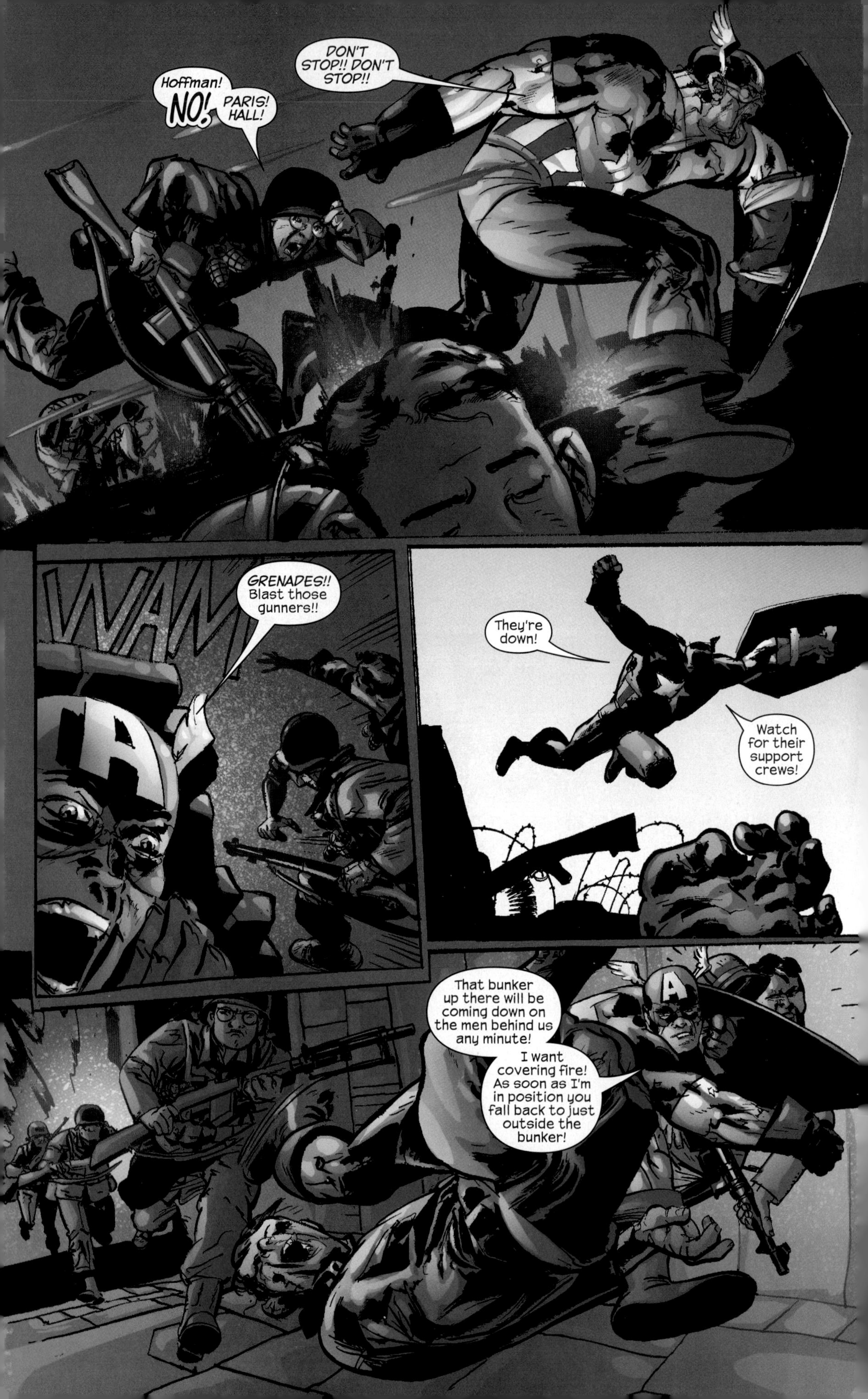

Hoffman! NO! PARIS! HALL!
DON'T STOP!! DON'T STOP!!
WAM
GRENADES!! Blast those gunners!!
They're down!
Watch for their support crews!
That bunker up there will be coming down on the men behind us any minute!
I want covering fire! As soon as I'm in position you fall back to just outside the bunker!

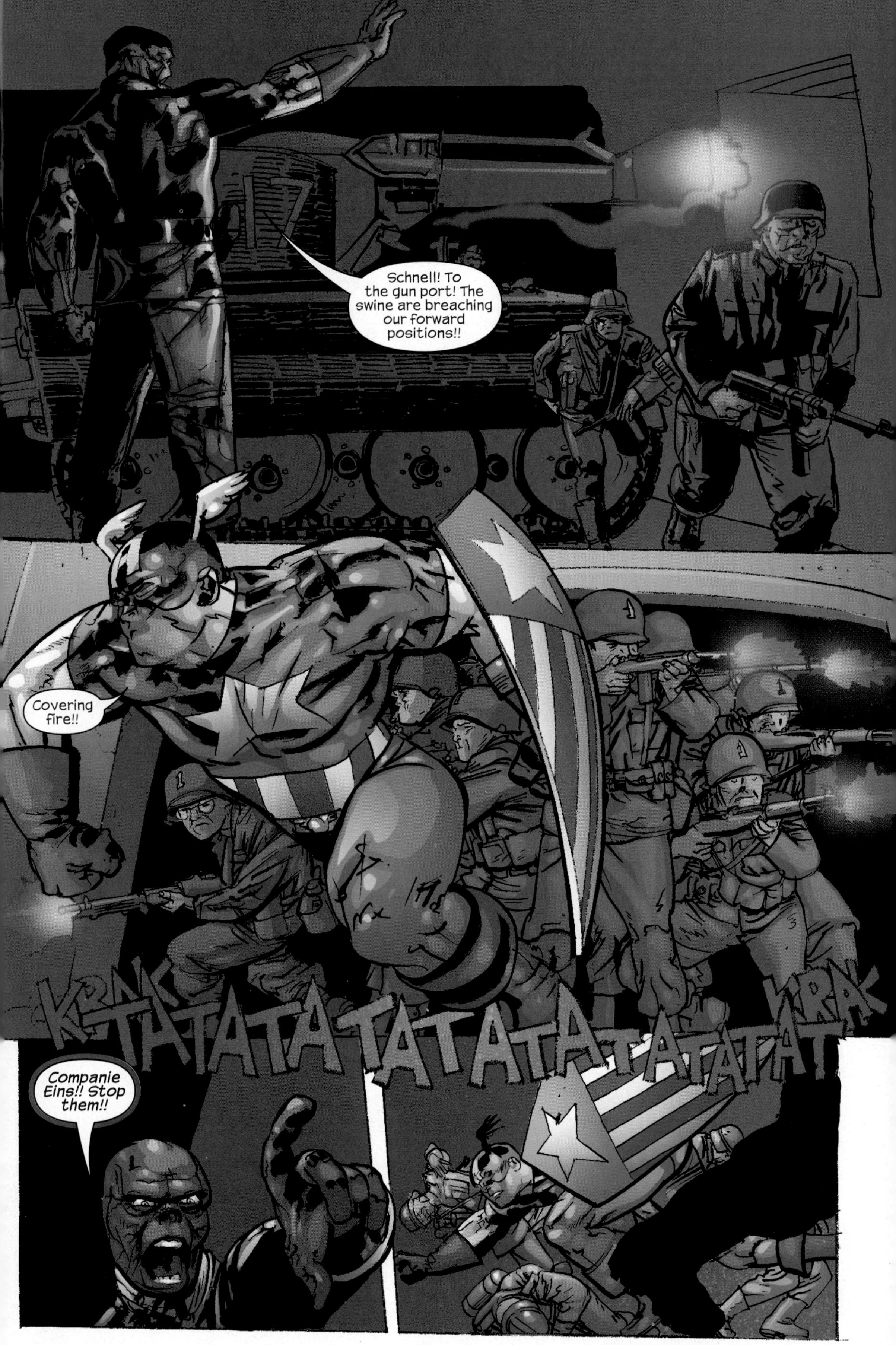

Schnell! To the gun port! The swine are breaching our forward positions!!
Covering fire!!
KRAK
TATATATATATATATATATATATAT
KRAK
Companie Eins!! Stop them!!

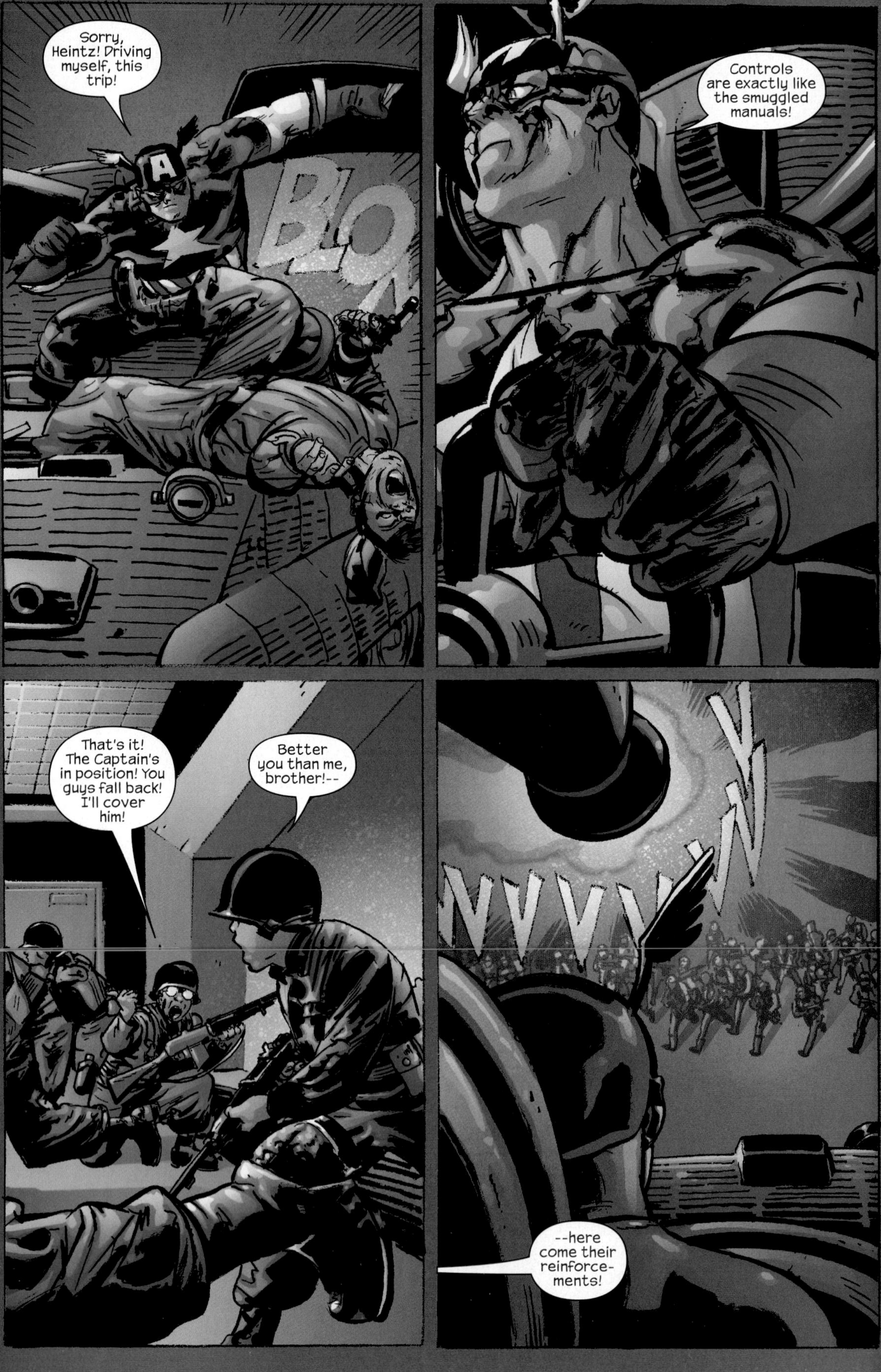
Sorry, Heintz! Driving myself, this trip!
BLOOM
Controls are exactly like the smuggled manuals!
That's it! The Captain's in position! You guys fall back! I'll cover him!
Better you than me, brother!--
--here come their reinforce-ments!

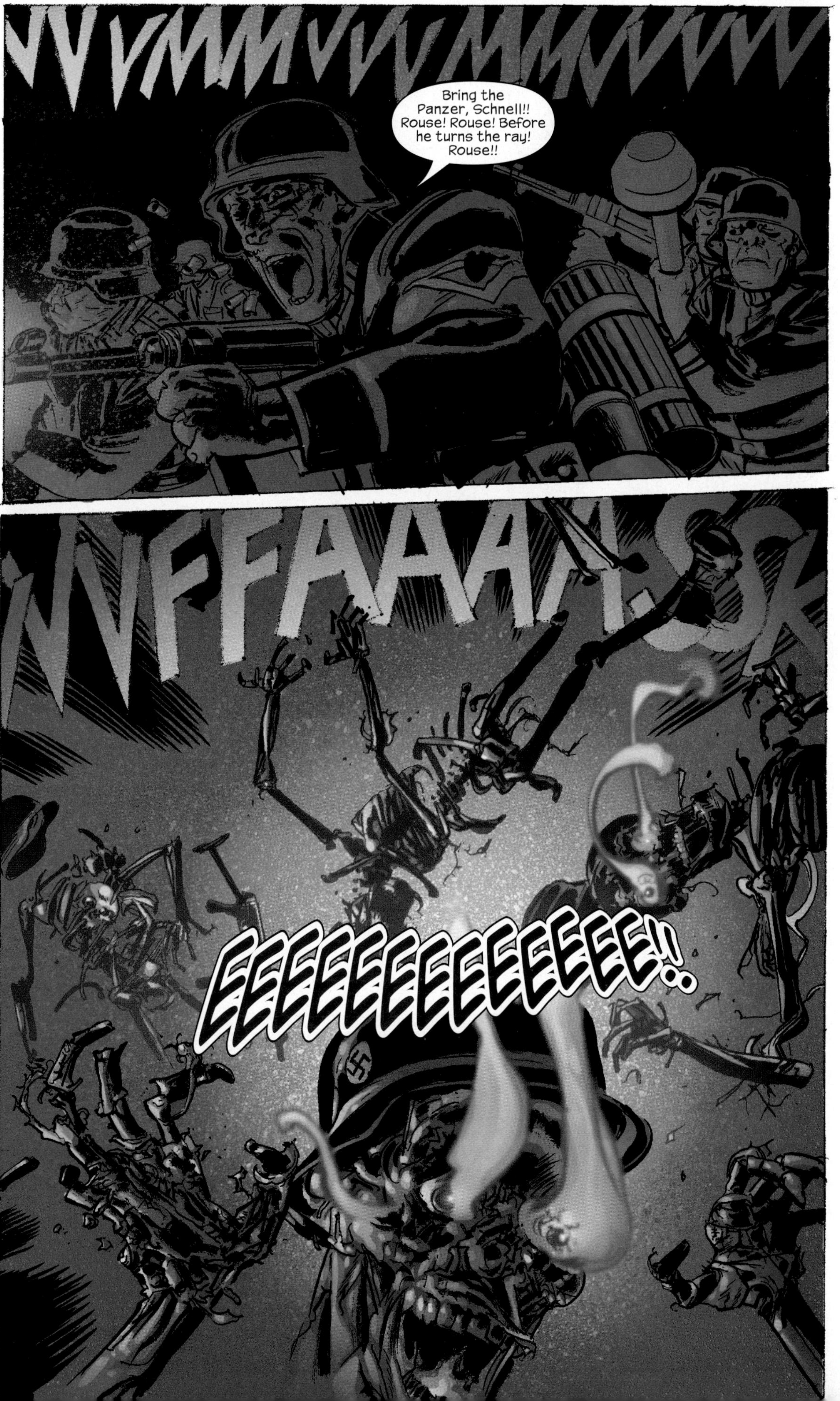
Bring the Panzer, Schnell!! Rouse! Rouse! Before he turns the ray! Rouse!!

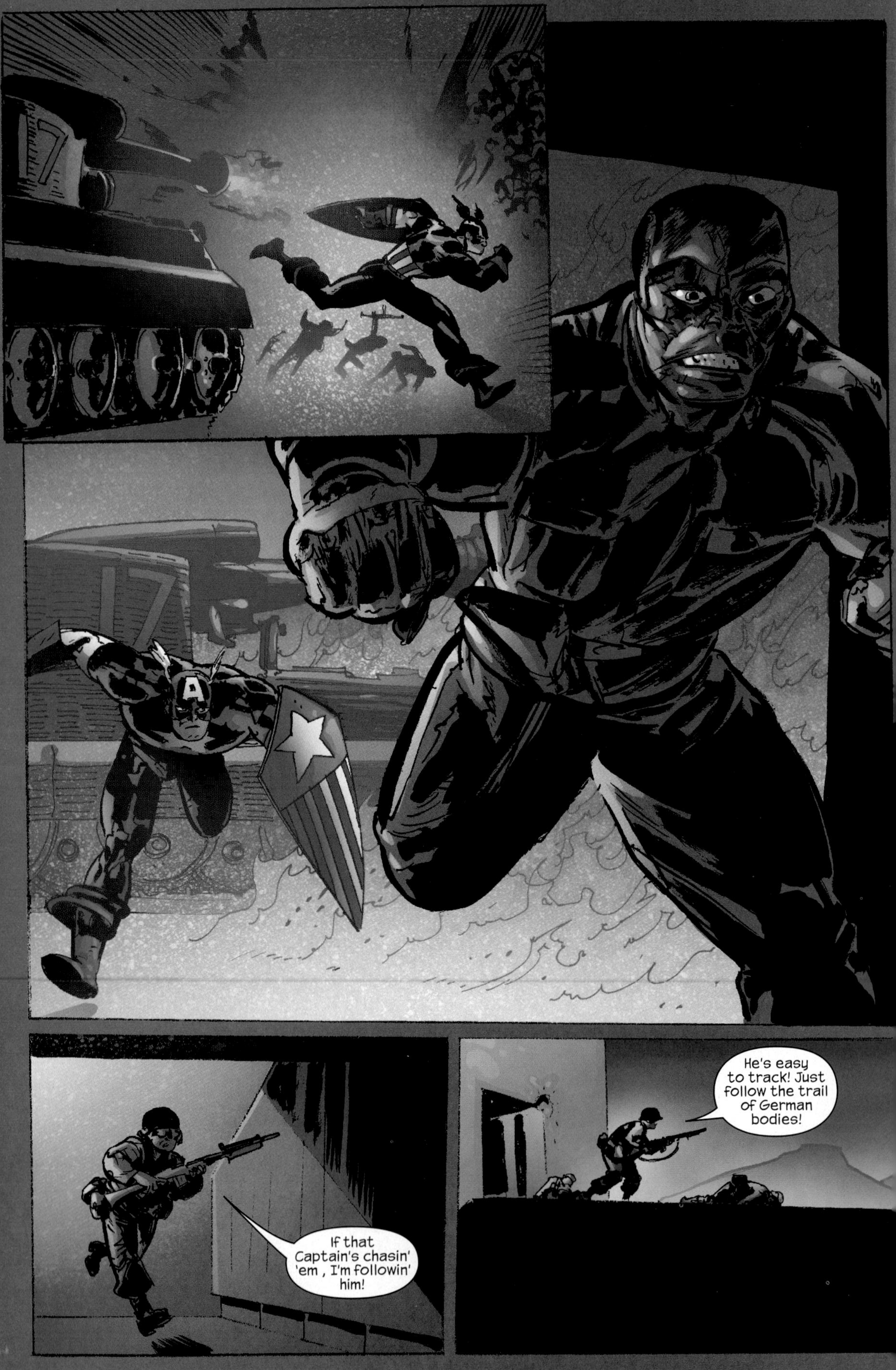
If that Captain's chasin' 'em , I'm followin' him!
He's easy to track! Just follow the trail of German bodies!